THE CLASSICS OF WESTERN SPIRITUALITY

THE CLASSICS OF WESTERN SPIRITUALITY
A Library of the Great Spiritual Masters

President and Publisher
Kevin A. Lynch, C.S.P.

EDITORIAL BOARD

IGNATIUS of LOYOLA
THE *SPIRITUAL EXERCISES* AND SELECTED WORKS

EDITED BY
GEORGE E. GANSS, S.J.

WITH THE COLLABORATION OF
PARMANANDA R. DIVARKAR, S.J., EDWARD J. MALATESTA, S.J., AND MARTIN E. PALMER, S.J.

PREFACE BY
JOHN W. PADBERG, S.J.

PAULIST PRESS
NEW YORK • MAHWAH

Cover art: NOREEN MALLORY was born in Brockville, Ontario, Canada, and is now living in Montréal with her husband of 33 years, the writer Hugh Hood. Noreen graduated from the Ontario College of Art in Toronto, studied at l'Ecôle des Beaux Arts and Concordia in Montréal and at Winchester School of Art in Winchester, England. Of her cover painting she says: "In the late '70s I was guided through the St. Ignatius of Loyola Spiritual Exercises by Sr. Marie Azzarello, C.N.D. at St. Augustine of Canterbury Parish in Montréal. In the beginning Ignatius seemed too stern, almost terrifying. But as the exercises unfolded, slowly his kindness and love began to emerge. When he suggested contemplating the subtle difference between a tear falling on a sponge and a tear falling on a stone as a means of discerning the power of Christ from the power of evil, the image struck me with great force. I have pondered it ever since, and used that image in the cover drawing as a tribute to St. Ignatius, whose loving gifts as a teacher in the service of Christ can still touch me and countless others, more than four centuries after his life on earth. The saint is depicted in the heavy black outer garment associated with the Jesuit 'Black Robes' in traditional Canadian legend."

Library of Congress Cataloging-in-Publication Data

Ignatius, of Loyola, Saint, 1491–1556.
    [Selections. English. 1991]
    Ignatius of Loyola: Spiritual exercises and selected works/edited by George E. Ganss; with the collaboration of Parmananda R. Divarkar, Edward J. Malatesta, and Martin E. Palmer; preface by John W. Padberg.
        p.   cm.—(The Classics of Western spirituality)
    Translated from the Latin.
    Includes bibliographical references and index.
    ISBN 0-8091-0447-4 (cloth)— ISBN 0-8091-3216-8 (pbk.)
    1. Ignatius, of Loyola, Saint, 1491–1556. 2. Christian saints—Spain—Biography. 3. Spiritual exercises—Early works to 1800.
I. Ganss, George E., 1905– . II. Title. III. Series.
BX4700.L7A25   1991
271'.53—dc20   90-22218
                                                                                          CIP

Published by Paulist Press
997 Macarthur Boulevard
Mahwah, New Jersey 07430

Printed and bound in the
United States of America

CONTENTS

CONTENTS

CONTENTS

REFERENCE MATTER

Editor of this Volume

GEORGE E. GANSS, S.J., is an editor in the Institute of Jesuit Sources at St. Louis University. From that university he received a doctorate in classical languages in 1934 and a licentiate in theology in 1938. After his Jesuit tertianship in Belgium he taught classics and theology at Marquette University, Milwaukee, from 1939 to 1962, where he also served as chairman of the department of classical languages. Meanwhile he published articles and two books, the *Sermons of St. Peter Chrysologus* in 1953 and *St. Ignatius' Idea of a Jesuit University* in 1954. In 1962 he became a professor of theology in the School of Divinity of St. Louis University. He was director of the Institute of Jesuit Sources from its inception in 1960 until 1986, during which time he edited over twenty-five scholarly books on Jesuit spirituality. From 1969 to 1986 he was editor of the periodical *Studies in the Spirituality of Jesuits* and chairman of the seminar which produced it. In 1970 he published *The Constitutions of the Society of Jesus*, a translation and a commentary.

Collaborators of this Volume

PARMANANDA R. DIVARKAR, S.J., is a member of the Jesuit province of Bombay, India. After his ordination to the priesthood in 1952 he taught philosophy in St. Xavier's College, a branch of the University of Bombay, where he became chairman of the department of philosophy and then rector of the college. He also served as Vice-Chancellor of the Jesuit Ecclesiastical Faculties. In 1975 he was elected a "General Assistant," one of the four chief advisors to Father General Pedro Arrupe, and served in that office in the Jesuit curia in Rome for nine years. He published two books on Jesuit spirituality: *A Pilgrim's Testimony* (1983), a translation of St. Ignatius's *Autobiography*, which is reprinted below in the present book; and *The Path of Interior Knowledge* (1983), on the dynamics of the *Spiritual Exercises*. In 1984 he returned to Bombay, where he is editor of *Ignis*, a periodical on Jesuit spirituality.

EDWARD J. MALATESTA, S.J., has been Director of the Institute for Chinese-Western Cultural History of the University of San Francisco since its inception in 1984. He received an M.A. in philosophy from Gonzaga University in 1955, the licentiate in theology from Les Fontaines, Chantilly, France, in 1962, and a doctorate in Sacred Scripture from the Pontifical Biblical Institute in 1975. He taught biblical spirituality at the Pontifical Gregorian University from 1966 to 1979, and has published books and articles in that field. He edited the twelve volumes of The Religious Experience Series (Abbey Press). For two years (1977–1979) he directed a Jesuit tertianship program at the Jesuit School of Theology in Berkeley. From 1979 to 1982, he engaged in

x

Chinese studies, and from 1982 to 1984 collaborated with Francis A. Rouleau, S.J., historian of the Jesuit missions in China.

MARTIN E. PALMER, S.J., is presently an editor at the Institute of Jesuit Sources and a teacher of the history of Christian thought in the College of Philosophy and Letters at St. Louis University. After philosophical studies at Berchmanskolleg, Munich, he received the degrees of M.A. in biblical languages and literature from Catholic University, Washington, and S.T.L. from Woodstock College, Maryland. After ordination to the priesthood in 1964 he received the degree of S.S.L. from the Pontifical Biblical Institute, Rome. Since then he has taught theology and the history of spirituality at St. Louis University and biblical spirituality at Creighton University, Omaha. He is preparing an English translation of selected early Directories of the Spiritual Exercises. He has served as an official translator at the worldwide Synods of Bishops held in Rome in 1985, 1987, and 1990.

Author of the Preface

JOHN W. PADBERG, S.J., is Director of the Institute of Jesuit Sources, Chairman of the Seminar on Jesuit Spirituality, and Editor of the journal *Studies in the Spirituality of Jesuits*. Born in 1926, Padberg received a bachelor's degree in classical languages (1949), a master of arts degree in modern European history (1954), and licentiates in both philosophy (1951) and theology (1959) from Saint Louis University. He received a Ph.D. in the history of ideas from Harvard University in 1965. After serving as professor of history and academic vice president at Saint Louis University, he was president (1975–1985) of Weston School of Theology, a national Jesuit theological center in Cambridge, Massachusetts. His major interest in recent years has been the history of the Society of Jesus and his publications include articles and monographs on that subject, such as *Colleges in Conflict: The Jesuit Schools in France from Revival to Suppression, 1815–1880* from Harvard University Press, and "The General Congregations of the Society of Jesus: A Brief Survey of Their History," in *Studies in the Spirituality of Jesuits*.

FOREWORD

September 27, 1990, was the 450th anniversary of the foundation of the Society of Jesus through the approval of Pope Paul III granted on that date; and the year 1991 will be the 500th anniversary of the birth of St. Ignatius of Loyola, according to the most probable date, 1491. The Society of Jesus and its friends will celebrate these events throughout the world by an Ignatian Year beginning on September 27, 1990, and ending on his feast day, July 31, 1991.

These celebrations will focus especially on his charism and his ministries. A charism is a gift of the Holy Spirit, different in different persons, for building up Christ's Mystical Body (1 Cor. 12:27–31; Ephes. 4:12). Special efforts will be made to penetrate more deeply the tenor of thought which runs through the writings Ignatius has left us and to explore the apostolic ministries he set in motion. How can these ideals and ministries be better understood and better adjusted to the circumstances of our present day? How can they be better achieved by the many persons, religious and lay, who share Ignatius' ideals and are cooperating toward their realization? It is this writer's hope that the present volume will be a modest contribution toward all these objectives.

Of Ignatius' five major works, two are presented here in their entirety: his *Autobiography* and *Spiritual Exercises*. From his *Spiritual Diary* and his *Constitutions of the Society of Jesus*, selections are given in a manner calculated to offer a conspectus of each complete work. Of his thousands of letters we can give only a few samples. The translators of the respective writings are listed in the Contents. The special introductions before each work and the endnotes were composed by the editor of this volume, Father Ganss, and he alone bears the responsibility for them—with one exception. All the work on the Deliberation on Poverty and the *Spiritual Diary* was done jointly by Father Ganss and Father Malatesta.

According to modern conventions superior numbers are not ordinarily used with display type. Ignatius, however, wrote his titles (or other words which modern editors in varying ways convert into titles

1

FOREWORD

or subheadings) before these conventions arose. Particularly in the case of the *Exercises*, his titles contain words which have his own highly technical meanings or nuances and do not reoccur in the text below. If such meanings or nuances are not explained immediately, uninitiated readers will misunderstand his thought. Hence for the purposes of this book we thought it best to make an exception to the modern convention and to use superior numbers with the display type.

Ignatius is ranked among the great educators of history. Hence one feature of this book merits attention. Scattered through it are groups of pages which, if combined together, amount to a monograph. They present, from the primary sources and within the context of Ignatius' worldview, his theory of Christian education and its application to practice in the system of colleges and universities he founded. These pages are: 48–49, 278–281, 293–302, 356–365, 451–452, and 457–464.

Although it is impossible to name in gratitude all those to whom this writer is indebted for valuable help, he desires to show his deep gratefulness explicitly to at least some of them: to Father John W. Padberg, for help of every sort toward carrying this work steadily forward; to Doctors John Farina of the Paulist Press and Bernard McGinn, editor of the series in which it appears, for their friendly cooperation, which injected so much pleasure into the task; to Jesuit Fathers Parmananda R. Divarkar, Edward J. Malatesta, and Martin E. Palmer for the translations they contributed; to Father Vincent J. O'Flaherty for scrutinizing my translation of and notes about the *Spiritual Exercises* and making valued suggestions which reflect his long experience as a director; to Father Philip C. Fischer for his competent editorial help, and to Mrs. Georgia J. Christo of Paulist Press for hers; to Sisters Elizabeth A. Johnson, C.S.J., who so carefully read the translation of the *Exercises*, and Frances Krumpelman, S.C.N., who similarly read the entire manuscript, to both of whom I am indebted for help particularly in regard to inclusive language. Finally, grateful acknowledgment is made to Father Pasquale Puca, Director of the Gregorian University Press in Rome, for permission to reprint Father Divarkar's translation of Ignatius' *Autobiography*, and to Marquette University Press, Milwaukee, for permission to reproduce, from my *St. Ignatius' Idea of a Jesuit University*, the Chart which appears with Chapter 12.

George E. Ganss, S.J.
Easter Sunday, April 15, 1990

PREFACE

It has taken a long time for Ignatius of Loyola really to become known, but this present volume in the Classics of Western Spirituality thoroughly and brilliantly changes that situation.

Only slowly over almost five centuries and only fully in the last one hundred years has it even been possible to know the richness of the personality of Ignatius, the variety of his gifts, the diversity of his accomplishments. Many reasons entered into this unusual situation.

First and paradoxically, Ignatius was too well known. Everyone knew him as the founder of the Jesuits. Even the briefest history of the era of the Protestant Reformation and the Catholic Reform would mention him as the founder of that supposedly prime agency of the Counter-Reformation, the Society of Jesus. Often, then, depending on the ecclesiastical allegiance of the writer, Ignatius would either be blamed or praised, usually for the same thing, his supposedly preternatural and dauntingly impersonal organizing and administrative abilities, as if that were his main characteristic. Those writers with a taste for the romantic or the martial might include a few lines on his early years as a courtier and soldier. However, the friend who with the most disparate kinds of men and women forged bonds that lasted across decades and beyond continents, the man of a love moved to tears, the man of mystical favors almost too deep for words, the Ignatius who was a teacher of the highest graces of prayer and the recipient of such graces beyond measure—that Ignatius, overshadowed by the conventional figure, was all but unknown until more recent times.

Another reason that Ignatius took so long to become truly known is that several of his own writings which best portrayed him were largely unavailable until comparatively recent times. The text of the *Spiritual Exercises*, of course, rapidly became widespread. The *Constitutions* were available in their Latin version, but full and accurate translations into the vernacular came only in the twentieth century, with the English version as late as 1970. The letters, with their extraordinarily varied array of correspondents and interests and insights and teaching, had to await the complete and critical editions of the *Monumenta Historica*. Selections in the vernacular did not become widespread until later, with several such compilations in English appearing only since the middle of this century.

Yet most astonishingly, the two works that are most particular and personal to the life of Ignatius, *The Autobiography* and *The Spiritual Diary*, are the very ones that remained least known and longest unavailable. The original 1554–1557 Spanish-Italian text of the *Autobiography* was put into Latin a few years later, but that translation sat unpublished in the archives for 170 years, until 1731. The original text had to wait almost 350 years, until 1904, to see the printed light of day, and only in 1963 did a fully critical text appear, more than 400 years after its writing. As for the *Spiritual Diary*, which "enables us to gaze directly into the depth of Ignatius' heart and the sublimity of his mysticism," while what we have of it was written in 1544–45, not until 1934 was the whole diary published. If this fragment of what was undoubtedly a larger work was indeed providentially preserved, it was also unaccountably stashed away on an archive shelf for almost 400 years. A very few Jesuit contemporaries of Ignatius knew of its existence; brief passages appeared in classic early biographies; in 1892 part of it was published but it took until 1938, a little more than fifty years ago, for the first study of the critically edited text. No wonder that it has taken a long time for Ignatius really to become known and for the sum total of his works to reveal him as simultaneously a man of apostolic action, one of the recipients of and guides to the widest and highest of God's graces, and a classic master of Christian spirituality.

This volume of the Classics of Western Spirituality now makes such an appreciation of Ignatius available to everyone, thanks to the collaborative work of all those involved in its preparation. Its editor and the translator of several of its selections, Father George E. Ganss, S.J., was founder and for many years the director of the Institute of Jesuit Sources. Seldom have the written sources for the knowledge of a great Christian man of prayer, activity, and spiritual guidance been better presented than in this volume. If the spiritual life and the work of Ignatius arose from his long experience of God, their presentation in this volume has arisen from the long experience of the life and works of Ignatius on the part of Father Ganss. Contemporaries of Ignatius de-

PREFACE

scribed him as capable of being simultaneously warm, affectionate, serious, stimulating. So is this selection and presentation of his writings.

John W. Padberg, S.J.
Director
Institute of Jesuit Sources
St. Louis, Missouri

GENERAL INTRODUCTION

GENERAL INTRODUCTION

St. Ignatius of Loyola (1491–1556) had a dynamic spirituality which was ordered toward both personal spiritual growth and energetic apostolic endeavor. It was firmly based on the chief truths in God's revelation, with a particular focus on God's plan for the creation, redemption, and spiritual development of the human beings who use their freedom wisely—that plan of salvation which St. Paul calls "the mystery of Christ."[1]

This Introduction will furnish background for reading Ignatius' works with better understanding. The keys for interpreting them correctly come largely from that background. A tourist who consults a guidebook and learns what to look for before a limited three-day visit to Rome will profit more than one who merely deplanes and begins to wander about. Much the same is true of a reader who first approaches a work of Ignatius. Here at the outset, therefore, we shall present a brief synthetic summary of his mature thought. It will let a reader know what to look for as she or he reads each work, and to see how it or any passage within it fits into the whole structure of his worldview.

Part I will briefly sketch Ignatius' historical environment and present an initial synthesis of his spirituality. Part II will be an intellectual and spiritual biography of Ignatius, tracing the process by which his expansive worldview was formed and showing the intellectual foundations on which it was eventually based, especially after his university studies in Paris. Part III will present a general introduction to his writings through which his worldview found expression, some keys for their correct interpretation, and a brief survey of the terminology about spirituality and mysticism which we shall employ.

It seems wise to introduce here some of Ignatius' chief associates from whom much of our information will be drawn: Diego Laínez, his close companion from the time when he made Ignatius' Exercises at Paris in 1534; Jerónimo Nadal, learned in theology, whom he considered a faithful interpreter of his mind; Juan de Polanco, his competent secretary, consultant, and alter ego from 1547 to 1556; Pedro de Ribadeneira, who lived with him in Rome for the last sixteen years of his life and gathered notes for the classic life of the founder which he later wrote; and Luis Gonçalves da Câmara, to whom he dictated the story of his life in 1553 and 1555.

PART I. BASIC ORIENTATIONS

A. The Historical Background

Ignatius lived in the era when feudalistic principalities were yielding place to the powerful central governments which were arising. Monarchs were growing strong by uniting centrifugal provinces into nations, as Ferdinand (1452–1516) and Isabella (1474–1504) strove to do in Spain. Other prominent kings during Ignatius' life were, in England, Henry VIII (king, 1509–1547); in France, Francis I (1515–1547); in Portugal, John III (1521–1557); in Spain, Charles I (king of Spain, 1516–1556; also Holy Roman Emperor as Charles V, 1519–1556). Overseas, Spain was enlarging her newly found empire and endeavoring to convert its natives to Christianity. She was also developing a system of centralized government for it through control by a king whose powers descended through a viceroy in many far-flung provinces or regions as distant as Mexico or Peru. This environment —or at least the same circumstances from which the arrangement developed—may have had some subconscious influence on the somewhat similar system of government Ignatius devised for his new supranational apostolic order, which he intended for apostolic service anywhere on earth. The authority a superior general held under the pope in Rome would descend through provincial superiors into their respective provinces. Yet within this monarchic structure, Ignatius included in his *Constitutions* representative functions and processes to a degree truly surprising in that era of absolute monarchs.

In northern Europe, religious unity was dissolving. Luther was excommunicated in 1521, the year of Ignatius' conversion at Loyola; and Henry VIII became head of the Anglican Church in 1531. Southern Europe was still one in faith; but there, as in the north, the people's ignorance of that faith and the consequent neglect of practice were often appalling. The Church was full of abuses and in need of reform "in head and members." In Corsica in 1552, none of the bishops of the island had been there for sixty years. Many of the priests did not correctly know the formula of consecration in the Mass and earned their living as laborers. It was almost unheard of that parish priests should preach. Many people did not know how to recite the Our Father or Hail Mary, and superstitions, hatreds, and immorality were rife among them.[2] The need for moral and administrative reforms along with doctrinal stabilization called for an Ecumenical Council within the Church. After many frustrating delays, Pope Paul III managed to open the Council of Trent on December 13, 1545. Among the people at large illiteracy was widespread. Probably less than 5 percent of the adults received education equivalent to that of seven-year-olds today.[3] Ignatius became very alert to these circumstances, and his desire to meet the needs of the Church played a large part in the formation of his spirituality.

B. An Initial Synthesis of His Spirituality

Convinced that he was being guided by God, Ignatius was led to form a worldview whereby he saw all things both as created by God and as the means by which men and women could make their way back to God. That is, by knowing, loving, and serving him on earth, they would achieve their supreme end hereafter: self-fulfillment by praising and enjoying God in the beatific vision. On earth they work out this ultimate end by means of many intermediate ends, such as upright living, helping their neighbors, and active membership in the Church. Ignatius developed an intense desire to be associated intimately with Christ, and to cooperate with him in achieving God's plan of creation, redemption, and spiritual growth as that plan was slowly unfolding in the history of salvation. Ignatius desired to play the role offered to him by God in that ongoing history. Further, his attachment was to the whole Christ, Christ present and functioning through his Mystical Body the Church in the 1500s and advancing it into the future. Ignatius' constant endeavor was to make all his activities result in praise or glory to God greater than would have accrued to him without them.

As a result, the "greater" praise or glory of God became the motivation which urged him on, and also the criterion by which he habitually made his decisions in deliberations about options he faced. In his usage, "glory," "praise," and "honor" to God are synonyms which constantly recur, and often they are linked with or imply "the service of God." For instance, there are some 140 such occurrences in his *Constitutions of the Society of Jesus* alone.[4]

One prominent characteristic of his spirituality, especially important for understanding his *Spiritual Exercises* and his *Constitutions*,[5] is his sharp focus on ends with accompanying means. His ends were clear in his mind and arranged in a series leading up to God.

The one supreme and inspiring end, the keystone to which all the other elements in the arch of his thought were support, was "the greater glory of God," with "glory" meaning praise and implying service. To pursue this single aim was his own constant endeavor, and he wanted the members of his Society to seek it by all their efforts toward personal sanctification and apostolic activities. God should be found in all one's actions, and one should order them all to his glory. To that supreme but simple end, as Joseph de Guibert has pointed out,[6] everything else served as means: material goods or evangelical poverty, work or repose, even prayer itself.

Ignatius spontaneously expressed that one same worldview through all his writings, as will appear in greater detail below. For example, in his *Spiritual Exercises* he applied it to aiding an individual person to discern how he or she can serve God best. In his *Constitutions of the Society of Jesus* he applied it to the inspiration and government of an apostolic religious institute; and in his letters he applied it to multifarious situations of daily life.

PART II. THE EVOLUTION OF IGNATIUS' SPIRITUAL WORLDVIEW

A. His Intellectual and Spiritual Biography

In May 1521, when the thirty-year-old Ignatius received the wound at Pamplona which occasioned his conversion to spiritual living at Loyola, he had little education. Yet less than two years later when he left Manresa in February 1523, he carried with him the first sketch of his later *Spiritual Exercises*. They were already structured around the chief truths of God's plan of salvation for human beings who use their freedom wisely, with particular attention to their creation by God and their redemption by Christ. Those pages also contained the incipient core of his worldview, which was to grow step by step with their continual revisions until about 1539. By then that core had grown into an outlook on life strongly motivating his own spiritual growth and his work for others. It had shaped his own personalized way of viewing God, the created universe, and the role of free human beings within God's plan for them. It had gradually matured into the spiritual doctrine and practices which he communicated through his conversations, writings, and other activities. In all this development he himself was convinced that God was treating him "just as a schoolmaster treats a child whom he is teaching" (*Autobiog*, 27).

What were the initiatives and instruments which the divine Schoolmaster used for this remarkable formation of the uneducated thirty-year-old soldier? By what cooperative procedures did Ignatius master the lessons which added up to this remarkable worldview? To answer those questions is our aim as we begin to sketch an intellectual and spiritual biography of Ignatius. It is a tale perhaps as fascinating as Augustine's *Confessions*.

The beginnings of Ignatius' spirituality must be sought in the Catholic faith, which he inherited with its sixteenth-century trappings amid the cultural environment of his youth. When he turned to serious spiritual living at the age of thirty, he began the lengthy formation of his personalized concept of God's redemptive plan by drawing particularly from writings of the Dominican, Carthusian, Cistercian, and Franciscan schools. We shall trace that process in his mind through six periods as he matured his spiritual outlook and expressed it in his writings.

1. Ignatius' Early Life, 1491–1521

Guipúzcoa, Ignatius' beautiful, mountainous homeland, lies in northern Spain, a little west of the French border. To the south lies Navarre with its capital, Pamplona, and beyond that in his day the Castile of King Ferdinand the Catholic, with which Guipúzcoa was in friendly alliance. The future founder of the Jesuits was born, almost certainly in 1491 and before October 23, in the ancestral castle of the noble Loyola family. It was situated on a farmland estate about a mile to the south of the village of Azpeitia. There in the parish church of San Sebastián he received the baptismal name of Iñigo (by which he was known until, between 1535 and 1540, he increasingly signed his name "Ignatius"). Here too he grew up while absorbing the traits characteristic of his Basque countrymen, known for their straightforward manners, their charitable readiness to be helpful, their tenacity, and their undiluted Catholic faith. In addition to the parish church of San Sebastián and the convent of Franciscan nuns in Azpeitia, shrines dotted the surrounding hillsides and valleys. Masses and Vespers were well attended, no doubt with the boy Ignatius often among the worshipers. In this environment he came to love music, dance, and songs both religious and secular. Although the Basques of his day had a strong, active, almost instinctive Catholic faith, they did not escape the moral laxity also widespread then in the rest of Europe. Among them were considerable instances of illicit marital unions, and feuding among either individuals or factions.

Somewhere near 1506, when Ignatius was about fifteen and knew how to read and write, he was sent to be trained for court life in the house of Juan Velázquez de Cuéllar, the high treasurer of King Ferdinand and Isabella. In that environment were factors likely to stimulate piety, and also others likely to be an occasion of loose morals or worldliness. Here Ignatius became acquainted with the literature of the flourishing Spanish Renaissance: religious and secular songs, and novels of chivalry (*libros de caballería*), which reflected the culture from which they sprang. One of these, *Amadis*, which Ignatius later told us he read (*Autobiog*, 17), gives us a concrete idea of the genre and its cultural environment. Its chief characters—King Lisuarte, Amadis, and his lady Oriana—are persons who converse quite naturally with priests and monks, strive for the exaltation of the holy Catholic faith, assist at Mass and Vespers. But the book also contained a few loose-living characters, salacious and scandalous incidents, and a false, exaggerated idealization of woman that *Amadis* dangerous reading for the young.[7]

In this atmosphere Ignatius passed into manhood, with ambitions for feats of arms and chivalry, interests in fine clothes and his personal appearance, and romantic episodes. He manifested certain characteristics: a desire for worldly praise and glory, eagerness to distinguish himself by daring or even reckless deeds against odds, and tenacity in reaching an objective once he had decided upon it. These traits, redirected to a higher end, were to last all his life.

He was never a professional soldier, but he took part in military expeditions when occasion required. He was eager to win the favor of the king and nobles and to distinguish himself in military glory. Such a case arose in 1521 when a large French army besieged Pamplona. Despite the opposition of other officers, Ignatius successfully urged a resistance which was hopeless. In the battle on May 17 a cannonball shattered the bone in one of his legs and inflicted a flesh wound in the other. Treated courteously by the French because of his bravery, he was carried on a litter to Loyola, which he reached in early June. After the surgery, which he bore with great fortitude, his condition deteriorated until he was near death, but after June 28, the vigil of Sts. Peter and Paul, he grew rapidly better. He attributed this to St. Peter.

Ignatius himself summed up his life from birth to Pamplona by telling us that until the age of twenty-six he was "a man given to the follies of the world, and what he enjoyed most was warlike sport, with a great and foolish desire to win fame" (*Autobiog*, 1). His associates give further details. Polanco states: "Although very much attached to the faith, he did not live in keeping with his belief or guard himself from sins; he was particularly careless about gambling, affairs with women, and the use of arms." When Ignatius was twenty-four, a magistrate of Azpeitia prosecuted him for misdemeanors which were "outrageous, committed at carnival time, at night."[8]

From 1491 to May 1521, therefore, Ignatius was a practicing Catholic, but no signs of intensive spirituality as yet appeared in him.

2. Conversion at Loyola, August, 1521–February, 1522

By early August, Ignatius' energy was returning but he still had to remain in bed. To while away the time he asked for novels of chivalry. "But in that house none of those that he usually read could be found, so they gave him a life of Christ and a book of the lives of the saints in Castilian" (*Autobiog*, 5).

As his reading grew increasingly meditative, he also began a practice he continued in later life, that of keeping spiritual notes. "As he very much liked those books, the idea came to him to note down briefly some of the more essential things from the life of Christ and the saints. So he set himself very diligently to write a book (because he was now beginning to be up and about the house a bit), with red ink for the words of Christ, blue ink for those of Our Lady, on polished and lined paper. . . . Part of the time he spent in writing, and part in prayer" (*Autobiog*, 11). His copybook of high-quality paper contained nearly 300 quarto pages.

a. The Lives of the Saints

The book containing the lives of the saints was the still popular *Golden Legend* (*Legenda aurea*) by the Dominican Jacobus de Voragine (d. 1298). These "golden things to be read" made up one of the most important books of the Middle Ages. It shows us much of the culture, outlook, and piety of the common folk in those centuries. Seventy-four editions in Latin are known before 1500 and numerous editions in at least six vernacular languages. It is a museum of sketches, each five to fifteen pages, which present the saints in a procession according to the order of their feasts in the Church year. Major feasts too are treated, such as the Nativity, Circumcision, Purification, Easter, and Pentecost. It is replete with tales, many of them about miracles, which are retold without any sense of critical scholarship; and its etymologies are fanciful. Yet beneath this exuberant foliage it also contained substantial historical and religious truth. The Christian message came through to the readers and fostered their genuine faith and with it a credulous piety.

The edition used by Ignatius was a Spanish version, probably that published in Toledo in 1511 with a Latin title, *Flos sanctorum*, in which the word "flower" really means the best or most important of the saints. It contained a prologue by the Cistercian Gauberto Vagad in which he enthusiastically spoke of the saints as the "knights of God" who did resplendent deeds in the service of the "eternal prince, Christ Jesus," whose "ever victorious banner" these knights were following. These ideas undoubtedly made a strong impression on Ignatius. They contain a fundamental idea which was to dominate the rest of his life: to give an outstanding service to Christ, following the banner of this King who has the saints as his knights. Desire to be an outstanding knight of Christ replaced his thoughts of chivalrous service to ladies.

However, he also let his mind wander back to worldly exploits, including three-hour daydreams about how he would charm a certain noble lady, unknown to us (*Autobiog*, 5, 6). Then he noticed that the thoughts about worldly affairs delighted him at first but left him dry and dissatisfied later, while those about holy practices had an opposite result. They consoled him while they were happening and also left him satisfied and joyful afterward. Thus "little by little he came to recognize the difference between the spirits that were stirring him, one from the devil, the other from God" (*Autobiog*, 8). Here we find the germ of what would become a prominent characteristic of his spirituality, discernment of spirits.

In his reading he was deeply impressed by two saints, and his reaction was: "St. Dominic did this, therefore, I have to do it. St. Francis did this, therefore, I have to do it" (*Autobiog*, 7). Two citations from Jacobus will make the background and atmosphere of Ignatius' thinking more concrete. For October 4 he wrote about Francis:

> Francis, the servant and friend of the Most High, was born
> in Assisi. He became a merchant, and until his twentieth year

spent his time in vain living. Then the Lord beset him with the scourge of sickness, and speedily transformed him into a new man, so that he began to manifest the spirit of prophecy. . . .

Once when out of piety he went to Rome, he laid aside his garments, put on those of a beggar, and sat among the mendicants at the door of St. Peter's church, grasping hungrily for food like any one of them; . . . The ancient Enemy strove to turn him away from his holy resolution. . . . But our Lord comforted him, and he heard the words: "Francis, put the bitter ahead of the sweet and despise thyself, if thou wouldst know Me." . . .

Once when he went into the church of St. Damian to pray, an image of the crucified Christ miraculously spoke to him and said: "Francis, go and repair my house, which, as thou seest, is falling in ruins! " . . .

Many men, nobles and of humble birth, clerics and laymen, put away the pomp of the world and followed in his footsteps, and these the holy father taught to live in evangelical perfection, to cling to poverty, and to walk in the way of holy simplicity. Moreover, he wrote a Rule according to the Gospel, for himself and the brethren whom he had and was to have; and this Rule our lord Pope Innocent approved. Thenceforth he began with even greater zeal to sow the seeds of the word of God, going about the cities and villages with admirable fervor.[9]

Jacobus' treatment of St. Dominic, for his feast on August 4, was similar:

Dominic, the illustrious founder and father of the Order of Preachers, was born in Spain, in the village of Calaroga. . . . Before he was born his mother dreamt that she bore in her womb a little dog, who held a lighted torch in his mouth, and when the dog came forth from her womb, he set the whole world afire with his torch. . . . He was sent to Palencia to make his studies, and such was his zeal for knowledge that for ten years he did not taste wine. . . . He devoted himself to study day and night, ceaselessly entreating God to grant him the grace to spend himself wholly for the salvation of his neighbor. . . .

He began to think upon the establishment of an Order whose mission it would be to go from place to place, preaching and strengthening the faith against the heretics. . . . In Rome he sought permission of Pope Innocent, for himself and his successors, to found an Order which would be called . . . the Order of Preachers. . . . The pope had . . . joyfully granted the petition of the man of God, advising him to return to his brethren and to choose some one of the approved Rules, and then to come back to him and receive his approval. Dominic therefore went back to his brethren, sixteen in number. . . . They, having invoked the Holy Spirit, with one mind chose the Rule of St. Augustine, doctor and preacher, adding thereto certain stricter practices which they determined to observe as constitutions.[10]

Still another passage which Ignatius may well have read is contained in Jacobus' life of St. Augustine:

At that time, the Goths had captured Rome and the idolaters and unbelievers were casting reproaches on the Christians. Therefore Augustine wrote his book, *The City of God*. In it he shows that the just are to be oppressed in this life and the wicked to flourish. He also treats of the two cities, Jerusalem and Babylon, and their kings, for Christ is the king of Jerusalem and the devil of Babylon. Two loves, he says, built these two cities for themselves; for the city of the devil has arisen from the love of self growing even to contempt of God, and the city of God from the love of God growing even to contempt of self.[11]

These ideas culled from Gauberto's preface and Jacobus' description of Augustine's *City of God* are highly similar to key thoughts in Ignatius' meditations on the Kingdom of Christ and on the Two Standards in his *Exercises* ([91–98 and 136–156]). It is plausible to conjecture that he had entered them in the copybook he carried with him to Manresa. Nadal tells us that both these exercises stem from Manresa. "There our Lord communicated the Exercises to him" and guided him "especially in two exercises, namely, that on the King and that on the Two Standards."[12]

b. Ludolph's Life of Christ

The life of Christ handed to Ignatius was a Spanish translation of the long *Vita Jesu Christi* by the Carthusian Ludolph of Saxony. This work was in the same literary tradition which had presented meditations on events in the Savior's life, such as Pseudo-Bonaventures's *Meditations on the Life of Christ*. Widely popular after its appearance, probably between 1360 and 1377, it circulated first in many manuscripts. The first printed edition came in 1472, followed by numerous new editions in continental Europe, and translations in French, Italian, Dutch, German, Bohemian, Catalan, and Spanish.

At the request of Ferdinand and Isabella, Ludolph's *Vita* was translated into Spanish by the Franciscan Ambrosio de Montesino. The Spanish *Vida* was published at Toledo in 1502–1503 in four large tomes totaling about 1,000 pages. This was the edition Ignatius used at Loyola.[13]

In contrast to *The Golden Legend*, the *Vita* was profound and scholarly. Ludolph (ca. 1300–1377) seems to have entered the Dominican order at eighteen. He became a Master of Theology and in about 1340 transferred to the Carthusians. Hitherto writers such as Pseudo-Bonaventure had composed meditations on episodes in the life of Christ, but no complete biography of the Savior had been attempted. Ludolph arranged his selected topics in a plausible chronological sequence of 181 long chapters which made it one continuous account of Christ's life up to his ascension; and he continued the narrative farther to take in the results of the last judgment. Thus his book contained the whole mystery of Christ, God's plan of salvation unfolding in a historical sequence. It began this drama of our salvation with the eternal generation of the Word in the Trinity, treated his Incarnation as the remedy for the sin of Adam, then progressed through his life, death, resurrection, and ascension, and onward into the last judgment, which results in hell or humankind's true destiny, heaven.

This succession of ideas in Ludolph's chosen topics is so important for studying the steps by which Ignatius formed his own spirituality, and so similar to the structure of his *Exercises* into which his thought flowed, that some further details of it should be indicated here. In Part I, with 92 chapters, Ludolph devotes his Introduction (*Prooemium*) to explaining methods for contemplating the events in Christ's life. Then follow: (in chapter 1), the divine generation of the Word in the eternity of the Trinity; (in 2), God's plan for the salvation of the fallen human

19

race; (in 5), the Annunciation; (in 10), the Circumcision; (in 13), the Flight; (in 16), the Hidden Life. Then come 127 chapters (in Parts I and II) on events of the Public Life, 18 chapters on the Passion, and 12 chapters on the Risen Life and the Ascension. The final seven chapters treat Pentecost, the Praise of God, the Last Judgment, and Heavenly Glory.[14]

This sequence contained in Ludolph's *Vita* became the nucleus of Ignatius' thought, which at Manresa he would soon express in his *Exercises*. A glance at their structure will also give us an initial idea of the depth of Ludolph's influence on the molding of his thought. In its central core the *Exercises* have meditations or contemplations on these topics: God's purpose in creating ([23]); in Week I, on the history of sin, the attempted frustration of God's plan ([45–72]); in Week II, on the Incarnation, Nativity, Presentation and Flight ([23]), Hidden Life, Finding of Jesus in the Temple, Call of the Apostles, Sermon on the Mount, Preaching in the Temple, Raising of Lazarus ([131–161]); in Week III, on Palm Sunday and the Passion ([190–209]); in Week IV, the risen life and Christ's appearance to his mother ([218]). Ludolph has a chapter on each of these topics, and in the same sequence as in Ignatius. Farther on too, in a sort of appendix to which the central core refers the reader, Ignatius had another list of fifty-one episodes (called "mysteries") which start with the Annunciation ([261]) and end with the Ascension ([312]). Virtually all these fifty-one topics are found also in the titles of Ludolph's 181 chapters, and in the same sequence as Ignatius'.

The manner of treatment, however, is totally different. Ludolph himself expounds on a topic at length, while Ignatius gives only brief points, original with himself, for an exercitant to expand in his own contemplation, according to his own needs and graces from God. All this suggests that at Loyola Ignatius had jotted down at least the titles and perhaps some sketchy ideas from Ludolph's chapters and written them, in changed, abbreviated wordings, in the copybook which he was still to have with him in Manresa.

Ludolph's *Vita* was a classic in the literature of devotion. He developed his topics by ideas and citations from the best scholarship of his day in Scripture, doctrinal and moral theology, patrology, devotional writings, and his own reflections. He mustered all this learning to further his controlling purpose: to stir up love and imitation of the Savior. Some treatments are imaginative reconstructions filling out

Gospel narratives. Legends too are present—often mentioning some earlier Fathers of the Church from whom they were drawn—but the sound doctrinal truth always shines through. The Carthusian school was characterized by practical mysticism. Ludolph, typically a writer of this school, wanted his readers to have a warm piety firmly based on sound doctrine, and he hoped to lead them toward salvation and rich spiritual development. In all this he exerted a deep formative influence on Ignatius' mentality by orienting him in the same direction.

Here too a few citations will show us more concretely the intellectual and spiritual formation Ignatius received during his convalescence. In these samples, few though they are, we shall see many ideas and attitudes which Ignatius absorbed and would later utilize in his *Exercises*, though expressed in his own new way.

Ludolph begins his own Introduction (*Prooemium*), which Ignatius almost certainly pondered, by stating that Christ is the only foundation for salvation. Thus:

> 2. First of all, a sinner who desires to escape from his misdeeds . . . should listen to God's invitation to forgiveness: "Come to me, all you who are burdened." . . . Let such a one come by means of deep contrition, careful confession, and firm will always to refrain from evil and do good.
>
> Secondly, let this sinner, now reconciled and made faithful in Christ, take diligent care to adhere to his Physician [Christ], and acquire familiarity with him by pondering his most holy life with all the devotion he can muster. . . .
>
> Let him return often to the most memorable episodes of Christ's life, such as his incarnation, nativity, circumcision, presentation in the temple, passion, resurrection, ascension, his sending the Holy Spirit, and his coming to judge the world. All these are topics for special recall, and exercise, and spiritual remembrance, and consolation. However, let him also read the life of Christ in such a manner that he endeavors to imitate him as far as he can. For it profits him little to read unless he also imitates.

These words show us the tenor of thought which colors all Ludolph's later chapters. For Ignatius they also established a sequence of steps which he was to follow later: repentance and confession at Montserrat, a preparation for constructive spiritual progress at Manresa. It was, finally, to reappear in the structure of his book of *Exercises* with its division into four "Weeks": one of repentance, then three of close association with Christ.

Farther on Ludolph gives directives for reading the life of Christ meditatively and prayerfully. This was the procedure used by Ignatius in his readings at Loyola, and it too was to reappear in his *Exercises*, but totally reworded and fitted to his own purposes. Especially noteworthy is Ludolph's insistence on the need to stop and relish interiorly the Savior's mysteries, words, and actions:

> 11. On my part I shall narrate [the things which Christ said or did] just as they occurred, or as they may be piously believed to have occurred, according to certain imaginative representations. . . .
>
> Your part will be, if you want to draw fruit from these sayings and deeds of Christ, to put aside all other preoccupations; and then, with all the affection of your heart, slowly, diligently, and with relish, make yourself present to what the Lord Jesus has said and done, and to what is being narrated, just as if you were actually there, and heard him with your own ears, and saw him with your own eyes; for all these matters are exceedingly sweet to one who ponders them with desire, and far more so to one who savors them. Although many of these facts are recounted as having taken place in the past, you nevertheless should meditate upon them as if they were taking place now, in the present; for from this you will surely experience great delight (*Prooem.*, no. 11, also 13. Compare *SpEx* [2, 69, 214]).

Ludolph's first chapter is entitled "On the Divine and Eternal Generation of Christ." It is a commentary on the prologue of St. John's Gospel. The Word is the revealer of the Father and the creator of humankind. Thus the Carthusian expounds the Son within the totality of the mystery of the Trinity. This chapter, as the italicized words in the following citations will show, contains many ideas which are foundational pillars of Ignatius' later spiritual doctrine. This establishes a probability that they were among the items on which he meditated deeply and even put into his copybook from which he was to derive much consolation at Manresa.

9. "The light shines" also "in the darkness" of this world, because *the Creator is seen in his creatures*. In heaven God is a mirror containing the creatures, in whom they shine forth, and in whom we shall see all things which will contribute to our joy. Similarly but conversely, in this life *creatures are a mirror reflecting the Creator, and in it we contemplate him*; for, as the Apostle says, "At present we see indistinctly, as in a mirror" (namely, the creatures); and elsewhere, "Ever since the creation of the world, God's invisible attributes . . . have been able to be understood and perceived in what he has made." . . .

10. When . . . you perceive that the Son is begotten by the Father, . . . contemplate that from that immense and brilliant Light *there arises a Splendor who is coeternal*, coequal, and consubstantial, One who is the highest Power and Wisdom, through whom the Father arranged all things from eternity, and *"through whom he created the universe"* (Heb. 1:1). And once it was created, he governs it and *orders it to his own glory*, partly through nature, and partly through grace, so that *he leaves nothing in this world which is not thus ordered*. (Emphasis added.)

Here the similarity of Ludolph's reverential thought and that of Ignatius is very striking. The Carthusian's words may well have been the germ of many features prominent in Ignatius' later Principle and Foundation (*SpEx* [23]), and his spirituality in general: (1) He saw creatures as coming from God and good, the means by which human beings come to know, reverence, and praise God; (2) he found God in all things, all creatures; (3) since all things are ordered to God and his glory, human persons too ought to order their own lives to the glory of God. To lead them to this ordering will become the very purpose of his *Exercises* ([21]); and further (4), this ordering is directed to the glory or praise of God—the central motivating thrust of his later spirituality; (5) Ignatius spoke of God reverentially as "God our Lord" and of the Son as "Christ our Lord." Similarly he developed a reverential habit of regarding Christ as the divine person become also a human being, our "Creator and Lord."[15] The similarity of ideas in this passage of Ludolph and in Ignatius' spiritual writings makes clear that the two are kindred souls.

Ludolph concluded all his chapters with a prayer which is their climax—much as Ignatius will later ask his exercitants to conclude their meditations by a "colloquy" expressed in their own words. The tender prayer placed by Ludolph at the end of this first chapter begins thus:

> Prayer
> Lord God, omnipotent Father, who before all the ages of time ineffably generated your Son as coeternal, coequal, and consubstantial with yourself, and with him and the Holy Spirit created all things visible and invisible, and also myself, a wretched sinner among these creatures, I adore you, *I praise you, I glorify you*. Be propitious to me, a sinner. (Emphasis added.)

This prayer occurs so early in Ludolph's book that it is very probable that Ignatius read it and perhaps wrote it into his copybook. He may well have absorbed it into his own heart, In this prayer, too, are the juxtaposed words "the praise and glory of God" which were to recur so often in his own writings. The ordering of all creatures to the glory of God was also in the passage which it concludes. This could have been the germ of his concern for the glory of God, the viewpoint which became his motivating ideal later on. Glory to God, in the sense of praise of God, was to become a central idea in his worldview. In the arch of thought to which his worldview can be compared, the glory of God is the keystone to which everything else leads. In his *Exercises* and his *Constitutions of the Society of Jesus*, "the greater glory of God" becomes his norm for making decisions. Nadal states that he conceived his zeal for God's glory already at Loyola: God "called Father Master Ignatius during his illness, and above all led him to desire, with great devotion, the greater honor and glory of His Divine Majesty."[16]

In what manner did Ignatius read these two books by Jacobus and Ludolph? He has not told us the details, but, as Leturia and De Guibert suggest,[17] a sequence somewhat as follows is plausible. He began by paging through the two books, sampling now this, now that. At first he was more influenced by Jacobus' lives; they were lighter reading and would be more attractive to one still seriously sick. Later he received a far deeper influence from his perusal of Ludolph—a warm devotional attitude of reverential admiration of the Savior, based on the Carthusian's extensive theological and scriptural knowledge. His reading became more and more meditative and prayerful. He did not have to read the whole of either lengthy work to absorb their spirit. He reread passages which inspired him.

Many ideas of Ludolph no doubt sank deeply into his memory; he could recall them at will, or they would spring forth spontaneously when some stimulus came. Other ideas sank profoundly into his subconscious mind; they became part of his fund of knowledge and formed his way of thinking and judging without his adverting to them, or knowing where he acquired them.

Precisely what influence Ludolph exerted upon him opens a question we cannot exhaust. Our prime concern here is not with that form of literary dependence which consists of passages transcribed almost verbatim from some previous author. As Codina and Leturia have pointed out, few if any verbatim quotations from Ludolph's *Life* are found in the *Exercises*.[18] Instead, our foremost interest is in the deep psychological influence which his Life exerted on Ignatius. It formed his mental habits of reading and praying, his way of looking at things, his mind-set. It put him on the way to discovering his methods of prayer which he was later to expound in the *Exercises*.

Ludolph also furnished him the organized core of structured thought which took in the whole history of salvation, from the Trinity and creation to the last judgment. Ignatius absorbed this sequence in his reading, probably without noticing the fact; but in this way God's salvific plan became the core of his thought and, like a rolling snowball, it picked up additions for the rest of his life. It was to become the viewpoint from which he appraised all things in life.

Further still, it was from Ludolph that Ignatius drew the detailed knowledge of Christ's life which so immensely strengthened his love of the Master, and around which his spirituality and his Exercises would henceforth grow. Surprisingly to us, that knowledge could not have come from the New Testament, because at Loyola and Manresa he did not know enough Latin to read it. Only about four years later when he left Barcelona for Alcalá was he to know enough Latin to use the Latin Vulgate. Although some translations into Spanish of sections of the New Testament existed in Spain in scattered manuscripts, because of the tight control of the Inquisition no Catholic Spanish translation of the New Testament was printed in Spain until 1793. Even the translation of the epistles and gospels of the Liturgy by Ambrosio de Montesino was blocked by the Inquisition.[19]

Through his readings and reflections Ignatius came to a firm determination to make a complete break with his past and to imitate the saints in a life of severe penance. He wanted to inaugurate this new life by a pilgrimage to Jerusalem (9). He felt great consolation while gazing long at the sky, "because he thus felt within himself a very great impulse to serve Our Lord. He . . . wished he were now wholly well so he could get on his way" (11). His brother tried to dissuade him from his proposals, but "he slipped away" (12). He would begin his new life with a pilgrimage, such as Ludolph had praised, first to Our Lady of Montserrat near Barcelona, then to Jerusalem, and after that perhaps lead the solitary life of a Carthusian.

In late February he set out for the shrine of the Black Virgin on the saw-toothed mountain, Montserrat. Hospitably received by the Benedictine monks, he asked for a confessor. Dom Juan Chanones came to him. He loaned the pilgrim a copy of the *Book of Exercises for the Spiritual Life* (*Ejercitatorio de la vida espiritual*) by García de Cisneros, once abbot of Montserrat. Ignatius used it, no doubt, in his preparations for his careful general confession, which lasted three days. It may have suggested to him later the title of his own book, and also some of the methods he proposed.

It had long been the custom for new knights to enter their chivalrous service to earthly lords by a prayerful vigil of arms. On March 24 he stealthily stripped off his fine clothing, replaced it with a pilgrim's tunic, and spent the whole night in prayer before Our Lady's statue. He was now formally dedicated to serving the Eternal King, and that under Mary's protection.

In summary, when Ignatius left Loyola in 1522 to take up his new life of total dedication, his spirituality was very generous and determined, but also inexperienced, uneducated, and indiscreet. Its thought content, however, was already oriented, far more than he was aware, toward prayerfully intimate cooperation with Christ and his redemptive plan. Henceforth he would desire more and more to order all things toward God's greater glory, in accordance with that divine plan for the spiritual growth and eventual self-fulfillment of free human beings in the joy of the beatific vision.

3. Deepening at Manresa, March, 1522–February, 1523

As he left Montserrat for Barcelona, Ignatius intended to tarry in nearby Manresa "a few days, . . . to note some things in his copybook; this he carried around very carefully, and he was greatly consoled by it"

(18). The few days, however, became a sojourn of eleven months of chiefly eremitical life. This stay, marked by the appearance of his gifts of infused contemplation, was to have immense importance for the formation of the major principles of his spirituality, for their first formulation in writing, and for the orientation of all his future work. His core of thought brought from Loyola was to be immensely deepened.

His interior development during these eleven months can be divided into three periods: (1) April and approximately May, 1522: a continuation of the same joy and discernment as at Loyola; (2) a severe struggle with doubts, scruples, and desolation—ended by late July; (3) August to mid-February, 1523: He receives marvelous divine illuminations and begins to write the notes which were eventually to become his *Exercises*.[20] After a few days of helping the sick in a hospital, he lived in a Dominican convent, from which he went for solitude to a nearby cave. It faced the River Cardoner and majestic Montserrat. Daily he attended Mass and the chanting of the Office. Clad in his pilgrim garment, he begged his food, catechized children, and conversed on spiritual matters with persons he met.

The first period was a time of prayer, spiritual joy, and penances in imitation of the saints. "His whole intention was to do such great external works because the saints had done so for the glory of God" (14). Still, he was "without . . . any knowledge of interior things of the spirit" (20). He was too much imitating their external deeds and austerities rather than the interior spirit from which their actions sprang, and often his penances were excessive. He relied too much on his own effort. Only slowly would he learn that holiness must be according to the measure God wants, and thus acquire the discretion so dear to him later.

Once again he experienced alternating periods of consolations and desolations. He was puzzled by visions of an attractive serpent (19–21). They made him curious about their origin and the results to which they led. He found himself experiencing strong temptations to abandon his new way of life because of the hardships it was bringing. He was developing the background of thought which he would eventually express about discernment of spirits (*SpEx* [313–317; 333]). He also felt an urge to share his experiences with others, and "in his speech he revealed great fervor and eagerness to go forward in God's service" (*Autobiog*, 21).

Also, "it was at Manresa," he told Câmara without making the time more precise, "that he first saw the *Gerzonçito* [the *Imitation of Christ*, then attributed to Gerson], and never afterwards did he wish to read another book of devotion. He recommended it to all those with whom he dealt, and read a chapter or two every day."[21] This little book, particularly in regard to many of its chief thrusts such as contempt of worldly values, docility to grace, and familiarity with God, deeply influenced him for the rest of his life.

The peace of soul characteristic of the first period of Manresa was interrupted, probably in June and July, by his struggle with scruples (22). He feared that some of his sins had to be confessed again. He found himself unaided by his confessor's advice. He felt disgust and deep despair, even a temptation to suicide. To beg God to free him he fasted excessively for a week. His confessor forbade him to continue. He obeyed, and for two days felt free from the scruples. Then they returned and with them his desolation. Reflection on these experiences brought further knowledge of the diversity of spirits. He thus decided not to confess anything from the past anymore; and henceforth "he remained free from those scruples" (25).

Daily he devoted seven hours to prayer, and spent more time "thinking about the things of God. . . . But when he went to bed, great enlightenment, great spiritual consolations, often came to him; so that they made him lose much . . . sleep. . . . He began to doubt, therefore, whether that enlightenment came from a good spirit." He decided to ignore it; he needed the sleep (26). Similarly he began to abstain from meat, but came to see this abstention as a temptation to what might lead to bad consequences (27). To eat the meat could be a good, just as truly as to abstain from it. Hence he viewed the abstention as originating, not from a good spirit, but from an evil one. The tactics characteristic of good and evil spirits were becoming still clearer to him.

a. Mystical Illuminations

Next come his transitional statements which mark the entrance into our third period. "God," he states, "treated him at this time just as a schoolmaster treats a child whom he is teaching. . . . Something of this can be seen from the five following points" (27). Then he begins his account of his divine illuminations. Many of his intimate companions considered them to be a high degree of mystical prayer; and in our own century studies of this topic by Hugo Rahner, Joseph de Guibert, and after them a host of modern experts have greatly deepened our knowledge of his divinely infused contemplation.[22] His own descriptions of his Manresan lights are so important for present purposes that we shall quote them at some length, italicizing some words which reveal the inner nature of these divine insights. They were predominantly intellectual experiences—insights, and not merely images. Images, however, were not wholly absent; he uses them at times as aids in his labored efforts to tell his experiences.[23]

First, they focused his devotion especially on the Trinity. "He had great devotion to the Most Holy Trinity, and so each day he prayed to the three Persons separately. . . . One day while he was saying the Office of Our Lady on the steps of the same monastery, *his understanding began to be elevated* so that he saw the Most Holy Trinity in the form [or harmony] of three musical keys. This brought on so many tears and so much sobbing that he could not control himself" (28).

Second, they gave him insights about God's act of creating. "Once, the manner in which God had created the world was *presented to his understanding* with great spiritual joy. He seemed to see something white, from which some rays were coming, and God made light from this"—but he could not well remember or explain these things while dictating them thirty years later.

Third, he increased in discretion, dropped some excessive penances, and "saw the fruit which he bore in dealing with souls." Also, "he saw clearly *with his understanding* . . . how Jesus Christ our Lord was there in that Most Holy Sacrament" (29).

Fourth, he gained new knowledge about Christ and Mary, two mediators whom he frequently begged to intercede for him. "Often and for a long time while at prayer, *he saw with interior eyes* the humanity of Christ. The form that appeared to him was like a white body, neither very large nor very small, but he did not see any distinction of members. He saw it at Manresa many times. . . . He has also seen Our Lady in a similar form" (29).

Fifth, he described the outstanding intellectual vision which unified all his previous knowledge.

> Once he was going out of devotion to a church situated a little more than a mile from Manresa; I believe it is called St. Paul's, and the road goes by the river. As he went along occupied with his devotions, he sat down for a little while

with his face toward the river, which ran down below. While he was seated there, *the eyes of his understanding* began to be opened; not that he saw any vision, but *he understood and learned* many things, both spiritual matters and matters of faith and of scholarship, and this with so great *an enlightenment* that everything seemed new to him.

The details that he *understood* then, though there were many, cannot be stated, but only that he experienced *a great clarity in his understanding*. This was such that in the whole course of his life, after completing sixty-two years, even if he gathered up all the various helps he may have had from God and all the various things he has known, even adding them all together, he does not think he had got as much as at that one time (30).

Several features of these illuminations are especially noteworthy. First, they repeated much the same topics which had loomed large in Ignatius' prayerful, reflective reading of Ludolph at Loyola, and in much the same order: the Trinity, creation of the world, Christ the incarnate mediator and his mother Mary—all prime elements in God's plan of creation and redemption. The same core of thought which Ignatius had drawn at Loyola from the lives of the saints and Ludolph's life of Christ was now being deepened and synthesized through graces of infused contemplation.

Second—to use the terminology[24] common to many theologians —Ignatius' experiences were not merely corporeal visions, by which a mystic gazes on an object, whether real or apparent, outside himself or herself; nor were they merely imaginative visions in which God so affects a mystic's imagination or "picturing faculty" that he or she sees an object not really present. Instead, Ignatius' experiences were predominantly intellectual visions, insights, in which God communicates himself in a way that leads a mystic to a better understanding of truths, experiences, or other matters previously known. God might do this, for example, by stirring up previously acquired ideas and/or modifying or coordinating them anew, or even by infusing new ideas. The terms which Ignatius used stress that the divine communications had been addressed chiefly to his understanding, as the terms italicized above indicate. His comparisons and figures followed afterward, and like those of other mystics, are inadequate to communicate their experiences, which were beyond his or their ability to describe well.

Third, particularly noteworthy is the account, in "Fifth," of his "outstanding illumination" (*eximia ilustración*). In it he states that if all the helps and insights he received from God in his more than sixty-two years were added together, they would not amount to "as much as at that one time." Was he really speaking about the quantity of things learned, or the intensity of the illumination? Because of some later statements by Ignatius, De Guibert thinks he means the intensity. That is, on no other one occasion did he ever receive illumination as intense as in that one beside the Cardoner. The supportive reasons for this opinion are indeed strong, for, as we shall see below, Ignatius' mystical experiences continued for the rest of his life, with perhaps some diminution during his years of "distraction" by study (1524–1535). But from 1535 to 1537 he advanced steadily along this path of infused union with God, and between 1538 and 1556 he was at the summit of his interior life (of which we get a glimpse in his *Spiritual Diary*). During the years of this summit Ignatius himself told Laínez, as the latter wrote in 1547: "What he received at Manresa . . . was little compared to what he was receiving then."[25]

After this outstanding illumination Ignatius saw everything in a new light. In later life, when others asked him why he had established this or that feature in his Society of Jesus—such as the omission of obligatory choir because it might impede apostolic activities—he often replied that it was "because of what I saw at Manresa,"[26] that is, in accordance with his insight there. This does not mean—as some have maintained—that he saw in detail the religious institute that he was to found. Instead, as Dalmases points out, what he saw was the new course his life was to take, and the consequences in a general way. He was not to remain a solitary pilgrim imitating the saints in prayer and penance, but to labor with Christ for the salvation of others. He also saw, somewhat dimly, that he ought to seek companions for this enterprise. As Nadal said of him, "he was being led gently toward something he himself did not know."[27]

Sometime during this third period—probably rather early in the seven months from early August of 1522 to mid-February of 1523, but after the *eximia ilustración* plausibly located after mid-September of 1522—Ignatius, making use of his copybook brought from Loyola, began to write the first pages of what was to become his *Spiritual Exercises*. He himself, questioned by Câmara as to how he drew them up, replied that "he had not composed the Exercises all at once, but that when he noticed some things in his soul and found them useful, he thought they might also be useful to others, and so he put them in writing" (99); and thus he traced such experiences all the way back to Loyola.

What Ignatius said here is of course important, yet surprisingly little for a matter which had played so important a part in his formation and apostolic activities from 1523 to his stating it in 1555. Fortunately, his companions make up for his modest brevity. They make clear that much of this work was done at Manresa. To cite one example, Polanco tells us that after the outstanding illumination "Ignatius began to make those exercises now contained in his book, and then to put them into writing for the instruction of others."[28] He was writing, not for publication, but notes for his own use as a spiritual diary and aids in his apostolic conversations.

The impact made upon Ignatius by the outstanding illumination beside the Cardoner was deep, lasting, and extraordinarily extensive. It took in matters not only of faith but also of learning, since no equally forceful experience came to him, even during his studies, up to 1555. It had extraordinary clarity and firmness; he was willing to die for it. He felt himself "another man with another intellect."[29]

What was included among the earlier elements synthesized in this mystical illumination? Undoubtedly among them were Ignatius' own experiences and reflections on them during his convalescence at Loyola, along with similar experiences in his first four months at Manresa. Also present was what he had learned from his readings at Loyola, especially in Jacobus' lives of the saints and Ludolph's life of Christ—including the descent of creatures from God, pretty much as presented in Ludolph's chapter 1 on the prologue of St. John. Through the illumination all these previous elements fell into place in a whole. His experiences of the purgative way became a starting point, and the events in Christ's life as told by Ludolph were seen in a new light. The problem of discerning the good and bad "spirits" or sources from which the consolations and desolations had originated, and also the problem of his election to persevere in his new way of living—these now became centered on Christ as King and the topic of the two banners of the contrasting leaders, Christ and Satan.

While this new organization of thought was forming, his way of viewing Christ was also transformed. Hitherto he had viewed him chiefly as the model to be imitated, in the way the saints had been doing for centuries. Now he saw him as the inspiring King sent by his Father on a mission to conquer the world, in order to win all humankind to faith and salvation; and calling for cooperators who would volunteer for this enterprise. They would follow him and his banner, and help to win over those who, following the banner of Satan, were caught by his characteristic snares. Ignatius' thought, hitherto oriented toward a contemplative manner of living, perhaps in a Carthusian monastery, was now becoming apostolic, with the whole world as its scope.

Further still, he soon felt an urge to share his illuminative experiences with others in Manresa, to learn new spiritual ideas from them, and to guide them to experiences similar to his own. He began his enthusiastic conversations by which he led others to repent and pray. This would naturally lead him to write notes about his recent experiences, and to refer to items from Jacobus and Ludolph in his copybook. Soon he had another handful of pages. He used it to refresh his own memory for the conversation he was about to have with one or another of his spiritual friends. It was now a means to aid himself in leading them to a sequence of prayerful activities. By means of these he was trying to lead them to goals such as to order their lives to God, generously search out how they could best serve and please him, discover his will for themselves, and make their decisions while free from disordered affections of nature or the tactics of Satan. Probably his goals were not yet this clear in his mind, but in some rudimentary fashion they were taking shape in this direction.

In this writing he transferred many passages from the copybook he had carried from Loyola, perhaps into a bundle of new sheets, those he was to call in Salamanca "his papers, which were the Exercises" (67), or perhaps into another copybook. He also made abbreviations or other changes, adjusting everything to the newly found purpose of what was becoming his Exercises. Soon he had at Manresa two sets of papers, the copybook from Loyola and a new set, whether bound or unbound—but the two were very different in character. The first had been made for himself at Loyola while he was preserving his first lights. The second consisted of jottings in the full light of the illumination beside the Cardoner and was intended for the help of others. The second set superseded the first. At some unknown time he let the first be lost, but he carefully preserved the second set of papers, and used it in guiding others. Throughout his years of study (1524–1535) and later he revised and recast it according to his growing experiences and university learning, until its printing in 1548.

Enroute to Barcelona and Jerusalem, Ignatius left Manresa in mid-February, 1523. He told his confessor "how much he wanted to seek perfection and whatever would be more to the glory of God" (36). This is the second time he himself mentions the "glory of God" in his *Autobiography* (see 14). Nadal has told us, as we saw above,[30] that his concern for the glory of God was conceived already at Loyola; and now at Manresa it recurs. It is taking on a central position in his thought, and will occur with increasing frequency.

What stage of growth had his Exercises reached when he left Manresa? "His papers," the experts substantially agree, contained in rudimentary form the fundamental meditations of these Exercises, divided into the sections called weeks. In the First Week were the two methods, general and particular, of examining one's conscience. After this, centered around the meditations on the King and the Two Standards, came meditations and contemplations on the life of Christ, linked together into a sequence aimed at achieving the purpose of the Exercises: to order one's life—and to do that without making one's decisions through some affection which is disordered. There was something about methods of praying mentally (drawn largely from Ludolph's Introduction and early chapters), such as the reasoning or discursive prayer with the memory, intellect, and will, and the contemplative gazing on persons, their words, and their actions. Present too in some sketchy form were ideas on the Election, and the Rules for the Discernment of Spirits for the First Week, and probably too the Principle and Foundation in some rudimentary form, though what it was then is hard to pin down with clear evidence.[31]

Still further and of striking importance for all his future work, when he left Manresa, the major ideas and thrusts of his spiritual doctrine were now formulated, at least in a sketchy form, both in his mind and to some little extent in writing. Henceforth his spiritual doctrine and his practice will mature side by side, with reciprocal influence. While applying his major principles, he will be revising them from his growing experience and learning, as we shall see in greater detail below. These principles will enable him to win companions, found the Society of Jesus, express them anew in its *Constitutions*, and exert great influence on individual persons and on society during his life and after.

b. The Pilgrimage

Ignatius left Manresa in late March, 1523. His pilgrimage to Jerusalem lasted until he arrived back in Barcelona in February, 1524. He reached Jerusalem on September 4, 1523, and with great devotion visited the places made sacred by Christ in Jerusalem, Bethlehem, and Jericho. "His firm intention was to remain in the Holy Land, continually visiting those sacred places; . . . he also planned to help souls" (45). But the dangerous political situation frustrated this desire.

He now saw the necessity of an academic foundation if he was to employ his learning and experience effectively in helping his neighbors. Hence he decided to remedy that deficiency. This resulted in ten years of university study. His apostolic endeavors were restricted, yet always progressing to the extent prudence allowed.

4. The Years of Study, 1524–1535

The lectures and textbooks used in teaching philosophy (then called "the arts") were all in Latin, hitherto totally unknown to Ignatius. Hence at the age of thirty-three in Barcelona he began to learn the rudiments of Latin under Master Jerónimo Ardèvol, who invited him to sit in his classes with the teenage boys. Meanwhile, as Laínez informs us, already in Barcelona Ignatius "gave meditations or spiritual exercises, in which he had special ability and efficacy, and the gift of discernment of spirits, and of helping and directing other souls."[32] After two years he went, in summer of 1526, to the University of Alcalá to begin philosophy.

There "he studied the logic of Soto, the physics of Albert, and the Master of the Sentences," Peter Lombard. He also "was engaged in giving spiritual exercises and teaching Christian doctrine, and this bore fruit for the glory of God" (57). His explanations of Christian doctrine attracted large crowds. Here, as previously in Manresa and Barcelona, he manifested a winning personality by which he attracted friends. Everywhere he went we find him winning others by his enthusiastic presentations of spiritual topics and spiritual conversations, which were often his Exercises.

However, these companions' activities in Alcalá brought them under suspicion from the Inquisition. The judges cleared them, but so inhibited them in their spiritual work that Ignatius moved to Salamanca in September, 1527. There similar difficulties reoccurred. Aware that he had learned only a little at Alcalá and Salamanca, especially because he had devoted too much time to his work for souls, he thought that by going to Paris he could study in a more concentrated way. His ignorance of French would prevent excessive apostolic work. He arrived in Paris on February 2, 1528, and stayed seven years until April, 1535.

He still felt that he lacked a "good foundation" (73), and therefore he repeated the humanities for a year and a half in the College of Montaigu. At the age of thirty-seven, he was once again "with the small boys, following the order and method of Paris" (73). This experience brought him great admiration of this method, and he later prescribed it for his own colleges and universities (*Cons*, [366, 446–451]). In May or June, 1529, he gave the Exercises to three of his friends.

At about that same time he became a boarder in the College of Sainte-Barbe, to begin his studies in arts under Master Juan Peña. Here he had as roommates Pierre Favre and Francisco de Javier, with whom he soon established warm friendships. In his third year Ignatius studied Aristotle's Physics, Metaphysics, and Ethics, and passed the examinations for his degree of Licentiate in Arts. He was ranked thirtieth in a class of 100 candidates. On March 15, 1533, he received this license to teach, at Paris and anywhere else in the world. Some students, such as Francis Xavier, received the degree of Master of Arts a few days after the licentiate. Ignatius, lacking the necessary money, put off his own "commencement" until March 14, 1535, when he received his diploma and became a Master of Arts.

During these studies, however, he was also busy with his friends whom he hoped might join him in his way of living. He gave the Exercises for a month to Favre early in 1534, to Laínez and Salmerón in spring, and a little later to Rodrigues and Bobadilla. Xavier, occupied with his teaching, postponed them to the fall. All six of these "through prayer," as Laínez later told, "had resolved to serve our Lord, leaving behind all worldly things." Probably they did this because of suggestions from Ignatius which were matured in prayer, with a decision either reached or confirmed in the "election" of the Exercises. These six generous youths and Ignatius now formed a group which Ignatius called "friends in the Lord."[33]

Ignatius' years in Paris were of great importance in giving his Exercises their final literary structure. Not long after his arrival in 1528 he gave them to other students who were not Spanish, and even to professors, for example, Doctor Martial Mazurier. This work brought on the necessity of a Latin text of the Exercises. Not surprisingly, the "First Version" in Latin appeared. This *Versio prima*, inelegant Latin of which Ignatius himself is the most likely author, was made between 1528 and 1535, probably in the earlier years of his Parisian sojourn.

Further still, he began to train his companions—Favre, Laínez, and Xavier—to give the Exercises, and this must have had a profound effect on the literary form of the book. It was becoming a manual, not for himself alone, but also for other directors—which it has been ever since. After Ignatius left Paris, Favre, Laínez, and Xavier, largely by means of the Exercises, won to their way of life new companions who were French: Codure, Jay, and Broët, whom they were to bring with them to Venice for their meeting with Ignatius in 1537.[34] By the time Ignatius left Paris in 1535 the literary structure of the Exercises was substantially set—about what it is today. It was the product of his experience and reflection, far more than of research in books and transcriptions from them, though it does to some extent mirror his reading and studies.

Through sharing their ideals, Ignatius and his friends reached an agreement which gave a new orientation to their lives. They were to live in strict poverty in imitation of Christ, and to devote themselves to the spiritual welfare of their fellow men and women. As a first step they would make a pilgrimage to Jerusalem, and for this purpose they would assemble in Venice in the spring of 1537. If circumstances throughout a year should make the journey impossible, they would offer themselves to the pope, that he might send them wherever he thought best.

All this was made the content of a vow which these seven friends pronounced on August 15, 1534, on the feast of Our Lady's Assumption in a small chapel dedicated to her on Montmartre, Paris. An item of great importance should be noticed here: the devotedness of the group to the pope, considered the vicar of Christ on earth.

Ignatius now took up his theological studies. He attended the lectures given in the Dominican convent on the rue Saint-Jacques and in the Franciscan convent nearby. To his lectures he had to bring the Bible and a commentary on Peter Lombard's *Sentences*. At Saint-Jacques between 1504 and 1526 four successive Dominicans had given a new orientation to theological studies by basing their commentaries on St. Thomas instead of on the *Sentences*. Ignatius' formation was basically Thomistic, and he conceived his preferential affection for St. Thomas, which later led him to prescribe "the scholastic doctrine of St. Thomas" for the scholastics of his Society (*Cons*, [464]). He also indicated his esteem for Peter Lombard ([466]).

What pages of Peter Lombard and Thomas Aquinas did Ignatius read? The answer would indeed be fascinating, but we lack the documentary evidence to give it with precision. However, it would be natural for Ignatius to seek further light on those ideas of his own which by now had become especially important to him. Hence our attention is

37

attracted to two passages from Peter Lombard which are similar to his own thought about rightness or purity of intention and about the whole content of the Principle and Foundation.

The very first pages of the *Sentences* expound a teaching of Augustine (*De doctrina christiana*, I, 3, 4): While tending toward beatitude, we enjoy creatures and should then also use them as aids to some further good, until eventually we reach God. Him we enjoy but do not use for anything higher. There is, however, a danger: On earth we may become so engrossed and distracted by some creature that we enjoy it for its own sake alone and thereby neglect its right use toward our true final goal. In this way Augustine, and Peter Lombard after him, showed all things arranged in a hierarchy of beings leading men to God.[35] This too was precisely how Ignatius viewed everything, whether he learned it from Peter, or from Augustine through Peter, or from some other source written or oral, or from his own reflection.[36] Even if Ignatius did not read these pages, they reveal to us the thought world in which he lived. Thus they furnish us with an important key to his spiritual outlook, to interpreting his spiritual writings, and to enriching their significance to ourselves by what we bring to them from our own resources and self-activity. That is the way he wanted his readers to use his texts, especially in the case of the *Exercises*.

Further, in the very first chapter of Book II is a passage which much helps us to see the depth of thought in the Principle and Foundation, the hub around which so much of Ignatius' thought revolves. In that passage Peter states that, in contrast with the incomplete notions of the Greeks and Aristotle, the Holy Spirit teaches that

> 3. God created the world at the beginning of time. . . .
> Therefore we should believe that there is no other cause of
> created beings . . . than the goodness of the Creator. . . . His
> goodness is so great that he wills others to be sharers of his
> eternal beatitude, which, he sees, can be communicated, but in
> no way diminished. . . .
> 4. . . . Therefore God made the rational creature which
> could know the supreme good, and by knowing it love it, and
> by loving it possess it, and by possessing it enjoy it. . . .
> 5. Consequently, if it is asked why man or angel was cre-
> ated, the brief reply can be given: because of God's goodness.
> . . .

6. And if it is asked for what destiny the rational creature was created, the answer is: to praise God, to serve him, and to enjoy him; and in all these activities the rational creature, not God, gains profit. For God, being perfect and full of all goodness, can be neither increased nor diminished. . . .

8. And just as man was made for God, that is, that he might serve God, so the world was made for man, that it might serve him. Therefore man was placed in the middle, that he might be served and in turn give service. . . . For God willed so to be served by man that by that service not God, but the man serving, might be aided; and He willed that the world should serve man, and that man might be aided by that too.[37]

In this citation we immediately notice the harmony of thought with that of Ignatius' Principle and Foundation. Peter's thought enriches the world-affirming character of Ignatius' spirituality, which views creatures as fundamentally good (despite the danger of our misusing them), as means through which human beings, if they use them wisely, can attain to God and to their own self-fulfillment by possessing him.

Other thoughts of great importance for appreciating Ignatius' spirituality are found in St. Thomas' comprehensive view of God's plan of creation and redemption. This plan forms the very structure of his *Summa theologiae*: the procession of creatures from God and their return to him through Christ.[38] The *Summa* can be succinctly summarized as follows. God created beings outside himself—including angels and human beings—not to increase his own glory and happiness, but to communicate his being and have his happiness shared and praised or glorified by these intelligent and volitional beings. "God seeks his glory not for his own sake" (as if the praise or glory from them were something which would increase his own happiness), "but for us," insofar as while operating for his own goodness he simultaneously gives us the opportunity to glorify or praise him and to be happy by doing it.[39] After Adam lost the supernatural life God gave him as a heritage to be handed on to his posterity, God again made it available to humankind through the Incarnation, redemptive death, and Resurrection of his Son.[40] The more a person merits by serving God here below, the greater will be his capacity or ability in heaven to enjoy him by praising him. In this heavenly beatitude, a person will know, love, and praise or enjoy God more perfectly in proportion to the charity he has practiced on earth.[41]

All those theological teachings of Peter Lombard and Thomas can be found also in Ignatius' complete writings. Whether he drew these concepts from the *Sentences*, or *Summa*, or Ludolph's Life of Christ, or his own conscious or subconscious memory, is a relatively unimportant problem. What matters most to us here is that they are part of his personalized concept of God's plan of creation and redemption, and are therefore keys to our deeper understanding and correct interpretation of his writings. They are "interpretative sources" which enable us to understand better the theological depth of Ignatius' thought.

The contagious enthusiasm with which he had for years explained Christian doctrine appeared also when he spoke about theological topics. "One doctor," Nadal states, "a distinguished person, said admiringly of our Father that he had not seen anyone who could discuss theological matters with such mastery and dignity."[42]

Ignatius' study of theology at Paris was cut short by illness. Complying with his physicians' orders, he departed in 1535 for his native air in Guipúzcoa, with the intention of rejoining his companions in spring, 1537.

The same line of spiritual thought which began at Loyola and deepened at Manresa continued and developed during this period of studies. He kept in the foreground of his thought the same basic outlook and goal he had conceived at Loyola and Manresa: to do everything for "the service and praise of His Divine Majesty," and to try "to procure the praise, honor, and service of God our Lord"; the need to direct and order our life for "the glory and praise of God." These and similar phrases appear with repeated emphases in his letter of November 10, 1532, to Isabel Roser, and in that to his brother Martín in the same year.[43]

5. Toward the Summit of His Spirituality, 1535–1540

From Spain Ignatius went to Venice. There, while awaiting the reunion with his companions, he spent the whole year of 1536 chiefly in the study of theology, but also in helping others, especially by spiritual conversations and giving the Exercises. Among his exercitants were Pietro Contarini, a Venetian cleric; Gasparo de' Dotti, the vicar of the papal nuncio to Venice; and Diego de Hoces, a priest from Spain who made an election to join Ignatius' group.

The companions from Paris arrived in Venice on January 8, 1537, hoping to carry out their pilgrimage, but in 1537 war with the Turks seemed imminent and not a single ship sailed for the Holy Land.

While waiting for this situation to clear, they prepared to receive Holy Orders. Seven of them, including Ignatius, were ordained on June 24, 1537.[44] Thereupon they dispersed in groups of two or three for ministerial work in nearby cities. Ignatius, Favre, and Laínez went to Vicenza. They spent forty days in prayer and penance, then preached in the piazzas.

For Ignatius this turned out to be a second Manresa. "At Vicenza," he tells us, "he had many spiritual visions and many quite regular consolations; the contrary happened when he was in Paris. In all that traveling he had great supernatural experiences like those he used to have when he was in Manresa, especially when he began to prepare for the priesthood in Venice and when he was preparing to say Mass" (95). His years of study were over and he could give his whole attention to finding God both by prayer and by spiritual work for others.

When their agreed-upon year of waiting had ended with no passage available, they journeyed to Rome to offer their services to the pope. They divided into three or four groups, and Ignatius traveled with Favre and Laínez. "On this journey he was visited very especially by God" (96).

a. The Vision at La Storta

In a small wayside chapel at La Storta on the outskirts of Rome Ignatius was favored with a mystical vision. It was an experience as important for this period of his life as was that beside the Cardoner at Manresa. During the journey he had many spiritual emotions, some of fear about the difficulties they might meet in Rome, but also many of confidence that God would protect his group. He had been "praying Our Lady to deign to place him with her Son. One day, a few miles before reaching Rome, he was at prayer in a church and experienced such a change in his soul and saw so clearly that God the Father placed him with Christ his Son that he would not dare to doubt it" (96).

To be "with Christ," in close association with him—that had long been Ignatius' ardent prayer. It also became the aspect of this vision which stood out in his mind when he was dictating his account to Câmara in 1555. However, he had also related other important aspects to his companions in 1537 while the vision was still fresh in his memory. They soon spread these other details of the vision, so that during his lifetime they were known to others in the Society. To get the complete picture we must piece together these features which his associates have left us, and which reveal the supportive impact of the vision on the early Jesuits.

Laínez wrote in 1559 that Ignatius "told me that it seemed to him that God the Father had impressed on his heart the following words: 'I shall be propitious to you in Rome'.... Then another time he said that it seemed to him that he saw Christ carrying a cross on his shoulder and the Eternal Father nearby who said to Christ: 'I want you to take this man for your servant.' And because of this, conceiving great devotion to this most holy name, he wished to name the congregation the 'Company of Jesus.' "[45]

Ignatius' vision at La Storta had a profound and confirming effect on the foundation of the Society and the shape it took. He perceived himself intimately united to Jesus, and he wanted to found a society totally dedicated to him, bearing his name, and carrying on his work. Its members should be intimately united to Jesus in prayer and enrolled under the banner of the cross, to ply in a corporate manner his work for the service and glory of God and the welfare of their fellow men and women. These are the ideas which would later be expressed at the very beginning of the Formula of the Institute of the new Society.

6. The Summit. His Mysticism, 1540–1556

The nineteen years between Ignatius' entrance to Rome in mid-November, 1537, and his death on July 31, 1556 were the most important in his life in regard to the maturing of his own spiritual life and also to his work of founding and governing the Society of Jesus. Through it his spiritual doctrine and practice were spread, during these last years of his life, throughout the world from Europe to India, Japan, and Brazil.

His strong interior life reached the mature form in which it has been ever since so inspirational to his followers. His infused divine favors, about which our sources are comparatively silent for the period of his "distraction" by studies, were back, and they remained abundantly present for the rest of his life. At La Storta his habitual ideas had just been synthesized around the idea of his intimate association with Christ, the Mediator through whom God's redemptive plan was being carried forward by the Church. Ignatius strove to fit himself into that plan as a cooperative servant. His spirituality was theocentric and trinitarian, aiming always at what might bring greater glory to God. At the same time it was Christ-centered, seeking to cooperate intimately and loyally with him. The Christ who appeared to him at La Storta was the glorified Christ who was still living and functioning in and through the Church, his mystical body, and specifically through his vicar, the pope. The spirit of loyalty to the pope, manifest already in the group at Montmartre, now flowed into a legislative formulation in the fourth vow of the professed members, to go anywhere the pope would send them and to do what he ordered.[46] Ignatius and his followers would ever afterward bear special devotion to this whole Christ. In no small measure the founder's later stress on obedience arose from his desire to secure among the members of his order effective and charitable cooperation toward apostolic success in the service of this Christ and his Mystical Body. He expected the members of his Society to love their Lord in contemplation and to manifest their love by deeds. He was singularly successful in motivating men to volunteer in the crusade for Christ's Kingdom and to strive for distinguished service in it. In his view, their apostolic effectiveness was to arise from their being human instruments intimately united with God (*Cons*, [813]).

Throughout this period his interior life progressed steadily and was marked by continually higher graces of infused contemplation. Laínez, writing about Ignatius in the period after the foundation of the Society, tells us of Ignatius' statement that "what he had received in Manresa . . . was little when compared to what he was receiving then. Those matters were the first rudiments and exercises of his novitiate, but quite different was the [present] impression made by the graces in his soul. What preceded was only a sketch, and something like an initiation."[47]

We shall see more about his mysticism when we treat his *Spiritual Diary* below. Meanwhile a brief citation will give an inkling of its nature. After describing his extraordinary experiences during his morning prayer on February 19, 1544, he continues:

As soon as Mass was over I offered a short prayer with the words: "Eternal Father, confirm me; Son, and so on, confirm me." Tears streamed down my face and my will to persevere in saying Their Masses grew stronger. . . . (*SpDiar*, [53]).

On that same day, even when I was walking in the city with great interior joy and when I saw three rational creatures, or three animals, or three other things, and so forth, I saw them as images reminding me of the Holy Trinity (ibid., [55]).

This and many similar characteristics of his infused contemplation, and the effect at times of these graces during his activities through the rest of the day, are what led Nadal to his now classic description of him:

> We know that Father Ignatius received from God the singular grace to enjoy freely the contemplation of the Trinity and to repose in it. . . . Father Ignatius enjoyed this kind of prayer by reason of a great privilege and in a most singular manner, and this besides, that in all things, actions, and conversations he perceived and contemplated the presence of God and an attraction to spiritual things, being a contemplative person even while in the midst of action.[48]

B. Effects of His Spirituality on His Work, 1538–1556

1. His Founding of the Society of Jesus

From the beginning of Ignatius' stay in Rome, his spiritual outlook found expression in his personal ministerial projects. They were many, such as work for catechumens, for fallen or endangered women, the sick, orphans, and other projects. The crowning work into which his spirituality flowered, however, was his founding of the Society of Jesus.

In an audience of late November, 1538, the companions offered themselves to Paul III, in accordance with their vow at Montmartre. "Why," he asked, "do you want so eagerly to go to Jerusalem? Italy is a good and true Jerusalem, if what you desire is to bring forth fruit in God's Church."[49] Clearly he was thinking of missioning them, singly or in small groups, to Italian cities, and it seemed that their group would be dispersed. This raised serious questions for deliberation. Should they, to retain some form of unity, elect one of their number as a superior, and vow to obey him? Should they form themselves into a new religious order?

From mid-March to June 24, 1539, they discussed the pros and cons of these and related problems, in meetings held at night that they might continue their ministries during the day. Their deliberations were an application of the directives for an election in the *Exercises*

[135, 169–188]. To the questions given above they reached unanimous affirmative answers.[50]

The first step toward giving juridical structure to their group was to compose a summary of the project for presentation to the pope. Ignatius was charged to do this, with some help from the others. He soon produced a document containing "Five Chapters" or sections of 200–400 words each and entitled "A First Sketch of the Institute of the Society of Jesus." It is permeated with the founder's ideas. The very first words, for example, reflect his enthusiasm over his vision at La Storta and his desire to be associated with Christ as still living in the Church:

> Whoever desires to serve as a soldier of God beneath the banner of the cross in our Society, which we desire to be designated by the name of Jesus, and in it to serve the Lord alone and his vicar on earth, should, after a solemn vow of chastity, keep what follows in mind.
>
> He is a member of a community founded chiefly to strive for the progress of souls in Christian life and doctrine, and for the propagation of the faith by means of the ministry of the word, the Spiritual Exercises, and works of charity, and specifically by the instruction of children and unlettered persons in Christianity.[51]

By early July Ignatius' friend Cardinal Gasparo Contarini presented these Five Chapters to Pope Paul III for approval. After two months of examination by members of the papal curia, Cardinal Contarini read the Five Chapters to the pope on September 3, 1539. "The finger of God is here," he remarked. He orally approved the Chapters and ordered the preparation of an official document. This led to a year of discussions in the papal curia about the proposals, but then the Five Chapters, revised only in a few small details, came back to Ignatius. They were encased within one paragraph of introduction and another of formal approval, in Paul III's bull of September 27, 1540, *Regimini militantis Ecclesiae*. Ignatius and his ten companions were now a new religious order of clerics regular in the Church, the Society of Jesus. The Five Chapters were its papal law and the Society's fundamental Rule.

On April 6, 1541, the companions elected Ignatius as their superior general, by unanimous vote except for his own. He accepted the charge on April 19, and on April 22 he and five companions made their solemn profession in the new Society. Through his remaining fifteen years he governed the Society with apostolic zeal, ingenuity, initiative, and much esteem. Through his trust in Providence he kept himself calm amid disappointments and successes. With Polanco's competent help he sent out his thousands of letters and, in steps we shall soon see, he completed his work on the Society's Constitutions. This document turned out to be a heritage of extraordinary value, simultaneously a classic of spirituality and of religious law. Since his death until now, it has spiritually inspired the Society, unified it, and directed its worldwide apostolic work.

2. The Rapid Growth of the Society

The fresh and zealous spirit of Ignatius and his companions and the tenor of thought of the Exercises flowed into their conversations, preaching, and everything they did. They were manifestly meeting widely felt needs of the era in a new way. Their enthusiasm resulted in a quickly expanding apostolate and an extraordinary growth in the number of recruits. By the time Ignatius died in 1556, his Society numbered approximately one thousand members. They resided in more than a hundred houses or colleges, and their work was expanding with their numbers.

They lived in twelve provinces gradually established by 1556: Portugal (1546), Spain (1547), India (1549), Italy apart from Rome (1551), Sicily (1553), Brazil (1553), Aragón, Andalusia, and Castile as new divisions of Spain (1554), France (1555), Lower Germany (1556), and Upper Germany (1556). While the Society had naturally encountered various instances of opposition, it also enjoyed much prestige with popes, bishops, kings, and others in many nations.[52]

3. The Apostolic Works and Ministries

In Europe most of the Jesuits' work in Ignatius' lifetime was directed to the spiritual welfare of individuals (by conversations and the Exercises), and of relatively small groups (by preaching or catechizing). Ignatius' aim in founding the Society was to promote the glory of God through the spiritual good of the neighbor—service to the Church under the pope as Christ's vicar, anywhere the pontiff would order them. However, the Church at the time was engaged in reforming itself internally and in opposing Protestantism without. As a result, the newly formed Society was drawn into both these endeavors and did play a considerable role in the Counter-Reformation—but that resulted from the purpose for which the Society was founded and was not the aim of the founding.

A good example is Germany. He sent there Favre, Bobadilla, and Jay between 1540 and 1543. The Jesuits working in Germany preached, catechized, gave the Exercises, conversed spiritually, carried on colloquies with the Protestants, and carried out any "missions" assigned to them either by the pope or Ignatius. Peter Canisius, too, found widespread success by his preaching, university lecturing, and the publication of his well-known *Catechism*. Similar ministries were carried on in Spain, Portugal, France, Italy, and elsewhere. At the request of Pope Paul III in February, 1546, three Jesuits participated in the Council of Trent: Jay, Laínez, Salmerón. Favre too had been assigned but died enroute.

Foreign missions also multiplied. The spiritual-minded King John III of Portugal asked Ignatius for Jesuits to be sent to Portuguese India. He sent Xavier, who arrived in Goa on May 6, 1542. A sample of his work exemplifies his procedures. On the Fishery Coast in southwest India he ministered to a Christian community of about 20,000 impoverished pearl fishers—converts of a few decades earlier who, largely because of language difficulties, were still almost totally uninstructed. Francis memorized in Tamil the Sign of the Cross, Creed, Our Father, Hail Mary, and Confiteor, and for over a year went from village to village instructing the natives. This activity stirred up a desire for Christianity among the people in neighboring Travancore. Their desire was mingled with hope that conversion would bring Portuguese protection from Mohammedan marauders. Advancing through fourteen villages, Francis baptized over 10,000 persons in one month. His reports about this work deeply stirred King John back in Portugal. It motivated him to provide a college at Coimbra where 100 Jesuits could live, and to help dispatch another 12 Jesuits to India in early 1546. Araoz, the provincial, informed Ignatius that Xavier was doing as much for the faith in Portugal as he was by his preaching in India. In the Molucca Islands and in Japan he firmly established the faith. When he died in 1552 he left behind Jesuits stationed along the seaways in a neatly organized pattern at Bassein, Ternate, Malacca, Cochin, Thana, and Chilon. Similar implantation of the faith was achieved across the

Atlantic by Jesuits Ignatius sent to Brazil. Their mission, begun in March 29, 1549, was preaching to the natives, pastoral care of the Portuguese, and Christian education.[53]

The Society's apostolate of education also quickly took on international importance. In that era cities and towns, dissatisfied with the haphazard results obtained from itinerant teachers, were becoming eager to establish schools if they could find teachers to man them. This led Ignatius into his first experiences with the ministry of Christian education at Gandía in 1545. Its success led citizens of Messina to request a college there for their youths. Drawing on his memories of "the order and method of Paris" (*Autobiog*, 73), Ignatius saw the opportunity and grasped it. The classes opened in 1548. The good results led him to throw all his organizational skill into this new work. He rapidly established other colleges at Palermo (1549), the Roman College (1551)—his most cherished school which he hoped would become a model throughout Christendom—Vienna (1553), and Billom in France (1556).

As his experience grew he reflected on it and gradually developed his theory of Christian education. He sent numerous letters about the colleges and their growth into universities. Especially noteworthy is one of December 1, 1551, which he commissioned Polanco to write to Araoz, provincial of Spain. It treated the manner of founding colleges, by first opening courses in humane letters and then philosophy when the students were ready for it. In its conclusion the letter told of the benefits which would accrue to the Society, the students, and the nation: "From among those who are now merely students, in time some will emerge to play diverse roles—some to preach and carry on the care of souls, others to the government of the land and the administration of justice, and others to other responsible occupations. Finally, since the children of today become the adults of tomorrow, their good education in life and doctrine will be beneficial to many others, with the fruit expanding more widely every day."[54] This letter shows his expansive vision and is an early sketch of the comprehensive philosophy of Christian secondary and higher education which he finally presented in Part IV of his *Constitutions*.

When Ignatius died in 1556 he had opened thirty-three colleges and approved six more.[55] They stretched from Goa throughout Europe to Brazil. All were governed according to the aims and procedures set forth in Part IV of his Constitutions. As a result, what the founder started soon became a widespread system of colleges and universities which shared common objectives, curriculum, procedural unity, evaluations of experience, and government from a central administration in Rome. Never before had the world seen so organized an educational system. The colleges continued to spread. They numbered 372 by 1675 and 612 by 1710. Shortly before the suppression of the Society, the Jesuits were directing fifteen universities. They also staffed 176 seminaries.[56]

All the success in these apostolates in Europe, in the foreign missions, and in education are in no small measure fruits of Ignatius' *Exercises*, Formula of the Institute, and *Constitutions*. They are also reasons why these writings are among the classics of western spirituality. Part IV of these Constitutions can itself be called a classic treatise on Christian education. Its influence on the theory and practice in this field is still functioning effectively today.

All this work was taking its toll on Ignatius as his years advanced. During his generalate in Rome he experienced alternating periods of good health and debilitating, painful illness. In early 1556 his increasing weakness and periods of sickness became more and more manifest to his associates. On July 31, 1556, Ignatius peacefully died. Esteem of his holiness, good example, and accomplishments, already widespread during his life, increased after his death. He and his close friend Francis Xavier were canonized together on March 12, 1622.

PART III. IGNATIUS' WRITINGS AND THEIR INTERPRETATION

A. *His Chief Works: Basic Descriptions*

All of Ignatius' extant writings have been published in the series entitled "The Historical Sources of the Society of Jesus" (*Monumenta Historica Societatis Iesu*), which now numbers 129 volumes. Of these, 27 volumes form a set called the *Monumenta Ignatiana*. They contain the texts of his writings, along with copious introductions, footnotes, and other primary sources about the founder.

His chief books, listed in the order in which he began their composition, are his *Spiritual Exercises* (1522); his almost 7,000 collected letters (from 1524 on, but most of them after 1547); his Deliberation on Poverty and related *Spiritual Diary* (1544); the *Constitutions of the Society of Jesus* (1546); and his *Autobiography* (1553).[57]

Ignatius also wrote numerous other small treatises; for example, the documents bearing titles such as The First Sketch of the Institute of the Society of Jesus (*Prima Societatis Iesu instituti summa*), the Constitutions for the Colleges, Rules for Scholastics, Rules for Priests, the Letter on Obedience, his brief Autograph Directory of the Spiritual Exercises, and the like. These treatises, relatively small, have been published in collections, but only now and then in the form of a book or pamphlet. In the present book we shall present the whole of the *Autobiography* and *Exercises*, and selections from his *Constitutions of the Society of Jesus*, *Spiritual Diary*, and letters. Basic introductory descriptions of them will now be given here, in the chronological order of their composition.

1. The *Spiritual Exercises* is beyond doubt the best-known among Ignatius' books. It is through it that most of those who have become followers of his spirituality have made their first acquaintance with its chief principles and inspirational force. This small book, begun in 1522, contains the marrow of his spiritual outlook and most quickly mirrors to us the synthesis of his principles. It reveals much of his personality as well. From 1522 to about 1541 his own spirituality developed side by side with his revisions of and additions to the pages which were to become the book published in 1548, twenty-six years after its inception.

Ignatius' *Exercises* in its final published form is not a treatise on the spiritual life, nor was it composed to communicate its message through reading by a retreatant. Instead, it is a manual to guide exercises which were to be carried out by an exercitant, ordinarily with counsel from a director. Thus it is comparable to a book on "how to play tennis"; almost all the intended benefit accrues, to one who not merely reads it, but carries out the practices suggested. Ignatius began the composition of the *Exercises* by writing notes meant as aids for himself in his spiritual conversations with others at Manresa in 1522 and Barcelona (*Autobiog*, 21, 32, 34, 37). He was enticing them to perform exercises of prayer, confession, and other activities of a more intensive spiritual life. In its later, more organized form the book became a guide also for other directors (such as those whom he trained to give his Exercises in Paris near to 1533) in their conversational presentation of topics, principles, methods of meditating and contemplating, directives for making a right-ordered choice or "election," and the like. Early directors sometimes left some points in writing with the retreatant. Since the printing of the book it has been used profitably by both directors and retreatants.

GENERAL INTRODUCTION

The book as a whole aims to furnish a director with the helps he or she needs for an ideal type of exercitant: a person who sincerely desires to discover how he or she can please and serve God best, and who for about thirty days can withdraw from ordinary occupations (whence arose the name "retreat"), in order to make four or five contemplations a day, alone with God in complete solitude.

However, Ignatius himself and his contemporary Jesuits continually used the book to direct persons who in numerous ways fell short of this ideal. He clearly intended the book to be a flexible guide from which a director would select and adapt what was likely to be most helpful to this particular retreatant in his or her circumstances (*SpEx* [18–20]). He and others whom he trained gave his Exercises to many kinds of persons and in many different ways; for example, for two or three days, or one week, or three, or four; to some persons who were deliberating about the choice of a state of life, and to others who had no such election to make. The topics and directions were presented in conversations between the director and the retreatant. The practice of preaching the topics to a group of retreatants was an adaptation which arose after Ignatius' death, often with great spiritual fruit. The preached retreat still continues. Each type of retreat, that individually directed and that preached to a group, has its own advantages and disadvantages.

The book opens with twenty introductory explanations, some chiefly for the director and others for the exercitant. Then it states the purpose of the Exercises: to order one's life toward God, without coming to a decision from some disordered attachment pleasing more to self than to him, even if this requires the conquering of self necessary when selfish urges would impede this goal. Then comes the Principle and Foundation, which presents the principles for the logic which functions through the rest of the book. It presents (1) an inspiring goal, eternal self-fulfillment as the purpose of life on earth; (2) the means to the goal, creatures rightly used; (3) a preliminary attitude for their wise use: making oneself "indifferent" or undecided until the sound reasons for choice appear; (4) a criterion of choice: Which option is likely to be more conducive to the end, greater praise or glory to God? The Exercises are indeed far more than an exercise in logic; but there is a logical sequence of ideas which runs through them all and links them together.

The remaining Exercises are divided into four groups, called "Weeks." The First Week consists of exercises characteristic of the purgative way, the purification of the soul to advance toward God. It views the whole history of sin and its consequences, the attempted wrecking of God's plan for human beings endowed with the freedom to give or refuse cooperation. It includes the exercitant's own role in this history, and God's loving mercy. The Exercises bring into play any or all the abilities any exercitant has, such as the intellect, will, imagination, and emotions. All these are stimulated, with a stress on each one at its own proper time.

The Second Week presents exercises proper to the illuminative way, the acquiring of virtues in imitation of Christ. The spirit of the week is set by means of an opening contemplation on Christ's call to participate with him in spreading his Kingdom. Then follow about three days devoted respectively to contemplations on the Incarnation, Nativity, and hidden life of Christ ([101–134]). They prepare the way for about six more days ([135–189]) when two series of exercises run concurrently: (1) contemplations on selected mysteries of the public life of Christ; and (2) principles (those drawn from the Principle and Foundation), applied now to "Three Times Suitable for Making a Sound Election" and the "Two Methods" of making it about some important matter, such as choice of a state of life. In series 1, during all the contemplations on the events in the life of Christ, the exercitant prayerfully strives to gain "an interior knowledge of our Lord, who has become man for me, that I may love him more and follow him more closely" ([104]). As an introduction to these two series, the fourth day of this week is devoted to three meditations aimed at attaining or confirming the necessary attitude for a rightly ordered decision: that of "indifference" (attained by suspending decision to avoid acting from mere impulse of likes or dislikes, or from some other disordered motive). The first meditation is on the two "Standards" (banners, flags), respectively of Christ and of Satan, to point out the opposite tactics of these two leaders. The second, on three "Classes" or categories of persons (postponers, half-hearted, and whole-heartedly decisive), fosters an adherence of the heart to total commitment, even if sacrifice is involved. The third consideration, on "Three Ways of Being Humble" which reach a climax in the third, evokes a desire to be as like to Christ as possible in an attitude of loving humility, no matter what the cost. This attitude is especially useful in an option where the pros and cons seem equal. These principles form a background which should function in all the contemplations on the public life for the rest of the Second Week.

Another important point about the principles for a good election should be noticed. Ignatius' text is focused concretely on one concrete case—that of someone deliberating about the choice of a state of life, but the principles and methods he gives are equally applicable to any options which occur in life. Further, not all retreatants are concerned with an election about something new. The Exercises should be adjusted to their condition, and for them Ignatius gives some suggestions about renewal of life. This, however, can be regarded as a species of election.

The Third and Fourth Weeks bring contemplations characteristic of the unitive or perfective way: activities to establish habitual and intimate union with God, through Christ. The exercitant associates himself or herself closely with Christ in his sufferings during the Third Week, and in his joys in the Fourth. By this sympathetic association he or she is confirmed in his or her choice (if this has been a retreat of election), or in whatever resolutions he or she has reached. The Exercises conclude with a contemplation to increase one's love of God. By now the exercitant has reviewed God's entire plan of creation and redemption evolving in the history of salvation, from creation, through the fall of the angels and Adam, the Incarnation, and redemption, which lead one all the way to one's destiny in the beatific vision. The exercitant, too, has been striving to fit himself or herself cooperatively into this divine plan. On many an exercitant this whole sequence of exercises has produced a powerful psychological impact and has given a new orientation of life.

Finally, as appendages at the end of his book Ignatius places sets of suggestions on a variety of topics: Three Methods of Praying; a list of Mysteries of Christ's life especially suitable for a time of retreat; Rules for the Discernment of Spirits; the Distribution of Alms; Thinking, Judging, and Feeling rightly within the Church; and the brief Notes on Scruples.

It is through the *Exercises* that Ignatius has exerted his most effective and widespread influence directly upon individual persons. During his own lifetime from Manresa onward he gave these Exercises continually to innumerable men and women with whom he dealt. By means of the Exercises, too, he won and trained the first followers with whom he founded the Society of Jesus. Thereupon they too directed innumerable others in making them. All the novices were obliged to make them for the full thirty days. For most of them probably no other element in their training was more effective in forming their outlook on life and their spiritual practices. From his day until now virtually all Jesuit priests, as well as some scholastics and brothers, have carried on the apostolate of the Exercises in various forms and adaptations. The book has been published unusually often. According to one plausible estimate worked out in 1948, by then the *Exercises* had been published, either alone or with commentaries, some 4,500 times—an average of once a month for four centuries—and the number of copies printed was around 4,500,000.[58] Throughout the world today the Exercises are being made by greater numbers than ever before.

2. *Ignatius' Letters.* Almost 7,000 of them are extant, dating from December 6, 1524, on and published in twelve volumes. There were many more, now lost. Only 173 of them are earlier than March, 1547. Shortly after this date Juan de Polanco became his secretary and the letters multiplied prodigiously.

Polanco had a clear and fluent style manifestly different from Ignatius' labored writing. In most cases Ignatius supplied the ideas and Polanco did the writing. Often he commissioned his secretary to compose the letter, but this does not detract from Ignatius' authorship, because he always meticulously corrected the drafts. Ribadeneira states of him: "He spent much time in considering what he was writing, in scrutinizing again and again the letters once written, examining every word, canceling and correcting. Sometimes he ordered to letter to be recopied."[59]

In his letters we see him applying his chief spiritual teachings and practices to all the affairs and situations of life. The ideas dominant in the *Exercises* and *Constitutions* reappear continually throughout this correspondence, often several times on a page. Spontaneously yet skillfully woven into the context are his ceaselessly recurring phrases: "the service of God," the "glory of God," the "service and praise of God," the "need to direct and order our life to the glory and service of God," "May it please the Sovereign Goodness that everything be ordered to his holy service and continual praise." Most of his letters have a conclusion similar to this: "I close by asking God through his infinite goodness to give us the perfect grace to know his most holy will and fulfill it completely."[60] These expressions are not mere clichés. Instead, they are his dominant thoughts springing spontaneously from his heart —a compressed expression of his spirituality under two prominent aspects, doctrine and practice.

3. The short Deliberation on Poverty, about three pages of human reasoning, and the *Spiritual Diary*, seventy pages of sublime mysticism

(pages 318–321 and 341–410 in *Obras completas*), are documents which complement each other and are best considered together. Both are written entirely in Ignatius' own hand and were intended for his own eyes alone. The *Diary* is the longest manuscript which we have directly from his own pen. In the Deliberation he lists his pros and cons and applies principles from the *Exercises* in view of election about the type of canonical poverty he was to prescribe in his future Constitutions: Would it be more to God's glory to allow fixed income[61] to the churches of the Society, or not? To obtain further light, he submitted the matter to God in daily contemplative prayer and during Mass. On pages meant for his own eyes alone he recorded the lights and favors he received in this prayer.

The *Diary* consists of two fascicles or copybooks. What we have is a fragment, which somehow escaped when the rest of his spiritual diaries were destroyed, probably by Ignatius himself. It is undoubtedly less than the "rather large bundle" which he showed to Câmara but would not let him read (*Autobiog*, 100–101). Copybook I consists of fourteen sheets which take in the forty days from February 2 to March 12, 1544, when he concluded his election. Copybook II records his spiritual experiences from March 13, 1544, to February 27, 1545. Both parts are his spontaneous notes recording his spiritual progress and the special graces of his mystical prayer.

The same tenor of thought which was present in his earlier life flows with strict continuity in the highly mystical life of these years in Rome. Everything is dominated and oriented by the thought of bringing glory or praise to God, of serving him, of learning his will and carrying it out, of living in accordance with the end of humankind as expressed in the Principle and Foundation. His chief ascetical principles, as expressed in his *Exercises*, and those running through his mystical life are identical.

There are many concepts, definitions, and theological theories connected with the elusive topic of mysticism, and divergent opinions about them tease the human intellect. No matter what theory or terminology about mysticism one may prefer, Ignatius will fit into it and have a high rank among those to whom God has given these gratuitous gifts.

4. The *Constitutions of the Society of Jesus* are the application of Ignatius' worldview to the organization, inspiration, and government of the religious institute he founded. They arose by stages.

When Ignatius and his companions decided in June, 1539, to form themselves into a new religious order, a plan of the new institute was needed as a first step toward obtaining papal approval. Hence the short document of about 2,000 words was produced, entitled "The First Sketch of the Institute of the Society of Jesus" (*Prima Societatis Iesu instituti summa*). Ignatius is quite surely the author, though he had some help from his companions. It contained "Five Chapters" or paragraphs, which are also called "The Formula of the Institute." With some slight revisions made in the papal curia it was incorporated into the bull *Regimini militantis Ecclesiae* of September 27, 1540, by which Pope Paul III approved the Society. These Five Chapters thus became the Society's fundamental Rule. It authorized the superior general and "his council" to compose statutes, called Constitutions, which would apply this Rule to extensive details.[62]

After Ignatius reluctantly acquiesced to his election as general on April 19, 1541, his companions entrusted this work to him and his associate Jean Codure, whose death in that same year left the task to Ignatius alone. Gradually he composed various drafts of details with a view to their experimental use, revision, and then incorporation into the final document. By about 1546 he completed a relatively short document called the "General Examen." It aimed to explain to candidates the Society's nature, end (the spiritual welfare of the members and all their fellow human beings), and the means of attaining the end.

In 1547 he appointed the able Juan de Polanco as his secretary, a competent writer who before joining the Society had been an amanuensis in the papal curia. He had a marked ability to organize thought and express it well. Immediately the work advanced rapidly. A first draft, text *a*, was revised into a second, text A. A group of professed fathers, summoned by Ignatius, made a few emendations and then approved it for promulgation and experimental use. Another text, called B, incorporated these emendations and was ready in 1552. Ignatius entrusted this mission of experimental promulgation to Nadal. From June 10, 1552, to September 22, 1554, he explained these Constitutions to Jesuit communities in Sicily, Spain, and Portugal; and from February to December, 1555, he did the same in Germany, Austria, and Sicily.

Meanwhile Ignatius had his own copy of text B, on which he continued to make corrections, chiefly verbal, until his death. Hence this corrected text B became known as the "Autograph." His Spanish original and a Latin translation made after his death chiefly by Polanco obtained their juridical validity through approval in 1558 by the Society's First General Congregation. Since then they have been and still are the governing law of the Society. Ignatius' classic text has been kept unchanged. However, around it has grown up a large body of interpretative and modifying decrees of thirty-three General Congregations.

What were the respective parts of Ignatius and Polanco in the composition of the *Constitutions?* To get a precise answer is impossible, but the heart of the matter is found in a statement of Ignatius recorded by Nadal: "With respect to the substance of the content, there is nothing of Polanco's in the Constitutions, unless something concerning the colleges and universities; and even that is according to his own thought."[63] Among all of Ignatius' published works, the *Constitutions* and some of his letters have the best style, and that style undoubtedly came from Polanco. Polanco, however, consulted Ignatius about all his doubts, and he in turn minutely examined and often revised all that his secretary wrote.

Through his *Constitutions of the Society of Jesus* the founder's inspirational and organizational ability has directly influenced all its members from his day till now, and indirectly, through them, all the people they have touched in their apostolic ministries. His spirituality has been a functioning factor in the life of the Church. Through these centuries, too, many founders and foundresses of religious institutes of men and of women, helped by Jesuits, adapted Ignatius' *Constitutions* and spirituality into their own charisms.

5. Ignatius' unfinished *Autobiography* takes in the founder's life from Pamplona (1521) through his first year in Rome (1538)—eighteen of his sixty-five years. Although this is the last of the books he produced, there are strong reasons for reading it first. It supplies extensive information indispensable for understanding the rest with accuracy and depth. Therefore we have placed it first among his works presented in this book.

From 1550 onward, many of Ignatius' collaborators, including Nadal, Câmara, and Ribadeneira, grew increasingly eager to obtain from him all the information they could, particularly about the evolution of his interior life and the foundation of the Society. In this way, they rightly sensed, they would learn much of the Society's spirit and charism. Nadal observed that Ignatius had received the three graces he had often begged of God: approval of the Institute of the Society by the Holy See; similar approval of the *Exercises*; and the completion of the Society's *Constitutions*. He feared that Ignatius might not live much longer. Hence sometime in 1552 he seized an opportunity and begged of him that he would "be kind enough to tell us how the Lord had guided him from the beginning of his conversion, so that his explanation could serve us as a testament and paternal instruction."[64] Ignatius was reluctant, but at length for the benefit of the Society he "decided . . . to narrate all that had occurred in his soul until now."[65] As the recipient of his narrations he chose the minister in charge of the house in Rome, Luis Gonçalves da Câmara, known for his excellent memory.

Consequently, in the full maturity of his spiritual life he retraced the chief events of his life for the eighteen years from 1521 to 1538. He modestly referred to himself as "the pilgrim," thus escaping use of the first personal pronoun. His chief purpose was to narrate the steps by which God had brought about the evolution of his spiritual and mystical life. The journeys and other external events were meant to present the occasions for these interior experiences, about which he had hitherto been rather reticent. He gave his accounts on three occasions: August and September of 1553; March of 1555; and September and October of 1555. Unfortunately, his narrations were interrupted by Câmara's departure for Portugal in October, 1555, and Ignatius never resumed them before his death in the following July. The details of his interior life for 1539–1556 must be pieced together from other sources, which fortunately are fairly numerous.

Câmara left his manuscript without a title. This lack led Nadal to write one on his own copy: The Deeds of Father Ignatius as Written by Father Gonçalves da Câmara. Modern editors and translators, finding this too cumbersome, have invented many titles of their own, using words such as The Pilgrim's Story, or Testament, or Autobiography. Among all these, *Autobiography* has by now in many languages come to serve as the most common title.

B. Interpretation of Ignatius' Writings

1. His Style

Ignatius was a warm, affective, communicative, and stimulating personality, afire with the love of God and the human persons with whom he conversed. He won their affections, even though at times he was very stern. "Those who were in his room," wrote Nadal, "were continually laughing."[66] If he had not been spontaneous and animated in his dealings with them, it is hard to see how he could have inspired the affection he so manifestly received. In his own way, too, he was a poetic soul. With emotion he contemplated the flowers, the starry heavens, and the deeds of Christ. A highly imaginative person himself, he tried to lead his retreatants to visualize the persons of the Gospel scenes and imaginatively reconstruct their probable words and deeds, and thus to penetrate more deeply the wonders of Christ. Traces of all these characteristics turn up occasionally in his writings, and more frequently in the writings of his friends to him or about him.

However, he was not a facile writer possessing a style easy to read. When he began to write, his spontaneity seemed to halt. He was a deep and accurate thinker, intent on expressing exactly what he wanted to say, but simultaneously preoccupied with precautions to be precise and complete. He slowly worked his thoughts into order. Sometimes he added qualifications, gerunds, participles, and relative clauses one after another so that the sentence as a whole became tangled and difficult to read. When he felt he had accurately expressed his thought, he dropped the matter and proceeded to whatever came next. He had little interest in going back to improve the form and make sentences smooth or polished. Hence his style is often difficult, complicated, succinct and sometimes elliptical, and long known for its "Spartan terseness." His diction too is plain, and he sometimes uses words in his own meanings. Time and close attention are required to understand his terminology.[67]

These deficiencies, however, are counterbalanced by other qualities through which he has won many satisfied readers from his day till now. His major works have won their worldwide circulation and influence, not because of their style, but through other features. Such are the depth of their Christian content, the inspiration which they stir up in those who study his writings rather than merely read them, and especially the expansive background of spiritual doctrine from which his treatment of single topics springs. This has brought the ever deepening satisfaction which many readers, exercitants, and scholars have experienced as they have ferreted out his messages. This work, often difficult, has fascinated them and made them eager to explore him farther. He repays their study and stimulates their own thought.

2. Keys to Interpretation

Clearly, therefore, the appeal of Ignatius' writings does not come from their style. Instead, it arises from such factors as the content of their thought, the further discoveries which he encourages readers to make for themselves, and the extraordinary effects his works have had in the history of spirituality and on the Church. All this points up the necessity of interpretative keys. The first key is obvious: to examine his words or phrases in their immediate context of the sentence or passage. A second key is also very important: to take account of other passages in his works where he treats any given topic. From the rich sources of thought consciously or subconsciously in his mind for any given topic, he habitually drew only what seemed most important for the occasion at hand. For example, he had a clear concept of religious obedience, but in writing for novices in Part III of his *Constitutions* he focused on some aspects, and on others when writing for formed Jesuits in Part VII. In neither place was his thought complete. To interpret either passage fully we must draw from the other, and beyond that also from his long letter of March 26, 1553, to the Jesuits in Portugal, the classic on the topic that has been so influential in religious institutes for some four centuries. A third key is the thought-world of his era: the ideas, conscious or unconscious assumptions, and attitudes which made up the intellectual, social, and spiritual milieu of the sixteenth century. To contribute toward meeting this need is one of the major aims of the notes in this book.

By far the most important key lies in the effort to fit any passage of his writings into the background into which it fit in his own mind: his worldview based (1) on the divine plan for the creation, redemption through Christ, and glorification of free human beings in the beatific vision, and (2) on his concept of the role which they have the opportunity to play within that plan as it is being applied to them as the history of salvation unfolds. Ignatius was trying to fit himself into that plan by his efforts to advance the reign of God and his Christ as vigorously as he could in the circumstances of his day. Hence as we read one of his works, or any passage in it, we often find great help by asking: How does this passage fit into the divine salvific plan? The answer often brings heartwarming light.

Finally, the more knowledge of updated biblical, doctrinal, and spiritual theology we bring to the reading and interpretation of his works, the more benefits both intellectual and spiritual do we get.

3. The Terms "Spirituality" and "Mysticism"

What is meant by spirituality? This question evokes many possible answers which cannot be explored in the present space. What can be done is to give an overview of the terms and viewpoints we shall employ.

For a century or more the English word *spirituality* has been used to designate a person's interior life, manner of praying, and other such practices. It also designates the spiritual doctrine and practices characteristically formulated in the writings of some person or group. Usually, too, the word connotes one's doing this with some intensity, a mounting above the merely obligatory into a more generous service and love of God and one's fellow human beings. This expresses itself in prayer of many kinds, various exercises, liturgical worship, and charitable actions both private and social. In this light, Christian spirituality is a lived experience, the effort to apply relevant elements in the deposit of Christian faith to the guidance of men and women toward their spiritual growth, that progressive development of their persons which flowers into a proportionally increased insight and joy in the beatific vision.

That body of revealed truth, however, is so extensive that no one can attend to all its aspects. Hence throughout history different persons have emphasized different elements in it to fit their own personalities and circumstances. In this way one develops a personalized set of doctrines, practices, and emphases. The spiritualities of St. John and St. Paul, for example, are basically one yet different in many accidental aspects and emphases. In subsequent centuries too, persons or groups adjusted to varying needs and opportunities. Thus the groups emerged which are commonly called schools of spirituality. Usually each new school formed around a perceptive and charismatic leader who inspired followers and cooperators in a spiritual enterprise. Pertinent examples are the founders of religious institutes, such as Benedict, Francis, Clare, Dominic, or Teresa of Avila.

Ignatius was the founder of such a school of spirituality, one with an emphasis directed especially toward personal spiritual growth and that of others. Emphasizing a desire to bring greater glory to God, here and hereafter, it has propagated a message of service through love and discernment. His spirituality—like that of others—is simply Christian spirituality with emphasis on those elements in the deposit of faith which he stressed.

Through the centuries, as persons discussed their lived experiences in the spiritual life, new concepts, terms, definitions, and categories of thought developed within the tradition of Western spirituality. To any one term, too, different writers attached variant meanings. They sometimes differed from one another about either the terms or the realities designated by them, so that by now the complexity is often puzzling. However, some categories and terms have been recurring so constantly for centuries that by now they have become rather classical. They lead us into the heart of the matter.

Spiritual theology guides persons toward their abundant spiritual development, called also perfection. It is called ascetical theology when it focuses on human activities in cooperation with God's ordinary graces, and mystical theology when it deals with activities performed with special graces such as infused contemplation or the extraordinary phenomena which sometimes accompany it. Spiritual theology devotes much study to the kinds of mental prayer characteristic of various stages of development.

Discursive mental prayer (also termed meditation) is predominantly characterized by multiple acts of reasoning, though there are also affections, resolutions, and communion with God. It is especially suitable for "beginners" (*incipientes*) in the "purgative" way or stage of growth in the spiritual life. They are purifying themselves from sin or disordered affections and need to develop basic convictions.

Affective mental prayer consists largely, even predominantly, of devout affections, particularly love. It is especially suited to "the advancing" (*progredientes*) who are in the "illuminative way" or stage. They are trying to learn and practice virtues in imitation of Christ.

In contemplative mental prayer the multiplied acts become simplified into a steady, loving gaze on God or some spiritual object or truth. Such prayer is especially suitable for those who are spiritually rather far developed, advanced, or matured and are in the "unitive way" or stage of spiritual growth. They are in union with God and love of him dominates their actions. In the traditional terminology they have been called the "*perfecti*," but this term can easily be misunderstood, sometimes with discouragement. On earth such persons are always capable of being developed or perfected further, and the "unitive" way would perhaps be better described as a "perfective" way. They will be completely developed or perfected only when they have attained the beatific vision.

In acquired contemplation (also called "active"), a person prays with his or her own initiative and with the aid of God's ordinary grace. She or he turns a loving, simplified gaze now on one object, now another. In infused contemplation (also termed passive, or mystical), the loving gaze is a gift infused by God through an extraordinary grace. He takes the initiative and deeply touches or even overwhelms a person, and he or she willingly and passively accepts it. This prayer, mystic in the strictest sense, is sometimes accompanied by extraordinary phenomena, such as visions, private revelations, charisms, levitations, tears of joy, stigmata, or the like. Infused contemplation transforms a person's outlook and practice.

A caution, however, is necessary. The above terms and categories present a typical, idealized case of steady advance, to make discussions and classifications easier. The cases in real life are not steady but indefinitely variant, unpredictable, and overlapping. One in the unitive stage or "way" still needs activities characteristic of the purgative way. In prayer, too, one form blends into another in ways as many as there are persons. For example, the form of "contemplation" of the persons, words, and actions which Ignatius teaches in *Spiritual Exercises* [101–117] consists in gazing by means of the imagination. It can be a form of affective mental prayer; but it can also be predominantly discursive meditation.

Elements of the classical terminology[68] described above are found in Ignatius' writings, and in treatises about them from his day till now. Hence to retain it in a book such as this has certain advantages. It helps us toward understanding his own works and others about them for almost five centuries. It gives us an anchor in the past which helps to understand new terms arising today. It is substantially what is used by the eminent expert in spiritual theology, Joseph de Guibert, whose historical study of Jesuit spiritual doctrine and practice is a masterful work. Since Vatican Council II there has been a proliferation of diverse terms used to describe the still constant core or data of lived spiritual experience. What is called spirituality by some is named mysticism by others. Close attention is necessary to discern what each writer means by his or her terms.[69]

In this elusive field full of divergent opinions, there is no terminology fully satisfying to all. In these circumstances we think it most practical to hold close to this traditional usage. It makes the terms and the realities they signify clear; and with that done, those who prefer another terminology can easily express those realities in their own way.

IGNATIUS' WRITINGS

A. THE AUTOBIOGRAPHY

THE AUTOBIOGRAPHY

INTRODUCTION

The *Autobiography* is the last of Ignatius' books. Here, however, we place it first because it furnishes so much information basic for the deeper understanding and interpretation of all the rest, particularly in regard to his mystical favors.

In a preface probably written in 1558, Câmara describes the procedure by which the book was produced. Ignatius "began to tell me about his whole life" (Preface no. 2). He narrated with such clarity that the past seemed to become present again. He "dictated while pacing about, as he had always done before" (no. 5). However, this was not a dictation intended for verbatim transcription. Instead, Câmara listened attentively and then immediately after the session he jotted down the main points of what he had heard. He strove "not to put down any words except those that I heard from the Father" (no. 3). Later—perhaps by some days—he expanded these points to what is our present text, and then dictated them to a secretary for verbatim transcription—in Spanish for sections 1–79a, in Italian for 79b–101 because he dictated this section in Genoa, where he had no Spanish amanuensis.

The *Autobiography* is a highly reliable historical source. Even though it is not verbatim transcription, its words approximate those used by Ignatius. He used a simple, straightforward manner of relating events. What resulted is our most fundamental testimony about his life. Most of the statements in the *Autobiography* are corroborated by other documents. Of course, as is often the case with historical sources, problems occur in the harmonization of details that seem to conflict, such as Ignatius' own statements about his age in *Autobiography* 1 and 30. Nevertheless, a statement by Ribadeneira well sums up the whole situation: "Ignatius was completely trustworthy in regard to the substance of his narrative, though in his advanced age he may have had slips of memory in recounting details long past."[1]

In manuscripts of the *Autobiography* there are marginal notes at twelve passages. No doubt they were written by Câmara himself. He added them at different times up to 1562 for various purposes: to supply something he forgot earlier, or to clarify a time or place, or to give something which may have come from Ignatius but at a time other than the narration. The notes on 8 and 30 could well be information obtained from Ignatius; but the others ought not to be cited as the founder's unless there is some proof.[2]

Copies of the finished portions of this work circulated among Jesuits in Rome before Câmara's departure for Portugal on October 23, 1554. Hence Ignatius probably saw them. In 1557 Nadal had a copy of the complete Spanish-Italian text, and he drew from it in exhortations in Spain, Portugal, and elsewhere. Hannibal du Coudret translated the Spanish-Italian text into Latin, probably between 1559 and 1561.[3] However, almost inexplicably to our modern mentality, the Autobiography remained unpublished until the Bollandist Jean Pien printed Coudret's Latin translation at Antwerp in 1731. What caused this long delay? Ribadeneira had been commissioned to write his lengthy life of Ignatius, which appeared in classical Spanish and Latin. The fathers general, probably thinking it more presentable than Ignatius' work, which was unfinished and deficient in literary style, recalled the copies of the *Autobiography* to Rome, where they remained in the Society's archives. Câmara's Spanish-Italian text was first published in the Monumenta Historica Societatis Iesu in 1904; then in a better critical text edited by D. F. Zapico and C. de Dalmases with copious explanatory notes in *Fontes Narrativi de S. Ignatio* I (1943): 67-323, and again by Dalmases in successive editions of *Obras completas de San Ignacio* after 1963. The English translation used here is that of Father Parmananda Divarkar, who for nine years was a General Assistant to Father General Pedro Arrupe and presently resides in St. Mary's, Mazagaon, Bombay, India. The commentary by way of footnotes is by the present editor, who drew heavily from the introduction and commentary of Dalmases in the *Obras completas* and from Joseph N. Tylenda's *A Pilgrim's Journey* (Wilmington, 1985).

*   *   *

Ch. 1. PAMPLONA AND LOYOLA
Mid-May, 1521–Late February, 1522

1. Up to the age of twenty-six[1] he was a man given to the vanities of the world; and what he enjoyed most was warlike sport, with a great and foolish desire to win fame.

And so, whilst in a fortress that the French were attacking, when all were of the view that they should surrender, with their lives safeguarded—for they saw clearly that they could not offer resistance—he gave so many reasons to the commander that he actually persuaded him to resist, even against this view of all the officers, who drew courage from his spirit and determination.

When the day came on which the bombardment was expected, he confessed to one of these companions in arms.[2] And after the bombardment had lasted a good while, a shot struck him on one leg, shattering it completely; and as the cannon ball passed between both legs, the other also was badly injured.

2. So with his fall those in the fortress soon surrendered to the French, who on taking possession of it treated the wounded man very well—treated him with courtesy and kindness. And after he had been in Pamplona for twelve or fifteen days, they took him home in a litter. Here he felt quite unwell. All the doctors and surgeons who were summoned from many places decided that the leg ought to be broken again and the bones reset, saying that because they had been badly set the other time, or had got broken on the road, they were out of place, and this way he could not mend. And once again this butchery was gone through. During it, as in all the others he underwent before or after, he never said a word nor showed any sign of pain other than to clench his fists tightly.

3. Yet he kept getting worse, not being able to eat, and with the other symptoms that usually point to death. When St. John's day came, because the doctors were far from confident about his health, he was advised to confess. He received the sacraments on the eve of St. Peter and St. Paul. The doctors said that if he did not feel any improvement by midnight, he could be taken for dead. It happened that this sick man was devoted to St. Peter, so Our Lord deigned that he should begin to get better that very midnight. His improvement proceeded so well that some days later it was judged that he was out of danger of death.

4. And his bones having knit together, one bone below the knee was left riding on another, which made the leg shorter. The bone protruded so much that it was an ugly business. He could not bear such a thing because he was set on a worldly career and thought that this would deform him; he asked the surgeons if it could be cut away. They said that it could indeed be cut away, but that the pain would be greater than all that he had suffered, because it was already healed and it would take a

while to cut it. And yet he chose on his own to make himself a martyr, though his elder brother was shocked and said that he himself would not dare suffer such pain; but the wounded man bore it with his wonted endurance.

5. After the flesh and excess bone were cut away, remedial measures were taken that the leg might not be so short. Ointment was often applied, and it was stretched continually with instruments that tortured him for many days. But Our Lord kept giving him health, and he felt so well that he was quite fit except that he could not stand easily on his leg and had perforce to stay in bed.

As he was much given to reading worldly books of fiction, commonly labeled chivalry, when he felt better he asked to be given some of them to pass the time. But in that house none of those that he usually read could be found, so they gave him a life of Christ and a book of the lives of the saints in Castilian.[3]

6. As he read them over many times, he became rather fond of what he found written there. But, interrupting his reading, he sometimes stopped to think about the things he had read and at other times about the things of the world that he used to think of before. Of the many foolish ideas that occurred to him, one had taken such a hold on his heart that he was absorbed in thinking about it for two and three and four hours without realizing it. He imagined what he would do in the service of a certain lady; the means he would take so he could go to the place where she lived; the quips—the words he would address to her; the feats of arms he would perform in her service. He became so infatuated with this that he did not consider how impossible of attainment it would be, because the lady was not of ordinary nobility; not a countess nor a duchess; but her station was higher than any of these.[4]

7. Nevertheless Our Lord assisted him, by causing these thoughts to be followed by others which arose from the things he read. For in reading the life of Our Lord and of the saints, he stopped to think, reasoning within himself, "What if I should do what St. Francis did, and what St. Dominic did?" Thus he pondered over many things that he found good, always proposing to himself what was difficult and burdensome; and as he so proposed, it seemed easy for him to accomplish it. But he did no more than argue within himself, saying, "St. Dominic did this, therefore I have to do it; St. Francis did this, therefore I have to do it." These thoughts also lasted a good while; then, other things coming in between, the worldly ones mentioned above returned, and he

also stayed long with them. This succession of such diverse thoughts lasted for quite some time, and he always dwelt at length on the thought that turned up, either of the worldly exploits he wished to perform or of these others of God that came to his imagination, until he tired of it and put it aside and turned to other matters.

8. Yet there was this difference. When he was thinking of those things of the world he took much delight in them, but afterwards, when he was tired and put them aside, he found himself dry and dissatisfied. But when he thought of going to Jerusalem barefoot, and of eating nothing but plain vegetables and of practicing all the other rigors that he saw in the saints, not only was he consoled when he had these thoughts, but even after putting them aside he remained satisfied and joyful.

He did not notice this, however; nor did he stop to ponder the distinction until the time when his eyes were opened a little, and he began to marvel at the difference and to reflect upon it, realizing from experience that some thoughts left him sad and others joyful. Little by little he came to recognize the difference between the spirits that were stirring, one from the devil, the other from God.[5]

[Marginal note of Câmara]: This was his first reflection on the things of God; and later, when he composed the Exercises, this was his starting point in clarifying the matter of diversity of spirits.

9. From this lesson he derived not a little light, and he began to think more earnestly about his past life and about the great need he had to do penance for it. At this point the desire to imitate the saints came to him, though he gave no thought to details, only promising with God's grace to do as they had done. But the one thing he wanted to do was to go to Jerusalem as soon as he recovered, as mentioned above, with as much of disciplines and fasts as a generous spirit, fired with God, would want to perform.

10. And so he began to forget the previous thoughts with these holy desires he had, and they were confirmed by a spiritual experience, in this manner. One night while he was awake he saw clearly an image of Our Lady with the holy Child Jesus. From this sight he received for a considerable time very great consolation, and he was left with such loathing for his whole past life and especially for the things of the flesh that it seemed to him that his spirit was rid of all the images that had been painted on it. Thus from that hour until August '53 when this was written, he never gave the slightest consent to the things of the flesh. For this reason it may be considered the work of God, although he did

not dare to claim it nor said more than to affirm the above. But his brother as well as all the rest of the household came to know from his exterior the change that had been wrought inwardly in his soul.

11. Not worried at all, he persevered in his reading and his good resolutions, and all his time of conversation with members of the household he spent on the things of God; thus he benefited their souls. As he very much liked those books, the idea came to him to note down briefly some of the more essential things from the life of Christ and the saints. So he set himself very diligently to write a book (because he was now beginning to be up and about the house a bit) with red ink for the words of Christ, blue ink for those of Our Lady, on polished and lined paper, in a good hand because he was a very fine penman.

[Câmara]: This had nearly 300 pages, all written quarto size. Part of the time he spent in writing and part in prayer. The greatest consolation he experienced was gazing at the sky and the stars, which he often did and for long, because he thus felt within himself a very great impulse to serve Our Lord. He often thought about his intention and wished he were now wholly well so he could get on his way.

12. And taking stock of what he might do after he returned from Jerusalem, so he could always live as a penitent, he thought he might enter the Carthusian house in Seville, without saying who he was, so that they would make little of him; and there never to eat anything but plain vegetables. But when he thought again of the penances he wished to do as he went about the world, the desire to enter the Carthusians cooled, with the fear that he would not be able to give vent to the hatred that he had conceived against himself. Still he instructed one of the household servants who was going to Burgos to get information about the rule of the Carthusians, and the information he obtained about it seemed good.

But for the reason mentioned above, and because he was wholly absorbed in the journey he was planning soon to make and that matter did not have to be dealt with until his return, he did not look much into it. Rather, finding now that he had some strength, he thought the time to depart had come; and he said to his brother, "Sir, the Duke of Nájera, as you know, is aware now that I am well. It will be good that I go Navarrete." (The duke was there at that time.)

[Câmara]: His brother and others at home suspected he was planning some drastic change.

His brother took him to one room and then another, and with much feeling begged him not to throw himself away; also, to consider what hopes had been placed in him by the people, and how much he could achieve, and other such words, all with the purpose of dissuading him from his good intention. But he answered in such a way that, without departing from the truth, for he was now very scrupulous about that, he slipped away from his brother.

Ch. 2. ROAD TO MONTSERRAT
Late February, 1522

13. And so, as he mounted a mule, another brother wished to go with him as far as Oñate. On the road he persuaded him to join in a vigil at Our Lady of Aránzazu. That night he prayed there that he might gain fresh strength for his journey. He left his brother in Oñate at the house of a sister he was going to visit, and himself went on to Navarrete.

[Câmara]: From the day he left home, he always took the discipline each night.

Remembering that a few ducats were owed him at the duke's household, he thought it would be well to collect them; for this he wrote out a bill for the treasurer. The treasurer said he had no money; and the duke hearing this said there might be a lack for everything but no lacking for Loyola—to whom he wanted to give a good position, if he would accept it, because of the reputation he had earned in the past. He collected the money and arranged that it be distributed among certain persons to whom he felt indebted, with a part for a statue of Our Lady that was in ill repair so it could be repaired and handsomely adorned. Then dismissing the two servants who had come with him, he set out alone on his mule from Navarrete for Montserrat.

14. On the way something happened to him which it would be well to record, so one may understand how Our Lord dealt with his soul, which was still blind, though greatly desirous of serving him as far as his knowledge went. Thus, he decided to do great penances, no longer with an eye to satisfying for his sins so much as to please and gratify God. So when it occurred to him to do some penance that the saints practiced, he determined to do the same and even more.

[Câmara]: He had such disgust of his past sins, and such a lively desire to do great things for love of God, that though he made no judgment that his sins were forgiven, he did not give them much attention in the penances that he undertook to perform.

From these thoughts he derived all his consolation, not looking to any interior thing, nor knowing what humility was or charity or patience, or the discretion that regulates and measures these virtues. His whole intention was to do such great external works because the saints had done so for the glory of God, without considering any more particular detail.

15. Well, as he was going on his way, a Moor came up to him riding on a mule. They went along chatting together and got to talking about Our Lady; and the Moor said it seemed to him that the Virgin had indeed conceived without a man, but he could not believe in her giving birth remaining a virgin. In support of this he cited the natural arguments that suggested themselves to him. The pilgrim, in spite of the many reasons he gave him, could not dislodge this opinion. The Moor then went ahead so quickly that he lost sight of him, and he was left pondering over what had transpired with the Moor.

At this, various emotions came over him and caused discontent in his soul, as it seemed that he had not done his duty. They also aroused his indignation against the Moor, for it seemed that he had done wrong in allowing the Moor to say such things about Our Lady, and that he ought to sally forth in defense of her honor. He felt inclined to go in search of the Moor and stab him with his dagger for what he had said. After a long engagement in this struggle of inclinations, he remained uncertain at the end, not knowing what he ought to do. The Moor, who had moved ahead, had told him that he was going to a place a little farther on the same road, very near the highway, though the highway did not pass through the place.

16. So, being tired of examining what would be best to do and not arriving at a definite conclusion, he decided as follows: to let the mule go with the reins slack as far as the place where the ways parted. And if the mule took the village road, he would seek out the Moor and stab him; if the mule did not go toward the village but took the highway, he would let him be. And doing as he had thought, Our Lord deigned that although the village was little more than thirty or forty paces away, and the road to it was very broad and very good, the mule took the highway and left the village road.

Coming to a large town before Montserrat, he decided to buy there the attire he had resolved to wear and use when going to Jerusalem. He bought cloth from which sacks are usually made, loosely woven and very prickly. Then he ordered a long garment to be made from it, reaching to his feet. He bought a pilgrim's staff and a small gourd and put everything in front by the mule's saddle.

[Câmara]: He also bought some slippers, of which he took just one; and this not for style but because he had one leg all tied up with a bandage and somewhat neglected, so much so that though he was mounted, each night he found it swollen; this foot he thought must be shod.

17. He went on his way to Montserrat, thinking as he always did of the exploits he would perform for the love of God. And as his mind was all full of tales like Amadís de Gaul and such books, the ideas that came to him were along those lines. Thus he decided to keep a vigil of arms one whole night, without sitting or lying down, but standing a while and kneeling a while, before the altar of Our Lady of Montserrat, where he had resolved to lay aside his garments and to don the armor of Christ. So leaving this place, he set off, thinking as usual of his resolutions.

On arrival at Montserrat, after praying and fixing an appointment with the confessor, he made a general confession in writing; it lasted three days.[6] He arranged with the confessor to have his mule taken in charge, and his sword and dagger placed in the church at the altar of Our Lady. This was the first man to whom he revealed his decision, because until then he had not revealed it to any confessor.

18. On the eve of the feast of Our Lady in March, at night, in the year 1522, he went as secretly as he could to a beggar and, stripping off all his garments, he gave them to the beggar. He dressed himself in his chosen attire and went to kneel before the altar of Our Lady. At times in this way and at other times standing, with his pilgrim's staff in his hand, he spent the whole night.

He left at daybreak so as not to be recognized and did not take the road that led straight to Barcelona, where he would come across many who would recognize and honor him, but turned off to a town called Manresa. Here he planned to stay in a hospice a few days and also to note some things in his book; this he carried around very carefully, and he was greatly consoled by it.

As he was gone about a league from Montserrat, a man who had been hurrying after him caught up and asked if he had given some clothes to a beggar, as the beggar affirmed. Answering that he had, tears flowed from his eyes in compassion for the beggar to whom he had given the clothes—in compassion, for he realized they were harassing him, thinking he had stolen them.

Yet as much as he avoided favorable notice, he could not remain long in Manresa before people had a big story to tell (their ideas coming from what happened at Montserrat). And soon the tale grew into saying more than the truth: That he had given up a large income, and the like.

Ch. 3. SOJOURN AT MANRESA
March 25, 1522–February 17–18? 1523

19. He begged alms in Manresa every day. He did not eat meat nor drink wine, even though they were offered to him. He did not fast on Sundays, and if they gave him a little wine, he drank it. Because he had been very fastidious in taking care of his hair, as was the fashion at that time (and his was handsome), he decided to let it go its way according to nature without combing or cutting it or covering it with anything by night or day. For the same reason he let the nails grow on toes and fingers because he had been fastidious in this too.

While in this hospice it often happened that in broad daylight he saw something in the air near him. It gave him great consolation because it was very beautiful—remarkably so. He could not discern very well the kind of thing it was, but in a way it seemed to him to have the form of a serpent with many things that shone like eyes, though they were not. He found great pleasure and consolation in seeing this thing, and the oftener he saw it the more his consolation grew. When it disappeared, he was displeased.[7]

20. Until this time he had remained always in nearly the same interior state of very steady joy, without having any knowledge of interior things of the spirit. The days while that vision lasted or somewhat before it began (for it lasted many days), a forceful thought came to trouble him by pointing out the hardships of his life, like a voice within his soul, "How will you be able to endure this life for the seventy years you have to live?" Sensing that it was from the enemy, he answered interiorly with great vehemence, "Wretch! Can you promise me an hour of life?" So he overcame the temptation and remained at peace. This was the first temptation that came to him after what is mentioned above. It happened when he was entering a church where he heard High Mass each day and Vespers and Compline, all sung, finding in this great comfort. Usually he read the Passion at Mass, always retaining his serenity.

21. But soon after the temptation noted above, he began to have great changes in his soul. Sometimes he felt so out of sorts that he found

no relish in saying prayers nor in hearing Mass nor in any other devotion he might practice. At other times quite the opposite of this came over him so suddenly that he seemed to have thrown off sadness and desolation just as one snatches a cape from another's shoulders. Now he started getting perturbed by these changes that he had never experienced before, and he said to himself, "What new life is this that we are now beginning?"

At this time he still conversed occasionally with spiritual persons who had regard for him and wanted to talk to him, because even though he had no knowledge of spiritual matters, yet in his speech he revealed great fervor and eagerness to go forward in God's service. At that time there was at Manresa a woman of great age, with a long record also as a servant of God, and known as such in many parts of Spain, so much so that the Catholic King had summoned her once to communicate something. One day this woman, speaking to the new soldier of Christ, said to him, "Oh! May my Lord Jesus Christ deign to appear to you some day." But he was startled at this, taking the matter quite literally, "How would Jesus Christ appear to me?" He persevered steadily in his usual confession and communion each Sunday.[8]

22. But here he began to have much trouble from scruples,[9] for even though the general confession he had made at Montserrat had been quite carefully done and all in writing, as has been said, still at times it seemed to him that he had not confessed certain things. This caused him much distress, because although he had confessed them all, he was not satisfied. Thus he began to look for some spiritual men who could cure him of these scruples, but nothing helped him. Finally a doctor of the cathedral, a very spiritual man who preached there, told him one day in confession to write down everything he could remember. He did so, but after confession the scruples still returned, becoming increasingly minute so that he was in great distress.

Although he was practically convinced that those scruples did him much harm and that it would be good to be rid of them, he could not break himself off. Sometimes he thought it would cure him if his confessor ordered him in the name of Jesus Christ not to confess anything of the past; he wanted his confessor to order him thus, but he did not dare say this to his confessor.

23. But without his saying so his confessor ordered him not to confess anything of the past, unless it was something quite clear. But since he found all those things to be very clear, this order was of no use to him, and so he continued with the difficulty. At this time he was

staying in a small room that the Dominicans had given him in their monastery. He persevered in his seven hours of prayer on his knees, getting up regularly at midnight, and in all the other exercises mentioned earlier. But in none of them did he find any cure for his scruples, and it was many months that they were tormenting him.

Once when he was very distressed by them, he began to pray, and roused to fervor he shouted out loud to God, saying, "Help me, Lord, for I find no remedy in men nor in any creature; yet if I thought I could find it, no labor would be hard for me. Yourself, Lord, show me where I may find it; even though I should have to chase after a puppy that it may give me the remedy, I will do it."

24. While he had these thoughts, the temptation often came over him with great force to throw himself through a large hole in his room, next to the place where he was praying. But realizing that it was a sin to kill oneself, he shouted again, "Lord, I will do nothing that offends you," repeating these words many times, as well as the previous ones. Then there came to his mind the story of a saint who, in order to obtain from God something that he wanted very much, went without eating many days until he got it. Thinking about this for a good while, he at last decided to do it, telling himself that he would not eat nor drink until God succored him, or until he saw that death was quite close. For should it happen that he found himself at the extreme limit, so that he would soon die if he did not eat, then he thought to ask for bread and to eat (as if indeed at that limit he would be able to ask or to eat).

25. This happened one Sunday after he had received Communion; he persevered the whole week without putting anything into his mouth, not ceasing to do his usual exercises, even going to divine office and saying his prayers on his knees, even at midnight, and the like. But when the next Sunday came and he had to go to confession, since he used to tell his confessor in great detail what he had done, he also told him how he had eaten nothing during that week. His confessor ordered him to break that fast; and though he still felt strong, he nevertheless obeyed his confessor. And that day and the next he felt free from scruples. But on the third day, which was Tuesday, while at prayer he began to remember his sins; and so, as in a process of threading, he went on thinking of sin after sin from his past and felt he was obliged to confess them again. But after these thoughts, disgust for the life he led came over him, with impulses to give it up.

In this way the Lord deigned that he awake, as from sleep. As he now had some experience of the diversity of spirits from the lessons

God had given him, he began to examine the means by which that spirit had come. He thus decided with great lucidity not to confess anything from the past anymore; and so from that day forward he remained free of those scruples and held it for certain that Our Lord had mercifully deigned to deliver him.

26. Besides his seven hours of prayer, he busied himself helping in spiritual matters certain souls who came there looking for him. All the rest of the day he spent thinking about the things of God that he had meditated upon or read that day. But when he went to bed, great enlightenment, great spiritual consolations, often came to him; so that they made him lose much of the time he had allotted to sleep, which was not much. Examining this several times, he thought to himself that he had ample time assigned for converse with God, and all the rest of the day as well; and he began to doubt, therefore, whether that enlightenment came from a good spirit. He concluded that it would be better to ignore it and to sleep for the allotted time. And so he did.[10]

27. He continued to abstain from eating meat and was so determined about it that he would not think of changing it for any reason; but one day, when he got up in the morning, edible meat appeared before him as if he saw it with his ordinary eyes, though no desire for it had preceded. At the same time he also had a strong inclination of his will to eat it from then on. Although he remembered his previous intention, he had no doubt about this, but rather a conviction that he ought to eat meat. Later when telling this to his confessor, the confessor told him to consider whether perhaps this was a temptation; but examining it carefully, he could never doubt about it.

God treated him at this time just as a schoolmaster treats a child whom he is teaching.[11] Whether this was because of his lack of education and of brains, or because he had no one to teach him, or because of the strong desire God himself had given him to serve him, he believed without doubt and has always believed that God treated him in this way. Indeed, if he were to doubt this, he would think he offended his Divine Majesty. Something of this can be seen from the five following points.

28. FIRST. He had great devotion to the Most Holy Trinity, and so each day he prayed to the three Persons separately. But as he also prayed to the Most Holy Trinity, the thought came to him: Why did he say four prayers to the Trinity? But this thought gave him little or no difficulty, being hardly important. One day while saying the Office of Our Lady on the steps of the same monastery, his understanding began to be elevated so that he saw the Most Holy Trinity in the form of three

musical keys.[12] This brought on so many tears and so much sobbing that he could not control himself. That morning, while going in a procession that set out from there, he could not hold back his tears until dinnertime; nor after eating could he stop talking about the Most Holy Trinity, using many comparisons in great variety and with much joy and consolation. As a result, the effect has remained with him throughout his life of experiencing great devotion while praying to the Most Holy Trinity.

29. SECOND. Once, the manner in which God had created the world was presented to his understanding with great spiritual joy. He seemed to see something white, from which some rays were coming, and God made light from this. But he did not know how to explain these things, nor did he remember too well the spiritual enlightenment that God was imprinting on his soul at the time.

THIRD. At Manresa too, where he stayed almost a year, after he began to be consoled by God and saw the fruit which he bore in dealing with souls,[13] he gave up those extremes he had formerly practiced, and he now cut his nails and his hair. One day in this town while he was hearing Mass in the church of the monastery mentioned above, at the elevation of the Body of the Lord, he saw with interior eyes something like white rays coming from above. Although he cannot explain this very well after so long a time, nevertheless, what he saw clearly with his understanding was how Jesus Christ our Lord was there in that Most Holy Sacrament.

FOURTH. Often and for a long time, while at prayer, he saw with interior eyes the humanity of Christ. The form that appeared to him was like a white body, neither very large nor very small, but he did not see any distinction of members. He saw it at Manresa many times. If he should say twenty or forty, he would not dare judge it a lie. He has seen this another time in Jerusalem and yet another while traveling near Padua.[14] He has also seen Our Lady in a similar form, without distinguishing parts. These things he saw strengthened him then and always gave him such strength in his faith that he has often thought to himself: If there were no Scriptures to teach us these matters of faith, he would be resolved to die for them, solely because of what he has seen.

30. FIFTH. Once he was going out of devotion to a church situated a little more than a mile from Manresa; I believe it is called St. Paul's, and the road goes by the river. As he went along occupied with his devotions, he sat down for a little while with his face toward the river, which ran down below. While he was seated there, the eyes of his

understanding began to be opened; not that he saw any vision, but he understood and learnt many things, both spiritual matters and matters of faith and of scholarship,[15] and this with so great an enlightenment that everything seemed new to him.

[Câmara]: This left his understanding so very enlightened that he felt as if he were another man with another mind.

The details that he understood then, though there were many, cannot be stated, but only that he experienced a great clarity in his understanding. This was such that in the whole course of his life, after completing sixty-two years, even if he gathered up all the various helps he may have had from God and all the various things he has known, even adding them all together, he does not think he had got as much as at that one time.[16]

31. After this had lasted for a good while, he went to kneel before a nearby cross to give thanks to God. There, the vision that had appeared to him many times but which he had never understood, that is, the thing mentioned above which seemed very beautiful to him, with many eyes, now appeared to him. But while before the cross, he saw clearly that the object did not have its usual beautiful color, and he knew very clearly with a strong agreement of his will that it was the devil. Later it would often appear to him for a long time; and by way of contempt he dispelled it with a staff he used to carry in his hand.[17]

32. Once while he was ill at Manresa, a very severe fever brought him to the point of death, and he fully believed that his soul was about to leave him. At this a thought came to him telling him that he was a just man, but this caused him so much trouble that he constantly rejected it and called his sins to mind. He had more trouble with this thought than with the fever itself, but no matter how much trouble he took to overcome the thought, he could not overcome it. Then somewhat relieved of the fever, he was no longer at the point of expiring, and he began to shout loudly to some ladies who had come there to visit him, that for the love of God, when they next saw him at the point of death, they should shout at him with loud voices, addressing him as sinner: Let him remember the offenses he had committed against God.

33. Another time, while he was going by sea from Valencia to Italy in a violent storm, the rudder of the ship was broken, and the situation reached such a pass that in his judgment and that of many others who sailed on the ship, they could not by natural means escape death. At this time, examining himself carefully and preparing to die, he could not feel afraid for his sins or of being condemned, but he did feel embarrassment

and sorrow, as he believed he had not used well the gifts and graces which God our Lord had granted him.

Another time, in the year '50, he was very bad with a very severe illness which in his opinion as well as in that of many others would be the last. At this time, thinking about death, he felt such joy and such spiritual consolation at having to die that he dissolved entirely into tears. This became so habitual that he often stopped thinking about death so as not to feel so much of that consolation.

34. When winter came he was down with a very severe illness, and for treatment the town put him in a house of the father of one Ferrera, who was later in the service of Baltasar de Faria. There he was cared for with great attention; and many prominent ladies, because of the deep regard they now had for him, came to watch over him by night. Though he recovered from this illness, he was still very weak and with frequent stomach pains. For these reasons, therefore, and because the winter was very cold, they made him dress up and wear shoes and cover his head; so they made him use two brown jackets of very coarse cloth and a cap of the same, something like a beret. At this time there was a long period during which he was very eager to converse on spiritual matters and to find persons who could deal with them. Meanwhile, the time was approaching when he planned to set out for Jerusalem.

35. So at the beginning of the year '23 he set out for Barcelona to take ship. Although various people offered to accompany him, he wanted to go quite alone, for his whole idea was to have God alone as refuge. One day some persons were strongly urging him to take a companion, since he did not know either the Italian or the Latin language. They told him how much this would help him and praised a certain person highly. He replied that even if the companion were the son or the brother of the Duke of Cardona, he would not go in his company. For he wanted to practice three virtues—charity, faith, and hope; and if he took a companion, he would expect help from him when he was hungry; if he fell down, the man would help him get up. He himself, too, would trust the companion and feel attachment to him on this account. But he wanted to place that trust, attachment, and expectation in God alone.

What he said in this way he felt just so in his heart. With these thoughts he not only had the desire to set out alone but to go without any provisions. When he began to arrange for his passage, he got round the master of the ship to carry him free, as he had no money, but on condition that he brought to the ship some biscuit for his sustenance; otherwise, for nothing in the world would they accept him.

36. When he went to obtain the biscuit, great scruples came over him: "Is this the hope and faith you had in God who would not fail you?" and the like. This was so powerful as to trouble him greatly; at last, not knowing what to do because he saw probable reasons on both sides, he decided to place himself in the hands of his confessor. So he told him how much he wanted to seek perfection and whatever would be more to the glory of God, and the reasons that caused him to doubt whether he ought to take any provisions. The confessor decided that he should beg what was necessary and take it with him.

As he begged from a lady, she asked where he was planning to travel. He hesitated a bit whether he would tell her, but at last he ventured to say no more than that he was going to Italy and to Rome. And as if in amazement, she said, "You want to go to Rome? Well, I don't know how those who go there come back." (She meant to say that in Rome one profited little in spiritual things.) Now the reason why he did not dare say that he was going to Jerusalem was fear of vainglory. This fear haunted him so much that he never dared say to what country or to what family he belonged. At last, having the biscuit, he went on board. But at the shore he found he had five or six *blancas*[18] left from what he was given begging from door to door (for he used to live that way). He left them on a bench that he came across there by the shore.

37. So he embarked, having been in Barcelona a little more than twenty days. While he was still in Barcelona before embarking, he sought out, as was his practice, all spiritual persons to converse with them, even though they lived in hermitages far from the city. But neither in Barcelona nor in Manresa during the whole time he was there did he find persons who could help him as much as he wished. He found in Manresa only that woman mentioned above, who told him she prayed God that Jesus Christ might appear to him. She alone seemed to him to enter more deeply into spiritual matters. Therefore, after leaving Barcelona, he completely lost this eagerness to seek out spiritual persons.

Ch. 4. PILGRIMAGE TO JERUSALEM
Mid-March–September 22, 1523

38. They had such a strong wind at the stern that they reached Gaeta from Barcelona in five days and nights, though they were all thoroughly frightened because of very rough weather. Throughout all

that region there was fear of the plague; but as soon as he disembarked he began the journey to Rome. Of those who came on the ship, a mother and her daughter whom she had in boy's clothing, and another youth, accompanied him. They joined him because they also were begging.

Having reached a lodge, they came upon a great blaze with many soldiers at it, who gave them to eat, and a good deal of wine, coaxing them as if they wanted to warm them up. Later they separated them, the mother and daughter being placed in a room above and the pilgrim and the youth in a stable. But at midnight he heard loud cries from that quarter above; getting up to see what it was, he found the mother and her daughter in the courtyard below, wailing and complaining that there was an attempt to violate them. At this such a strong feeling came over him that he began to shout, saying: "Must one put up with this?" and similar protests. He uttered these words with such force that all those in the house were alarmed. No one did him any harm. The youth had already fled, and though it was still night, all three got going.

39. When they arrived at a nearby city, they found it closed. Unable to enter, the three of them spent the night in a leaky church there. In the morning they would not allow them into the city, and they found no alms outside, even though they went to a castle which could be seen nearby. There the pilgrim felt weak, as much from the hardships of the sea and of others similar. Unable to travel farther, he remained there. The mother and her daughter went on to Rome.

That day many people came out of the city. Learning that the lady of the place was coming there he approached her, saying that he was ill only from weakness. He asked her to let him enter the city to seek some cure. She readily granted it, and he began to beg through the city and obtained a fair amount. After two days of recovery, he set out on his journey again and arrived in Rome on Palm Sunday.

40. Here all who spoke to him, on discovering that he did not carry any money for Jerusalem, began to dissuade him from making that trip, asserting with many arguments that it was impossible to find passage without money. But he had great assurance in his soul and he could not doubt but that he would in fact find a way to go to Jerusalem. After receiving the blessing of Pope Adrian VI, he set out for Venice eight or nine days after Easter. He did have six or seven ducats which had been given him for the passage from Venice to Jerusalem; he had accepted them, being somewhat overcome by the fears suggested to him that he would not otherwise make the passage. But two days after leaving Rome, he began to realize that this was a lack of trust on his part, and it

greatly bothered him that he had accepted the ducats. So he wondered if it would be good to be rid of them. He finally decided to give them generously to those who approached him, who were beggars usually. He so managed that when he eventually arrived in Venice, he had no more than a small amount which he required that night.

41. While on the journey to Venice, he slept in doorways because of the guards against the plague. It happened once that when he got up in the morning he ran into a man who, with one look, fled in horror, presumably because he saw him so very pale. Traveling in this way, he came to Chioggia, and with some companions who had joined him, he learned that they would not be allowed to enter Venice. His companions decided to go to Padua to obtain a certificate of health there, so he set out with them. But he could not keep up for they went very fast, leaving him at nightfall in a large field.

While he was there, Christ appeared to him in the manner in which he usually appeared to him, as we have mentioned above, and this brought him much comfort. Consoled in this way, the next morning, without forging a certificate as (I believe) his companions had done, he came to the gates of Padua and entered without the guards asking anything of him. The same thing happened when he left. This greatly astonished his companions who had just got a certificate to go to Venice, about which he did not bother.

42. When they arrived at Venice, the guards came to the boat to examine them all, one by one, as many as were in it, but him alone they let be. He maintained himself in Venice by begging, and he slept in St. Mark's Square. But he would never go to the house of the emperor's ambassador, nor did he take any special care to seek the means for his passage. He had a great assurance in his soul that God would provide a way for him to go to Jerusalem. This gave him such confidence that no arguments or fears suggested to him could make him doubt.

One day he ran into a rich Spaniard who asked him what he was doing and where he wanted to go. Learning his purpose, the man took him home to dinner, and kept him a few days till all was set for the departure. Ever since Manresa the pilgrim had the habit when he ate with anyone never to speak at table except to answer briefly; but he listened to what was said and noted some things which he took as the occasion to speak about God, and when the meal was finished, he did so.

43. This was the reason why the worthy gentleman and all his household were so attached to him and wanted him to stay and made an

effort to keep him there. This same host brought him to the doge of Venice so he could speak to him; that is, he obtained entrance and an audience for him. When the doge heard the pilgrim, he ordered that he be given passage on the ship of the governors who were going to Cyprus.

Although many pilgrims had come that year for Jerusalem, most of them had returned home because of the recent event which had occurred, the capture of Rhodes. Even so there were thirteen on the pilgrim ship which sailed first, and eight or nine remained for the governors' ship.[19]

As this was about to leave, our pilgrim had a severe bout of fever; but after troubling him a few days, it left him. The ship was sailing on the day he had taken a purge. The people of the house asked the doctor if he could embark for Jerusalem, and the doctor said that indeed he could embark, if he wanted to be buried there. But he did embark and sail that day; and he vomited in such a way that he felt much relieved and began to recover completely. He severely condemned some obscenities and indecencies that were openly practiced on the ship.

44. The Spaniards who were there warned him not to do so, because the ship's crew were planning to leave him on some island. But Our Lord deigned that they arrive quickly at Cyprus. Leaving the ship there, they went overland to another port called Las Salinas, ten leagues away. They boarded the pilgrim ship, and here too he brought no more for his maintenance than his hope in God, as he had done on the other.

During all this time, Our Lord appeared to him often, giving him great consolation and determination; but what he seemed to see was something round and large, as though it were of gold: and this was what presented itself to him.

Having left Cyprus, they arrived at Jaffa. Moving on to Jerusalem on their little donkeys, as is usually done, two miles before they reached Jerusalem a Spaniard—a noble it would seem, named Diego Manes— suggested with great devotion to all the pilgrims that since in a little while they would reach the place from which they could see the Holy City, it would be well for all to prepare their consciences and go in silence.

45. This seemed good to them all, and each one began to recollect himself. A little before coming to the place from where it could be seen, they dismounted, because they saw the friars with the cross, awaiting them. On seeing the city the pilgrim felt great consolation; and as the others testified, this was common to them all, with a joy that did not

seem natural. He always felt this same devotion on his visits to the holy places.[20]

His firm intention was to remain in Jerusalem, continually visiting those holy places; and in addition to this devotion, he also planned to help souls.[21] For this purpose he had brought letters of recommendation for the Guardian and gave them to him. He told him of his intention to remain there because of his devotion; but not the second part, about wanting to help souls, because he had not told this to anyone, although he had frequently made public the first. The Guardian answered that he did not see how he could stay because the house was in such need that it could not support the friars; for that reason he had decided to send some with the pilgrims, to these parts. The pilgrim replied that he wanted nothing from the house, except only that when he came sometimes to confess, they would hear his confession. With that the Guardian told him that such an arrangement might work, but he would have to wait for the coming of the provincial (I believe he was the head of the order in that area), who was at Bethlehem.

46. By this promise the pilgrim was reassured and began to write letters to Barcelona to spiritual persons. Having already written one and while writing another on the eve of the departure of the pilgrims, he received a summons from the provincial (for he had arrived) and the Guardian. The provincial spoke kindly to him, saying that he knew of his good intention to remain in those holy places, and he had given much thought to the matter; but because of the experience he had with others, he judged that it was not expedient. For many had that desire, but some had been captured and others killed, and the order had later been obliged to ransom the captives. Therefore he should prepare to leave the next day with the pilgrims.

He replied to this that he was very firm in his purpose and was resolved that on no account would he fail to carry it out. He frankly gave them to understand that even though the provincial thought otherwise, if there was nothing binding him under sin, he would not abandon his intention out of any fear. To this the provincial replied that they had authority from the Apostolic See to have anyone leave the place, or remain there, as they judged, and to excommunicate anyone who was unwilling to obey them; and that in this case they thought that he should not remain, and so forth.

47. He wanted to show him the bulls giving them power to excommunicate, but he said he did not need to see them, as he believed their Reverences; inasmuch as they had so decided with the authority

they had, he would obey them.[22] When this was over, returning to where he had been before, he felt a strong desire to visit Mount Olivet again before leaving, since it was not Our Lord's will that he remain in those holy places. On Mount Olivet there is a stone from which Our Lord rose up to heaven, and his footprints are still seen there; this was what he wanted to see again.

So without saying anything or taking a guide (for those who go without a Turk as guide run a great risk), he slipped away from the others and went alone to Mount Olivet. But the guards would not let him enter. He gave them a penknife that he carried, and after praying with great consolation, he felt the desire to go to Bethphage. While there he remembered that he had not noted on Mount Olivet on what side the right foot was, or on what side the left. Returning there, I think he gave his scissors to the guards so they would let him enter.

48. When it was learned in the monastery that he had gone like that without a guide, the friars took steps to find him. So as he was coming down from Mount Olivet he ran into a "belted"[23] Christian who served in the monastery. He had a large staff and with a great show of annoyance made as if to strike him. When he came up to him he grabbed him tightly by the arm, and he readily let himself be led. The good man, however, never let him go. As he went along this way, held thus by the "belted" Christian, he felt great consolation from Our Lord, and it seemed to him that he saw Christ over him continually. This lasted all through in great abundance until he reached the monastery.

Ch. 5. THE RETURN VOYAGE
October 23, 1523–February, 1524

49. The next day they set out, and after arriving at Cyprus, the pilgrims dispersed in different ships. In the port there were three or four ships bound for Venice. One was Turkish, another was a very small vessel, and the third was a very rich and powerful ship belonging to a wealthy Venetian. Some pilgrims asked the master of this ship kindly to take the pilgrim; but when he learned that he had no money, he did not want to, even though many made petition, praising him, and so on. The master answered that if he was a saint, he should travel as St. James had done,[24] or something like that. These same petitioners very easily succeeded with the master of the small vessel.

They set out one day with a good wind in the morning; but in the afternoon a storm came upon them, and they got separated one from the other. The big one was wrecked near those same Islands of Cyprus, and only the people escaped; in the same storm the Turkish ship was lost and all the people with it. The small vessel had great trouble, but in the end they reached land somewhere in Apulia. This was in the depth of winter, and it was very cold and snowing. The pilgrim had no clothing other than some breeches of coarse cloth (knee-length and leaving the legs bare), shoes and doublet of black cloth opened by many slashes at the shoulders, and a jacket that was short and quite thin.

50. He arrived in Venice in mid-January of the year '24, having been at sea from Cyprus the whole months of November and December and what was gone of January. In Venice, one of the two who had welcomed him in their homes before he set out for Jerusalem met him and gave him as alms fifteen or sixteen *giulii* and a piece of cloth, which he folded many times and put over his stomach because of the great cold.

After the pilgrim realized that it was not God's will that he remain in Jerusalem, he continually pondered within himself what he ought to do. Eventually he was rather inclined to study for some time so he would be able to help souls, and he decided to go to Barcelona. So he set out from Venice for Genoa. One day, whilst going through his devotions in the principal church of Ferrara, a beggar asked him for alms and he gave him a *marchetto*,[25] which is a coin of five or six *quatrini*. After that another came, and he gave him another small coin that he had, somewhat larger; and to a third he gave a *giulio*, having nothing but *giulii*. The beggars, seeing that he was giving alms, kept coming and so all he had was finished. Finally many beggars came together seeking alms. His response was to ask pardon, as he had nothing left.

51. So he left Ferrara for Genoa. On the road he met some Spanish soldiers who treated him well that night; but they were much surprised that he traveled that road, because one had to pass practically between the two armies, the French and the Imperial.[26] They urged him to leave the highway and to take another safe road that they showed him. But he did not take their advice. Instead, traveling straight on he came upon a burned and destroyed village; and so till night he found no one to give him anything to eat.

But at sunset he reached a walled place where the guards immediately seized him, thinking he was a spy. They put him in a cabin next to the gate and began to question him, as is usual when there is some suspicion, but he replied to all their questions that he knew nothing. They stripped him and searched him down to his shoes, and all over his body, to see if he was carrying any letters. Unable to learn anything by any means, they took hold of him that he might appear before the captain—he would make him talk. He asked them to take him clothed in his jacket, but they refused to give it to him and took him in the breeches and doublet mentioned above.

52. On the way the pilgrim had some sort of impression of when Christ was led away, but this was not a vision like the others. He was led through three main streets, and he went without any sadness, but rather with joy and satisfaction. It was his custom to speak to any person, no matter who it might be, using "you,"[27] piously holding that Christ and the apostles had spoken in this way, and so forth. As he was going thus through the streets, it crossed his fancy that it would be wise to give up that custom in this situation and address the captain as "Sir." This because of some fear of the tortures they might inflict, and the like. But recognizing that this was a temptation, "Since it is such," he said, "I will not address him as Sir nor do him reverence nor take off my cap to him."

53. They reached the captain's headquarters and left him in a lower room. A while later the captain spoke to him. Without using any form of courtesy, he answered in a few words, with a noticeable interval between one and the next. The captain took him for a madman and said so to those who had brought him: "This man is not in his senses. Give him his things and throw him out." Just on leaving the headquarters he met a Spaniard who lived there; he took him to his house and gave him something to break his fast and all the necessaries for that night.

Setting out in the morning, he traveled until evening, when two soldiers in a tower saw him and came down to seize him. They took him to their captain, who was French; the captain asked him, among other things, from what country he came, and learning that he was from Guipúzcoa, he said to him, "I come from near there," apparently from near Bayonne. Then he said, "Take him and give him supper and treat him well." On this road from Ferrara to Genoa he had many other little experiences.

At last he reached Genoa, where a Vizcayan named Portundo, who had spoken with him on other occasions when he served in the court of the Catholic King, recognized him. This man got him passage on a ship going to Barcelona, in which he ran great danger of being captured by Andrea Doria,[28] who gave chase, being then on the French side.

Ch. 6. BARCELONA AND ALCALÁ
February or March, 1524–June 21, 1527

54. When he arrived at Barcelona he made his wish to study known to Isabel Roser[29] and to a Master Ardèvol[30] who taught grammar. To both this seemed a very good idea; he offered to teach him for nothing, and she to give him what he needed to support himself. In Manresa the pilgrim had known a friar (of the order of St. Bernard, I think), a very spiritual man; he wanted to be with this person to learn and to be able to give himself more easily to the spirit, as also to be of help to souls. So he replied that he would accept the offer if he did not find in Manresa the facilities he was looking for. But when he went there, he found that the friar was dead.

So, returning to Barcelona, he began to study with great diligence. But one thing hampered him very much. It was that when he started memorizing, as one needs to do in the beginnings of grammar, there came to him new insights into spiritual matters and fresh delights, to such an extent that he could not memorize, nor could he drive them away no matter how much he resisted.

55. So, thinking often about this, he said to himself, "Not even when I engage in prayer and am at Mass do such vivid insights come to me." Thus, little by little, he came to realize that this was a temptation. After praying he went to Our Lady of the Sea, near the master's house, having asked that he kindly listen to him for a few moments in that church. So when they were seated, he told him exactly all that went on in his soul and what little progress he had made until then for that reason. But he promised this same master, saying: "I promise you never to fail to listen to you these two years, so long as I can find bread and water in Barcelona with which I might support myself." As he made this promise with great determination, he never again had those temptations.[31] The stomach pain that afflicted him in Manresa, for which reason he wore shoes, was gone, and he had felt well in the stomach ever since he set out for Jerusalem. For this reason, while he was studying at Barcelona he had the desire to resume his previous penances and so he began to make a hole in the soles of his shoes, which he kept widening little by little so that when the winter cold came, he was wearing only the uppers.

56. After two years of study during which, so they said, he had made great progress, his master informed him he could now study the

liberal arts and should go to Alcalá. Even so, he had himself examined by a doctor of theology who gave him the same advice. So he set out alone for Alcalá, though he already had some companions,[32] I think.

When he arrived at Alcalá, he began to beg and to live on alms. After he had lived in this fashion for ten or twelve days, a cleric and others who were with him, seeing him beg alms one day, began to laugh at him and to utter some insults, as one usually does to those who, being healthy, go begging. At that moment the superintendent of the new hospice of Antezana passed by, and expressing regret at this, called him and took him to the hospice where he gave him a room and all he needed.

57. He studied at Alcalá almost a year and a half. Since he had arrived in Barcelona in the year '24 during Lent, and had studied there for two years, it was in the year '26 that he reached Alcalá. He studied the logic of Soto, the physics of Albert, and the Master of the Sentences.[33] While at Alcalá, he was engaged in giving spiritual exercises[34] and teaching Christian doctrine, and this bore fruit for the glory of God. There were many persons who came to a deep understanding and relish of spiritual things; but others had various temptations. For example, there was one such who wanted to take the discipline but could not do so, as though the hand were held, and other similar cases. These gave rise to talk among the people, especially because of the great crowd that gathered wherever he was explaining doctrine.

[Câmara]: I will recall the fright that he himself got one night.[35]

Soon after he arrived in Alcalá, he became acquainted with Don Diego de Guia,[36] who was staying with his brother, a printer in Alcalá who was quite well off. So they helped him with alms to support the poor. The pilgrim's three companions were lodged in his house. Once, when he came to ask alms for some needs, Don Diego said he had no money, but he opened for him a chest in which he had various objects, and then gave him bed coverings of different colors and some candlesticks and suchlike things. Wrapping them all in a sheet, the pilgrim put them on his shoulders and went off to aid the poor.

58. As mentioned above, there was much talk throughout that region about the things happening at Alcalá; some spoke one way, some another. The thing reached the inquisitors at Toledo. When these came to Alcalá, the pilgrim was alerted by their host, who told him that they were calling them "ensayalados"[37] and, I believe, "alumbrados,"[38] and that they would butcher them. So they began at once to investigate and

examine their life; but finally they returned to Toledo without summoning them, though they had come for that sole purpose.

They left the trial to the vicar Figueroa,[39] who is now with the emperor. A few days later he summoned them and told them how an investigation and examination of their life had been made by the inquisitors and that no error had been found in their teaching nor in their life, and therefore they could go on doing the same as they did without any hindrance. But since they were not religious, it did not seem right for them to go about all in the same habit. It would be well, and he so ordered, that two of them, pointing to the pilgrim and Arteaga, dyed their clothes black; and that the other two, Calixto and Cáceres, dyed theirs brown; Juanito,[40] who was a French lad, could stay as he was.

59. The pilgrim says they will do what they are ordered. "But," he says, "I do not know what benefit these inquisitions bring; the other day a priest did not want to give the sacrament to someone because he went to Communion every eight days; and they were objecting to me, too. We would like to know if they have found any heresy in us." "No," says Figueroa, "for if they did, they would burn you." "They would burn you too," says the pilgrim, "if they found heresy in you." They dyed their clothing, as they were ordered, and fifteen or twenty days later Figueroa ordered the pilgrim not to go barefoot but to wear shoes; and so he did without fuss, as in all matters of this sort that he was ordered.

Four months later Figueroa himself again began an investigation of them. Besides the usual reasons, I believe this was also something of a factor, that a married woman of rank had special regard for the pilgrim. In order not to be noticed, she came to the hospice at dawn, wearing a veil, as is the custom in Alcalá de Henares. On entering she removed her veil and went to the pilgrim's room. But they did nothing to them this time either, nor did they say anything to them.

[Câmara]: R. I must remember what Bustamante told me.

60. After another four months, he being now in a cabin outside the hospice, a policeman came to his door one day and called him, saying, "Just come with me." He put him in jail and said to him, "You may not leave here until you are ordered otherwise." This was in the summertime, and as he was not confined, many people came to visit him.

[Câmara]: Mª [Miona?], and was confessor.

He did the same things as when he was free, teaching and giving exercises. Never would he have an advocate or attorney, though many

offered themselves. He especially remembers Doña Teresa de Cár-
denas, who sent someone to visit him and frequently offered to get him
out; but he accepted nothing, always answering, "He for whose love I
got in here will get me out, if he is served thereby."

61. He was in prison seventeen days without being examined or
knowing the reason for it. At the end of that time Figueroa came to the
jail and examined him about many things, even asking him if he enjoined
observance of the Sabbath. He also asked whether he knew two particular women, a mother and her daughter,[41] and to this he answered yes;
and further, whether he had known of their departure before they had
set out. He replied no, with appeal to the oath he had sworn. The vicar
then placed a hand on his shoulder, manifesting joy, and said, "This is
the reason why you were brought here."

Among the many persons who followed the pilgrim there were a
mother and her daughter, both widowed. The daughter was very young
and very attractive. They had made great spiritual progress, especially
the daughter. So much so that though they were noble women, they had
gone to the Verónica of Jaén on foot, possibly begging and unaccompa-
nied. This caused considerable gossip in Alcalá, and Doctor Ciruelo,
who had some responsibility for them, thought that the prisoner had
persuaded them and for this reason had him arrested.

Having taken in the vicar's words, the prisoner said to him,
"Would you like me to speak more at length about this affair?" He said,
"Yes." "Then you should know," said the prisoner, "that these two
women have often insisted with me that they wanted to go about the
world serving the poor in one hospital and then in another. I have
always dissuaded them from this plan, because the daughter is so young
and so attractive, and so forth. And I have told them that when they
wanted to visit the poor, they could do so in Alcalá, and could accompany the Blessed Sacrament." When this conversation was finished,
Figueroa left with his notary, taking a complete written statement.

62. At that time Calixto was in Segovia, and learning of his imprisonment came at once, though but recently recovered from a serious
illness, and got into jail with him. He for his part suggested it would be
better to go and call on the vicar, who received him kindly and manifested the intention to send him to jail; for that is where he had to be till
those women returned, in order to see if they confirmed what had been
said. Calixto remained in jail a few days, but when the pilgrim saw that
this harmed his bodily health, because he was not yet entirely well, he
had him released with the help of a doctor, a great friend of his.

From the day the pilgrim entered jail until they let him out, forty-two days passed. At the end of that time, as the two pious women returned, the notary came to the jail to read the sentence: He should go free, and they should dress like the other students, and should not speak about matters of faith until they had studied for four more years, because they had no education. This was true, for the pilgrim was the one who knew the most, and that was with little foundation. This was the first thing he used to say whenever they examined him.

63. Because of this sentence he was somewhat doubtful what he should do, for seemingly they were closing the door for him to help souls, without giving him any reason except that he had not studied. At last he decided to go to Fonseca, the archbishop of Toledo, and put the case in his hands. He set out from Alcalá and found the archbishop in Valladolid. Faithfully recounting the affair to him, he said that even though he was not now in his jurisdiction nor obliged to abide by the sentence, still he would do whatever he commanded in this matter. (He addressed him as "you" as was his custom with everyone.) The archbishop received him very well, adding he had friends and a college in Salamanca too, all of which he put at his disposal. Just as he was leaving, he had four *escudos* given to him.

Ch. 7. TROUBLES AT SALAMANCA
Mid-July–Mid-September, 1527

64. On arrival in Salamanca, while he was praying in a church, he was recognized by a devoted friend of the group (for his four companions had been there some days already). She asked him his name and then took him to the lodgings of his companions. When the sentence had been given in Alcalá that they should dress like students, the pilgrim said, "When you ordered us to dye our clothes, we did so; but now we cannot do this, because we do not have the means to buy them." So the vicar himself provided them with clothing and caps and all the other student gear. Dressed in this fashion, they had left Alcalá.

At Salamanca he went to confession to a Dominican friar at St. Stephen's. Ten or twelve days after his arrival the confessor said to him one day, "The Fathers of the house would like to speak with you." He said, "In the name of God." "Then," said the confessor, "it would be well if you came here to dine on Sunday; but I warn you of one thing, that they will want to know many things from you." So on Sunday he came with Calixto.

After dinner, the subprior, in the absence of the prior, together with the confessor and I think with another friar, went with them to a chapel. With great cordiality the subprior began to say what good reports they had of their life and ways; that they went about preaching in apostolic fashion; and that they would be pleased to learn about these things in greater detail. So he began asking what they had studied. The pilgrim replied, "Of all of us, I am the one who has studied the most," and he gave a clear account of the little he had studied and with what little foundation.

65. "Tell, then, what do you preach?" "We do not preach," said the pilgrim, "but we do speak familiarly with some people about the things of God; for example, after dinner with some people who invite us." "But," said the friar, "what things of God do you speak about? That is just what we would like to know." "We speak," said the pilgrim, "sometimes of one virtue, sometimes of another; and do so, praising it; sometimes of one vice, sometimes of another, condemning it." "You are not learned men," said the friar, "and you speak about virtues and vices; but no one can speak about these except in one of two ways: either through learning or through the Holy Spirit. If not through learning, then through the Holy Spirit."[42]

[Câmara]: What comes from the Holy Spirit—that is what we want to know about.

At this the pilgrim was somewhat on his guard, because that kind of argument did not seem good to him. After being silent a while, he said it was not necessary to speak further of these matters. The friar insisted, "Well, now that there are so many errors of Erasmus[43] and of so many others who have deceived the world, you do not wish to explain what you say?"

66. The pilgrim said, "Father, I will say no more than I have said, except before my superiors who can oblige me to do so." Before this the friar had asked why Calixto came dressed as he was. He wore a short tunic and a large hat on his head, with a staff in his hand and boots almost halfway up the leg; and being very tall, he looked the more grotesque. The pilgrim related how they had been imprisoned in Alcalá and had been ordered to dress like students and that his companion, because of the great heat, had given his gown to a poor cleric. At this the friar seemed to mutter to himself, indicating that he was not pleased: "Charity begins at home."

Well, to get back to the story, the subprior, unable to get any other word out of the pilgrim but that, said, "Then remain here, and we will indeed make you tell all." So all the friars left with some haste. The pilgrim first asked if they wanted them to remain in that chapel, or where did they want them to remain. The subprior answered that they should remain in the chapel. The friars then closed all the doors and, as it appears, took the matter up with the judges. Still the two of them were in the monastery for three days, eating in the refectory with the friars, without anything being said to them in the name of the court. Their room was almost always full of friars who came to see them. The pilgrim always spoke on his usual topics; as a result there was already some division among them, many showing that they were sympathetic.

67. At the end of three days a notary came and took them to jail. They were not put down below with the criminals but in an upper room where, because it was old and unused, there was much dirt. They were both bound with the same chain, each one by his foot. The chain was attached to a post in the middle of the house and would be ten or thirteen palms long. Each time that one wanted to do something, the other had to accompany him. All that night they kept awake. The next day, when their imprisonment was known in the city, people sent to the jail something on which they could sleep and all that was needed, in abundance. Many people came continually to visit them, and the pilgrim kept up his practice of speaking about God, and so forth.

The bachelor Frías[44] came to examine each of them separately, and the pilgrim gave him all his papers, which were the Exercises,[45] to be examined. Asked if they had companions, they said they did, and where they were. Straightaway some went there on the bachelor's orders and brought Cáceres and Arteaga to the jail; and they left Juanito, who later became a friar. However, they did not put them above with the other two but down where the common prisoners were. Here too he would not have an advocate or attorney.

68. Some days later he was summoned before four judges: the three doctors, Sanctisidoro, Paravinhas, and Frías; and the fourth was the bachelor Frías. All of them had already seen the Exercises. Now they asked him many things not only about the Exercises, but also about theology, for example, about the Trinity and the Eucharist, and how he understood these articles. He first made his introduction but then, pressed by the judges, he spoke in such a manner that they had no reason to fault him. The bachelor Frías, who on these points had throughout been to the fore, also asked him about a canonical case.[46] He was required to answer everything, but he always said first that he did not know what scholars said about those matters.

Then they ordered him to explain the first commandment in the way he usually explained it. He started to do so and took so long and said so many things about the first commandment that they were not inclined to ask him more. Before this, when they were speaking about the Exercises, they insisted a good deal on one point only in them, which was at the beginning: When a thought is a venial sin and when it is mortal. The question was why he, without studies, was deciding that. He answered, "If this is true or not, decide that; and if it is not true, condemn it." But in the end they left without condemning anything.

69. Among the many who came to speak to him in jail was Don Francisco de Mendoza, who now has the title of Cardinal of Burgos, came with the bachelor Frías. In a friendly way he asked him how he was getting on in prison and if it bothered him to be imprisoned. He replied, "I will answer what I answered today to a lady who, on seeing me in prison, spoke words of compassion. I said to her, 'By this you show that you do not wish to be imprisoned for the love of God. Does imprisonment seem to be such a great evil to you?' Well, I will tell you that there are not so many fetters and chains in Salamanca that I do not want more for the love of God."

At this time it happened that all the prisoners in the jail fled, but the two companions who were with them did not flee. In the morning when they were found there alone without anyone, with the doors open, all were deeply edified, and there was much talk in the city; so they gave them an entire mansion that was nearby, as a prison.

70. After twenty-two days of imprisonment, they were summoned to hear the sentence, which was that no error was found in their life or teaching. Therefore they could do what they had been doing, teaching doctrine and speaking about the things of God, so long as they never defined that this is a mortal sin or this is venial, until they had spent four years in further studies. After the sentence was read, the judges displayed great affection, apparently wishing to make it acceptable. The pilgrim said he would do everything the sentence ordered, but he did not find it acceptable, because without condemning him for anything they shut his mouth so he might not help his neighbors in what he could. Although Doctor Frías urged and showed himself very well disposed, the pilgrim said no more—only that as long as he was in the jurisdiction of Salamanca he would do what had been ordered.

Then they were released from jail, and he began to commend the matter to God and to think about what he ought to do. He found great difficulty in remaining in Salamanca, for it seemed to him that the door had been closed to helping souls by this prohibition not to determine mortal and venial sin.

71. So he decided to go to Paris to study. When the pilgrim was considering in Barcelona whether he should study and how much, his one concern had been whether, after he had studied, he would enter a religious institute or go about the world. When thoughts of entering an institute came to him, then he also had the desire to enter a decadent and not quite reformed one (if he were to be a religious) so that he would suffer more in it, and thinking also that perhaps God would help them. And God gave him great confidence that he would endure easily all the insults and injuries they might inflict.

Now, at the time of his imprisonment in Salamanca, he still felt the same desire that he had to help souls, and for that reason to study first and to gather some others with the same idea, and to keep those he had. So he decided to go to Paris, and he arranged with them that they wait there while he went to see if he could find some means by which they might study.

72. Many important persons urged strongly that he should not go, but they could never dissuade him. Rather, fifteen or twenty days after leaving prison, he set out alone, taking some books on a little donkey. When he arrived at Barcelona, all those who knew him advised him against the journey to France because of the fierce wars, recounting very specific instances, even telling him that they put Spaniards on spits. But he never had any kind of fear.

Ch. 8. AT THE UNIVERSITY OF PARIS
February 2, 1528–April, 1535

73. So he set out for Paris, alone and on foot. He reached Paris in the month of February or thereabouts and, as he estimates, this was in the year 1528 or '27.[47] He lodged in a house with some Spaniards and went to study humanities at Montaigu. The reason was that as they had made him advance with such haste in studies, he found himself very deficient in fundamentals. He studied with children, following the order and method of Paris.[48]

[Câmara]: When he was imprisoned in Alcalá, the Prince of Spain was born; and from this one can calculate everything, even previous events.

When he first came to Paris, a merchant gave him twenty-five escudos on a draft from Barcelona. These he gave to one of the Spaniards in those lodgings to keep, but in a short time the latter spent them and had not the means to pay him. So after Lent the pilgrim had nothing left, both because the other had spent the money and because of the reason mentioned above. He was compelled to beg and even to leave the house where he was staying.

74. He got admission into the hospice of Saint-Jacques, beyond the Innocents. He was greatly inconvenienced in study because the hospice was a good distance from the college of Montaigu, and in order to find the door open one had to return at the sound of the Angelus and to leave in daylight. Thus he could not attend his classes properly. Having to beg alms to support himself was another obstacle.

It was almost five years now that he felt no stomach pains, so he began to subject himself to greater penances and fasts. After some time, in this life of hospice and begging, seeing that he was making little progress in studies, he began to consider what he should do. Seeing that there were several who served some of the regents in the colleges and had time to study, he decided to seek a master.

75. He found great consolation in the following reflection and resolution which he entertained, imagining that the master would be Christ, that one of the students he would call St. Peter and another St. John, and so with each one of the apostles: "When the master orders me, I will think that Christ orders me; when another orders me, I will think that St. Peter orders me." He tried hard to find a master; as one attempt, he spoke to the bachelor Castro, and as another to a Carthusian friar who knew many teachers, and to others; but never could they find him a master.

76. At last, as he found no solution, a Spanish friar told him one day that it would be better for him to go each year to Flanders and spend two months or even less to secure the means to study the whole year. After commending this to God, it seemed good to him. Following this advice, each year he brought back from Flanders enough to carry on in some way. Once he also went over to England and fetched more alms than he usually did in other years.[49]

77. The first time he returned from Flanders he got more involved than usual in spiritual contacts, and he gave exercises almost simultaneously to three persons, namely, Peralta, the bachelor Castro who was at the Sorbonne, and a Vizcayan named Amador,[50] who was at Sainte-Barbe. These were quite transformed and so gave all they had to the poor, even their books, and began to beg alms through Paris. They went

to lodge in the hospice of Saint-Jacques, where the pilgrim had stayed before but which he had now left for the reasons mentioned above.

This caused great commotion in the university, for the first two were distinguished persons and well known. The Spaniards then began a campaign against the two masters; but with their much argument and persuasion they were unable to convince them to return to the university. Hence one day many went armed and dragged them out of the hospice.

78. When they were brought to the university, an agreement was arrived at that they could carry out their plans after they had finished their studies. The bachelor Castro later came to Spain and preached at Burgos for some time and then became a Carthusian friar in Valencia. Peralta set out on foot as a pilgrim to Jerusalem. In these circumstances he was captured in Italy by a captain, a relative of his, who took steps to bring him to the pope, whom he got to order him to return to Spain. These things did not happen immediately but some years later.

Great complaints arose in Paris, especially among the Spaniards, against the pilgrim. Our Master de Gouvea, saying that he had caused Amador, who was in his college, to go mad, decided and stated that the first time he came to Sainte-Barbe he would subject him to a drubbing as a seducer of the students.

79. The Spaniard with whom he had stayed at the beginning and who had spent his money without paying it back set out for Spain by way of Rouen. While awaiting passage at Rouen, he fell sick. While he was thus ill, the pilgrim learned this from a letter of his and felt the desire to visit and help him. He also thought that in those circumstances he could win him over to leave the world and give himself completely to the service of God.[51]

In order to achieve this he felt the desire to walk the twenty-eight leagues from Paris to Rouen barefoot, without eating or drinking. As he prayed over this, he felt very afraid. At last he went to St. Dominic's, and there he decided to go in the manner just mentioned, the great fear he had of tempting God having now passed.

He got up early the next day, the morning that he was going to set out. As he began to dress, such a great fear came over him that he seemed almost unable to dress himself. In spite of that repugnance he left the house and the city too, before it was quite daylight. Still the fear was with him constantly and persisted as far as Argenteuil, a walled town three leagues from Paris on the way to Rouen, where the garment of Our Lord is said to be. He passed the town with that spiritual distress, but as he came up to a rise the thing began to go away. He felt great consolation and spiritual strength, with such joy that he began to shout through the fields and to speak to God, and so forth.

He lodged that evening with a poor beggar in a hospice, having traveled fourteen leagues that day. The next day he sought shelter in a barn. The third day he reached Rouen, all this time without eating or drinking and barefoot, as he had determined. In Rouen he consoled the sick man and helped him board a ship to go to Spain. He also gave him letters directing him to the companions who were in Salamanca, namely, Calixto, Cáceres, and Arteaga.

80. Not to have to speak further of these companions, their lot was this. While the pilgrim was in Paris he wrote frequently to them, as they had agreed, about the scant facilities he had to bring them to Paris to study. Still, he undertook to write to Doña Leonor de Mascarenhas[52] to assist Calixto with letters to the court of the King of Portugal so he could obtain one of the scholarships which the King of Portugal gave in Paris. Doña Leonor gave Calixto the letters and a mule to ride and money for his expenses. Calixto went to the court of the King of Portugal, but in the end he did not come to Paris. Rather, returning to Spain, he went to the Imperial Indies with a certain spiritual woman. He returned to Spain later but went to the same Indies once more and this time returned to Spain a rich man, surprising all in Salamanca who had known him before.

Cáceres returned to Segovia, which was his hometown, and there began to live in such a manner that he seemed to have forgotten his earlier resolution.

Arteaga was made a *comendador*.[53] Later when the Society was already in Rome, he was offered a bishopric in the Indies. He wrote to the pilgrim that it be given to one of the Society, but the answer was in the negative, so he went to the Imperial Indies as a bishop and died there in strange circumstances. That is, when he happened to be ill, there were two water bottles to refresh him, one with water which the doctor had ordered for him, the other with Water of Soliman, a poison—the latter was given him by mistake and killed him.

81. The pilgrim returned to Paris from Rouen and discovered that because of the affair of Castro and Peralta there was much talk regarding him and that the inquisitor had issued a summons for him. But he would not wait further and went to the inquisitor, to whom he said that

he understood he was looking for him, and that he was prepared for anything he might wish (the inquisitor was our Master Ory, a Dominican friar). But he would request that he expedite it, because he had in mind to enroll in the arts course at the coming feast of St. Remy.[54] He wanted to get this business over first so he would be better able to attend to his studies. The inquisitor did not summon him further, only telling him it was true that they had spoken of his doings, and so forth.

82. A short time after this came the feast of St. Remy, that is, the first of October, and he enrolled in the arts course under a teacher named Master Juan Peña. He enrolled with the idea of retaining those who had decided to serve the Lord, but not to go farther in search of others, so that he could study more easily.

As he began attending the lectures of the course, the same temptations began to come to him that had come when he studied grammar in Barcelona. Whenever he was at a lecture, he could not pay attention because of the many spiritual thoughts that came to him. Realizing that in this way he made little progress in study, he went to his master and promised he would never fail to follow the whole course, so long as he could find bread and water for his sustenance. After making this promise, all that devotion which came to him out of time left him, and he went on quietly with his studies.[55]

At this time he associated with Master Pierre Favre and Master Francis Xavier, whom he later won for God's service by means of the Exercises.[56]

At that stage in his course they did not harass him as before. With reference to this, Doctor Frago once told him how he marveled that he went about so peacefully without anyone giving him trouble; and he replied, "The reason is because I do not speak to anyone of the things of God; but once the course is over, we'll be back to business as usual."

83. While the two were speaking together, a friar came to ask Doctor Frago that he try to find him a house, because in the one where he had lodging many people had died of the plague, he thought (for the plague was then beginning in Paris). Doctor Frago and the pilgrim wished to go to see the house. They took a woman well versed in these matters, and on entering she confirmed that it was the plague. The pilgrim also chose to enter. Coming upon a sick person, he comforted him and touched his sore with his hand.

After he had comforted and encouraged him a while, he went off alone. His hand began to hurt so that it seemed he had caught the plague.

This fancy was so strong that he could not overcome it until he thrust his hand forcefully into his mouth and moved it about inside, saying, "If you have the plague in the hand, you will also have it in the mouth." When he had done this, he was rid of the fancy and of the pain in the hand.

84. But when he returned to the college of Sainte-Barbe, where he then had lodging and was attending the course, those in the college who knew that he had entered the plague-ridden house fled from him and would not let him enter. So he was forced to remain out for some days.

It is the custom in Paris for those who are studying arts in the third year, in order to receive the baccalaureate, "to take a stone,"[57] as they say. And because one has to spend an *escudo* for that, those who are very poor cannot do so. The pilgrim began to wonder whether it would be good for him to take it. Finding himself in great doubt and undecided,[58] he determined to put the matter in the hands of his master, who advised him to take it, and he did so. There were not lacking, however, some critics—at least one Spaniard who commented upon it.

In Paris already by this time he was quite unwell in the stomach, so that every fifteen days he had a stomachache which lasted over an hour and gave him a fever.[59] Once the stomachache lasted sixteen or seventeen hours. At this time he had already finished the arts course and studied theology for some years,[60] and gathered the companions. His trouble kept getting worse and worse, and he could not find a cure, though many were tried.

85. The doctors said there was nothing left that might help him except his native air—just that. Moreover, the companions gave him the same advice and pressed him hard. Already by this time they had all determined what they would do, namely, go to Venice and to Jerusalem, and spend their lives for the good of souls; and if they were not given permission to remain in Jerusalem, then return to Rome and present themselves to the Vicar of Christ, so that he could make use of them wherever he thought it would be more for the glory of God and the good of souls. They also planned to wait a year in Venice for passage; but if there was no passage for the East that year, they would be free of their vow about Jerusalem and approach the pope, and so forth.[61]

In the end, the pilgrim let himself be persuaded by the companions, and also because the Spaniards among them had some business which he could settle.[62] It was agreed that when he felt well he should go and attend to their business, and then proceed to Venice where he would wait for the companions.

86. This was the year '35, and the companions were to set out, according to the agreement, in the year '37 on the day of the conversion of St. Paul (though in fact, because of the outbreak of war, they eventually left in November of the year '36).

As the pilgrim was about to set out, he learned that he had been accused before the inquisitor, with a case brought against him. Knowing this but seeing that they did not summon him, he went to the inquisitor[63] and told him what he had heard and that he was about to set out for Spain and that he had companions. Would he please pass sentence. The inquisitor said it was true there was an accusation, but that he did not find anything of importance in it. He only wanted to see his manuscript of the Exercises. When he saw it he praised it very much and asked the pilgrim to let him have the copy; and he did so. Nevertheless, the pilgrim again insisted that the case be carried through to the sentence. As the inquisitor excused himself, the pilgrim brought a public notary and witnesses to the inquisitor's house, and obtained a testimonial on this whole affair.

Ch. 9. FAREWELL TO SPAIN
October–November, 1535

87. With that done, he mounted a pony the companions had bought him and set out alone homeward. Along the way he felt much better. When he arrived in the Province,[64] he left the highway and took the mountain road, which was more secluded. Having moved along a bit, he saw two armed men who were approaching him (that road is somewhat notorious for assassins). A little after they had passed him, they turned about and came toward him in great haste, and he was a little afraid. All the same he spoke to them, and learned that they were servants of his brother, who had sent them to meet him, because, as it seems, he had news of his coming from Bayonne in France, where the pilgrim was recognized.

So they went ahead, and he went the same way. Just before he got to the place, he came upon the same men, who were approaching him. They were very insistent about taking him to his brother's house, but they could not constrain him. So he went to the hospice and later, at a convenient hour, went to seek alms in the locality.

88. In this hospice he began to speak with many who came to visit him of the things of God, by whose grace much fruit was derived. As soon as he arrived, he decided to teach Christian doctrine every day to

children, but his brother strongly objected to this, saying that no one would come. He replied that one would be enough. But after he began to do it, many came continually to hear him, and even his brother.

Besides Christian doctrine, he also preached on Sundays and feasts with profit and help to the souls who came many miles to hear him. He also made an attempt to eliminate some abuses, and with God's help some were set right. For example, he persuaded the one administering justice to have an effective ban on gambling. There was also another abuse there. That is, the girls in that region always go about with head uncovered and do not cover it until they are married. But there are many who have become concubines of priests and other men, and are faithful to them as though they were their wives. This is so common that the concubines are not at all ashamed to say that they have covered their heads for so and so, and are acknowledged as such.

89. Much evil results from this custom. The pilgrim persuaded the governor to make a law that all those who covered the head for anyone, and were not wives, should be legally punished. And so this abuse began to be corrected. He got an order to be given that the poor should be provided for officially and regularly, and that bells should be rung three times at the Angelus, that is, morning, noon, and evening, so that the people might pray as in Rome.

But though he had felt well at the beginning, he later fell seriously ill. Once he had recovered, he decided to set out to attend to the affairs his companions had entrusted to him, and to set out without money. At this his brother was very upset, and ashamed that he should go on foot. By evening the pilgrim was willing to settle for this: to go on horseback with his brother and his relatives to the border of the Province.

90. But when he left the Province he got to his feet without taking anything and went toward Pamplona, and thence to Almazán, Father Laínez's home, and then to Siguenza and Toledo and from Toledo to Valencia. In all these native places of his companions he would not take anything, although they offered him much with great insistence.

In Valencia he spoke with Castro, who was a Carthusian monk. He wanted to sail to Genoa, but good friends in Valencia begged him not to do so, because they said Barbarossa was on the sea with many ships, and so on. Although they did say many things, enough to frighten him, nevertheless nothing made him hesitate.

91. Boarding a large ship, he passed through the storm mentioned above,[65] when it was said that he was on the point of death three times.

When he arrived at Genoa he took the road to Bologna,[66] on which he suffered much, especially on one occasion when he lost his way and began to walk alongside a river. It was down below and the path, which was high above it, became ever more narrow the farther he went along it. It got so narrow that he could no longer go forward or turn back. So he began to crawl along and in this way he covered a great distance in great fear, because each time he moved he thought he would fall into the river. This was the greatest physical stress and strain that he ever experienced, but finally he got through.

Making his way into Bologna and having to cross over a wooden footbridge, he fell off the bridge. Then, as he got up covered with mud and water, he made many bystanders laugh. Entering Bologna he began to beg alms, but not one small coin did he get though he sought everywhere. He was ill for some time in Bologna, but afterward he went on to Venice, always in the same fashion.

Ch. 10. VENICE AND VICENZA
January, 1536–November, 1537

92. During that time in Venice, he busied himself giving the Exercises and in other spiritual contacts. The most distinguished persons to whom he gave them were Master Pietro Contarini and Master Gasparo de' Dotti, and a Spaniard whose name was Rozas. There was also another Spaniard there called the bachelor Hoces,[67] who was in close touch with the pilgrim and also with the bishop of Cette. Although he had some desire to make the Exercises, still he did not put it into execution.

At last he decided to begin making them. And having made them for three or four days, he spoke his mind to the pilgrim, telling him that because of the things someone had told him, he had been afraid that he would be taught some evil doctrine in the Exercises. For this reason he had brought with him certain books so he could have recourse to them, if perchance he tried to deceive him. He was helped very much by the Exercises and in the end resolved to live the pilgrim's way. He was also the first one to die.

93. In Venice the pilgrim also endured another persecution, with many saying that his effigy had been burned in Spain and in Paris. This business went so far that a trial was held and sentence was given in favor of the pilgrim.

The nine companions came to Venice at the beginning of '37. There they separated to serve in various hospices. After two or three months, they all went to Rome to obtain the blessing for the journey to Jerusalem. The pilgrim did not go because of Doctor Ortiz and also because of the new Theatine cardinal.[68] The companions returned from Rome with drafts for 200 or 300 *escudos*, which had been given to them as alms for the journey to Jerusalem. They did not want to take anything except in drafts; later, not being able to go to Jerusalem, they gave them back to the donors.

The companions returned to Venice in the fashion they had gone, that is, on foot and begging, but divided into three groups and in such a way that they were always of different nationalities. There in Venice, those who were not ordained were ordained priests,[69] and the nuncio who was then in Venice (and who was later known as Cardinal Verallo) gave them faculties. They were ordained *ad titulum paupertatis*[70] and all made vows of chastity and poverty.

94. In that year no ships sailed for the East because the Venetians had broken with the Turks. So, seeing that their hope of sailing was put off, they dispersed within the Venetian region, with the intention of waiting the year they had decided upon, and if it expired without possibility of travel, they would go to Rome.

It fell to the pilgrim to go with Favre and Laínez to Vicenza. There they found a certain house outside the city, which had neither doors nor windows. They stayed in it, sleeping on a little straw that they had brought. Two of them always went out to seek alms in the city twice a day, but they got so little they could hardly maintain themselves. They usually ate a little toasted bread when they had it, and the one who remained at home saw to its toasting. In this way they spent forty days, not engaging in anything other than prayer.

95. After the forty days, Master Jean Codure arrived; and the four together decided to begin to preach. The four went to different piazzas and began to preach on the same day and at the same hour, first shouting loudly and summoning the people with their caps. Their preaching caused a great stir in the city, and many persons were moved with devotion, and they received in greater abundance the material goods they needed.

During the time he was at Vicenza, he had many spiritual visions and many quite regular consolations; the contrary happened when he was in Paris. In all that traveling he had great supernatural experiences like those he used to have when he was in Manresa, especially when he began to prepare for the priesthood in Venice and when he was preparing to say Mass.[71]

While he was still at Vicenza, he learned that one of the companions, who was at Bassano, was ill to the point of death.[72] At the same time he too was ill with fever. Nevertheless he set out and walked so vigorously that Favre, his companion, could not keep up with him. On that journey he had assurance from God, and he told Favre so, that the companion would not die of that illness. On their arriving at Bassano, the sick man was much comforted and soon recovered. Then they all returned to Vicenza; and all ten were there for some time, and some used to go seeking alms in the towns around Vicenza.

96. Then, the year being over and no passage available, they decided to go to Rome—even the pilgrim, because on the other occasion when the companions had gone, those two about whom he had doubts[73] had shown themselves very kind. Divided into three or four groups, the pilgrim with Favre and Laínez, they went to Rome. On this journey he was visited very especially by God.

He had decided to spend a year without saying Mass after he became a priest, preparing himself and praying Our Lady to deign to place him with her Son. One day,[74] a few miles before reaching Rome, he was at prayer in a church and experienced such a change in his soul and saw so clearly that God the Father placed him with Christ his Son that he would not dare doubt it—that God the Father had placed him with his Son.

[Câmara]: And I who am writing these things said to the pilgrim, when he told me this, that Laínez recounted it with other details —so I understood. He told me that everything that Lainez said was true, because he did not recall it in such detail, but that at the moment when he narrated it he was certain that he had said nothing but the truth. He said the same to me about other things.

97. Then on arriving in Rome[75] he told the companions that he saw the windows were closed, meaning to say that they would have to meet many contradictions. He also said, "We must be very much on our guard, and not have contacts with women, unless they are prominent." While on this subject, later in Rome Master Francis was confessor to a woman and sometimes visited her to treat of spiritual matters, and she was subsequently found to be pregnant. But the Lord deigned that the one who had done the mischief should be discovered. The same sort of thing happened to Jean Codure, with a spiritual daughter who was caught with a man.

Ch. 11. THE FIRST YEAR IN ROME
1538

98. From Rome the pilgrim went to Monte Cassino to give the Exercises to Doctor Ortiz.[76] He was there forty days, and on one of them he saw the bachelor Hoces as he entered heaven. This brought him many tears and great spiritual consolation. He saw this so clearly that if he said the contrary he would feel he was lying. From Monte Cassino he brought with him Francis de Strada;[77] and returning to Rome he busied himself helping souls. They were still living at the vineyard. He gave the Spiritual Exercises to various people at the same time, one of whom lived at St. Mary Major, the other at Ponte Sesto.

Then the persecutions began.[78] Miguel [Landívar] began to give trouble and to speak badly of the pilgrim, who caused him to be summoned before the governor. He first showed the governor a letter of Miguel's, in which he praised the pilgrim very much. The governor examined Miguel, and ended by banishing him from Rome.

Mudarra and Barreda then began their persecution, saying that the pilgrim and his companions were fugitives from Spain, from Paris, and from Venice. In the end both of them confessed in the presence of the governor and the legate, who was then in Rome, that they had nothing bad to say about them, neither regarding their ways nor regarding their teaching. The legate ordered silence to be imposed on the whole affair, but the pilgrim did not accept that, saying he wanted a definite sentence. This did not please the legate nor the governor nor even those who at first favored the pilgrim. At last, after some months, the pope came to Rome. The pilgrim went to speak to him at Frascati and gave him several reasons; thus informed, the pope ordered sentence to be given, and it was given in his favor, and so on.

With the help of the pilgrim and his companions some pious works such as the Catechumens, Saint Martha, the Orphans,[79] and so forth were begun in Rome. Master Nadal can recount the rest.[80]

99. After these things had been recounted, I asked the pilgrim on October 20 about the Exercises and the Constitutions, as I wanted to know how he had drawn them up. He told me that he had not composed the Exercises all at once, but that when he noticed some things in his soul and found them useful, he thought they might also be useful to others, and so he put them in writing, for example, the examination of conscience with that arrangement of lines, and so forth. He told me that he derived the elections in particular from that diversity of spirit and

thoughts which he had at Loyola when he was still suffering in the leg. He told me he would speak to me about the Constitutions in the evening.

The same day he summoned me before supper, with the air of a person who was more recollected than usual, and made a sort of protestation to me, the sum of which was to show the intention, the sincerity with which he had related these things. He said he was quite sure that he had not exaggerated; and that, although he had committed many offenses against Our Lord after he began to serve him, he had never consented to mortal sin. Rather, he had always grown in devotion, that is, ease in finding God, and now more than ever in his whole life. Every time, any hour, that he wished to find God, he found him. And even now he often had visions, especially those mentioned above in which he saw Christ as the sun. This often happened while he was engaged in important matters, and that gave him confirmation.[81]

100. He also had many visions when he said Mass, and when he was drawing up the Constitutions too, he had them very often. He can now affirm this more easily because every day he wrote down what went on in his soul and he had it now in writing. He then showed me a rather large bundle of writings,[82] of which he read me a good bit. Most were visions that he saw in confirmation of some of the Constitutions, at times seeing God the Father, at times all three Persons of the Trinity; at times Our Lady—who interceded and at times confirmed.

In particular he spoke to me about precisions over which he spent forty days, saying Mass each day, and each day with many tears. The question was whether a church would have any fixed income[83] and whether the Society should make use of that.

101. I wished to see all those papers on the Constitutions, and asked him to let me have them a while. But he would not.

THE END

B. THE SPIRITUAL EXERCISES

ABBREVIATED CONTENTS OF THE *SPIRITUAL EXERCISES*

THE FOURTH WEEK

*   *   *

RULES AND NOTES

INTRODUCTION

Ignatius completed his last substantial revisions of the Spiritual Exercises in Rome between 1539 and 1541. The texts of the three chief editions, critically edited by the expert Cándido de Dalmases, are printed in parallel columns on pages 140–415 in the 850 pages of Volume 100 (1969) in the series Historical Sources of the Society of Jesus.[1] Their designations and names are:

A, The Autograph text in Spanish, Ignatius' own copy containing some thirty-two minor corrections, left at his death in 1556;

P¹, the *Versio prima* or first translation into scholastic Latin, made in Paris by 1534 probably by Ignatius himself; and

V, the *Versio Vulgata*, made from the Spanish Autograph into stylistic classical Latin to present it along with A to Pope Paul III for approval, which was granted in 1548. Ignatius used it from 1548 to 1556. It was named *Vulgata* because it was spread in a printed edition of 500 copies. It was the text in greatest use until Jan Roothaan's new Latin version of the Autograph in 1835.

Most modern scholars think that the Autograph, text A, best reproduces Ignatius' thought and its nuances. However, since texts P¹ and V were used by Ignatius, they have approval by him and are substantial helps for interpreting A in passages where obscurities occur. The present new translation of the *Exercises* is based chiefly on this critical text A published by Dalmases in 1969, with aid from the Latin versions printed in his parallel columns. There is, however, more to say.

Recently Dalmases himself updated and adjusted his previous critical text for practical use as a manual by directors, retreatants, and students of the *Exercises*, for whom the earlier volume of 850 pages was too unwieldy. He left this small book virtually complete when he died in 1986, and it was posthumously published by his colleague Father Manuel Ruiz Jurado with the title: Ignacio de Loyola, *Ejercicios Espirituales: Introducción, texto, notas y vocabulario* por Cándido de Dalmases, S.J. (Santander: Sal Terrae, 1987), to which we refer hereafter as *Dalm-Man*. His introductions, brief interpretative footnotes, and dictionary (*vocabulario*) of selected Ignatian terms were a great help for both the translation and the explanatory footnotes. Similar help was also obtained from the recent French translation: Ignace de Loyola, *Exercices Spirituels: Traduction du texte Autographe* par Edouard Gueydan, S.J. (Paris, 1986). This version is the result of teamwork by an editorial committee and its consultation with experts, among whom was Father Dalmases. Another team of experts cooperating with the first group has recently completed, under the leadership of Roberto Busa in Milan, a computerized concordance of all the words used in Ignatius' works (except his Letters, on which the work is far advanced). Beyond doubt this concordance will stimulate numerous studies of Ignatius' terminology. We also acknowledge extensive help obtained from the information on the *Exercises* furnished by Ignacio Iparraguirre in the well-known *Obras completas de San Ignacio* in the Series Biblioteca de autores cristianos.

Like Dalmases' manual edition, the present translation is intended for practical use, especially by directors, retreatants, and those who are reading the *Exercises* for the first time. For these users this translator thought it best to aim, not at a literal translation strictly so called, but rather at one of "functional equivalence." That is, the ideal and aim of the present version is to express Ignatius' ideas altogether accurately, with no concept added to or subtracted from his own thought in the Autograph text of his *Exercises*. However, it does not seek to do this by "formal equivalence," namely, word for word, clause for clause, and participle by participle, pretty much in the sentence structure of the original language. Instead it takes a middle path by endeavoring to reproduce the thought of the original more as a modern English-speaking writer would be likely to express it. Its aim is to adjust Ignatius' Spanish to the thought patterns and habits of English-speaking persons in such a way that a reader can grasp the thought accurately and with reasonable ease, usually on the first reading.

Each of these two types of translation has, for its respective purposes, advantages and disadvantages the other lacks; and whichever is chosen, the translator must sacrifice something if he is to achieve his particular goals. Usually the version of functional equivalence is better for quick intelligibility in practical use or for popular audiences, but the strictly literal version is better and even indispensable for scholarly investigation of technicalities and nuances. What our translation loses is some traits of Ignatius' style. It may make him appear to be more concerned with form and more literary than he really was.

Several excellent literal translations of the *Exercises* exist, such as those by E. Mullan (1909), J. Morris (1913), W. H. Longridge (1919), and others. We by no means seek to replace or disparage the more literal versions. Rather, if in some instances a reader wonders whether our translation has missed a nuance of Ignatius' thought, we invite him or her to investigate the matter with the help of a more literal version.

While the ideals of translation mentioned above were being pursued, many difficulties were met which required arbitrary decisions. The use of nondiscriminatory language has been sincerely sought but at times found difficult in practice. In numerous instances whatever remedy was tried pleased some and displeased others. To please all in this matter seems impossible today.

According to modern editorial conventions, headings in a text should ordinarily match the listings in a table of contents, and superior numbers should not be used with display type. We follow that procedure in the main Table of Contents at the front of the book, but make an exception to if in the abbreviated contents located on the reverse of divider pages which introduce each of Ignatius' works. These abbreviated tables are intended merely as guideposts to let readers know where they are going, and do not pretend to be exact reproductions of all the subheadings below.

Directories

When the *Exercises* appeared in print in 1548, the book stimulated many requests from Jesuits for further directives about its use in practice. Successive sets of such directives arose, each called a "Directory." Ignatius himself started to work on this problem, especially because of questions raised by Polanco, but by 1556 he had completed only a few fragments and had given some instructions orally, which others wrote down.[2] After 1556 the First General Congregation, the early generals, and various committees or prominent persons such as Miró and Polanco produced Directories. During the generalate of Claudio Aquaviva (1581–1615) this work was brought to a synthesis. In 1599 he sent to all the provinces an official *Directory*, intended to be a guide useful to all directors of the Exercises.[3] It contains forty short chapters. All these Directories enshrine the early traditions and are great helps for the interpretation and use of the *Exercises*.

Since Ignatius' style was so terse and his book was intended for flexible use, differing opinions about its meanings and proper use have been abundant from the first appearance of the book in print. In these controversies, usually neither protagonist fully convinced his opponent, but both parties felt their efforts well repaid by all they had learned during their discussions. A fortunate result has been an ever growing insight into the inexhaustible spiritual treasures hidden in Ignatius' little book. Only a few of these varying opinions, worthy though they are, can be mentioned in our limited pages of notes, and we apologize to those whose favorite theories must be left in silence.

In these notes our foremost hope is to aid in the accurate understanding and interpretation of Ignatius' text. In the cases of differing opinions we aimed to give always a position which is solidly based and gets to the heart of the matter, to indicate on occasions some of the differing views, and to give some bibliographical aids for those who wish to explore them farther.

In judging such opinions and in studying the *Exercises*, we should distinguish carefully between two questions: (1) In any given passage, precisely what did Ignatius mean? and (2), what are the uses which we today can legitimately make of his thought? Since he intended his brief remarks to set exercitants on the way to thinking things out for themselves,[4] there is wide room for directors, exercitants, and students to enrich his texts by the knowledge they bring to it, for example, from updated writings in systematic, spiritual, or biblical theology. In general, the more such knowledge one brings to his text the more one gets from it.[5] Many exercitants have found treasures in Ignatius' book of which he himself was unaware; and precisely that was his hope. In many a case, the discoveries made in prayer during the Exercises have led to enriching study through the rest of life. Furthermore, since the *Exercises* present a comprehensive view of God's whole plan for the salvation of human beings, growing insight into the *Exercises* brings deepening understanding of the deposit of faith itself. Although Ignatius never intended the *Exercises* to be a well-rounded treatise on the spiritual life, no other work of his introduces us better into the chief principles of his spirituality. All the rest of his writings can be considered to be commentaries on the *Exercises*.

The Spiritual Exercises

[1]

IHS

**INTRODUCTORY EXPLANATIONS,[1] TO GAIN
SOME UNDERSTANDING OF THE SPIRITUAL
EXERCISES WHICH FOLLOW, AND TO AID
BOTH THE ONE WHO GIVES THEM AND
THE ONE WHO RECEIVES THEM.**

The First Explanation. By the term Spiritual Exercises we mean every method of examination of conscience, meditation, contemplation, vocal or mental prayer, and other spiritual activities, such as will be mentioned later. For, just as taking a walk, traveling on foot, and running are physical exercises, so is the name of spiritual exercises given to any means of preparing and disposing our soul to rid itself of all its disordered affections[2] and then, after their removal, of seeking and finding God's will in the ordering of our life for the salvation of our soul.

[2]   *The Second.* The person who gives to another the method and procedure for meditating or contemplating should accurately narrate the history contained in the contemplation or meditation, going over the points with only a brief or summary explanation. For in this way the person who is contemplating, by taking this history as the authentic foundation, and by going over it and reasoning about it for oneself, can thus discover something that will bring better understanding or a more personalized concept of the history—either through one's own reasoning or to the extent that the understanding is enlightened by God's grace. This brings more spiritual relish and spiritual fruit than if the one giving the Exercises had lengthily explained and amplified the meaning of the history. For, what fills and satisfies the soul consists, not in knowing much, but in our understanding the realities profoundly and in savoring them interiorly.

[3]   *The Third.* In all the following Spiritual Exercises we use the acts of the intellect in reasoning and of the will in eliciting acts of the affections. In regard to the affective acts which spring from the will we should note that when we are conversing with God our Lord or his saints vocally or mentally, greater reverence is demanded of us than when we are using the intellect to understand.

[4]   *The Fourth.* Four Weeks are taken for the following Exercises, corresponding to the four parts into which they are divided. That is, the First Week is devoted to the consideration and contemplation of sins; the Second, to the life of Christ our Lord up to and including Palm Sunday; the Third, to the Passion of Christ our Lord; and the Fourth, to the Resurrection and Ascension. To this week are appended the Three Methods of Praying. However, this does not mean that each week must necessarily consist of seven or eight days. For during the First Week some persons happen to be slower in finding what they are seeking, that is, contrition, sorrow, and tears for their sins. Similarly, some persons work more diligently than others, and are more pushed back and forth and probed by different spirits.[3] In some cases, therefore, the week needs to be shortened, and in others lengthened. This holds as well for all the following weeks, while the retreatant is seeking for what corresponds to their subject matter. But the Exercises ought to be completed in thirty days, more or less.

[5]   *The Fifth.* The persons who receive the Exercises will benefit greatly by entering upon them with great spirit and generosity toward their Creator and Lord, and by offering all their desires and freedom to him so that his Divine Majesty can make use of their persons and of all they possess in whatsoever way is according to his most holy will.

[6]   *The Sixth.* When the one giving the Exercises notices that the person making them is not experiencing any spiritual motions[4] in his or her soul, such as consolations or desolations, or is not being moved one way or another by different spirits, the director should question the exercitant much

about the Exercises: Whether the exercitant is making them at the appointed times, how they are being made, and whether the Additional Directives are being diligently observed. The director should ask about each of these items in particular. Consolation and desolation are treated in [316–324], the Additional Directives in [73–90].

[7]   *The Seventh.* When the giver of the Exercises sees that the recipient is experiencing desolation and temptation, he or she should not treat the retreatant severely or harshly, but gently and kindly. The director should encourage and strengthen the exercitant for the future, unmask the deceptive tactics of the enemy of our human nature, and help the retreatant to prepare and dispose himself or herself for the consolation which will come.

[8]   *The Eighth.* According to the need perceived in the recipient with respect to the desolations and deceptive tactics of the enemy, and also the consolations, the giver of the Exercises may explain to the retreatant the rules of the First and Second Weeks for recognizing the different kinds of spirits, in [313–327 and 328–336].

[9]   *The Ninth.* This point should be noticed. When an exercitant spiritually inexperienced is going through the First Week of the Exercises he or she may be tempted grossly and openly, for example, by being shown obstacles to going forward in the service of God our Lord, in the form of hardships, shame, fear about worldly honor, and the like. In such a case the one giving the Exercises should not explain to this retreatant the rules on different kinds of spirits for the Second Week. For to the same extent that the rules of the First Week will help him or her, those of the Second Week will be harmful. They are too subtle and advanced for such a one to understand.

[10]   *The Tenth.* When the one giving the Exercises perceives that the recipient is being assailed and tempted under the appearance of good, the proper time has come to explain to the retreatant the rules of the Second Week mentioned just

above. For ordinarily the enemy of human nature tempts under the appearance of good more often when a person is performing the Exercises in the illuminative life, which corresponds to the Exercises of the Second Week, than in the purgative life, which corresponds to those of the First Week.[5]

[11]   *The Eleventh.* It is helpful for a person receiving the Exercises of the First Week to know nothing about what is to be done in the Second, but to work diligently during the First Week at obtaining what he or she is seeking, just as if there were no anticipation of finding anything good in the Second.

[12]   *The Twelfth.* The one giving the Exercises should insist strongly with the person receiving them that he or she should remain for a full hour in each of the five Exercises or contemplations which will be made each day; and further, that the recipient should make sure always to have the satisfaction of knowing that a full hour was spent on the exercise—indeed, more rather than less. For the enemy usually exerts special efforts to get a person to shorten the hour of contemplation, meditation, or prayer.

[13]   *The Thirteenth.* This too should be noted. In time of consolation it is easy and scarcely taxing to remain in contemplation for a full hour, but during desolation it is very hard to fill out the time. Hence, to act against the desolation and overcome the temptations, the exercitant ought to remain always a little longer than the full hour, and in this way become accustomed not merely to resist the enemy but even to defeat him.

[14]   *The Fourteenth.* If the one giving the Exercises sees that the exercitant is proceeding with consolation and great fervor, he or she should warn the person not to make some promise or vow which is unconsidered or hasty. The more unstable the director sees the exercitant to be, the more earnest should be the forewarning and caution. For although it is altogether right for someone to advise another to enter religious life, which entails the taking of vows of obedience,

poverty, and chastity; and although a good work done under a vow is more meritorious than one done without it; still one ought to bestow much thought on the circumstances and character of each person, and on the helps or hindrances one is likely to meet with in carrying out what one wishes to promise.

[15]   *The Fifteenth.* The one giving the Exercises should not urge the one receiving them toward poverty or any other promise more than toward their opposites, or to one state or way of life more than to another. Outside the Exercises it is lawful and meritorious for us to counsel those who are probably suitable for it to choose continence, virginity, religious life, and all forms of evangelical perfection. But during these Spiritual Exercises when a person is seeking God's will, it is more appropriate and far better that the Creator and Lord himself should communicate himself to the devout soul, embracing it with love, inciting it to praise of himself, and disposing it for the way which will most enable the soul to serve him in the future. Accordingly, the one giving the Exercises ought not to lean or incline in either direction but rather, while standing by like the pointer of a scale in equilibrium, to allow the Creator to deal immediately with the creature and the creature with its Creator and Lord.

[16]   *The Sixteenth.* For this purpose—namely, that the Creator and Lord may with greater certainty be the one working in his creature—if by chance the exercitant feels an affection or inclination to something in a disordered way, it is profitable for that person to strive with all possible effort to come over to the opposite of that to which he or she is wrongly attached. Thus, if someone is inclined to pursue and hold on to an office or benefice,[6] not for the honor and glory of God our Lord or for the spiritual welfare of souls, but rather for one's own temporal advantages and interests, one should try to bring oneself to desire the opposite. One should make earnest prayers and other spiritual exercises and ask God our Lord for the contrary; that is, to have no desire for this office or benefice or anything else unless his Divine Majesty has put proper order into those desires, and has by this means so

changed one's earlier attachment that one's motive in desiring or holding on to one thing rather than another will now be only the service, honor, and glory of his Divine Majesty.

[17]   *The Seventeenth.* Although the one giving the Exercises should not endeavor to ask about or know the personal thoughts or sins of the exercitant, it is very advantageous for the director to be faithfully informed about the various agitations and thoughts which the different spirits stir up in the retreatant. For then, in accordance with the person's greater or lesser progress, the director will be able to communicate spiritual exercises adapted to the needs of the person who is agitated in this way.

[18]   *The Eighteenth.* The Spiritual Exercises should be adapted to the disposition of the persons who desire to make them, that is, to their age, education, and ability.[7] In this way someone who is uneducated or has a weak constitution will not be given things he or she cannot well bear or profit from without fatigue.

Similarly exercitants should be given, each one, as much as they are willing to dispose themselves to receive, for their greater help and progress.

Consequently, a person who wants help to get some instruction and reach a certain level of peace of soul can be given the Particular Examen ([24–31]), and then the General Examen ([32–43]), and farther, the Method of Praying for a half hour in the morning on the Commandments ([238–243]), the Capital Sins[8] ([244–245]), and other such procedures ([238; 246–260]). Such a person can also be encouraged to weekly confession of sins and, if possible, to reception of the Eucharist every two weeks or, if better disposed, weekly. This procedure is more appropriate for persons who are rather simple or illiterate. They should be given an explanation of each of the commandments, the seven capital sins, the precepts of the Church, the five senses, and the works of mercy.

Likewise, if the one giving the Exercises sees that the recipient is a person poorly qualified or of little natural capacity from whom much fruit is not to be expected, it is preferable to give to such a one some of these light Exercises until he or she has confessed, and then to give ways of examining one's conscience and a program for confession more frequent than before, that the person may preserve what has been acquired. But this should be done without going on to matters pertaining to the Election or to other Exercises beyond the First Week. This is especially the case when there are others with whom greater results can be achieved and time is insufficient to do everything.

[19]   *The Nineteenth.* A person who is involved in public affairs or pressing occupations but educated or intelligent may take an hour and a half each day to perform the Exercises.[9] To such a one the director can explain the end for which human beings are created. Then he or she can explain for half an hour the particular examen, then the general examen, and the method of confessing and receiving the Eucharist. For three days this exercitant should make a meditation for an hour each morning on the first, second, and third sins ([45–53]); then for another three days at the same hour the meditation on the court-record of one's own sins ([55–56]); then for a further three days at the same hour the meditation on the punishment corresponding to sins ([65–72]). During these three meditations the ten Additional Directives ([73–90]) should be given the exercitant. For the mysteries of Christ our Lord this exercitant should follow the same procedure as is explained below and at length throughout the Exercises themselves.

[20]   *The Twentieth.* A person who is more disengaged, and who desires to make all the progress possible, should be given all the Spiritual Exercises in the same sequence in which they proceed below. Ordinarily, in making them an exercitant will achieve more progress the more he or she withdraws from all friends and acquaintances, and from all earthly concerns; for example, by moving out of one's place of residence and taking a different house or room where one can live in the greatest possible solitude, and thus be free to attend Mass and Vespers

daily without fear of hindrance from acquaintances. Three principal advantages flow from this seclusion, among many others.

First, by withdrawing from friends and acquaintances and likewise from various activities that are not well ordered, in order to serve and praise God our Lord, we gain much merit in the eyes of his Divine Majesty.

Second, by being secluded in this way and not having our mind divided among many matters, but by concentrating instead all our attention on one alone, namely, the service of our Creator and our own spiritual progress, we enjoy a freer use of our natural faculties for seeking diligently what we so ardently desire.

Third, the more we keep ourselves alone and secluded, the more fit do we make ourselves to approach and attain to our Creator and Lord; and the nearer we come to him in this way, the more do we dispose ourselves to receive graces and gifts from his divine and supreme goodness.

SPIRITUAL EXERCISES

[21]

TO OVERCOME ONESELF,[10]
AND TO ORDER ONE'S LIFE,[11]
WITHOUT REACHING A DECISION
THROUGH SOME DISORDERED AFFECTION.[12]

[22]

PRESUPPOSITION

That both the giver and the receiver of the Spiritual Exercises may be of greater help and benefit to each other, it should be presupposed that every good Christian ought to be more eager to put a good interpretation on a neighbor's statement than to condemn it. Further, if one cannot interpret it favorably, one should ask how the other means it. If that meaning is wrong, one should correct the person with love; and if this is not enough, one should search out every appropriate means through which, by understanding the statement in a good way, it may be saved.[13]

THE FIRST WEEK[14]

[23] ## PRINCIPLE AND FOUNDATION

Human beings are created to praise, reverence, and serve God our Lord,[15] and by means of this to save their souls.[16]

The other things on the face of the earth are created for the human beings, to help them in working toward the end for which they are created.

From this it follows that I should use these things to the extent that they help me toward my end, and rid myself of them to the extent that they hinder me.

To do this, I must make myself indifferent[17] to all created things, in regard to everything which is left to my freedom of will and is not forbidden. Consequently, on my own part I ought not to seek health rather than sickness, wealth rather than poverty, honor rather than dishonor, a long life rather than a short one, and so on in all other matters.

I ought to desire and elect only the thing which is more conducive to the end for which I am created.[18]

[24] ## DAILY PARTICULAR EXAMINATION OF CONSCIENCE.[19]
It comprises three times in the day and two examinations of conscience.

The First Time is in the morning. Upon arising the person should resolve to guard carefully against the particular sin or fault he or she wants to correct or amend.

[25] *The Second Time* is after the noon meal.[20] One should ask God our Lord for what one desires, namely, grace to recall how often one has fallen into the particular sin or fault, in order to correct it in the future. Then one should make the first examination, exacting an account of oneself with regard to the particular matter one has decided to take for correction

and improvement. One should run through the time, hour by hour or period by period, from the moment of rising until the present examination. On the upper line of the G═══²¹ one should enter a dot for each time one fell into the particular sin or fault. Then one should renew one's resolution to do better during the time until the second examination which will be made later.

[26]   *The Third Time* is after supper. The person should make the second examination, likewise hour by hour starting from the previous examination down to the present one. For each time he or she fell into the particular sin or fault, a dot should be entered on the lower line of the g═══.

[27]   **FOUR ADDITIONAL DIRECTIVES**
to help toward quicker riddance
of the particular sin or fault.

    The First Directive. Each time one falls into the particular sin or fault, one should touch one's hand to one's breast in sorrow for having fallen. This can be done even in public without its being noticed by others.

[28]   *The Second*. Since the upper line of the G═══ represents the first examination and the lower line the second, the person should look at night to see if there was any improvement from the first line to the second, that is, from the first examination to the second.

[29]   *The Third*. The person should compare the second day with the first, that is, the two examinations of each day with those of the previous day, to see whether any improvement has been made from one day to the next.

[30]   *The Fourth*. The person should compare this week with the previous one, to see if any improvement has been made during the present week in comparison with the one before.

[31]   It should be noted that the first large G═══ on the top line indicates Sunday, the second and smaller g═══ Monday, the third Tuesday, and so on.

G═══════════════.
g═══════════════════.
g═══════════════════.
g═══════════════════.

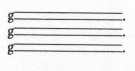

[32] **GENERAL EXAMINATION OF CONSCIENCE**
to purify oneself, and to make a better confession.[22]

I assume that there are three kinds of thoughts in myself. That is, one kind is my own, which arises strictly from my own freedom and desire; and the other two come from outside myself, the one from the good spirit and the other from the evil.[23]

[33] ### Thoughts

There are two ways in which I can merit from an evil thought that comes from outside myself.

The first occurs when a thought of committing a mortal sin comes to me, and I resist it immediately, and it remains banished.

[34] The second way to merit occurs when this same bad thought comes to me, and I resist it, but it keeps coming back and I resist it continually, until it is overcome and goes away. This second way gains more merit than the first.

[35] I sin venially when this same thought of committing a mortal sin comes to me and I give some heed to it—dwelling on it somewhat or experiencing some pleasure in the senses; or when there is some slackness in repulsing the thought.

[36] There are two ways of sinning mortally. The first occurs when I consent to the bad thought, intending at that time to carry out what I have assented to, or to do so if it becomes possible.

[37] The second way of sinning mortally occurs when one actually carries out the sin. This is graver, for three reasons: the longer time involved, the greater intensity, and the worse harm to the two persons.

[38] ### Words

It is not permissible to swear, either by God or by a creature, unless it is done with truth, necessity, and reverence. With necessity, that is, to affirm with an oath, not just any truth at all, but only one of some importance for the good of the soul, or the body, or temporal interests. With reverence, that is, when in pronouncing the name of our Creator and Lord one acts with consideration and manifests that honor and reverence which are due to him.

[39]　　In an unnecessary oath, it is a more serious sin to swear by the Creator than by a creature. However, we should note, it is harder to swear by a creature with the proper truth, necessity, and reverence than to swear by the Creator, for the following reasons.

The First. When we desire to swear by a creature, our very desire to name a creature makes us less careful and cautious about speaking the truth or affirming it with necessity than is the case when our urge is to name the Lord and Creator of all things.

The Second. When we swear by a creature, it is not as easy to maintain reverence and respect for the Creator as it is when we swear by the name of the Creator and Lord himself. For our very desire to name God our Lord carries with it greater respect and reverence than desire to name a creature. Consequently, to swear by a creature is more permissible for persons spiritually far advanced than for those less advanced. The perfect, through constant contemplation and enlightenment of their understanding, more readily consider, meditate, and contemplate God our Lord as being present in every creature by his essence, presence, and power. Thus when they swear by a creature, they are more able and better disposed than the imperfect to render respect and reverence to their Creator and Lord.

The Third. To swear continually by a creature brings a risk of idolatry that is greater in the imperfect than in the perfect.

[40]　　It is not permissible to speak idle words. I take this to mean words that are of no benefit to myself or anyone else, and are not ordered toward such benefit. Consequently, words that benefit or are intended to benefit my own or another's soul, body, or temporal goods are never idle. Nor are they idle merely because they are about matters outside one's state of life; for example, if a religious talks about wars

or commerce. However, in all that has been mentioned, there is merit if the words are ordered to a good end, and sin if they are directed to a bad end, or by one's talking uselessly.

[41]   We may not say anything to harm the reputation of others or to disparage them. If I reveal another person's mortal sin that is not publicly known,[24] I sin mortally; if a venial sin, venially; if a defect, I expose my own defect.

When one has a right intention, there are two cases where it is permissible to speak about someone else's sin or fault.

The first. When the sin is public, for example, in the case of a known prostitute, a judicial sentence, or a public error infecting the minds of those with whom we live.

The second. When a hidden sin is revealed to another person so that he or she can help the sinner arise from this state. But in that case there must be conjectures or probable reasons to think that this person will be able to help the sinner.[25]

[42]   **Deeds**

Here the subject matter takes in the ten commandments, the precepts of the Church, and the official recommendations of our superiors. Any action performed against these three headings is a sin, more serious or less in accordance with its nature. By official recommendations of our superiors I mean, for example, the bulls about crusades and other indulgences, such as those for peaceful reconciliations on condition of confession and reception of the Eucharist. For it is no small sin to act or cause others to act against these pious exhortations and recommendations of our superiors.

[43]   **A METHOD FOR MAKING THE GENERAL
             EXAMINATION OF CONSCIENCE.[26]
             It contains five points.**

The First Point is to give thanks to God our Lord for the benefits I have received from him.

The Second is to ask grace to know my sins and rid myself of them.

The Third is to ask an account of my soul from the hour of rising to the present examen, hour by hour or period by period; first as to thoughts, then words, then deeds, in the same order as was given for the particular examination [in 25].

The Fourth is to ask pardon of God our Lord for my faults.

The Fifth is to resolve, with his grace, to amend them. Close with an Our Father.

[44]

GENERAL CONFESSION, WITH HOLY COMMUNION

For a person who voluntarily desires to make a general confession, to make it here in the time of retreat will bring three benefits, among others.

The First. It is granted that a person who confesses annually is not obliged to make a general confession. Nevertheless, to make it brings greater profit and merit, because of the greater sorrow experienced at present for all the sins and evil deeds of one's entire life.

The Second. During these Spiritual Exercises one reaches a deeper interior understanding of the reality and malice of one's sins than when one is not so concentrated on interior concerns. In this way, by coming to know and grieve for the sins more deeply during this time, one will profit and merit more than was the case on earlier occasions.

The Third. As a result of having made a better confession and come to a better disposition, one is worthier and better prepared to receive the Holy Sacrament. Furthermore, the reception of it helps, not only to avoid falling into sin, but also to preserve the increase of grace.

The general confession is best made immediately after the Exercises of the First Week.

THE FIRST EXERCISE

IS A MEDITATION[27]
BY USING THE THREE POWERS
OF THE SOUL ABOUT THE FIRST,
SECOND, AND THIRD SINS.
It contains, after a preparatory prayer
and two preludes,
three main points and a colloquy.

[46]   *The Preparatory Prayer*[28] is to ask God our Lord for the grace that all my intentions, actions, and operations[29] may be ordered purely to the service and praise of his Divine Majesty.

[47]   *The First Prelude* is a composition[30] made by imagining the place. Here we should take notice of the following. When a contemplation or meditation is about something that can be gazed on, for example, a contemplation of Christ our Lord, who is visible, the composition consists of seeing in imagination the physical place where that which I want to contemplate is taking place. By physical place I mean, for instance, a temple or a mountain where Jesus Christ or Our Lady happens to be, in accordance with the topic I desire to contemplate.

When a contemplation or meditation is about something abstract and invisible, as in the present case about the sins, the composition will be to see in imagination and to consider my soul as imprisoned in this corruptible body, and my whole compound self as an exile in this valley [of tears] among brute animals. I mean, my whole self as composed of soul and body.[31]

[48]   *The Second Prelude* is to ask God our Lord for what I want and desire.[32] What I ask for should be in accordance with the subject matter. For example, in a contemplation on the Resurrection, I will ask for joy with Christ in joy; in a

contemplation on the Passion, I will ask for pain, tears, and suffering with Christ suffering.

In the present meditation it will be to ask for shame and confusion about myself, when I see how many people have been damned for committing a single mortal sin, and how many times I have deserved eternal damnation for my many sins.

[49]   *Note.* All the contemplations or meditations ought to be preceded by this same preparatory prayer, which is never changed, and also by the two preludes, which are sometimes changed in accordance with the subject matter.

[50]   *The First Point* will be to use my memory, by going over the first sin, that of the angels; next, to use my understanding, by reasoning about it; and then my will.[33] My aim in remembering and reasoning about all these matters is to bring myself to greater shame and confusion, by comparing the one sin of the angels with all my own many sins. For one sin they went to hell; then how often have I deserved hell for my many sins!

In other words, I will call to memory the sin of the angels: How they were created in grace and then, not wanting to better themselves by using their freedom to reverence and obey their Creator and Lord, they fell into pride, were changed from grace to malice, and were hurled from heaven into hell. Next I will use my intellect to ruminate about this in greater detail, and then move myself to deeper affections by means of my will.

[51]   *The Second Point* will be meditated in the same way. That is, I will apply the three faculties to the sin of Adam and Eve. I will recall to memory how they did long penance for their sin, and the enormous corruption it brought to the human race, with so many people going to hell.

Again in other words, I will call to memory the second sin, that of our first parents: How Adam was created in the plain of Damascus[34] and placed in the earthly paradise; and how Eve was created from his rib; how they were forbidden to eat of the tree of knowledge, but did eat, and thus sinned; and then, clothed in garments of skin and expelled from paradise, they lived out their whole lives in great hardship and penance, deprived of the original justice which they had lost.

Next I will use my intellect to reason about this in greater detail, and then use the will, as is described just above.

[52]   *The Third Point* will likewise be to use the same method on the third sin, the particular sin of anyone who has gone to hell because of one mortal sin; and further, of innumerable other persons who went there for fewer sins than I have committed.

That is, about this third particular sin too I will follow the same procedure as above. I will call to memory the gravity and malice of the sin against my Creator and Lord; then I will use my intellect to reason about it—how by sinning and acting against the Infinite Goodness the person has been justly condemned forever. Then I will finish by using the will, as was described above.

[53]   *Colloquy.*[35] Imagine Christ our Lord[36] suspended on the cross before you, and converse with him in a colloquy: How is it that he, although he is the Creator, has come to make himself a human being? How is it that he has passed from eternal life to death here in time, and to die in this way for my sins?

In a similar way, reflect on yourself and ask: What have I done for Christ? What am I doing for Christ? What ought I to do for Christ?

In this way, too, gazing on him in so pitiful a state as he hangs on the cross, speak out whatever comes to your mind.

[54]   A colloquy is made, properly speaking, in the way one friend speaks to another, or a servant to one in authority—now begging a favor, now accusing oneself of some misdeed, now telling one's concerns and asking counsel about them. Close with an Our Father.

[55]

THE SECOND EXERCISE
IS A MEDITATION ON OUR OWN[37] SINS.
It comprises, after the preparatory prayer and preludes, five points and a colloquy.

The Preparatory Prayer will be the same.
The First Prelude will be the same composition of place.

The Second Prelude will be to ask for what I desire. Here it will be to ask for growing and intense sorrow and tears for my sins.

[56]   *The First Point* is the court-record[38] of my sins. I will call to memory all the sins of my life, looking at them year by year or period by period. For this three things will be helpful: first, the locality or house where I lived; second, the associations which I had with others; third, the occupation I was pursuing.

[57]   *The Second Point* is to ponder these sins, looking at the foulness and evil which every mortal sin would contain in itself, even if it were not forbidden.

[58]   *The Third Point.* I will reflect upon myself, by using examples which humble me:

First, what am I when compared with all other human beings?

Second, what are they when compared with all the angels and saints in paradise?

Third, what is all of creation when compared with God? and then, I alone—what can I be?

Fourth, I will look at all the corruption and foulness of my body.

Fifth, I will look upon myself as a sore or abscess from which have issued such great sins and iniquities and such foul poison.

[59]   *The Fourth Point.* I will consider who God is against whom I have sinned, by going through his attributes and comparing them with their opposites in myself: his wisdom with my ignorance, his omnipotence with my weakness, his justice with my iniquity, his goodness with my malice.

[60]   *The Fifth Point.* This is an exclamation of wonder and surging emotion, uttered as I reflect on all creatures and wonder how they have allowed me to live and have preserved me in life. The angels: How is it that, although they are the swords of God's justice, they have borne with me, protected me, and prayed for me? The saints: How is it that they have interceded and prayed for me? Likewise, the heavens, the sun, the moon, the stars, and the elements; the fruits, birds,

fishes, and animals. And the earth: How is it that it has not opened up and swallowed me, creating new hells for me to suffer in forever?

[61] *I will conclude with a colloquy* of mercy—speaking and giving thanks to God our Lord for giving me life until now, and proposing, with his grace, amendment for the future. Our Father.

[62]
THE THIRD EXERCISE
IS A REPETITION OF THE FIRST AND
SECOND EXERCISES, BY MAKING
THREE COLLOQUIES.

After the preparatory prayer and two preludes, this exercise will be a repetition[39] of the first and the second exercises. I should notice and dwell on those points where I felt greater consolation or desolation, or had a greater spiritual experience. Then I will make three colloquies in the manner which follows.

[63] *The First Colloquy* will be with Our Lady, that she may obtain for me from her Son and Lord grace for three things:

First, that I may feel an interior knowledge of my sins and also an abhorrence of them;

Second, that I may perceive the disorder in my actions, in order to detest them, amend myself, and put myself in order;

Third, that I may have a knowledge of the world,[40] in order to detest it and rid myself of all that is worldly and vain. Then I will say a Hail Mary.[41]

The Second Colloquy. I will make the same requests to the Son, asking him to obtain these graces for me from the Father. Then I will say the prayer Soul of Christ.[42]

The Third Colloquy. I will address these same requests to the Father, asking that he himself, the eternal Lord, may grant me these graces. Then I will say an Our Father.

[64]
THE FOURTH EXERCISE
IS TO MAKE A RÉSUMÉ OF THE THIRD.

I have used the word résumé because the intellect, without rambling, should strive assiduously to recall the matters contemplated in the previous exercises. It concludes with the same three colloquies.

[65]
THE FIFTH EXERCISE
IS A MEDITATION ON HELL.
It contains, after the preparatory prayer and two preludes, five points and a colloquy.

The Preparatory Prayer will be the same as usual.

The First Prelude, the composition of place. Here it will be to see in imagination the length, breadth, and depth of hell.

The Second Prelude, to ask for what I desire. Here it will be to ask for an interior sense of the pain suffered by the damned, so that if through my faults I should forget the love of the Eternal Lord, at least the fear of those pains will serve to keep me from falling into sin.

[66] *The First Point* will be to see with the eyes of the imagination the huge fires and, so to speak, the souls within the bodies full of fire.

[67] *The Second Point.* In my imagination I will hear the wailing, the shrieking, the cries, and the blasphemies against our Lord and all his saints.

[68] *The Third Point.* By my sense of smell I will perceive the smoke, the sulphur, the filth, and the rotting things.

[69] *The Fourth Point.* By my sense of taste I will experience the bitter flavors of hell: tears, sadness, and the worm of conscience.

[70] *The Fifth Point.* By my sense of touch, I will feel how the flames touch the souls and burn them.

[71] *The Colloquy.* I will carry on a colloquy with Christ our Lord. I will call to mind the souls who are in hell: Some are there because they did not believe in Christ's coming; and others who, although they believed, did not act according to his commandments. I will group these persons into three classes.

First, those lost before Christ came.

Second, those condemned during his lifetime.

Third, those lost after his life in this world.

Thereupon I will thank Christ because he has not, by ending my life, let me fall into any of these classes. I will also thank him because he has shown me, all through my life up to the present moment, so much pity and mercy. I will close with an Our Father.[43]

[72] *Note.* The first exercise will be made at midnight; the second, soon after arising in the morning; the third, before or after Mass, but always before the noon meal; the fourth, at the time of Vespers; and the fifth, an hour before the evening meal. This distribution of the hours is intended to be followed, more or less, throughout the four Weeks. The norm is the help found by the exercitant in making the five exercises or fewer, in accordance with his or her age, disposition, and health.

[73]
ADDITIONAL DIRECTIVES[44]
FOR MAKING THE EXERCISES BETTER AND FINDING MORE READILY WHAT ONE DESIRES.

The First Directive. Upon going to bed at night, just before I fall asleep, I will think for the length of a Hail Mary about the hour when I should arise, and for what purpose; and I will briefly sum up the exercise I am to make.

[74] *The Second.* Upon awakening, while keeping out any other thoughts, I will immediately turn my attention to what I will contemplate in the first exercise, at midnight. I will strive to feel shame for my many sins, by using examples, such as that of a knight who stands before his king and his whole court, shamed and humiliated because he has grievously offended him, from whom he had received numerous gifts and favors.

Similarly, in the second exercise I will imagine myself as a great sinner in chains; that is, as if I were being brought in chains to appear before the supreme and eternal Judge; taking as an example how chained prisoners, already deserving death, appear before their earthly judge. As I dress I will keep thoughts like these in mind, or others proper to the subject matter.

[75]   *The Third.* A step or two away from the place where I will make my contemplation or meditation, I will stand for the length of an Our Father. I will raise my mind and think how God our Lord is looking at me, and other such thoughts. Then I will make an act of reverence or humility.

[76]   *The Fourth.* I will enter upon the contemplation, now kneeling, now prostrate on the floor, or lying face upward, or seated, or standing—but always intent on seeking what I desire. Two things should be noted. First, if I find what I desire while kneeling, I will not change to another posture; so too, if I find it while prostrate, and so on.

Second, if in any point I find what I am seeking, there I will repose until I am fully satisfied, without any anxiety to go on.[45]

[77]   *The Fifth.* After finishing the exercise, for a quarter of an hour, either seated or walking about, I will examine how well I did in the contemplation or meditation. If poorly, I will seek the reasons; and if I find them, I will express sorrow in order to do better in the future. If I did well, I will thank God our Lord and use the same procedure next time.

[78]   *The Sixth.* I should not think about pleasant or joyful things, such as heavenly glory, the Resurrection, and so forth. For if we desire to experience pain, sorrow, and tears for our sins, any thought of happiness or joy will be an impediment. Instead, I should keep myself intent on experiencing sorrow and pain; and for this it is better to think about death and judgment.

[79]   *The Seventh.* For the same purpose I will deprive myself of all light, by closing the shutters and doors while I am in my room, except for times when I want to read the office or other matters, or eat.

[80]   *The Eighth.* I should not laugh, or say anything that would arouse laughter.

[81]   *The Ninth.* I should restrain my sight, except to receive or say goodbye to someone with whom I speak.

[82]   *The Tenth.* This pertains to penance, which is divided into interior and exterior. Interior penance is grieving for one's sins with a firm intention not to commit those or any

other sins again. Exterior penance, a fruit of the former, is self-punishment for the sins one has committed. This is done in three principal ways.

[83] The first way pertains to eating. That is, when we abstain from what is superfluous we are practicing, not penance, but temperance. We practice penance when we abstain from what is ordinarily suitable. And the more we subtract the better is the penance, provided that we do not weaken our constitution or bring on noteworthy illness.

[84] The second way pertains to our manner of sleeping. Again, when we abstain from the superfluous in things delicate and soft, this is not penance. But we do practice penance when we deprive ourselves of what is ordinarily suitable; and the more we so deprive ourselves, the better is the penance, provided we do not harm ourselves or weaken our constitution. However, we should not deprive ourselves of the amount of sleep ordinarily good for us, except perhaps in an effort to find the right mean when one has a bad habit of sleeping too much.

[85] The third way is to chastise the body, that is, to inflict pain on it, by wearing hairshirts, cords, or iron chains; by scourging or wounding oneself; and by similar austerities.

[86] *Note.* The best and safest form of penance seems to be that which produces physical pain but does not penetrate to the bones, so that it brings pain but not illness. Therefore the most suitable form of penance is to hurt oneself with light cords that inflict the pain on the surface, rather than some other manner which might cause noteworthy illness inside.

[87] *A First Observation.* Exterior penances are performed chiefly for three purposes.

First, to satisfy for one's past sins.

Second, to overcome ourselves; that is, to keep our bodily nature obedient to reason and all our bodily faculties[46] subject to the higher.

Third, to seek and obtain some grace or gift which one wishes and desires, such as interior contrition for one's sins, abundant tears because of them or of the pains and sufferings which Christ our Lord underwent in his Passion; or to obtain a solution to some doubt in which one finds oneself.

[88]   *A Second Observation.* The first and second additional directives should be used for the exercises at midnight and early morning, but not for those which will be made at other times. The fourth additional directive will never be practiced in church in the presence of others, but only privately, for example, in one's house, and so forth.

[89]   *A Third Observation.* When someone making the Exercises fails to find what he or she desires, such as tears, consolation, and the like, it is often useful to make some change in eating, sleeping, and other forms of penance, so that we do penance for two or three days, and then omit it for two or three days. Furthermore, for some persons more penance is suitable, and for others less. Further still, on many occasions we give up penance because of love of our bodies and judge erroneously that a human being cannot endure such penance without notable illness. On the other hand, we sometimes do excessive penance, thinking that the body can bear it. Now since God our Lord knows our nature infinitely better than we do, through changes of this sort he often enables each of us to know what is right for her or him.

[90]   *A Fourth Observation.* The particular examination should be made to get rid of faults and negligences pertaining to the exercises and Additional Directives. This holds true also during the Second, Third, and Fourth Weeks.

THE SECOND WEEK

[91]

THE CALL OF THE TEMPORAL KING, AS AN AID TOWARD CONTEMPLATING THE LIFE OF THE ETERNAL KING.[47]

The Preparatory Prayer will be as usual ([46]).

The First Prelude. A composition by imagining the place. Here it will be to see with the eyes of the imagination the synagogues, villages, and castles[48] through which Christ our Lord passed as he preached.

The Second Prelude is to ask for the grace which I desire. Here it will be to ask grace from our Lord that I may not be deaf to his call, but ready and diligent to accomplish his most holy will.

[92] *The First Point.* I will place before my mind a human king, chosen by God our Lord himself, whom all Christian princes and all Christian persons reverence and obey.[49]

[93] *The Second Point.* I will observe how this king speaks to all his people, saying, "My will is to conquer the whole land of the infidels. Hence, whoever wishes to come with me has to be content with the same food I eat, and the drink, and the clothing which I wear, and so forth. So too he or she must labor with me during the day, and keep watch in the night, and so on, so that later they may have a part with me in the victory, just as they have shared in the toil."[50]

[94] *The Third Point.* I will consider what good subjects ought to respond to a king so generous and kind; and how, consequently, if someone did not answer his call, he would be scorned and upbraided by everyone and accounted as an unworthy knight.

[95]   **THE SECOND PART OF THIS EXERCISE**
consists in applying the above parable of a temporal
king to Christ our Lord, according to the three
points just mentioned.[51]

The First Point. If we give consideration to such a call
from the temporal king to his subjects, how much more
worthy of consideration it is to look on Christ our Lord, the
eternal King, and all the world assembled before him. He calls
to them all, and to each one in particular he states: "My will is
to conquer the whole world and all my enemies, and thus to
enter into the glory of my Father. Therefore, whoever wishes
to come with me must labor with me, so that through following me in the pain he or she may follow me also in
the glory."[52]

[96]   *The Second Point.* This will be to reflect that all those
who have judgment and reason will offer themselves whole-
heartedly for this labor.

[97]   *The Third Point.* Those who desire to show greater devotion and to distinguish themselves in total service to their
eternal King and universal Lord will not only offer their
persons for the labor, but go further still. They will work
against[53] their human sensitivities[54] and against their carnal
and worldly love, and they will make offerings of greater
worth and moment, and say:

[98]   "Eternal Lord of all things, I make my offering, with
your favor and help. I make it in the presence of your infinite
Goodness, and of your glorious Mother, and of all the holy
men and women in your heavenly court. I wish and desire,
and it is my deliberate decision, provided only that it is for
your greater service and praise, to imitate you in bearing all
injuries and affronts, and any poverty, actual[55] as well as
spiritual, if your Most Holy Majesty desires to elect and
receive me into such a life and state."

[99]   *First Note.* This exercise will be made twice during the
day, that is, on rising in the morning and an hour before the
noonday or the evening meal.

[100]   *Second Note.* During the Second Week, and also the
following weeks, it is profitable to spend occasional periods

in reading from *The Imitation of Christ*, the Gospels, or lives of the saints.

[101]
THE FIRST DAY.
ON IT THE FIRST CONTEMPLATION[56]
IS DEVOTED TO THE INCARNATION.[57]
It contains, after the preparatory prayer,
three preludes, three points, and a colloquy.

The usual Preparatory Prayer.

[102]   *The First Prelude* is to survey the history[58] of the matter I am to contemplate. Here it is how the Three Divine Persons gazed on the whole surface or circuit of the world, full of people; and how, seeing that they were all going down into hell, they decided in their eternity that the Second Person would become a human being, in order to save the human race. And thus, when the fullness of time had come, they sent the angel St. Gabriel to Our Lady (as in [262] below).

[103]   *The Second Prelude* is a composition, by imagining the place. Here it will be to see the great extent of the circuit of the world, with peoples so many and so diverse; and then to see in particular the house and rooms of Our Lady, in the city of Nazareth in the province of Galilee.

[104]   *The Third Prelude* will be to ask for what I desire. Here it will be to ask for an interior knowledge of our Lord, who became human for me, that I may love him more intensely and follow him more closely.

[105]   *Note.* It should be noted here that this same preparatory prayer, without any change, should be made throughout this and the following weeks, as was stated at the beginning. Similarly the same three preludes are to be made throughout this and the following weeks; but their content is changed in accordance with the subject matter.

[106]   *The First Point.* I will see the various persons, some here, some there.

First, those on the face of the earth, so diverse in dress and behavior: some white and others black, some in peace and others at war, some weeping and others laughing, some healthy and others sick, some being born and others dying, and so forth.

Second, I will see and consider the Three Divine Persons, seated, so to speak, on the royal throne of their Divine Majesty. They are gazing on the whole face and circuit of the earth; and they see all the peoples in such great blindness, and how they are dying and going down to hell.

Third, I will see Our Lady and the angel greeting her. Then I will reflect on this to draw some profit from what I see.

[107]   *The Second Point.* I will listen to what the persons on the face of the earth are saying; that is, how they speak with one another, swear and blaspheme, and so on. Likewise, I will hear what the Divine Persons are saying, that is, "Let us work the redemption of the human race," and so forth. Then I will listen to what the angel and Our Lady are saying. Afterward I will reflect on this, to draw profit from their words.

[108]   *The Third Point.* Here I will consider what the people on the face of the earth are doing: How they wound, kill, go to hell, and so on. Similarly, what the Divine Persons are doing, that is, bringing about the most holy Incarnation, and other such activities. Likewise, what the angel and Our Lady are doing, with the angel carrying out his office of ambassador and Our Lady humbling herself and giving thanks to the Divine Majesty. Then I will reflect on these matters, to draw some profit from each of them.

[109]   *Colloquy.* At the end a colloquy should be made. I will think over what I ought to say to the Three Divine Persons, or to the eternal Word made flesh, or to our Mother and Lady. I will beg favors according to what I feel in my heart, that I may better follow and imitate Our Lord, who in this way has recently become a human being. Our Father.

[110]   ## THE SECOND CONTEMPLATION IS ON THE NATIVITY.

The Preparatory Prayer as usual.

[111]   *The First Prelude* is the history. Here it will be to recall how our Lady and Joseph left Nazareth to go to Bethlehem and pay the tribute which Caesar imposed on all those lands

([264]). She was pregnant almost nine months and, as we may piously meditate, seated on a burro; and with her were Joseph and a servant girl, leading an ox.

[112]   *The Second Prelude.* The composition, by imagining the place. Here it will be to see in imagination the road from Nazareth to Bethlehem. Consider its length and breadth, whether it is level or winds through valleys and hills. Similarly, look at the place or cave of the nativity: How big is it, or small? How low or high? And how is it furnished?

[113]   *The Third Prelude.* This will be the same as in the preceding contemplation, and have the same words ([104]).

[114]   *The First Point.* This is to see the persons; that is, to see Our Lady, Joseph, the maidservant, and the Infant Jesus after his birth. I will make myself a poor, little, and unworthy slave, gazing at them, contemplating them, and serving them in their needs, just as if I were there, with all possible respect and reverence. Then I will reflect upon myself to draw some profit.

[115]   *The Second Point.* I will observe, consider, and contemplate what they are saying. Then, reflecting upon myself, I will draw some profit.

[116]   *The Third Point.* This is to behold and consider what they are doing; for example, journeying and toiling, in order that the Lord may be born in greatest poverty; and that after so many hardships of hunger, thirst, heat, cold, injuries, and insults, he may die on the cross! And all this for me! Then I will reflect and draw some spiritual profit.

[117]   *Colloquy.* Conclude with a colloquy, as in the preceding contemplation, and with an Our Father.

[118]   ## THE THIRD CONTEMPLATION WILL BE A REPETITION OF THE FIRST AND SECOND EXERCISES.

After the preparatory prayer and the three preludes, the exercitant should make a repetition of the first and second exercises. Always he or she will note some more important points where some insight, consolation, or desolation was experienced. Also, at the end a colloquy should be made, and an Our Father recited.

[119]   *Note.* In this repetition, and in all those which follow, the order of procedure will be the same as what was used in the repetitions of the First Week ([62–65]). The subject matter is changed but the same procedure is kept.

[120]
THE FOURTH CONTEMPLATION
WILL BE A REPETITION OF THE FIRST AND SECOND CONTEMPLATIONS,
just as in the preceding repetition.

[121]
THE FIFTH CONTEMPLATION
WILL BE AN APPLICATION OF THE FIVE SENSES[59]
to the subject matter of the first and second contemplations.

After the preparatory prayer and the three preludes, it is profitable to use the imagination and to apply the five senses to the first and second contemplations, in the following manner.

[122]   *The First Point.* By the sight of my imagination I will see the persons, by meditating and contemplating in detail all the circumstances around them, and by drawing some profit from the sight.

[123]   *The Second Point.* By my hearing I will listen to what they are saying or might be saying; and then, reflecting on myself, I will draw some profit from this.

[124]   *The Third Point.* I will smell the fragrance and taste the infinite sweetness and charm of the Divinity, of the soul, of its virtues, and of everything there, appropriately for each of the persons who is being contemplated. Then I will reflect upon myself and draw profit from this.

[125]   *The Fourth Point.* Using the sense of touch, I will, so to speak, embrace and kiss the places where the persons walk or sit. I shall always endeavor to draw some profit from this.

[126]   *Colloquy.* Conclude with a colloquy, as in the first and second contemplations ([109–117]), and with an Our Father.

[127]

NOTES

The First Note. For this and the following weeks this should be observed. I should read only about the mystery which I shall immediately contemplate. In this way I will avoid reading about a mystery foreign to my contemplation for that day or that hour. The purpose is to keep the consideration of one mystery from interfering with that about another.

[128]   *Second Note.* The first exercise, that on the Incarnation, will be at midnight; the second exercise, on awakening in the morning; the third, near the hour of Mass; the fourth, at the hour of Vespers; and the fifth, before the evening meal. The exercitant should remain for an hour in each of these five exercises. This same order of the day should be followed on all the remaining days.

[129]   *Third Note.* This too should be noted. If the one making the Exercises is aged or weak, or even if he or she is strong but has been left somewhat weakened by the First Week, during the Second Week it is better for this person not to arise at midnight, at least sometimes. Instead one contemplation should be made in the morning, a second at the hour of Mass, a third before the noon meal, the repetition near the hour of Vespers, and the application of the senses before the evening meal.

[130]   *Fourth Note.* In the observance of the ten Additional Directives given in the First Week, during the Second Week modifications should be made in the second, sixth, seventh, and part of the tenth.

The second Additional Directive ([74]) will be that when I awaken I should call to mind the contemplation I am about to make in my desire to know better the eternal Word made flesh, so that I may better serve him and follow him.

The sixth ([75]) will be frequently to call to mind the life and mysteries of Christ our Lord, from his Incarnation up to the place or mystery I am presently contemplating.

The seventh ([79]) will become this: I should make use of darkness or light, good weather or its opposite, to the extent that I find them profitable for myself and helpful toward finding what I desire.

In regard to the tenth Additional Directive ([82]), the exercitant ought to adjust his or her practice of penance in accordance with the mysteries being contemplated. For some of them call for penance, and others do not.

In this way all ten Additional Directives should be carried out with great care.

[131] *Fifth Note.* In all the exercises, except those at midnight and in the morning, the equivalent of the second Additional Directive ([74]) should be observed in the following way.

As soon as I recall that the time to make the exercise has come, before I begin it I will call to mind where I am going and before whom I shall appear, and I will briefly survey its subject matter. Then I will carry out the third Additional Directive ([75]) and begin the exercise.

[132] ## THE SECOND DAY

On the second day, for the first and second contemplations the exercitant should take the Presentation in the Temple ([268]) and the Flight into exile in Egypt ([269]). The two repetitions will be made about this pair of contemplations, and then an application of the senses to them. This is done in the same way as on the preceding day ([101–121]).

[133] *Note.* On this second day and through the fourth day, it is sometimes profitable, even when an exercitant is strong and well-disposed, to make changes in procedure, to help him or her in finding what is desired. One contemplation might be taken at dawn, another near the hour of Mass, and the repetition at the hour of Vespers, and the application of the senses before the evening meal.

[134] ## THE THIRD DAY

On the third day the exercitant will contemplate how the child Jesus was obedient to his parents at Nazareth ([271]), and next how they found him in the temple ([275]). After this will come the two repetitions and the application of the senses.

[135]   ## INTRODUCTION TO THE CONSIDERATION ON STATES OF LIFE.[60]

We have already considered the example which Christ our Lord gave us for the first state of life, which consists in the observance of the commandments. He gave this example when he lived in obedience to his parents.

We have also considered the example he gave us for the second state, that of evangelical perfection,[61] when he remained in the temple, separating himself from his adoptive father and human mother in order to devote himself solely to the service of his eternal Father.

While continuing our contemplations of his life, we now begin simultaneously to explore and inquire: In which life or state does his Divine Majesty wish us to serve him?

Therefore to gain some introduction to this matter, we shall in our next exercise observe the intention of Christ our Lord, and in contrast, that of the enemy of human nature. We shall also think about how we ought to dispose ourselves in order to come to perfection in whatsoever state of life God our Lord may grant us to elect.

[136]   ## THE FOURTH DAY
A MEDITATION ON TWO STANDARDS,[62] THE ONE OF CHRIST, OUR SUPREME COMMANDER AND LORD, THE OTHER OF LUCIFER, THE MORTAL ENEMY OF OUR HUMAN NATURE.

The Preparatory Prayer will be as usual.

[137]   *The First Prelude.* This is the history. Here it will be to consider how Christ calls and desires all persons to come under his standard, and how Lucifer in opposition calls them under his.

[138]   *The Second Prelude.* A composition, by imagining the place. Here it will be to imagine a great plain in the region of Jerusalem, where the supreme commander of the good people is Christ our Lord; then another plain in the region of Babylon, where the leader of the enemy is Lucifer.

[139]   *The Third Prelude.* It is to ask for what I desire. Here it will be to ask for insight into the deceits of the evil leader, and for help to guard myself against them; and further, for insight into the genuine life which the supreme and truthful commander sets forth, and grace to imitate him.[63]

PART I. THE STANDARD OF SATAN.

[140]   *The First Point.* Imagine the leader of all the enemy in that great plain of Babylon. He is seated on a throne of fire and smoke, in aspect horrible and terrifying.

[141]   *The Second Point.* Consider how he summons uncountable devils, disperses some to one city and others to another, and thus reaches into the whole world, without missing any provinces, places, states, or individual persons.

[142]   *The Third Point.* Consider the address he makes to them: How he admonishes them to set up snares and chains; how first they should tempt people to covet riches (as he usually does, at least in most cases), so that they may more easily come to vain honor from the world, and finally to surging pride. In this way, the first step is riches, the second is honor, and the third is pride;[64] and from these three steps the enemy entices them to any other vices.

PART II. THE STANDARD OF CHRIST.

[143]   Similarly, in contrast, gaze in imagination on the supreme and true leader, who is Christ our Lord.

[144]   *The First Point.* Consider how Christ our Lord takes his place in that great plain near Jerusalem, in an area which is lowly, beautiful, and attractive.

[145]   *The Second Point.* Consider how the Lord of all the world chooses so many persons, apostles, disciples, and the like. He sends them throughout the whole world, to spread his doctrine among people of every state and condition.

[146]   *The Third Point.* Consider the address which Christ our Lord makes to all his servants and friends whom he is sending on this expedition. He recommends that they endeavor to aid all persons, by attracting them, first, to the highest degree of spiritual poverty and also, if his Divine Majesty would be served and pleased to choose them for it, to no less a degree of

actual poverty;[65] second, by attracting them to a desire of reproaches and contempt, since from these results humility.

In this way there will be three steps: the first, poverty in opposition to riches; the second, reproaches or contempt in opposition to honor from the world; and the third, humility in opposition to pride. Then from these three steps they should induce people to all the other virtues.[66]

[147]   *The First Colloquy* should be with Our Lady. I beg her to obtain for me grace to be received under the standard of her Son and Lord; that is, to be received, first, in the highest degree of spiritual poverty and also, if his Divine Majesty would be served and if he should wish to choose me for it, to no less a degree of actual poverty; and second, in bearing reproaches and injuries, that through them I may imitate him more, if only I can do this without sin on anyone's part and without displeasure to his Divine Majesty. Then I will say a Hail Mary.

The Second Colloquy. It will be to ask the same grace from the Son, that he may obtain it for me from the Father. Then I will say the Soul of Christ.

The Third Colloquy will be to ask the same grace from the Father, that he may grant it to me. Then I will say an Our Father.

[148]   *Note.* This exercise will be made at midnight and again after arising. There will also be two repetitions of it, one near the hour of Mass and one near that of Vespers. Each of these exercises will close with the three colloquies: one with Our Lady, one with the Son, and one with the Father. Then, before the evening meal, the exercise on the Three Classes of Persons will be made, as follows.

[149]   # ON THIS SAME FOURTH DAY, A MEDITATION[67] IS MADE ON THREE CLASSES OF PERSONS.[68]
It should be made as an aid toward embracing what is better.

The Preparatory Prayer will be as usual.

[150]   *The First Prelude.* It is the history,[69] that of three classes of typical persons. Each of them has acquired ten thousand

ducats, but not purely or properly for the love of God. Each desires to save his or her soul and to find God our Lord in peace, by discarding the burden and obstacle to this purpose which he or she finds this affection for the acquired money to be.[70]

[151]   *The Second Prelude.* A composition, by seeing the place. Here it will be to imagine myself as standing before God and all his saints, that I may desire and know what will be more pleasing to his Divine Goodness.

[152]   *The Third Prelude.* It will be to ask for what I desire. Here I will ask for the grace to choose that which is more to the glory of his Divine Majesty and the salvation of my soul.[71]

[153]   *Persons Typical of the First Class* would like to get rid of the attachment[72] which they have for this acquired money, in order to find God in peace and be able to save their souls. But these persons do not take the means, even to the hour of death.

[154]   *Persons Typical of the Second Class* also desire to get rid of the attachment, but in such a way that they will keep the acquired money, so that God will come to where they desire. These persons do not decide to relinquish the money in order to go to where God is, even though that would be the best state for them.

[155]   *Persons Typical of the Third Class* desire to get rid of the attachment, but in such a way that they have no inclination either to keep the acquired money or to dispose of it. Instead they desire to keep it or dispose of it solely according to what God our Lord will move[73] their will to choose, and also according to what they themselves will judge to be better for the service and praise of his Divine Majesty.

Meanwhile they strive to imagine that, as far as their attachment is concerned,[74] they have abandoned all of it. They strive earnestly not to desire that money or anything else, except when they are motivated solely by the service of God our Lord; in such a way that the desire to be able to serve God our Lord better is what moves them to take or reject any object whatsoever.[75]

[156]   *Colloquy.* The same three colloquies should be made as in the preceding contemplation on the Two Standards ([147]).

[157]   *Note.* When we feel an inclination or repugnance against

157

actual poverty, or when we are not indifferent to poverty or riches, a great help toward overcoming this disordered inclination is to beg the Lord in the colloquies to choose oneself to serve him in actual poverty (even though it is contrary to our lower nature); and further that one desires it, begs for it, and pleads for it, provided only that it would be for the service and praise of his Divine Goodness.

[158]

THE FIFTH DAY

The contemplation will be on the departure of Christ our Lord from Nazareth for the river Jordan, and how he was baptized (see [273]).[76]

[159]

First Note. This contemplation will be made once at midnight, and a second time in the early morning. Then there will be two repetitions of it, one near the hour of Mass and one near that of Vespers, and an application of the five senses before the evening meal. In each of these five exercises the usual preparatory prayer and three preludes will be used, in the manner explained for the contemplation on the Incarnation ([102]) and the Nativity ([111]). Moreover, the triple colloquy should be that of the Three Classes of Persons ([147]), or according to the note which follows that meditation ([157]).[77]

[160]

Second Note. The particular examination of conscience after the noonday and evening meals will be about one's faults and negligences during the day in regard to the exercises and the Additional Directives. This same procedure should be used also for the following days.

[161]

THE SIXTH DAY

The contemplation will be on how Christ our Lord went from the river Jordan to the desert inclusively, and on his temptations there ([274]). The same manner of proceeding should be followed as on the fifth day.

THE SEVENTH DAY

How St. Andrew and others followed Christ our Lord ([275]).

THE EIGHTH DAY

The Sermon on the Mount, which is on the eight beatitudes ([278]).

THE NINTH DAY

How Christ our Lord appeared to his disciples on the waves of the sea ([280]).

THE TENTH DAY

How Christ our Lord preached in the temple ([288]).

THE ELEVENTH DAY

On the raising of Lazarus ([285]).

THE TWELFTH DAY

On Palm Sunday ([287]).

[162]   *First Note.* In this Second Week the number of the contemplations can be increased or lessened, according to the number of days each exercitant wants to spend in this Week or finds profitable. If the week is to be prolonged, one can take the mysteries of Our Lady's visitation to Elizabeth, the Shepherds, the Circumcision of the Infant Jesus, the Three Kings, and others similar. If the week is to be shortened, even some of those which were assigned can be omitted. For the purpose of these meditations is to furnish an introduction and a method for meditating and contemplating, that one may do this better and more completely later on.

[163]   *Second Note.* The exposition of the material pertaining to an election will be begun on the Fifth Day, the day devoted to the contemplation of Christ's departure from Nazareth for the Jordan, in accordance with the explanations given below ([169–189]).

[164]   *Third Note.* Before entering into the deliberations about an election, an exercitant who desires to become lovingly attached to the genuine teaching of Christ our Lord will profit much from considering and pondering the three ways of being humble[78] which are described immediately be-

low. One should mull them over from time to time through-out the whole day,[79] and make colloquies, as will be ex-plained ([168]).

THREE WAYS OF BEING HUMBLE

[165]   *The First Way of Being Humble* is necessary for eternal salvation, and consists in this. I so lower and humble myself, as far as is in my power, that in all things I may be obedient to the law of God our Lord.

Consequently, even though others would make me lord of all the creatures in the world, or even though to save my temporal life, I would not enter into deliberation about vio-lating a commandment either human or divine which binds me under mortal sin.

[166]   *The Second Way of Being Humble* is more perfect than the first. It is what I have when I find myself in this disposition: When the options seem equally effective for the service of God our Lord and the salvation of my soul, I do not desire or feel myself strongly attached to have wealth rather than pov-erty, or honor rather than dishonor, or a long life rather than a short one.[80]

Furthermore, neither for all creation nor to save my life would I enter into deliberation about committing a venial sin.

[167]   *The Third Way of Being Humble* is the most perfect, and consists in this. When I possess the first and second ways, and when the options equally further the praise and glory of God, in order to imitate Christ our Lord better and to be more like him here and now, I desire and choose poverty with Christ poor rather than wealth; contempt with Christ laden with it rather than honors. Even further, I desire to be re-garded as a useless fool for Christ, who before me was re-garded as such, rather than as a wise or prudent person in this world.[81]

[168]   *Note.* One who desires to obtain this third way of being humble will profit much by making the colloquies of the meditation on the Three Classes of Persons, as presented above ([149–156]). In order to imitate and serve our Lord better, he or she should beg him to be chosen for this third,

greater, and better way of being humble, if the service and praise to his Divine Majesty would be equal or greater.

INTRODUCTION TO THE MAKING OF AN ELECTION[82]

[169]   In every good election insofar as it depends on us, the eye of our intention ought to be single. I ought to focus only on the purpose for which I was created, to praise God our Lord and to save my soul. Accordingly, anything whatsoever that I elect ought to be chosen as an aid toward that end, without my ordering or dragging the end into subjection to the means, but with my ordering the means to the end.

It happens, for example, that many first choose to marry, which is the means, and in the second place to serve God our Lord in marriage, which service of God is the end. Similarly, others first seek to possess benefices, and afterward to serve God in them. Hence these do not go directly to God, but desire God to come to their disordered affections. As a result they transform the end into a means and the means into the end; and what they should fasten on in the first place they take up in the last. For I ought to take up first my desire to serve God, which is the end, and in the second place the benefice or marriage, and whether it is more suitable for myself, which is the means to the end.

Therefore nothing whatever ought to move me to choose such means or deprive myself of them, except one alone, the service and praise of God our Lord and the eternal salvation of my soul.[83]

[170]   ## [A CONSIDERATION][84] TO ACQUIRE KNOWLEDGE OF THE MATTERS ABOUT WHICH AN ELECTION SHOULD BE MADE.
It contains four points and one note.

The First Point. It is necessary that all the matters about which we wish to make an election should in themselves be either indifferent or good, so that they function constructively within our Holy Mother the hierarchical Church, and are not bad or opposed to her.[85]

[171]   *The Second.* Some matters fall under the heading of an unchangeable election, such as priesthood, marriage, and the like. Others fall under the heading of a changeable election; for example, we may take or leave benefices; we may take or reject temporal goods.

[172]   *The Third.* In the case of an unchangeable election, once it has been made there is nothing further to elect, since the first one cannot be undone. Examples are marriage, priesthood, and the like. But if this election was not made properly and in a rightly ordered way, free from disordered affections, the one thing that can be considered is to repent and then explore how to lead a good life within the decision made. An election of this kind does not seem to be a divine vocation, since it is something disordered and devious. This is a way in which many are in error; for they take up a predisposed or bad choice and then regard it as a divine vocation. For every vocation from God is something pure, stainless, and without mingling of the flesh or any other disordered affection.

[173]   *The Fourth.* In regard to matters under the heading of a changeable election, if someone has made one in a proper and well-ordered way, and with no admixture of the flesh or the world, there is no reason to make a new election. Instead one should perfect oneself in accordance with it as much as possible.

[174]   *Note.* This too should be noticed. If such a changeable election was made but not in a sincerely and rightly ordered way, then, if one desires fruits to spring from it which are noteworthy and very pleasing to God our Lord, it is profitable to make it anew in a properly ordered way.

[175]   ## THREE TIMES SUITABLE FOR MAKING A SOUND AND GOOD ELECTION.

The First Time is an occasion when God our Lord moves and attracts the will in such a way that a devout person, without doubting or being able to doubt, carries out what was proposed. This is what St. Paul and St. Matthew did when they followed Christ our Lord.[86]

[176]   *The Second Time* is present when sufficient clarity and knowledge are received from the experience of consolations and desolations, and from experience in the discernment of various spirits.[87]

[177]   *The Third Time* is one of tranquility. I consider first the end for which I was born, namely, to praise God our Lord and save my soul; then, desiring this, as the means I elect a life or state of life within the bounds of the Church, in order to be helped in the service of my Lord and the salvation of my soul.[88]

By a time of tranquility I mean one when the soul is not being moved one way and the other by various spirits and uses its natural faculties in freedom and peace.

[178]   If an election is not made in the first or second time, two methods are given below for making it in this third time.

THE FIRST METHOD
OF MAKING A SOUND AND
GOOD ELECTION.
It contains six points.

The First Point is to put before myself the matter about which I wish to make an election, for example, an office or a benefice to be taken or left or any other thing which falls under the heading of a changeable election.

[179]   *The Second Point.* It is necessary to keep as my objective the end for which I am created, to praise God our Lord and save my soul. Furthermore, I ought to find myself indifferent,[89] that is, without any disordered affection, to such an extent that I am not more inclined or emotionally disposed toward taking the matter proposed rather than letting go of it, nor more toward letting it go rather than taking it.

Rather, I should find myself in the middle, like the pointer of a balance, in order to be ready to follow that which I perceive to be more to the glory and praise of God our Lord and the salvation of my soul.

[180]   *The Third Point.* I should beg God our Lord to be pleased to move my will and to put into my mind what I ought to do in regard to the matter proposed, so that it will be more to his

praise and glory. I should beg to accomplish this by reasoning well and faithfully with my intellect, and by choosing in conformity with his most holy will and good pleasure.

[181]   *The Fourth Point.* I should consider and reason out how many advantages or benefits accrue to myself from having the office or benefice proposed, all of them solely for the praise of God our Lord and the salvation of my soul; and on the contrary I should similarly consider the disadvantages and dangers in having it. Then, acting in the same manner in the second part, I should consider the advantages and benefits in not having it, and contrarily the disadvantages and dangers in not having it.[90]

[182]   *The Fifth Point.* After I have considered and thought out every aspect of the proposed matter, I should see to which side reason more inclines. It is in this way that I ought to come to a decision[91] about the matter proposed, namely, in accordance with the preponderating motion of reason, and not from some motion[92] arising from sensitive human nature.

[183]   *The Sixth Point.* When that election or decision has been made, the person who has made it ought with great diligence to go to prayer before God our Lord, to offer him that election, and to beg his Divine Majesty to receive and confirm it, provided it is conducive to his greater service and praise.

[184]   ## THE SECOND METHOD OF MAKING A SOUND AND GOOD ELECTION.[93]
It contains four rules and a note.

The First Rule. That love which moves me and brings me to choose the matter in question should descend from above, from the love of God; in such a way that the person making the election should perceive beforehand that the love, whether greater or less, which he or she has for the matter being chosen, is solely for the sake of our Creator and Lord.

[185]   *The Second Rule.* I will imagine a person whom I have never seen or known. Desiring all perfection for him or her, I will consider what I would say in order to bring such a one to act and elect for the greater glory of God our Lord and the

greater perfection of his or her soul. Then, doing the same for myself, I will keep the rule which I set up for another.

[186] *The Third Rule.* I will consider, as if I were at the point of death, what procedure and norm[94] I will at that time wish I had used in the present election. Then, guiding myself by that norm, I should make my decision on the whole matter.

[187] *The Fourth Rule.* Imagining and considering in what condition I will find myself on judgment day, I will think how at that time I will wish I had decided in regard to the present matter. And the rule which I will then wish I had followed is what I shall apply now, in order that then I may be in complete contentment and joy.

[188] *Note.* After I have observed the rules presented above for my salvation and eternal contentment, I shall make my election and offer it to God our Lord, in the manner described in point six of the First Method of Making an Election ([183]).

[189] ## TO AMEND AND REFORM ONE'S LIFE AND STATE.[95]

In regard to those persons who are established in an ecclesiastical office or in the state of matrimony (whether they possess an abundance of temporal goods or not), there is either no possibility of a change, or else no ready will to make an election about matters subject to a changeable election.

For them it is very profitable to present, in place of an election, a form and method for each one of them to improve and reform his or her life and state, by setting before them the purpose of each one's creation, life, and state of life: the glory and praise of God our Lord and the salvation of their own soul.

To make progress toward this end and attain to it, one ought to consider and work out in detail, during the Exercises and by means of the Methods of Making an Election as explained above ([175–188]), how large a house and how many persons in it one ought to maintain, how one ought to direct and govern its members, and how to teach them by word and example. So too persons such as these should examine their resources, how much they ought to assign for the house and household, and how much for the poor and other good works. In all this and by it, each one should desire and seek nothing except the greater praise and glory of God our Lord.

For everyone ought to reflect that in all spiritual matters, the more one divests oneself of self-love, self-will, and self-interests, the more progress one will make.[96]

THE THIRD WEEK[97]

THE FIRST CONTEMPLATION,
at Midnight.
HOW CHRIST OUR LORD WENT FROM BETHANY TO JERUSALEM FOR THE LAST SUPPER.
It contains the preparatory prayer, three preludes, six points, and a colloquy ([289]).

The Preparatory Prayer is as usual.

[191]   *The First Prelude* is to survey the history. Here it is to recall how Christ our Lord sent two disciples from Bethany to Jerusalem to prepare the supper, and later went there himself with his other disciples; and how, after eating the Paschal Lamb and finishing the meal, he washed their feet and gave his Most Holy Body and Precious Blood to his disciples; and further, how he addressed his farewell discourse to them, after Judas had left to sell his Lord.

[192]   *The Second Prelude.* A composition, by imagining the place. Here it will be to see in imagination the road from Bethany to Jerusalem, whether it is broad, or narrow, or level, and so on. In similar manner, imagine the room of the supper, whether it is large, or small, or arranged in one way or another.

[193]   *The Third Prelude* is to ask for what I desire. Here it will be to ask for heartfelt sorrow and confusion, because the Lord is going to his Passion for my sins.

[194]   *The First Point* is to see the persons at the Supper; and then, by reflecting on myself, to endeavor to draw some profit from them.

The Second Point is to listen to what they are saying, and similarly to draw profit from that.

The Third Point is to see what they are doing, and to draw profit from it.

167

[195]   *The Fourth Point.* Consider what Christ our Lord suffers in his human nature, or desires to suffer, according to the passage being contemplated. Then one should begin here with much effort to bring oneself to grief, sorrow, and tears, and in this same manner to work through the points which follow.

[196]   *The Fifth Point.* Consider how his divinity hides itself; that is, how he could destroy his enemies but does not, and how he allows his most holy humanity to suffer so cruelly.

[197]   *The Sixth Point.* Consider how he suffers all this for my sins, and so on; and also to ask: What ought I to do for him?[98]

[198]   *The Colloquy.* Finish with a colloquy to Christ our Lord, and at its end recite an Our Father.

[199]   *Note.* Attention should be called to a matter which was partially explained before ([54]). In the colloquies we ought to converse and beg according to the subject matter. That is, in accordance with whether I find myself tempted or consoled, desire to possess one virtue or another, or to dispose myself in one way or another, or to experience sorrow or joy over the matter I am contemplating. And finally I ought to ask for what I more earnestly desire in regard to some particular matters.

In carrying out this procedure, we may make one colloquy to Christ our Lord or, if the topic or devotion moves us, make three colloquies, one to the Mother, one to the Son, and one to the Father—using the same procedure that was explained in the Second Week in the Meditation on the Three[99] Classes ([156]) and the note after it ([157]).

[200]   ## THE SECOND CONTEMPLATION,
in the Morning.
FROM THE SUPPER TO THE GARDEN, INCLUSIVELY ([290]).

The Preparatory Prayer will be as usual.

[201]   *The First Prelude* is the history. Here it will be how Christ our Lord descended with his eleven disciples from Mt. Sion, where the Supper had been eaten, into the Valley of Jehoshaphat. He left eight of them in one part of the valley and three in an area of the garden. He began to pray, and his

sweat became like drops of blood. After he had prayed three times to his Father and awakened his disciples, his enemies fell back at his words. Then Judas gave him the kiss of peace and St. Peter cut off the ear of Malchus, but Christ put it back in place. He was arrested as a malefactor, and his captors led him down the valley and up its other side to the house of Annas.

[202]   *The Second Prelude* is to imagine the place. Here it will be to consider the road from Mt. Sion down into the Valley of Jehoshaphat, and the Garden, whether it is small or large, whether of one appearance or another.

[203]   *The Third Prelude* is to ask for what I desire. Here it is what is proper for the Passion: sorrow with Christ in sorrow; a broken spirit with Christ so broken; tears; and interior suffering because of the great suffering which Christ endured for me.

[204]   *First Note.* In this second contemplation, after the preparatory prayer and the three preludes already mentioned, the exercitant will follow the same manner of proceeding through the points and colloquy as in the first contemplation on the Supper. At the hour of Mass and of Vespers two repetitions will be made, and after that, but before the evening meal, an application of the senses to both the contemplations mentioned above. The preparatory prayer and the three preludes will always be used, adjusted to the subject matter, in the same manner of proceeding indicated and explained above in the Second Week ([19, 152; see also 72]).

[205]   *Second.* According to what is most helpful in view of the exercitant's age, disposition, and temperament, there will be five exercises each day or fewer.

[206]   *Third.* During this Third Week the second and sixth Additional Directives will be changed in part.

The second will be that as soon as I awaken I will think of where I am going and for what purpose. In my mind I will briefly run over the coming contemplation I intend to make, in accordance with the mystery at hand. While I am arising and dressing, I will endeavor to make myself sad and sorrowful over the great sorrow and suffering of Christ our Lord.

The sixth will be adjusted thus. I will not admit joyful thoughts, even though they are good and holy, such as those about the Resurrection and heavenly glory. Instead, I will try to foster an attitude of sorrow, suffering, and heartbreak, by calling to mind often the labors, fatigue, and sufferings which Christ our Lord suffered, from his birth up to whatever mystery of his Passion I am contemplating at the time.

[207]   *Fourth.* The Particular Examination of Conscience will be made about the exercises and the Additional Directives for the present, just as it was in the past week ([160]).

[208]   **THE SECOND DAY**

At midnight, the contemplation will be about the events from the Garden to the house of Annas, inclusively ([291]); and in the morning, on those from the house of Annas to that of Caiaphas, inclusively ([292]). The two repetitions and the application of the senses will follow, according to what has been already stated ([204]).

THE THIRD DAY

At midnight, from the house of Caiaphas to that of Pilate, inclusively ([293]); and in the morning, from Pilate to Herod ([294]); and later the two repetitions and application of the senses, by using the same procedure already described ([204]).

THE FOURTH DAY

From Herod to Pilate ([293]). The contemplation at midnight will take in half the mysteries in the house of Pilate, and the later one, in the morning, the remaining events which took place in the same house. The repetitions and application of the senses will be done as was described above ([204]).

THE FIFTH DAY

At midnight, what happened from the house of Pilate up to the crucifixion ([296]), and in the morning, from the raising of the cross until Christ expired ([297]). Then the two repetitions and the application of the senses.

THE SIXTH DAY

At midnight, from the taking down from the cross to the burial in the sepulcher, exclusively; and in the morning, from the placing in the tomb ([298]) to the house where Our Lady went after the burial of her Son.

THE SEVENTH DAY
A CONTEMPLATION OF ALL THE PASSION TAKEN AS A WHOLE
during the exercise at midnight and in the morning.

In place of the repetitions and application of the senses, the exercitant should consider, throughout the day and as frequently as possible, how the Most Holy Body of Christ our Lord was separated from his soul and remained apart from it, and how it was buried. Consider, too, Our Lady's loneliness along with her deep grief and fatigue; then, on the other hand, the fatigue of the disciples.

[209]   *Note.* If someone wishes to extend the time spent on the Passion, in each contemplation he or she should take fewer mysteries. That is, in the first contemplation ([290]) only the Supper (point 1); in the second, the washing of the feet (ibid., point 2); in the third, Christ's institution of the Holy Eucharist (ibid., point 3); in the fourth, his farewell discourse to his apostles; and so on through the other contemplations and mysteries.

Similarly, after finishing the Passion such a one should devote one full day to half of it, another day to the other half, and a third day to a review of the whole. On the contrary, one who wants to abbreviate the time spent on the Passion will take: at midnight, the Supper; in the morning, the Garden; at the hour of Mass, the house of Annas; at the hour of Vespers, the house of Caiaphas; and during the hour before the evening meal, the house of Pilate. In this way the exercitant, omitting the repetitions and the application of the senses, will make five distinct exercises; and in each exercise, a distinct mystery of Christ our Lord will be taken.

When the whole Passion has been completed, he or she can take another day to review it as a whole, either in one

171

exercise or in several, according to what will seem to be more fruitful.

[210] ## RULES[100] TO ORDER ONESELF HENCEFORTH IN THE TAKING OF FOOD.[101]

The First Rule. In regard to bread there is less need to abstain, because it is not a food to which the appetite ordinarily urges us in a disordered way, or to which we are tempted as strongly as we are to other foods.

[211] *The Second.* In regard to drink more attention seems to be required than about eating bread. Therefore, we ought to consider much more carefully what is better for us, in order to accept it, and what is harmful to us, to reject it.

[212] *The Third.* In regard to foods, greater and more complete abstinence ought to be practiced. For in this area just as the appetite is more prone to become disordered, so is temptation more likely to assail us. Hence, toward avoiding what is disordered in the taking of food, abstinence can be practiced in two ways. One is to accustom oneself to eating ordinary foods, and the other, if the foods are dainties, to take them in small quantity.

[213] *The Fourth.* Provided care is taken not to fall into sickness, the more one abstains from what is ordinarily sufficient, the sooner will one find the right mean to keep for oneself in eating and drinking, for two reasons: First, by making this progress and disposing oneself through it, on many occasions one will more clearly perceive interior lights, consolations, and divine inspirations which guide one to the mean suitable to oneself. Second, if in abstinence of this sort one finds oneself lacking in the physical energy and disposition to carry on the present spiritual exercises, one will soon be able to judge what is more suitable to one's own bodily sustenance.

[214] *The Fifth.* While one is eating, it is good to imagine Christ our Lord eating in company with his apostles, and to observe how he eats, how he drinks, how he looks about, and how he converses, and then to try to imitate him. In this way one's mind will be occupied chiefly with the consideration of Our Lord and less with the sustenance of the body. Thus one

gains a better method and order in regard to how one ought to conduct and govern oneself.

[215] *The Sixth.* At another time, while one is eating one can use a different consideration, drawn from a life of the saints, or some pious contemplation, or some spiritual project at hand. When the attention is thus directed to some good object, a person will be less concerned with the sensible pleasure from the bodily food.

[216] *The Seventh.* Above all, one should be on guard against being totally absorbed in what one is eating or letting oneself be completely dominated by the appetite. Rather, one should be master of oneself, both in the manner of eating and the amount one takes.

[217] *The Eighth.* To rid oneself of disordered excess it is very profitable, after dinner or supper or at some other hour when the appetite to eat or drink is not strong, to settle with oneself how much food is to be taken at the next dinner or supper, and further, to do this every day. Then one should not exceed this amount either because of appetite or of temptation, but overcome every occurrence of disordered appetite and of temptation from the enemy, whether his temptation is to take more food or less.[102]

THE FOURTH WEEK

[218]

THE FIRST CONTEMPLATION:
HOW CHRIST OUR LORD APPEARED
TO OUR LADY ([299]).[103]

The usual Preparatory Prayer.

[219]   The *First Prelude* is the history. Here it is how, after Christ died on the cross, his body remained separated from his soul but always united with his divinity. His blessed soul, also united with his divinity, descended to hell.[104] Then, releasing the souls of the just from there, returning to the sepulcher, and rising again, he appeared in body and soul to his Blessed Mother.[105]

[220]   *The Second Prelude.* A composition, by imagining the place. Here it will be to see the arrangement of the holy sepulcher; also, the place or house where Our Lady was, including its various parts, such as a room, an oratory, and the like.

[221]   *The Third Prelude.* It is to ask for what I desire. Here it will be to ask for the grace to be glad and to rejoice intensely because of the great glory and joy of Christ our Lord.[106]

[222]   *The First, Second, and Third Points* will be respectively the usual ones which were used about the Last Supper of Christ our Lord ([194]).

[223]   *The Fourth Point.* Consider how the divinity, which seemed hidden during the Passion, now appears and manifests itself so miraculously in this holy Resurrection, through its true and most holy effects.

[224]   *The Fifth Point.* Consider the office of consoler which Christ our Lord carries out, and compare it with the way friends console one another.

[225]   *Colloquy.* Finish with a colloquy, according to the subject matter, and recite the Our Father.

[226]   *First Note.* In the following contemplations, the exercitant should proceed through all the mysteries of the Resurrection and Ascension in the manner indicated immediately below ([227]). The procedure and method throughout the week on the Resurrection should be the same as they were in the whole week on the Passion ([204]). Therefore, the first contemplation on the Resurrection should be taken as a guiding model in regard to the preludes, which are varied according to the subject matter. The five points should remain the same as immediately above, as do also the Additional Directives which are given below ([229]). In everything else the exercitant can be guided by the procedure used in the week on the Passion; for example, in regard to the repetitions, applications of the five senses, the shortening or lengthening of the time devoted to the mysteries, and the like ([204, 205]).

[227]   *Second Note.* Ordinarily in this Fourth Week it is more suitable to make four exercises a day instead of five than it was in those which preceded. The first exercise should be made shortly after rising in the morning; the second, near the hour of Mass or near the noonday meal, in place of the first repetition; the third, at the hour of Vespers, in place of the second repetition; the fourth, before the evening meal, should be an application of the senses to the preceding exercises of the day. The retreatant ought to note and dwell reflectively on the principal places where he or she has experienced greater interior motions and spiritual relish.

[228]   *Third Note.* Although a fixed number of points, such as three or five, is presented as the subject matter in all the contemplations, the person who is contemplating may prepare more or fewer points, according to what is found better. Before the contemplation is begun, however, it is highly profitable to determine and choose a definite number of points to be used.

[229]   *Fourth Note.* During the Fourth Week, among the ten Additional Directives, changes should be made in the second, sixth, seventh, and tenth.

The second will become: Upon awakening, I will think of the contemplation I am about to make, and endeavor to feel joyful and happy over the great joy and happiness of Christ our Lord ([221]).

The sixth. I will call into my memory and think about things which bring pleasure, happiness, and spiritual joy, such as those about heavenly glory.

The seventh. I will avail myself of light or the pleasant features of the seasons, such as the refreshing coolness in summer or the sun or heat in winter, as far as I think or conjecture that this will help me to rejoice in Christ my Creator and Redeemer.

The tenth. In place of penance, I will attend to temperance and moderation in all things. However, an exception must be made here if the Church has prescribed days of fast and abstinence, unless there is some proper excusing cause.

[230]

CONTEMPLATION TO ATTAIN LOVE.[107]

Note. Two preliminary observations should be made.

First. Love ought to manifest itself more by deeds than by words.[108]

[231]   Second. Love consists in a mutual communication between the two persons. That is, the one who loves gives and communicates to the beloved what he or she has, or a part of what one has or can have; and the beloved in return does the same to the lover.[109] Thus, if the one has knowledge, one gives it to the other who does not; and similarly in regard to honors or riches. Each shares with the other.

[232]   *The usual Preparatory Prayer.*

The First Prelude. A composition. Here it is to see myself as standing before God our Lord, and also before the angels and saints, who are interceding for me.

[233]   *The Second Prelude* is to ask for what I desire. Here it will be to ask for interior knowledge of all the great good I have received, in order that, stirred to profound gratitude, I may become able to love and serve his Divine Majesty in all things.[110]

[234]   *The First Point.*[111] I will call back into my memory the gifts I have received—my creation, redemption, and other gifts particular to myself. I will ponder with deep affection how much God our Lord has done for me, and how much he

has given me of what he possesses, and consequently how he, the same Lord, desires to give me even his very self, in accordance with his divine design.

Then I will reflect on myself, and consider what I on my part ought in all reason and justice to offer and give to his Divine Majesty, namely, all my possessions, and myself along with them. I will speak as one making an offering with deep affection, and say:

"Take, Lord, and receive all my liberty, my memory, my understanding, and all my will—all that I have and possess. You, Lord, have given all that to me. I now give it back to you, 0 Lord. All of it is yours. Dispose of it according to your will. Give me your love and your grace, for that is enough for me."[112]

[235]   *The Second Point.* I will consider how God dwells in creatures; in the elements, giving them existence; in the plants, giving them life; in the animals, giving them sensation; in human beings, giving them intelligence; and finally, how in this way he dwells also in myself, giving me existence, life, sensation, and intelligence; and even further, making me his temple, since I am created as a likeness and image of his Divine Majesty. Then once again I will reflect on myself, in the manner described in the first point, or in any other way I feel to be better. This same procedure will be used in each of the following points.

[236]   *The Third Point.* I will consider how God labors and works for me in all the creatures on the face of the earth; that is, he acts in the manner of one who is laboring. For example, he is working in the heavens, elements, plants, fruits, cattle, and all the rest—giving them their existence, conserving them, concurring with their vegetative and sensitive activities, and so forth. Then I will reflect on myself.

[237]   *The Fourth Point.* I will consider how all good things and gifts descend from above; for example, my limited power from the Supreme and Infinite Power above; and so of justice, goodness, piety, mercy, and so forth—just as the rays come down from the sun, or the rains from their source.[113] Then I will finish by reflecting on myself, as has been explained. I will conclude with a colloquy and an Our Father.

THREE METHODS OF PRAYING.[114]

THE FIRST METHOD.

This first manner of praying takes as its subject matter the ten commandments, the seven capital sins, the three faculties of the soul, and the five senses of the body.

This method of praying aims chiefly to give a manner of proceeding—a method along with exercises in it[115]—so that persons may become better able to profit from the exercises and to find their prayer a pleasing experience.[116] That is its aim rather than to give a new procedure or method of prayer.[117]

1. ON THE TEN COMMANDMENTS[118]

First of all, something should be done which is the equivalent of the Fifth Note[119] of the Second Week ([131]). That is, before entering into the prayer, I should briefly recollect myself in spirit, either seated or pacing to and fro, as I find better; and I should consider where I am going and for what. This same Additional Directive ([75, 131]) will be used for all three of these Methods of Praying ([250, 258]).

A Preparatory Prayer. For example, I will ask God our Lord that I may be able to know how I have failed against the ten commandments. Similarly I will ask for grace and aid to amend myself for the future. I will beg, too, for a complete understanding of the commandments, in order to keep them better for greater glory and praise of his Divine Majesty.

For the First Method of Praying, a suitable procedure for the first commandment is to consider and think over in what I have kept it and in what I have failed, measuring this reflection by the time required to recite three Our Fathers and three Hail Marys. If I discover my faults within this time, I will ask forgiveness and pardon for them and say an Our

Father. Then I will follow the same procedure with each of the ten commandments.

[242]   *First Note.* It should be observed that if one begins reflection on a commandment which he or she has no habit of violating, one need not dwell long on it. But if one considers a commandment which she or he breaks often, sometimes more and sometimes less, accordingly more or less time should be taken in considering and scrutinizing this commandment. The same procedure should be used with the capital sins.

[243]   *Second Note.* After finishing the examination of all the commandments in the manner described above, I should accuse myself accordingly and beg grace and help to amend myself for the future. Then I should finish with a colloquy, according to the subject matter.

[244]   ## 2. ON THE CAPITAL SINS

With regard to the seven capital sins,[120] after the Additional Directive ([75, 239]) has been changed in the manner described ([240]), the Preparatory Prayer should be made. The only change is that the subject matter here consists of the sins to be avoided, whereas there it was the commandments which should be observed. Likewise the same procedure and measuring of the time should be followed, and a colloquy made.

[245]   To know better the faults springing from the capital sins, one should consider their contrary virtues. Through this, to avoid the faults better a person should propose and strive by holy exercises to acquire and retain the seven virtues contrary to these sins.

[246]   ## 3. ON THE THREE POWERS OF THE SOUL

In regard to the three powers[121] of the soul, the same procedure and measuring of time should be observed as with the commandments, by following the additional directive ([239] and making the Preparatory Prayer and colloquy ([240–243]).

[247]   ## 4. ON THE FIVE SENSES OF THE BODY

In regard to the five senses of the body, the same procedure will always be observed, but the subject matter will be
changed to them.

[248]   *Note.* If I wish to imitate Christ our Lord in the use of
my five senses, I should commend myself to his Divine Majesty in the Preparatory Prayer, and after the consideration of
each sense, recite a Hail Mary and an Our Father.

If I wish to imitate Our Lady in the use of these senses, I
should commend myself to her in the Preparatory Prayer, and
ask her to obtain for me that grace from her Son. Then after
the consideration of each sense I should recite a Hail Mary.

[249]   ## THE SECOND METHOD OF PRAYING CONSISTS IN CONTEMPLATING THE MEANING OF EACH WORD OF A PRAYER.

[250]   *The Same Additional Directive* is followed as in the First
Method ([239]).

[251]   *The Preparatory Prayer* will be made in conformity with
the person to whom the prayer is addressed.

[252]   *The Second Method of Praying*[122] is practiced as follows.
One may sit or kneel accordingly as one feels better disposed
or finds greater devotion, but should keep the eyes closed or
intent on one place, and not allow them to wander. Then the
person should say the word *Father*, and continue to consider
the word as long as meanings, comparisons, relish, and consolations connected with it are found. The same procedure
should be continued with each word of the Our Father, or of
any other prayer which one wishes to use in this manner.

[253]   *First Rule.* The person will remain for an hour in this
manner of praying, going through the whole of the Our Father. At the end he or she should say a Hail Mary, Creed, Soul
of Christ, and Hail Holy Queen, vocally or mentally in the
customary way.

[254]   *Second Rule.* If the person who is contemplating finds in
one or two words matter which yields thought, relish, and
consolation, he or she ought not to be concerned to move

forward, even though the whole hour is consumed on what he finds. At the end, he will say the rest of the prayer in the customary manner.

[255] *Third Rule.* If one has dwelt for a full hour on one or two words of the Our Father, on another day when she or he wishes to return to the prayer, he should say the word or words in the customary manner. Then he should begin the contemplation on the word immediately following, and proceed according to what was stated in the second rule.

[256] *First Note.* It should be noted that if the Our Father has been finished in one or several days, one should use the same method with the Hail Mary and then with other prayers, in such a way that one is always engaged for a certain time on one of them.

[257] *Second Note.* When the prayer is finished, one should turn to the person to whom it is directed and ask for the virtues or graces for which greater need is felt.

[258] ## THE THIRD METHOD OF PRAYING IS TO PRAY ACCORDING TO RHYTHMIC MEASURES.

The Same Additional Directive will be followed as in the first and second methods of praying ([239, 250]).

The Preparatory Prayer will be the same as in the second method of praying ([251]).

In this Third Method of Praying, with each breath taken in or expelled, one should pray mentally, by saying a word of the Our Father, or of any other prayer which is recited. This is done in such a manner that one word of the prayer is said between one breath and another. In between these two breaths one reflects especially on the meaning of that word, or on the person to whom the prayer is being recited, or on one's own lowliness, or on the distance between that person's dignity and our lack of it. The same procedure and measure of time will be used on the words of the Our Father; and the other prayers—the Hail Mary, Soul of Christ, Creed, and Hail Holy Queen—will be recited in the usual manner.[123]

[259]   *First Rule.* When one wishes to pray again on another day or at another hour, one should say the Hail Mary according to the rhythmic measures, and the other prayers in the customary way. The same procedure may be used with the other prayers.

[260]   *Second Rule.* One who wishes to spend a longer time in this prayer according to rhythmic measures may use it with all the prayers mentioned above, or on some of them. The same order of rhythmic breathing explained in [258] should be used.

THE MYSTERIES OF THE LIFE
OF CHRIST OUR LORD

Note. In all the following mysteries,[124] all the words enclosed in quotation marks[125] are from the four Gospels, but not the other words. For each mystery, at least in most instances, three points are given, to make it easier to meditate and contemplate on them.

[THE INFANCY AND HIDDEN LIFE]

[262] ## THE ANNUNCIATION TO OUR LADY
St. Luke 1:26–38[126]

First Point.[127] The angel, St. Gabriel, greets Our Lady and announces to her the conception of Christ our Lord: "The angel entered the place where Mary was, greeted her, and said: 'Hail, full of grace. You will conceive in your womb and give birth to a Son.'"

Second Point. The angel confirms what he said to Our Lady by telling her about the conception of St. John the Baptist: "And behold your cousin Elizabeth, she also has conceived a son in her old age."

Third Point. Our Lady replied to the angel: "Behold the handmaid of the Lord. Be it done to me according to your word."

[263]

THE VISITATION OF OUR LADY
TO ELIZABETH
St. Luke 1:39–56

First Point. When Our Lady visited Elizabeth, St. John the Baptist, still in his mother's womb, perceived the visitation Our Lady made. "When Elizabeth heard the salutation of Mary, the infant leaped in her womb. And Elizabeth, filled with the Holy Ghost, cried out with a loud voice and said: 'Blessed are you among women, and blessed is the fruit of your womb.'"

Second point. Our Lady breaks into her canticle, exclaiming: "My soul magnifies the Lord!"

Third Point. "Mary abode with Elizabeth about three months; and then she returned to her own house."

[264]

THE NATIVITY OF CHRIST OUR LORD
St. Luke 2:1–14

First Point. Our Lady and her spouse St. Joseph journey from Nazareth to Bethlehem: "Joseph also went up from Galilee to Bethlehem, to express his obedience to Caesar, with Mary his espoused wife, who was with child."

Second Point. "And she brought forth her first-born Son, and wrapped him up in swaddling clothes, and laid him in a manger."

Third Point. "There was . . . a multitude of the heavenly army saying: 'Glory to God in the heavens.'"

[265]

THE SHEPHERDS
St. Luke 2:15–20

First Point. The birth of Christ is made known to the shepherds by an angel: "I bring you good news of great joy, for this day is born to you the Savior of the world."

Second Point. The shepherds go to Bethlehem: "They came with haste; and they found Mary and Joseph and the Infant lying in the manger."

Third Point. "The shepherds returned, glorifying and praising God."

[266]
THE CIRCUMCISION
St. Luke 2:21

First Point. They circumcised the child Jesus.

Second Point. "His name was called Jesus, which was called by the angel before he was conceived in the womb."

Third Point. They handed the child back to his mother, who felt compassion because of the blood that he shed.

[267]
THE THREE KINGS
St. Matthew 2:1–12

First Point. The three kings, guided by the star, came to adore Jesus, saying: "We have seen his star in the East, and have come to adore him."

Second Point. They adored him and offered him gifts: "Falling prostrate on the ground they adored him and offered him gifts: gold, frankincense, and myrrh."

Third Point. "Having received an answer in sleep that they should not return to Herod, they went back another way to their own country."

[268]
THE PURIFICATION OF OUR LADY AND
THE PRESENTATION OF THE INFANT JESUS
St. Luke 2:21–40

First Point. They carry the Infant Jesus to the temple, to present him as the first-born to the Lord, and they offer for him "a pair of turtledoves and two young pigeons."

Second Point. Simeon, coming to the temple, "took him into his arms" and said: "Now you dismiss your servant, O Lord, in peace."

Third Point. Afterward Anna, "coming in, confessed to the Lord and spoke of him to all who looked for the redemption of Israel."

[269]
THE FLIGHT INTO EGYPT
St. Matthew 2:13–18

First Point. Herod wanted to kill the Infant Jesus and therefore slew the Innocents. But before their death an angel warned Joseph to flee into Egypt: "Arise, and take the child and his mother, and flee into Egypt."

Second Point. He arose by night, and departed for Egypt.

Third Point. He remained there until the death of Herod.

[270]
HOW CHRIST OUR LORD RETURNED FROM EGYPT
St. Matthew 2:19-23

First Point. The angel tells Joseph to return to Israel: "Arise, and take the child and his mother, and go into the land of Israel."

Second Point. He arose and went into the land of Israel.

Third Point. Because Archelaus, son of Herod, was reigning in Judaea, he retired to Nazareth.

[271]
THE LIFE OF CHRIST OUR LORD FROM THE AGE OF TWELVE TO THIRTY
St. Luke 2:50-52

First Point. He was obedient to his parents, and "Jesus advanced in wisdom, and age, and grace."

Second Point. It seems that he practiced the trade of carpenter, as St. Mark seems to indicate (6:3): "Is not this the carpenter?"

[272]
CHRIST'S VISIT TO THE TEMPLE AT THE AGE OF TWELVE
St. Luke 2:41-50

First Point. Christ our Lord at the age of twelve went up from Nazareth to Jerusalem.

Second Point. Christ our Lord remained in Jerusalem, and his parents did not know it.

Third Point. After three days, they found him seated among the doctors and conversing with them. When his parents asked him where he had been, he replied: "Did you not know that I must be about my Father's business?"

[THE PUBLIC LIFE]

[273]
HOW CHRIST WAS BAPTIZED
St. Matthew 3:13-17

First Point. Christ our Lord, after his farewell to his Blessed Mother, came from Nazareth to the river Jordan, where St. John the Baptist was.

Second Point. St. John baptized Christ our Lord; and when he sought to excuse himself because he thought himself unworthy to baptize him, Christ said to him: "Allow it now, for thus it is fitting for us to fulfill all justice."

Third Point. The Holy Ghost descended upon him, and the voice of the Father came from heaven and testified: "This is my Beloved Son, in whom I am well pleased."

[274]
HOW CHRIST WAS TEMPTED
St. Luke 4:1-13; St. Matthew 4:1-11

First Point. After he had been baptized, he went into the desert, where he fasted forty days and forty nights.

Second Point. He was tempted by the enemy three times. "The tempter came to him and said: 'If you are the Son of God, command that these stones be made bread. Cast yourself down from here. I will give you all these kingdoms if you will adore me.' "

Third Point. "Angels came and ministered to him."

[275]
THE CALLING OF THE APOSTLES

First Point. It seems that St. Peter and St. Andrew were called three times; first, to some knowledge, as is evident from St. John (1:35-42); second, to follow Christ to some extent, but with an intention to return to the possession of what they had left behind, as St. Luke tells us (5:1-11); third, to follow Christ our Lord forever (Matt. 4:18-30; Mark 1:16-18).

Second Point. He called Philip (John 1:43), and Matthew, as St. Matthew himself tells us (9:9).

Third Point. He called the other Apostles, although the Gospels do not mention the particular instances.

Three other things too should be considered: first, how they came from a rude and lowly type of living; second, the dignity to which they were so gently called; and third, the gifts and graces by which they were raised above all the Fathers of the New Testament and the Old.

[276]
THE FIRST MIRACLE, WORKED AT THE MARRIAGE FEAST IN CANA OF GALILEE
St. John 2:1–12

First Point. Christ our Lord was invited with his disciples to the wedding feast.

Second Point. His Mother points out to her Son the shortage of the wine: "They have no wine." Then she orders the waiters, "Do whatever he tells you to do."

Third Point. "He changed the water into wine, and he manifested his glory, and his disciples believed in him."

[277]
HOW CHRIST OUR LORD CAST THE SELLERS OUT OF THE TEMPLE
St. John 2:13–25

First Point. He drove all the sellers out of the Temple with a whip made of cords.

Second Point. He overturned the tables and spilled the money of the rich money-changers who were in the Temple.

Third Point. To the poor people who sold doves, he gently said: "Take these things hence, and do not make my Father's house a marketplace."

[278]
THE SERMON ON THE MOUNT
St. Matthew 5:1–48

First Point. To his beloved disciples he speaks apart about the eight beatitudes: "Blessed are the poor in spirit, the meek, the merciful, they who mourn, those who hunger and thirst for justice, the clean of heart, the peacemakers, and those who suffer persecution."

Second Point. He exhorts them to make good use of their talents: "So let your light shine before men that they may see your good works and glorify your Father who is in heaven."

Third Point. He shows that he is not a transgressor of the Law, but the one who has come to fulfill it, by explaining the precepts: Do not kill, or commit adultery, or swear falsely; and love your enemies: "I say to you, 'Love your enemies, do good to them who hate you.' "

[279]

HOW CHRIST OUR LORD CALMED THE STORM
St. Matthew 8:23–27

First Point. While Christ our Lord was on the lake, asleep, a great tempest arose.

Second Point. His frightened disciples awaken him; and he reprehends them for their little faith: "Why are you afraid, O you of little faith?"

Third Point. He commanded the winds and the sea to cease, and the sea grew calm. The disciples marveled at this, and asked: "What sort of man is this, for even the winds and the sea obey him?"

[280]

HOW CHRIST WALKED ON THE WATERS
St. Matthew 14:22–33

First Point. While Christ our Lord remained on the mountain, he ordered his disciples to go before him in the little boat. Then he dismissed the multitude and began to pray alone.

Second Point. The little boat was tossed by the waves. Christ came toward it, walking on the waters; and the disciples thought they saw a ghost.

Third Point. Christ said to them, "It is I, do not fear." At his command St. Peter came to him, walking on the water. He doubted, and began to sink. But Christ our Lord saved him, and reprehended him for his little faith. Then he entered into the boat and the wind ceased.

[281]

HOW THE APOSTLES WERE SENT
TO PREACH
St. Matthew 10:1-15

First Point. Christ calls his beloved disciples, and gives them power to drive devils out of human bodies and to heal all kinds of infirmities.

Second Point. He teaches them about prudence and patience: "Behold I am sending you like sheep in the midst of wolves. Therefore be shrewd as serpents and simple as doves."

Third Point. He tells them how they are to go: "Do not seek to possess gold or silver; freely have you received, freely give." And he gave them the matter to preach: "Go and preach, saying, 'The kingdom of heaven is at hand.'"

[282]

THE CONVERSION OF MAGDALEN
St. Luke 7:36-50

First Point. Magdalen enters where Christ our Lord is seated at table in the house of the Pharisee. She was bringing an alabaster jar full of ointment.

Second Point. Staying behind the Lord at his feet, she began to wash them with her tears, and to wipe them with the hair of her head. She kissed his feet, and anointed them with ointment.

Third Point. When the Pharisee accuses Magdalen, Christ speaks in her defense: "Many sins are forgiven her, because she has loved much." And he said to the woman: "Your faith has made you safe, go in peace."

[283]

HOW CHRIST OUR LORD FED FIVE
THOUSAND PERSONS
St. Matthew 14:13-21

First Point. When evening was near, the disciples ask Christ to dismiss the multitude of those who are with him.

Second Point. Christ our Lord commanded the disciples to bring him some loaves, and ordered the crowd to sit down. He blessed and broke the loaves and gave them to his disciples, and the disciples gave them to the multitude.

Third Point. They ate and were filled, and they took up what remained, twelve full baskets.

[284]

THE TRANSFIGURATION OF CHRIST
St. Matthew 17:1–13

First Point. Christ our Lord took his beloved disciples Peter, James, and John and was transfigured, and his face shone like the sun, and his garments became white as snow.
Second Point. He conversed with Moses and Elijah.
Third Point. When St. Peter proposed that they should make three tents, a voice sounded from heaven, saying: "This is my beloved Son; listen to him." His disciples heard this voice and fell on their faces through fear, and Christ our Lord touched them and said to them, "Arise and do not be afraid. Do not tell the vision to anyone until the Son of Man is risen from the dead."

[285]

THE RESURRECTION OF LAZARUS
St. John 11:1–44

First Point. Martha and Mary inform Christ our Lord about the illness of Lazarus. After he heard this news he remained where he was for two days, to make the miracle more evident.
Second Point. Before raising him he asks the two sisters to believe, saying: "I am the resurrection and the life; whoever believes in me, even if he dies, will live."
Third Point. He raises him, after he has wept and prayed; and the manner in which he raised him was by his command: "Lazarus, come forth."

[286]

THE SUPPER IN BETHANY
St. Matthew 26:1–13

First Point. Our Lord eats supper in the house of Simon the leper, together with Lazarus.
Second Point. Mary pours the perfumed oil on the head of Christ.
Third Point. Judas murmurs, saying, "To what purpose is this waste of perfumed oil?" But he again excuses Magda-

len, with the words: "Why do you trouble this woman? For she has done a good thing for me."

[287]
PALM SUNDAY
St. Matthew 21:1–11

First Point. Our Lord sends for the ass and the colt, saying, "Untie them, and bring them here to me; and if anyone should say anything to you, reply, 'The master has need of them.' Then he will let them go."

Second Point. He mounted the ass, which was covered with the cloaks of the Apostles.

Third Point. The people come out to meet him, and spread their cloaks and branches of trees on the road, and shout: "Hosanna to the Son of David! Blessed is he who comes in the name of the Lord. Hosanna in the highest!"

[288]
CHRIST'S PREACHING IN THE TEMPLE
St. Luke Chapter 19; also 21:37–38

First Point. During each day he was teaching in the temple.

Second Point. When he had finished preaching, since there was no one to receive him in Jerusalem, he returned to Bethany.

[THE PASSION]

THE SUPPER

[289]
St. Matthew 26:17–30; St. John 13:1–17

First Point. He ate the paschal lamb with his twelve Apostles, and he foretold his death to them: "Amen, I say to you that one of you will betray me."

Second Point. He washed his disciples' feet, even those of Judas. He began with St. Peter; and Peter, thinking of the

Lord's majesty and his own lowliness, was reluctant to consent. "Lord," he asked, "are you going to wash my feet?" But Peter failed to understand that the Lord was giving an example of humility, and therefore the Lord said: "I have given you an example, so that as I have done, so you also should do."

Third Point. He instituted the most holy sacrifice of the Eucharist, as the greatest sign of his love. "Take and eat," he told them. When the supper was finished, Judas went out to sell Christ our Lord.

[290]   ## THE MYSTERIES ENACTED FROM THE SUPPER TO THE GARDEN, INCLUSIVELY
St. Matthew 26:30–46; St. Luke 22:39–46;
St. Mark 14:26–42

First Point. Our Lord, after finishing the supper and singing a hymn, went to Mount Olivet with his disciples, who were full of fear. He left eight of them in Gethsemane, and said, "Sit here while I go over there and pray."

Second Point. Accompanied by St. Peter, St. James, and St. John, he prayed three times to the Lord, saying, "My Father, if it is possible, let this cup pass from me; yet, not as I will, but as you will." And being in agony, he prayed the longer.

Third Point. He came to a fear so great that he said, "My soul is sorrowful even unto death," and he sweated blood so copiously that St. Luke says: "His sweat became like drops of blood falling on the ground." This supposes that his clothes were already full of blood.

[291]   ## THE MYSTERIES ENACTED FROM THE GARDEN TO THE HOUSE OF ANNAS, INCLUSIVELY
St. Matthew 26:47–56; St. Luke 22:47–53;
St. Mark 14:42–53; St. John 18:1–22

First Point. Our Lord allowed himself to be kissed by Judas, and to be arrested like a thief by the crowd, to whom he said, "You have come out as against a robber with swords and clubs to seize me. Day after day I was teaching in the temple, and you did not arrest me." And when he asked, "Whom are you seeking?" his enemies fell to the ground.

Second Point. St. Peter wounded a servant of the high priest; and the meek Lord said to him, "Put your sword back into its sheath." Then he healed the servant's wound.

Third Point. Abandoned by his disciples, he is dragged before Annas, where St. Peter, who had followed him from afar, denied him once, and a blow was given to Christ by a servant who said to him, "Is this the way you answer the high priest?"

[292]

THE MYSTERIES FROM THE HOUSE OF ANNAS TO THE HOUSE OF CAIAPHAS, INCLUSIVELY
St. Matthew 26:57–68; St. Mark 14:53–72; St. Luke 22:54–62; St. John 18:24–27

First Point. They take him bound from the house of Annas to that of Caiaphas, where St. Peter denied him twice. When our Lord looked at him, he went out and wept bitterly.

Second Point. Jesus remained bound all that night.

Third Point. Besides this, those who held him prisoner mocked him, struck him, blindfolded him, and slapped him, and asked him: "Prophesy for us: Who it is that struck you?" They also uttered similar blasphemies against him.

[293]

FROM THE HOUSE OF CAIAPHAS TO THAT OF PILATE, INCLUSIVELY
St. Matthew 27:1–27; St. Luke 23:1–5; St. Mark 15:1–16

First Point. The whole multitude of the Jews bring Christ to Pilate, and before him they accuse him, saying: "We have found this man misleading our people. He forbids payment of taxes to Caesar."

Second Point. Pilate, after having examined him again and again, says, "I find no guilt in him."

Third Point. Barabbas the robber was preferred before him. "They cried: 'Not this man, but Barabbas.' "

[294]

FROM THE HOUSE OF PILATE
TO THAT OF HEROD
St. Luke 23:6–12

First Point. Pilate sent Jesus the Galilean to Herod, the tetrarch of Galilee.

Second Point. Through curiosity Herod questioned him at length, but he gave him no answer. Meanwhile the scribes and priests unceasingly accused him.

Third Point. Herod and his soldiers mocked him and clothed him in a white garment.

[295]

FROM THE HOUSE OF HEROD
TO THAT OF PILATE
St. Matthew 26:21–30; St. Luke 23:11–23;
St. Mark 15:15–19; St. John 19:1–11

First Point. Herod sends him back to Pilate, and because of this they become friends, although previously they had been enemies.

Second Point. Pilate took Jesus, and scourged him. Then the soldiers wove a crown out of thorns, and placed it on his head, and they clothed him in a purple cloak; and they came before him and said, "Hail, king of the Jews!" And they struck him repeatedly.

Third Point. Pilate brought him out into the presence of all. So Jesus came out, wearing the crown of thorns and the purple cloak, and Pilate said to them: "Behold, the Man." When the priests saw him, they cried out: "Crucify, crucify him!"

[296]

FROM THE HOUSE OF PILATE TO THE
CROSS, INCLUSIVELY
St. John 19:13–22

First Point. Pilate, seated like a judge, handed Jesus over to be crucified, after the Jews had denied him as their king: "We have no king but Caesar."

Second Point. He carried the cross on his shoulders, and as he could not carry it, Simon of Cyrene was compelled to carry it behind Jesus.

Third Point. They crucified him in the middle between two thieves, and placed this title above him: "Jesus of Nazareth, the King of the Jews."

[297]
THE MYSTERIES ON THE CROSS
St. John 19:23–37

First Point. He spoke seven words on the cross: He prayed for those who were crucifying him; he forgave the thief; he commended St. John to his mother and his mother to St. John; he said with a loud voice, "I thirst," and they gave him gall and vinegar; he said that he was forsaken; he said, "It is finished"; he said, "Father, into your hands I commend my spirit."

Second Point. The sun was darkened, the rocks were split, the tombs were opened, the veil of the temple was torn in two from top to bottom.

Third Point. They blaspheme him, saying, "You who would destroy the temple of God, come down from the cross." His garments were divided. His side was pierced by the lance, and water and blood flowed out.

[298]
THE MYSTERIES FROM THE CROSS TO THE SEPULCHER, INCLUSIVELY
St. John 19:38–42

First Point. He was taken down from the cross by Joseph and Nicodemus in the presence of his sorrowful Mother.

Second Point. His body was carried to the tomb, anointed, and buried.

Third Point. Guards were stationed.

[THE RISEN LIFE]

[299] THE RESURRECTION OF CHRIST OUR LORD, AND HIS FIRST APPARITION

First Point. He appeared to the Virgin Mary. Although this is not stated in Scripture, still it is considered as understood by the statement that he appeared to many others. For Scripture supposes that we have understanding, as it is written: "Are even you without understanding?" [Matt. 15:16].

[300] THE SECOND APPARITION
St. Mark 16:1–11

First Point. Very early in the morning Mary Magdalen, Mary the mother of James, and Salome go to the tomb, saying: "Who will roll back the stone for us from the entrance to the tomb?"

Second Point. They see the stone rolled back, and the angel, who says, "You seek Jesus of Nazareth. He is already risen; he is not here."

Third Point. He appeared to Mary, who remained near the tomb after the other women had departed.

[301] THE THIRD APPARITION
St. Matthew 28:8–10

First Point. These Marys went away from the tomb with fear and great joy, eager to announce the Resurrection of the Lord to the disciples.

Second Point. Christ our Lord appeared to them on the way, and greeted them: "Hail to you." They approached, placed themselves at his feet, and adored him.

Third Point. Jesus says to them, "Do not be afraid. Go, tell my brothers to go into Galilee, and there they will see me."

[302]
THE FOURTH APPARITION
St. Luke 24:9–12, 33–34; St. John 20:1–10

First Point. When St. Peter had heard from the women that Christ had risen, he got up and ran to the tomb.

Second Point. Entering the tomb, he saw only the burial cloths with which the body of Christ our Lord had been covered, and nothing else.

Third Point. While St. Peter was thinking on these things, Christ appeared to him. Because of this the Apostles said, "The Lord is truly risen and has appeared to Simon."

[303]
THE FIFTH APPARITION
St. Luke 24:13–35

First Point. He appears to the disciples, who were going to Emmaus, and were conversing about Christ.

Second Point. He upbraids them, showing from the Scriptures that Christ had to die and to rise again: "Oh, how foolish you are and slow of heart to believe all the things which the prophets have spoken. Was it not necessary that Christ should suffer these things and thus enter into his glory?"

Third Point. At their urging he remained there and was with them until he gave them Communion and then disappeared. They returned and told the disciples how they had recognized him in the Communion.

[304]
THE SIXTH APPARITION
St. John 20:19–23

First Point. The disciples, except St. Thomas, were assembled, "through fear of the Jews."

Second Point. Jesus appeared to them when the doors were locked. He stood in their midst and said: "Peace be with you."

Third Point. He gives them the Holy Spirit, saying to them: "Receive the Holy Spirit; whose sins you forgive are forgiven them."

THE SEVENTH APPARITION
St. John 20:24–29

[305]

First Point. St. Thomas, unbelieving because he was absent from the preceding apparition, says: "Unless I see, I will not believe."

Second Point. Eight days after that Jesus appears to them, although the doors are locked, and he says to St. Thomas, "Put your finger here and see the truth, and do not be unbelieving, but believe."

Third Point. St. Thomas believed, and said: "My Lord and my God." Christ says to him: "Blessed are those who have not seen and have believed."

THE EIGHTH APPARITION
St. John 21:1–17

[306]

First Point. Jesus reveals himself to seven of his disciples who were fishing, after they had caught nothing during the whole night. They cast forth the net at his bidding, and "were unable to pull it in because of the number of the fish."

Second Point. Through this miracle St. John recognized him and said to St. Peter: "It is the Lord." Thereupon St. Peter jumped into the sea, and came to Christ.

Third Point. He gave them part of a roasted fish and a honeycomb to eat. He asked St. Peter three times about his love for him, and then he entrusted his sheep to him: "Feed my sheep."

THE NINTH APPARITION
St. Matthew 28:16–20

[307]

First Point. At the command of the Lord the disciples go to Mt. Tabor.

Second Point. Christ appears to them, and says: "All power in heaven and on earth has been given to me."

Third Point. He sent them to preach throughout the whole world, saying: "Go, therefore, and teach all nations, baptizing them in the name of the Father and of the Son and of the Holy Spirit."

[308]
THE TENTH APPARITION
1 Corinthians 15:6

"After that he appeared to more than five hundred brethren at once."

[309]
THE ELEVENTH APPARITION
1 Corinthians 15:7

After that he appeared to James.

[310]
THE TWELFTH APPARITION

He appeared to Joseph of Arimathea, as may be piously meditated, and as we read in the Lives of the Saints.

[311]
THE THIRTEENTH APPARITION
1 Corinthians 15:8

After his ascension he appeared to St. Paul: "Last of all, as to one born out of due time." He appeared also in his soul to the holy fathers in limbo; and after he had freed them, and taken up his body again, he appeared to the disciples on many occasions, and discoursed with them.

[312]
THE ASCENSION OF CHRIST OUR LORD
Acts 1:1–12

First Point. After Christ our Lord had manifested himself for forty days to the Apostles, giving many proofs and signs and speaking about the Kingdom of God, he commanded them to wait in Jerusalem for the Holy Spirit who had been promised them.

Second Point. He led them out to Mt. Olivet, and in their presence he was lifted up, and a cloud took him from their sight.

Third Point. While they are looking up to heaven the angels say to them, "Men of Galilee, why are you standing there looking up at the sky? This Jesus who has been taken up from you into heaven will return in the same way as you have seen him going into heaven."[128]

[RULES FOR THE DISCERNMENT OF SPIRITS.¹²⁹]

[313]   RULES TO AID US TOWARD PERCEIVING
AND THEN UNDERSTANDING,¹³⁰ AT LEAST
TO SOME EXTENT, THE VARIOUS
MOTIONS¹³¹ WHICH ARE CAUSED¹³² IN THE
SOUL¹³³: THE GOOD MOTIONS THAT THEY
MAY BE RECEIVED, AND THE BAD THAT
THEY MAY BE REJECTED.
These rules are more suitable to the First Week.¹³⁴

[314]   *The First Rule.* In the case of persons who are going
from one mortal sin to another, the enemy ordinarily proposes to them apparent pleasures. He makes them imagine
delights and pleasures of the senses, in order to hold them fast
and plunge them deeper in their sins and vices.

But with persons of this type the good spirit uses a
contrary procedure. Through their habitual sound judgment
on problems of morality¹³⁵ he stings their consciences with
remorse.

[315]   *The Second.* In the case of persons who are earnestly
purging away their sins, and who are progressing from good
to better in the service of God our Lord, the procedure used
is the opposite of that described in the First Rule. For in this
case it is characteristic of the evil spirit to cause gnawing
anxiety, to sadden, and to set up obstacles. In this way he
unsettles them by false reasons aimed at preventing their
progress.

But with persons of this type it is characteristic of the
good spirit to stir up courage and strength, consolations,
tears, inspirations, and tranquility. He makes things easier
and eliminates all obstacles, so that the persons may move
forward in doing good.

[316]   *The Third*, about spiritual consolation.[136] By [this kind of] consolation I mean that which occurs when some interior motion is caused within the soul through which it comes to be inflamed with love[137] of its Creator and Lord. As a result it can love no created thing on the face of the earth in itself, but only in the Creator of them all.

Similarly, this consolation is experienced when the soul sheds tears which move it to love for its Lord—whether they are tears of grief for its own sins, or about the Passion of Christ our Lord, or about other matters directly ordered to his service and praise.

Finally, under the word consolation I include every increase in hope, faith, and charity, and every interior joy which calls and attracts one toward heavenly things and to the salvation of one's soul, by bringing it tranquility and peace in its Creator and Lord.

[317]   *The Fourth*, about spiritual desolation.[138] By [this kind of] desolation I mean everything which is the contrary of what was described in the Third Rule; for example, darkness of soul, turmoil within it, an impulsive motion toward low and earthly things, or disquiet from various agitations and temptations. These move one toward lack of faith and leave one without hope and without love. One is completely listless, tepid, and unhappy, and feels separated from our Creator and Lord.

For just as consolation is contrary to desolation, so too the thoughts which arise from consolation are likewise contrary to those which spring from desolation.

[318]   *The Fifth*. During a time of desolation one should never make a change. Instead, one should remain firm and constant in the proposals and in a decision in which one was on the day before the desolation, or in a decision in which one was during a previous time of consolation.

For just as the good spirit is chiefly the one who guides and counsels us in time of consolation, so it is the evil spirit who does this in time of desolation. By following his counsels we can never find the way to a right decision.

[319]   *The Sixth*. It is taken for granted that in time of desolation we ought not to change our former plans. But it is very helpful to make vigorous changes in ourselves as counterat-

tack against the desolation, for example, by insisting more on prayer, meditation, earnest self-examination, and some suitable way of doing penance.

[320]   *The Seventh.* When we are in desolation we should think that the Lord has left us in order to test us, by leaving us to our own natural powers so that we may prove ourselves by resisting the various agitations and temptations of the enemy. For we can do this with God's help, which always remains available, even if we do not clearly perceive it. Indeed, even though the Lord has withdrawn from us his abundant fervor, augmented love, and intensive grace, he still supplies sufficient grace for our eternal salvation.

[321]   *The Eighth.* One who is in desolation should strive to preserve himself or herself in patience. This is the counterattack against the vexations which are being experienced. One should remember that after a while the consolation will return again, through the diligent efforts against the desolation which were indicated in the Sixth Rule.

[322]   *The Ninth.* There are three main reasons for the desolation we experience.

The first is that we ourselves are tepid, lazy, or negligent in our spiritual exercises. Thus the spiritual consolation leaves us because of our own faults.

The second reason is that the desolation serves to test how much we are worth, that is, how far we will go in the service and praise of God, even without much compensation by way of consolations and increased graces.

The third reason is to give us a true recognition and understanding, in order to make us perceive interiorly that we cannot by ourselves bring on or retain increased devotion, intense love, tears, or any other spiritual consolation; and further, that all these are a gift and grace from God our Lord; and still further, that they are granted to keep us from building our nest in a house which belongs to Another, by puffing up our minds with pride or vainglory through which we attribute the devotion or other features of spiritual consolation to ourselves.

[323]   *The Tenth.* One who is in consolation should consider how he or she will act in future desolation, and store up new strength for that time.

[324]   *The Eleventh.* One who is in consolation ought to humble and abase himself or herself as much as possible, and reflect how little he is worth in time of desolation when that grace or consolation is absent.

In contrast, one who is in desolation should reflect that with the sufficient grace already available he or she can do much to resist all hostile forces, by drawing strength from our Creator and Lord.

[325]   *The Twelfth.* The enemy conducts himself like a woman. He is weak against physical strength but strong when confronted by weakness.[139]

When she is quarreling with a man and he shows himself bold and unyielding, she characteristically loses her spirit and goes away. But if the man begins to lose his spirit and backs away, the woman's anger, vindictiveness, and ferocity swell almost without limit.

In the same way, the enemy characteristically weakens, loses courage, and flees with his temptations when the person engaged in spiritual endeavors stands bold and unyielding against the enemy's temptations and goes diametrically against them. But if, in contrast, that person begins to fear and lose courage in the face of the temptations, there is no beast on the face of the earth as fierce as the enemy of human nature when he is pursuing his damnable intention with his surging malice.

[326]   *The Thirteenth.* Similarly the enemy acts like a false lover, insofar as he tries to remain secret and undetected. For such a scoundrel, speaking with evil intent and trying to seduce the daughter of a good father or the wife of a good husband, wants his words and solicitations to remain secret. But he is deeply displeased when the daughter reveals his deceitful words and evil design to her father, or the wife to her husband. For he easily infers that he cannot succeed in the design he began.

In a similar manner, when the enemy of human nature turns his wiles and persuasions upon an upright person, he intends and desires them to be received and kept in secrecy. But when the person reveals them to his or her good confessor or some other spiritual person who understands the enemy's deceits and malice, he is grievously disappointed. For he quickly sees that he cannot succeed in the malicious project he began, because his manifest deceptions have been detected.

[327]   *The Fourteenth.* To use still another comparison, the enemy acts like a military commander who is attempting to conquer and plunder his objective. The captain and leader of an army on campaign sets up his camp, studies the strength and structure of a fortress, and then attacks at its weakest point.

In the same way, the enemy of human nature prowls around and from every side probes all our theological, cardinal, and moral virtues. Then at the point where he finds us weakest and most in need in regard to our eternal salvation, there he attacks and tries to take us.

[RULES FOR THE SECOND WEEK[140]]

[328]   ## RULES FOR THE SAME PURPOSE, WITH A MORE PROBING DISCERNMENT OF SPIRITS.
These rules are more suitable for the Second Week.[141]

[329]   *The First Rule.* It is characteristic of God and his angels, by the motions they cause, to give genuine happiness and spiritual joy, and thereby to banish any sadness and turmoil induced by the enemy.

It is characteristic of the enemy to fight against this happiness and spiritual consolation, by using specious reasonings, subtleties, and persistent deceits.

[330]   *The Second.* Only God our Lord can give the soul consolation without a preceding cause. For it is the prerogative of the Creator alone to enter the soul, depart from it, and cause a motion in it which draws the person wholly into love of his Divine Majesty. By "without [a preceding] cause" I

mean without any previous perception or understanding of some object by means of which the consolation just mentioned might have been stimulated, through the intermediate activity of the person's acts of understanding and willing.[142]

[331]   *The Third.* With or by means of a preceding cause,[143] both the good angel and the evil angel are able to cause consolation in the soul, but for their contrary purposes. The good angel acts for the progress of the soul, that it may grow and rise from what is good to what is better. The evil angel works for the contrary purpose, that is, to entice the soul to his own damnable intention and malice.

[332]   *The Fourth.* It is characteristic of the evil angel, who takes on the appearance of an angel of light, to enter by going along with the devout soul and then to come out by his own way with success for himself. That is, he brings good and holy thoughts attractive to such an upright person and then strives little by little to get his own way, by enticing the soul over to his own hidden deceits and evil intentions.

[333]   *The Fifth.* We should pay close attention to the whole train of our thoughts. If the beginning, middle, and end are all good and tend to what is wholly good, it is a sign of the good angel. But if the train of the thoughts which a spirit causes ends up in something evil or diverting, or in something less good than what the soul was originally proposing to do; or further, if it weakens, disquiets, or disturbs the soul, by robbing it of the peace, tranquility, and quiet which it enjoyed earlier, all this is a clear sign that it comes from the evil spirit, the enemy of our progress and eternal salvation.

[334]   *The Sixth.* When the enemy of human nature has been perceived and recognized by his serpent's tail and the evil end to which he is leading, a new procedure becomes profitable for the person who was tempted in this way. He or she should examine immediately the whole train of the good thoughts which the evil spirit brought to the soul, including their beginning, and then how little by little the evil spirit endeavored to bring the soul down from the sweetness and spiritual joy in which it had been, and finally brought it to his evil intention. Thus the person, by understanding this experience and taking note of it, can be on guard in the future against these characteristic snares.

[335]   *The Seventh.* In the case of those going from good to better, the good angel touches the soul gently, lightly, and sweetly, like a drop of water going into a sponge. The evil spirit touches it sharply, with noise and disturbance, like a drop of water falling onto a stone.

In the case of those who are going from bad to worse, these spirits touch the souls in the opposite way. The reason for this is the fact that the disposition of the soul is either similar to or different from the respective spirits who are entering. When the soul is different, they enter with perceptible noise and are quickly noticed. When the soul is similar, they enter silently, like those who go into their own house by an open door.

[336]   *The Eighth.* When the consolation is without a preceding cause, no deception can be present in it, since it is coming only from God our Lord, as was stated above ([330]). However, the spiritual person to whom God gives this consolation ought with great vigilance and attention to examine his or her experience and to distinguish the time when the consolation itself was present from the time after it, in which the soul remains still warm and favored with the gifts and aftereffects of the consolation which has itself passed away. For very often during this later period the person, through either his or her own reasoning which springs from one's own habits and from conclusions reached by one's own concepts and judgments, or through the influence of either an angel or a devil, forms various proposals and convictions which are not coming immediately from God our Lord. Hence these need to be very carefully examined before they are fully accepted or carried into effect.[144]

[337]   **IN THE MINISTRY OF DISTRIBUTING ALMS[145] THE FOLLOWING RULES OUGHT TO BE FOLLOWED.**

[338]   If I make the distribution to my relatives or friends or persons for whom I feel affection, there are four things which I ought to observe. They have been treated in part above ([184–187]) in the matters on which an election is made.

The First Rule. That love which moves me and brings me

to give the alms should descend from above, from the love of God our Lord, in such a way that I perceive beforehand that the love, whether greater or less, which I have for the persons is for God, and that God may shine forth in the reason for which I have a preferential love for these persons.

[339]   *The Second.* I will imagine a person whom I have never seen or known. Desiring all perfection for him or her in his ministry and state of life, I will consider how I would wish him to hold to a good mean in his manner of distributing alms, for the greater glory of God and the perfection of his soul. Then I, acting in the same way, neither more nor less, will keep the rule and norm which I would desire and judge proper for this other person.

[340]   *The Third.* I will consider, as if I were at the point of death, what procedure and norm I will at that time wish I had used in the duty of my administration. Then, guiding myself by that norm, I will apply it in the acts of my distribution.

[341]   *The Fourth.* Imagining how I will find myself on judgment day, I will think well how at that time I will wish that I had carried out this office and duty of my ministry. The rule which I will then wish I had used is what I will follow now.

[342]   *The Fifth.* When I perceive myself inclined and affectionately attached to others to whom I want to distribute alms, I should delay and think over the four rules mentioned above in [184-187]. I should examine and test my affection by means of them, and not give the alms until, in conformity with those rules, the inordinate affection has been completely removed and banished.

[343]   *The Sixth.* There is clearly no fault in accepting the goods[146] of God our Lord in order to distribute them, when one has been called by our God and Lord to that ministry of distributing alms. However, there is place for doubt about culpability and excess in regard to the amount one takes and applies to oneself from what one holds for distribution to others. Hence one can reform one's way of living in his state, by means of the rules mentioned above ([338-342]).

[344]   *The Seventh.* For the reasons already mentioned and many others, in regard to our own persons and household arrangements it is always better and safer to curtail and re-

duce our expenses. The more we do this, the more do we draw near to our high priest, model, and rule, who is Christ our Lord. In conformity with this the Third Council of Carthage (at which St. Augustine was present) decided and ordered that the furniture of the bishops should be inexpensive and poor.

The same consideration should be applied to all the styles of living, in accordance with the person's condition and state. For example, in that of marriage we have Sts. Joachim and Anne. They divided their possessions into three parts, gave the first to the poor, the second to the ministry and service of the Temple, and kept the third for their own support and that of their family.[147]

[345] ## TOWARD PERCEIVING AND UNDERSTANDING SCRUPLES AND THE ENTICEMENTS OF OUR ENEMY THE FOLLOWING NOTES[148] ARE HELPFUL.

[346] *The First Note.* People commonly apply the word scruple to something which comes from our own judgment and free will, for example, when I take something that is not sinful and freely build it up into a sin. This happens, for example, if someone accidentally steps on a cross made by straws and afterward forms the judgment that he or she has sinned. This, strictly speaking, is an erroneous judgment and not a scruple in the proper sense of the term.

[347] *The Second Note.* After I have stepped on that cross, or after I have thought or said or done something else similar, there comes to me from without the thought that I have sinned; but on the other hand I think I have not sinned. However, in all this I feel disturbed, that is, at one moment I doubt and at another I do not. This is a scruple in the proper sense of the term, and a temptation brought on by the enemy.

[348] *The Third Note.* The first scruple, that described in the first note, should be strongly abhorred, since it is totally error. But the second, described in the second note, can for a limited period of time be profitable to a person performing spiritual exercises. For it greatly purifies and cleanses a soul,

and separates it far from every semblance of sin, in accordance with Gregory's maxim: "It is characteristic of good souls to see a fault where none exists."[149]

[349]   *The Fourth Note.* The enemy considers attentively whether one has a lax or a delicate conscience. If a conscience is delicate, the enemy strives the harder to make it delicate even to an extreme, in order to trouble it more and eventually thwart it.

For example, if he sees that a person does not consent to any sin, whether mortal or venial or even merely an appearance of deliberate sin, since he cannot make the person fall into what even appears sinful, he brings him or her to judge as sinful something in which no sin exists; for example, in some unimportant word or thought.

But if a person has a lax conscience, the enemy works to make it still more lax. For example, if a soul makes little or nothing of venial sins, he tries to bring it to similar unconcern about mortal sins; and if previously it did have some concern about them, he now tries to make the concern less or to banish it.

[350]   *The Fifth Note.* A person who desires to make progress in the spiritual life ought always to proceed in a manner contrary to that of the enemy. In other words, if the enemy seeks to make a soul lax, it should try to make itself more sensitive. In the same way, if the enemy seeks to make a soul too sensitive, in order to entice it to an extreme, the soul should endeavor to establish itself staunchly in a correct mean and thus arrive at complete peace.

[351]   *The Sixth Note.* Sometimes a good soul of this type wishes to say or do something which, in conformity with the Church or the mind of our superiors, contributes to the glory of God our Lord. But it gets a thought or temptation from without not to say or do it. Specious reasons of vainglory or other similar things are brought up. In such a case we ought to raise our minds to our Creator and Lord; and if we see that it is for his due service, or at least not opposed to it, we ought to act diametrically against the temptation. We should reply as St. Bernard: "I did not begin because of you, and neither will I desist for you."[150]

[352] **[RULES[151] FOR THINKING, JUDGING, AND FEELING WITH THE CHURCH.[152]] TO HAVE THE GENUINE ATTITUDE[153] WHICH WE OUGHT TO MAINTAIN IN THE CHURCH MILITANT,[154] WE SHOULD OBSERVE THE FOLLOWING RULES.**

[353]   *The First Rule.* With all judgment of our own put aside, we ought to keep our minds disposed and ready to be obedient in everything to the true Spouse of Christ our Lord, which is our Holy Mother the hierarchical Church.[155]

[354]   *The Second.*[156] We should praise confession to a priest, reception of the most blessed Sacrament once a year, and much more once a month, and still more every week, always with the required and proper conditions.

[355]   *The Third.* We should praise frequent attendance at Mass; also, chants, psalmody, and long prayers inside and outside the church; and further, the schedules setting the times for the Divine Office as a whole, for prayers of every kind, and for all the canonical hours.

[356]   *The Fourth.* We should strongly praise religious institutes, virginity and continence, and marriage too, but not as highly as any of the former.

[357]   *The Fifth.* We should praise the vows of religion, obedience, poverty, chastity, and vows to perform other works of supererogation which conduce to perfection. We should remember, too, that just as a vow is made in regard to matters which lead toward evangelical perfection, so vows ought not to be made with respect to matters that withdraw one from it, such as to enter business, to get married, and the like.

[358]   *The Sixth.* We should praise relics of saints, by venerating the relics and praying to the saints. We should extol visits to stational churches, pilgrimages, indulgences for jubilees and crusades, and the lighting of candles in churches.

[359]   *The Seventh.* We should praise precepts of fast and abstinence, for example, in Lent, on ember days, vigils, Fridays and Saturdays; also penances, not only interior but also exterior.

[360]   *The Eighth.* We ought to praise the ornamentations and structures of churches; also images, and their veneration according to what they represent.

[361]   *The Ninth.* Lastly, we should praise all the precepts of the Church, while keeping our mind ready to look for reasons for defending them and not for attacking them in any way.

[362]   *The Tenth.*[157] We ought to be more inclined to approve and praise the decrees, recommendations, and conduct of our superiors[158] than to speak against them. For although some of these acts are not or were not praiseworthy, to speak against them either by preaching in public or by conversing among the ordinary people would cause more murmuring and scandal than profit. And through this the people would become angry at their officials, whether civil or spiritual. However, just as it does harm to speak evil about officials among the ordinary people while they are absent, so it can be profitable to speak of their bad conduct to persons who can bring about a remedy.

[363]   *The Eleventh.* We ought to praise both positive theology and scholastic theology.[159] For just as it is more characteristic of the positive doctors, such as St. Jerome, St. Augustine, St. Gregory, and the rest to stir up our affections toward loving and serving God our Lord in all things, so it is more characteristic of the scholastic teachers, such as St. Thomas, St. Bonaventure, the Master of the Sentences, and so on to define and explain for our times the matters necessary for salvation, and also to refute and explain all the errors and fallacies. For the scholastic teachers, being more modern, can avail themselves of an authentic understanding of Sacred Scripture and the holy positive doctors. Further still they, being enlightened and clarified by divine influence, make profitable use of the councils, canons, and decrees of our Holy Mother Church.

[364]   *The Twelfth.* We ought to be on our guard against comparing those of us who are still living with the blessed of the past.[160] For no small error is made when one says, for example, "He knows more than St. Augustine," or "He is another St. Francis, or even more," or "He is another St. Paul in goodness, holiness, and the like."

[365] *The Thirteenth.*[161] To keep ourselves right in all things, we ought to hold fast to this principle: What I see as white, I will believe to be black if the hierarchical Church thus determines it.[162] For we believe that between Christ our Lord, the Bridegroom, and the Church, his Spouse, there is the one same Spirit who governs and guides us for the salvation of our souls. For it is by the same Spirit and Lord of ours who gave the ten commandments that our holy Mother Church is guided and governed.

[366] *The Fourteenth.* It is granted that there is much truth in the statement that no one can be saved without being predestined and without having faith and grace. Nevertheless great caution is necessary in our manner of speaking and teaching about all these matters.

[367] *The Fifteenth.* We ought not to fall into a habit of speaking much about predestination. But if somehow the topic is brought up on occasions, it should be treated in such a way that the ordinary people do not fall into an error, as sometimes happens when they say: "It is already determined whether I shall be saved or damned, and this cannot now be changed by my doing good or evil." Through this they grow listless and neglect the works which lead to good and to the spiritual advancement of their souls.

[368] *The Sixteenth.* In the same way we should notice with caution that by speaking much and emphatically about faith, without any distinction and explanation, we may give the people an occasion to grow listless and lazy in their works, either before or after these persons have a faith which is informed by charity.

[369] *The Seventeenth.* Similarly, we ought not to speak so lengthily and emphatically about grace that we generate a poison harmful to freedom of the will. Hence one may speak about faith and grace as much as possible, with God's help, for the greater praise of his Divine Majesty; but not in such ways or manners, especially in times as dangerous as our own, that works and free will are impaired or thought worthless.

[370] *The Eighteenth.* It is granted that we should value above everything else the great service which is given to God because of pure love. Nevertheless we should also strongly

213

praise fear of his Divine Majesty. For not only is filial fear something pious and very holy, but so also is servile fear. Even if it brings a person nothing better or more useful, it greatly aids him or her to rise from mortal sin; and once such a one has risen, one easily attains to filial fear, which is wholly acceptable and pleasing to God our Lord, since it is inseparably united with love of him.

C. THE DELIBERATION ON POVERTY

and

Selections from

THE SPIRITUAL DIARY

ABBREVIATED CONTENTS

1. INTRODUCTION TO THE DELIBERATION ON POVERTY

Ignatius wrote his Deliberation on Poverty either simultaneously with the first week of his *Spiritual Diary* or perhaps a little before it. Already on the seventh day of the *Diary*, February 8, 1544, he refers in [8] to "reading it" and finding it well thought out (*bien escrito*). In both documents he shows by example (although he never intended this) how he applied the principles of the *Exercises* to problems arising in his daily life. In particular we see him making an election about a problem much on his mind since March, 1541: In the future Constitutions which he was charged to compose, what prescriptions was he to insert for the canonical poverty of the Society's churches and their sacristies? In the three pages of the Deliberation we observe his mind working according to the "Third Time for Making a Sound Election" (*SpEx* [177]), when one is in tranquility and can reason clearly about the pros and cons. In the seventy pages of the *Diary* we watch his whole inmost person functioning according to the "Second Time" ([176]), "from the experience of consolations and desolations, . . . and the discernment of spirits." Taken together these two documents are perhaps the best exemplification we have of Ignatius' own use of the "Three Times," as well as a very authentic commentary on them.

We place the Deliberation before the *Diary* because it furnishes background necessary to understand the *Diary* well. From it, too, we come to understand some obscure terminology which has often misled or at least puzzled many readers of both documents.

a. *Juridical Evangelical Poverty*

To understand either the Deliberation or the *Diary* well it is important to have fresh in memory a sketch of the previous history of (1) the Church's evolving canon law on evangelical poverty and also (2) the immediate circumstances of 1544 amid which Ignatius was writing.

During the centuries previous to the thirteenth the monks could not own property individually but the monastery could. The practice of poverty was contained only implicitly in the monk's promise of "stability, fidelity to monastic life (*conversatio morum suorum*), and obedience."[1] In the thirteenth century the mendicant orders arose, the Franciscans, Dominicans, Carmelites, and Augustinians. They forbade the possession, even in common, of (1) immovable property, except in some cases for the monastery or convent in which the members lived, and (2) all fixed income, that is, regularly recurring revenues, so that the friars had to live from alms alone. Some goods are necessary, however, both stable goods like the house and the church, and movable goods, like furniture, clothing, and food. Among the Dominicans, the order (that is, the community or convent) kept both the ownership and the use of these goods. Originally the Franciscans kept only the use, transferring to the Holy See the ownership of all their property, of which they remained the administrators. St. Francis forbade the acceptance of money. In 1260 the Friars Minor introduced poverty as an explicit vow.[2] By Ignatius' time a distinction had become commonly recognized in Franciscan poverty between fixed revenues with a right to defend them in court and fixed revenues without that right. These latter could be considered as alms.[3]

b. The Juridical Poverty of the Society of Jesus

Since their vow at Montmartre in 1534, Ignatius and his companions had been living in evangelical poverty, endeavoring to imitate the itinerant life of Christ and his apostles preaching in poverty (Luke 8:1–2; Matt. 10:5–10; see also *SpEx* [281]). Like Francis and Dominic before them, they were particularly opposed even to any appearance of the avarice which was working much harm in the Church. In their Deliberations from mid-March to June 24, 1538, they decided to band themselves into a religious order. Thus they had to encase their charismatic tenor of thought into some form of juridical poverty which would win papal approval. They determined on June 11, 1538, that

> We may receive houses with a church attached, but without any right to ownership of their property, so that those who give us their use may freely take them back if they so wish; furthermore, we shall have no right to claim them in court . . . against anyone whatsoever, even if they take them unjustly.[4]

These ideas were rephrased into the First Sketch of the Institute of the Society of Jesus by early July, 1539, and then into *Regimini,* the bull of September 27, 1540, which approved the Society.[5] Therefore the Society's members could have no civil right to own stable goods or property like a house or a church, but would be merely the administrators of it. They could have no civil right to annual crops or to other fixed income to buy needed movable goods such as food, furniture, travel, books, postage, and the like, but they could receive alms, either in the form of money or of other gifts which they could sell and use the price received to buy food and other necessities.[6]

On March 4, 1541, Ignatius and five of his professed companions met to discuss the contents of the bull and its further determinations in the future constitutions. Beginning with poverty, they agreed that "the sacristy may have fixed income (*renta*) for all things necessary, from those revenues which will not be for the professed."[7] Three months later Pope Paul III, on June 24, 1541, handed over to the Society the Church of Our Lady of the Way, and applied to its sacristy the fixed revenues which it previously possessed.[8] Since the professed could receive no fixed revenues, was this inconsistent with the Bull *Regimini?* No, because the church or sacristy was considered as a moral person, distinct from the Society; and this moral person was the holder of the civil rights to the fixed revenues. Hence they were permissible.[9]

But as 1544 began Ignatius, now general since April 19, 1541, was uneasy about the decision of March 4, 1541, to accept fixed income for the sacristies. He feared that it was a departure from the strict poverty the companions had determined to practice. Therefore he decided to reexamine the pros and cons deeply before the Lord. As one result we have what he left us in his Deliberation on Poverty and his *Diary.*

c. *The Terminology of the Deliberation and the* Spiritual Diary

The Deliberation, like the *Diary,* contains much difficult terminology which it is best to learn before reading either document. In both of them Ignatius was not writing to communicate his thought to others, but solely to think out for himself a problem filled with technicalities, while viewing it from various angles in his sometimes convoluted way. In both documents he used shorthand phrases such as "in part" (*en parte*), "in whole" (*en todo*), "nothing" (*no nada*), and others. They were catchwords perfectly clear to Ignatius himself amid the circumstances so thoroughly familiar to him, but precisely what did he mean by them? In his environment, precisely to whom or what did they apply? His word *income* (*renta*), for example, is a trap which has misled many North Americans, to whom it usually means receipts of any kind, such as donations, or wages, or interest—anything they must list in their income-tax report. In the three successive Formulas of the Institute, however, Ignatius' Deliberation, *Diary*, and *Constitutions*, income (*renta*) always means fixed or regularly recurring revenues—for example, annual crops, interest from a church benefice, and the like.[10] It is wise to remember, too, that the term *society* meant its professed members (at that time no more than ten) and not those who were still in their period of training, the scholastics. To retrace the history of this evolving terminology from 1538 to 1544 is the best key to these words or phrases.

Codure's record of the early companions' deliberations of March 4, 1541 contains the following items.[11]

> First we must think of poverty: How it is to be understood, keeping in mind the statement in the bull approving the Society that it cannot have any civil right to anything, either in common or in private.
>
> For the present, we raise these questions:
> 1. If it will be good to have no fixed income at all (*no aver renta ninguna*);
> 2. If it will be good to have fixed income for all the things (*renta por todas las cosas*);
> 3. If it will be good to have fixed income for some things and for others not (*renta por algunas, y por algunas no*).

Their answer to question 1 was:

> The present professed should not be able to possess anything of fixed revenue, either as individuals or in common (*no puedan aver nada*).

No answer to question 2 was recorded here, probably because they thought that the answer to question 1 was also the answer to 2. However, they acted wisely in discussing the question, for theoretically an affirmative answer would have been permissible. In the mitigated Franciscan poverty (1) fixed income *with* a civil right to defend it was not allowed, but (2) fixed income *without* a civil right was permissible. It was considered alms.[12] Therefore a residence of the professed along with its church could have fixed income without civil right. Further, it could be permissible "to have fixed income in whole" (*aver renta en todo*) applicable to "all the things" under consideration.

Their answer to 3, most pertinent here, was:

> The sacristy should be able to have fixed income for all things necessary (*aver renta para todas las casas de menester*), from those revenues which will not be for the professed.

Another decision gives us information about the concrete circumstances.

> The founder can leave the care of the sacristy to some person who is not professed, such as the aforementioned administrator of the church of Jesus. The Society will hold the superintendency, be able to dismiss him, or after his death to replace him. If a disagreement should arise between him and the Society, the Society should explain its case without a trial in court.

Clearly, the six were thinking about the church of Our Lady of the Way which had been given to the Society in 1541, and about the neighboring house then under construction for the professed members of the Society. This situation was a model which could be applied to future residences and their churches.

From the solutions to the problems cited above[13] we gather the meanings of the terms which Ignatius used in the headings of the Deliberation and throughout the *Diary*. In this context:

1. "To have nothing"   means   to have no fixed income.
   No tener nada   means   *no aver renta fija.*
2. "To have in whole"   means   to have fixed income without limitation.

   Tener todo or *en todo* means   *renta fija sin limitación.*

That is, although this fixed income could be considered as alms and theoretically could be applied to (1) the Society (namely, the professed members), and (2) its churches and sacristies, this option 1 had already been rejected by the answer to question 1 of March 4, 1541 (above).

3. "To have in part"   means   to have fixed income limited to the
                                    churches and their sacristies.
    Tener en parte   means   *renta fija limitada a las iglesias y*
                                    sacristias de ellas.

d. Simplifying the Statement of the Question

In writing his headings Ignatius approached the options first from one viewpoint and then from its opposite. This too confuses some readers. However, it is possible to reduce his deliberation to one simple proposition and its pros and cons, as follows.[14]

THE QUESTION

Shall We Permit Fixed Income to the Churches or Sacristies of the Society's Houses for Its Professed Members?

THE PROS

I. The reasons for *having* a fixed income are:
  1. The Society will maintain itself better.
  2. Its members will cause less annoyance by begging.
And so on for the rest of the pros.

THE CONS

II. The reasons for *rejecting* the fixed income are:
  1. The Society will have greater spiritual strength for apostolic work and be more like to Christ.
  2. It will be less tempted to avarice.
And so on for the rest of the cons.

Ignatius' entries already in the first week of his *Diary* lead us to think that he reached at least a tentative conclusion against fixed income for the churches by his reasoning according to the "Third Time" of the *Exercises* ([177]). Already during the first week he writes for February 8 that his "will was more moved . . . not to have any fixed income." In any case, he submitted the matter to God according to the "Second Time" ([176]) and sought further light "from the experience of spiritual consolations and desolations" in mental prayer of many days which was often highly mystical. The recorded experiences we have began on February 2, and only on March 12 was his conclusion against any fixed income for his churches and sacristies firm. It is indicated by one word which seems like a final punctuation mark: "It is finished" (*finido*).

e. The Present Translation of the Deliberation and Diary

The present translation of both the Deliberation on Poverty and the selections from the *Spiritual Diary* is a project of mutual cooperation between Fathers Edward J. Malatesta and George E. Ganss. Since Ignatius was not writing either of these documents to communicate his thought to others, he paid no attention to style. He simply jotted down his ideas just as they came to mind. In preclassical Spanish he piled together gerunds, participles, infinitives, or other parts of speech, often without including a finite verb (which generally, however, is easily understood). To reproduce all these traits of his style would result in unnatural and often puzzling English. Hence the translators thought it best to use the same principles of "functional equivalence" which were utilized with the *Exercises*, and were explained above on pages 118–119. Our hope is to enable the reader to grasp Ignatius' thought with accuracy and reasonable ease. The Introductions and notes were composed by Father Ganss. As a final step, Father Malatesta reviewed the entire work and made valuable suggestions which improved it. The notes draw heavily on the similar running commentaries by Adolf Haas, Maurice Giuliani, Ignacio Iparraguirre, Peter Knauer, and Joseph Munitiz, whose books on the *Diary* are listed in our Bibliography and to whom this writer expresses his deep gratitude.

The translation is based on the critical text of both documents by Arturo Codina,[15] but great aid was also received from the editorial helps supplied by Iparraguirre in *Obras completas de San Ignacio*. He points out that even the words or passages which Ignatius crossed out reveal his first thought and are often important helps toward interpreting his final text. Hence Iparraguirre took those items from Codina's critical apparatus and smoothly worked them into the text itself with the following signs:[16]

THE DELIBERATION ON POVERTY

[   ] square brackets indicate editorial additions to Ignatius'
text.

⟨   ⟩ angular brackets indicate something which Ignatius
wrote but crossed out and replaced with something else
nearby.

In numerous instances we shall use the same procedures and signs.

2. THE DELIBERATION ON POVERTY

THE DISADVANTAGES[1] OF HAVING NO FIXED INCOME ARE ALSO THE ADVANTAGES OF HAVING SUCH INCOME EITHER IN PART[2] OR IN WHOLE.[3]

1. It seems that the Society, by having a fixed income in part or in whole, would maintain itself better.

2. Having a fixed income, the members would not be annoying or disedifying to others by having to beg, especially since those begging would be clerics.

3. Having a fixed income, they will not experience so many troubled motions[4] toward a disordered solicitude in seeking alms.

4. They will be able to devote themselves in a more orderly and peaceful way to their duties and set prayers.

5. The time that would be spent in asking or seeking could be used for preaching, hearing confessions, and other pious works.

6. It seems that the church would be kept cleaner, adorned, and more apt to move to devotion, and would have the possibility of renovation.

7. Similarly, they will be able to devote themselves more to study and thus provide more spiritual help to their neighbors and take better care of their own physical health.

8. After two members of the Society had considered the matter, all the others approved.[5]

THE DISADVANTAGES IN HAVING A FIXED INCOME ARE ALSO THE ADVANTAGES OF HAVING NONE WHATEVER; THAT IS TO SAY:

1. Having a fixed income, they would not be so diligent in helping their neighbors, nor be so disposed to travel and endure hardships. Also they would be less able to lead their neighbors to true poverty and self-abnegation in all things, as is explained in what follows regarding the advantages of not having any fixed income.

⟨The disadvantages in having a fixed income in part (in addition to the fact that they are also the advantages in having no fixed income whatever) are the following: First, one and the same person would be superior of those who have a fixed income[6] because of his holding the superintendency over it, and superior also of those who do not have any fixed income. Also he would take from the same house[7] what is necessary for himself and for those of the Society; that does not sound right.⟩[8]

ADVANTAGES AND REASONS FOR HAVING NO FIXED INCOME

1. The Society receives greater spiritual strength and greater devotion by resembling and contemplating the Son of the Virgin, our Creator and Lord, so poor and in so many adversities.

2. Not to desire any assured income better puts to shame all worldly avarice.

2. [*sic*] It seems that we are united to the Church with greater affection, by being uniform in not having anything ourselves while we are contemplating Christ poor in the sacrament [of the Eucharist].

3. It facilitates our efforts to place our hope for everything in God our Lord, when we separate ourselves from everything belonging to the world.

4. This helps more to humiliate us and to unite ourselves more with the One who humbled himself the most beyond all others.

4. [*sic*] [The Society] lives more oblivious of all worldly consolation.

5. It lives more in continual divine hope and with greater diligence in God's service.

6. There is greater edification in general, since it is apparent that it is seeking nothing of this world.

7. It speaks of all spiritual things with greater freedom of spirit and with greater effectiveness for the greater progress of souls.

8. Because it receives daily alms, it is helped and encouraged more to assist souls spiritually.

9. It will better persuade others to true poverty by observing it in the form Christ our Lord recommended, when he said: "If anyone has left father," and so on.

10. It seems they will be more diligent in helping the neighbor and more ready to travel and endure hardships.

11. The poverty which has no fixed income is more perfect than that which has one in part or in whole.[9]

12. Jesus, the Lord of us all, chose this poverty for himself and taught the same to his apostles and beloved disciples, when he sent them to preach ([Matt. 10:51; Luke 8:1–2]).

13. When all ten of us chose this, with no one objecting, we took as our head Jesus himself, our Creator and Lord, to go out under his banner to preach and exhort, which is our vocation.

14. With this understanding of poverty we requested and obtained the papal bull; and after waiting one year for it to be expedited during which we remained firm in our understanding, it was confirmed by His Holiness.[10]

15. It is characteristic of God our Lord to be unchangeable, and of the enemy to be changeable and inconstant.

⟨16. There are three ways to preserve the Society: (1) that all or nearly all the members have studied; (2) for the scholastics, in what concerns clothes, lodging, and food, it seems that some provision could be made; (3) for furnishings and other things the Society needs, even some of those who will probably enter could help.⟩[11]

3. INTRODUCTION TO THE *SPIRITUAL DIARY*

a. Special Characteristics

When we pass from the Deliberation into the *Spiritual Diary* we enter a new world. Of all Ignatius' writings, the *Diary* enables us to gaze most directly into the depths of his heart in his intimate dealing with God. It also best reveals the sublimity of his mysticism.

The pages of the *Exercises* and *Constitutions* seem at first reading to pertain more to the realm of asceticism than of mysticism. That is, they do not by themselves reveal that Ignatius was highly gifted with infused contemplation—even though they are in fact the carefully reasoned thought which has proceeded from a great mystic who has habitually submitted all his important topics to God in prayerful discernment. His *Autobiography* was dictated thirty-two years after his mystical experiences at Manresa when his memory had dimmed on some details. In it (especially in 28–30, 96, 99–101), for the benefit of his fellow Jesuits he told *about* his many visions, mystical illuminations, and some of their content. From it we learn the fact that Ignatius was gifted by God with infused contemplation; and we also get glimpses of what he learned in his meetings with God in 1522. In this *Diary*, however, intended for his own eyes alone, for months he jotted down his fresh and totally uninhibited thoughts, his most intimate conversations with God, and the overwhelming mystical experiences he received. If these pages had not been providentially preserved when the rest of his diary was destroyed, these sublime peaks of his interior life would have remained unknown throughout all of time.

Câmara and perhaps a few others of Ignatius' contemporaries knew of the existence of the *Diary* but never read it (*Autobiog*, 100–101). Jesuits after 1556 knew only a few short passages which appeared in the lives of Ignatius by Ribadeneira and Bartoli. Otherwise the *Diary* remained a handwritten document in archives until 1892, when Juan de la Torre published most of the first copybook.[1] The first critical text of the Deliberation and whole *Diary* was published by

Codina in 1934.[2] Shortly later came (in 1938) the first study in depth of the *Diary*, Joseph de Guibert's masterful article "Mystique ignatienne."[3] This inaugurated a steadily increasing stream of studies on it and on Ignatius' mystical life,[4] which was inadequately treated in earlier biographies.

b. Ignatius' Mystical Life

He usually penned the entries into the *Diary* during the same day on which the experiences occurred, while they were fresh in his memory. Many of its statements are manifestly his feeble attempt to describe what was clearly a vivid mystical experience or a vision beyond his power of adequate explanation. On occasions he even gives us hints that he is trying to record such a gift from God. This is an unintended result of his encircling some passages as especially meaningful to himself—as he did, for example, in [52 or 87]. The *Diary*, therefore, is his own extended record of these divine invasions into his soul. It reveals the peaks and characteristics of his mystic prayer, and the extraordinary mystical phenomena which often accompanied it—for example, infused tears, usually of reverential joy (*lagrimas*), insights (*inteligencias*), visions (*visiones*), visitations (*visitaciones*), touches (*tocamientos*), affectionate awe (*acatamiento*), (*reverencia*), loving humility (*humildad amorosa*), and speech (*loquela*). For putting ourselves into the best frame of mind to read the *Diary*, it is hard to improve upon de Guibert's oft-quoted description:

> We are in the presence of a mystical life in the strictest sense of this term. We are in the company of a soul that is being led by God in the ways of infused contemplation to the same degree, though not in the same manner, as a St. Francis of Assisi or a St. John of the Cross. To assure ourselves of this as we read the relevant texts [in the *Diary*], it is enough to focus our attention on the distinctive characteristics of infused contemplation—those traits on which theologians agree in describing as the characteristics of infused contemplation, in spite of the different explanations of them which they give. Such traits are: an experience of God as being present under a form of knowledge which is simultaneously general and obscure yet rich and satisfying; an experience of love penetrating and dominating the soul in its innermost depths, in a manner

connected with passivity; the mystic's experiencing this passivity while he is under the all-powerful control of God; his
complete impotence to awaken, prolong, or renew these experiences, or even to foresee their approach or their end; also,
his inability to translate what he has experienced into forms of
current language or, above all, to give an idea of them which
is fairly clear to one who has never experienced anything
similar.[5]

Most but not all of the mystical experiences recorded in the *Diary*
occurred during Ignatius' prayer in the morning. This prayer, including
the Mass on which it was centered, seemingly lasted one to three hours
daily.[6] For the rest of the day throughout these almost thirteen months
he engaged in his ordinary apostolic activities. He was governing the
Society, which now had members in Portugal, Spain, Germany, Italy,
and India. He had spiritual care of the women living in the House of St.
Martha and was confessor to the household of Margaret of Austria, who
in 1543 had given him help in his work for the catechumens from
Judaism. His secretary at the time, Domènech, wrote that on some days
he heard confessions from morning to evening without taking time to
eat. He made visits to the papal curia to negotiate a new papal bull which
would remove the limitation of the Society to sixty professed members,
and also prepared material for the Constitutions.[7] The *Diary* contains
indications of some of these activities in [22, 42, 55, 74, 89, 110, 124].
His prayer in the morning coupled with his activities during the day
show very concretely what Nadal meant by describing him in Thomistic terminology as being "a contemplative person even while he was in
action" (*simul in actione contemplativus*).[8] His mysticism was not confined to loving union with God in prayer but was oriented toward
execution and loving service.[9]

c. The Spiritual Diary *as Teaching by Example*

The Deliberation and the *Diary* taken together are a remarkable
instance of teaching by example. They show how Ignatius himself
applied to the problems arising in his own daily life the principles and
procedures which he taught to others in the *Exercises*. We understand
far more concretely what he meant when he wrote of colloquies and
triple colloquies, his mediators, spiritual consolation and desolation; and
particularly, how in making an Election he flexibly interwove the Third

and Second Times (*SpEx* [177 and 176]). His procedure in this is very authentic commentary on his statements in the *Exercises*.

We see further how the master lines of his thought in his earlier life, whether ascetical or mystical, flow with strict continuity into the highly mystical life of his years in Rome. Everything is dominated and orientated by the thought of bringing greater glory or praise to God, of serving him, of learning his will and carrying it out, of living in accordance with the end of humankind as expressed in the First Principle and Foundation.

d. The Reading and Study of the Diary

It must be admitted, however, that to many the first reading of the *Diary* brings a feeling of wandering in a forest without guideposts. After three or four pages, "one finds only more and more of the same." This, of course, is true also about many other mystical writers who have tried to record their experiences, for in bestowing his favors God does not confine himself to any preconceived human outline. Ignatius jotted down his experiences in the order in which they came, merely to keep alive his memory of them and his gratitude. Hence his *Diary*, to be understood in depth, must be studied rather than merely read. Authors who have done this since its first publication in 1934 have produced somewhat different outlines which have progressively advanced our understanding of its contents.

Some writers have found their clarifying divisions, classifications, and terminology by attending chiefly to God's activity in Ignatius' soul. Thus Adolf Haas, for example, in an excellent study, has found four stages by which God led Ignatius in the journey recorded in the *Diary*: (1) from the Divine Persons contemplated one by one to the unity of their circuminsession in the Trinity ([1–64], February 2–22, 1544); (2) from Jesus as man to Jesus as God ([65–88], February 23–28); (3) from the unity by circuminsession to the Divine Essence ([89–125], February 29–March 6); (4) a mysticism of reverential love ([126–490], March 7, 1544–February 27, 1545).[10]

Ignacio Iparraguirre has approached the study of the *Diary* from a different viewpoint. By focusing on the human activities and preoccupations which Ignatius brought to his prayer, Iparraguirre devised a different outline which is a truly helpful guide to many.[11] Comparing the contents of the *Diary* to the movement or rhythm of a symphony, he found in it six major divisions or tempos. We shall build on this approach, but we shall change his metaphor to that of a journey made in six stages, each of which is accomplished in four to ten segments, as will appear below.

A full forty days passed before Ignatius concluded his election. Why did it take him so long? Two different plans, it seems, were involved, his own and that of God, and each plan had its own time schedule. For a while Ignatius thought himself ready to conclude his election within a week or two. God, however, intended not only to help with the election but also to teach him lessons far more extensive, especially total submission of himself to God in affectionate awe (*acatamiento*) before God and in habitual loving humility (*humildad amorosa*). That would require a longer time.

According to Ignatius' own teaching (*SpEx* [175–189]), such an election would entail several steps: consideration of the pros and cons according to the Third Time ([177]), seeking light from experience of consolation and desolation according to the Second Time ([176]), offering the election to God in prayer which begs for confirmation ([183]), and thanksgiving for the graces received (as his practice shows). He began on February 2 and already on February 10 (in Stage I of the *Diary*) he felt that the pros and cons clearly favored no fixed revenue. He made this election and offered it to God for confirmation (*SpDiar* [13]), and on February 11 he felt confirmed ([14–18]). Then doubts arose and unsettled him ([18]). This same process was repeated several times (in Stages II–IV). On February 17 he resolved to conclude the election the next day ([42]). He hoped to finish in a blaze of confirming consolation ([49, 147]). (In this—as he understood later on [146, 147] —he was seeking more what he wanted than what God desired; his indifference had become faulty.) God let him experience deep desolation ([44]).

Meanwhile the Divine Pedagogue was beginning to teach his own lessons. Ignatius was led to be conformed to whatever path the Holy Trinity would choose for him ([79–82, 142, 147]). The pupil was slowly growing more interested in the lessons and peacefully content with the Master's pace ([54]). On February 23 (in Stage IV) he received brilliant clarity through Jesus ([67–70]). On February 27 he realized the importance of affectionate awe (*acatamiento*) coupled with reverential love of God ([83]). He confided everything to God's initiative ([92–96]). On March 12 he concluded the election (in Stage V [150]). The Teacher, however, had still further lessons to impart.

The entire Second Copybook from March 13, 1544, to February 27, 1545 (Stage VI, [154–490]) can be considered a description of Ignatius' walking along that new spiritual path, affectionate awe which grew into loving humility. First he awakened anew, on March 14, to the propriety of affectionate awe. It was the path which the Lord had wanted to point out to him, so that he ought to attach greater value to this grace and knowledge than to all the other graces he had received in the past ([157 with 139]). This path was "the best of all and the one I ought to follow always" ([162]). He came to see further that humility was the basis from which the awe sprang. At every word which names God he was "deeply penetrated by an affectionate awe and an admirable reverential humility which seem impossible to explain" ([164]). He begged God, "Give me loving humility, and with it reverence and affectionate awe" ([178]). He received this loving humility not merely as a grace toward which the entire process had been tending, but also as the new path along which he should henceforth walk ([178]).

This loving humility, with the complete conformity to God's will which it implies and in its context of reverential awe, can be regarded as the summit of Ignatius' spiritual experience narrated in the *Diary*. He makes this conformity explicit in [189–190]. It is strikingly similar to the Third Way of Being Humble (*SpEx* [167]), considered by many to be a synthesis of the graces of the *Exercises* up to that point.[12] God confirmed Ignatius' efforts to walk along this new path by the further mystical gifts recorded from March 30, 1544, to February 27, 1545 ([178–490]), especially the infused tears of joy and the *loquela* ([221–240]).

e. An Outline of Ignatius' Mystical Journey

The progression of Ignatius' spiritual journey can now be glimpsed in the outline ahead, and then seen more clearly in the *Diary* itself.

4. IGNATIUS' MYSTICAL JOURNEY AS RECORDED IN HIS *SPIRITUAL DIARY*

PART I, The First Copybook
THE PROCEDURES OF ELECTION.
February 2 to March 12, 1544.

STAGE I. HE CONSIDERS THE PROS AND CONS OF HIS ELECTION AND OFFERS IT TO GOD FOR APPROVAL. FEBRUARY 2–12.

Segment 1. He examines the options [1–6].
2. He offers his tentative conclusion to God [7–14].
3. He feels confirmed in his election according to the Third Time [15].
4. He again offers the conclusion to God [16–18].
5. He begins acts of thanksgiving [19–22].

STAGE II. HE REPEATS THE ELECTION, OFFERING, AND THANKSGIVING. FEBRUARY 13–18.

1. He again reviews the options [23–35].
2. He makes the offering a third time [36–38].
3. He gives thanks to God [39–43].
4. Instead of confirmation, he experiences aridity and loss of confidence [44].

STAGE III. HE RENEWS HIS OFFERING AND GIVES THANKS. FEBRUARY 18–22.

1. Through his mediators he approaches the Trinity and begs to renew his offering [45–46].
2. He again feels confirmed and makes the offering a fourth time [47].
3. He begs its acceptance from God [48–50].
4. He decides to seek further [51].

THE SPIRITUAL DIARY

5. Before, during, and after Mass he receives great insights into the Holy Trinity [52–64].

STAGE IV. BRILLIANT CLARITY THROUGH
MEDIATION OF JESUS. FEBRUARY 23–MARCH 4.

1. He receives confirmation from Jesus in an unexpected way [65–70].
2. He experiences, through Jesus, divine confirmation of that clarity [71–73].
3. He clearly sees a past error [74–78].
4. Through prayer to Jesus he conforms to whatever spiritual way will be most pleasing to the Trinity [79–82].
5. The Mediation of Jesus and visions confirm him in this new attitude [83–91].
6. He leaves everything to the divine initiative [92–96].
7. Devotion and love toward the Trinity [97–102].
8. Intense love for the Holy Trinity [103–110].

STAGE V. HE EXPERIENCES LUMINOUS AND WARM DEVOTION,
FEELS RECONCILED, AND DECIDES. MARCH 5–12.

1. In humility he feels complete reconciliation with the Trinity [111–116].
2. He has rest after labor [117–120].
3. He perceives the Divine Essence and the Divine Persons amid Intense Brightness [121–126].
4. He looks below and sees the Divine Essence reflected in creatures [127–133].
5. He experiences devotion and contentment in this new attitude of humble conformity to God's will [134–144].
6. In spiritual desolation, he submits to whatever is more pleasing to God and then receives spiritual consolation [145–149].
7. He definitively concludes and experiences God's full confirmation [150–153].

THE SPIRITUAL DIARY

PART II, The Second Copybook.
A RECORD IN GRATITUDE FOR MYSTICAL FAVORS.

STAGE VI. WALKING ALONG A NEW PATH: LOVING HUMILITY
AND AFFECTIONATE AWE. MARCH 13, 1544 TO FEBRUARY 27, 1545.

1. Contentment and peace of soul [154–155].
2. Affectionate awe and reverence [156–160].
3. Confirming an election by the new way of affectionate awe and reverence (161–171).
4. Visions and realization that affectionate awe is God's gift [172–176].
5. Reverence, affectionate awe, and the further gift of loving humility [177–182].
6. He understands the relation of these new gifts to his fidelity or infidelity [183–188].
7. In mystical prayer he conforms himself totally to God's will [189–190].
8. He lists instances of the infused gift of tears [191–220].
9. He receives a final mystical gift: *loquela* [221–240].
10. He lists further occurrences of the gift of tears, May 29, 1544, to February 27, 1545

Our desire is to present a conspectus of the *Diary* as a whole, and for this purpose the above division based on Ignatius' human activities seems to furnish the most practical arrangement for the selections given here. We shall provide guideposts by placing the stages and their segments as captions above the selections. This will enable the reader to see how each passage fits into the *Diary* as a whole, have some idea of what is in the passages omitted, know at what stage or step of the journey he or she is, and in this journey through a pleasant forest be able to distinguish the trees from the forest itself.

These divisions are not exclusive, however, and must be used with caution. Each guidepost points out something prominent or even predominant in a given passage, but simultaneously there may be features from any other heading. Neither God nor Ignatius was proceeding rigidly according to a preconceived human plan.

Selections from
THE SPIRITUAL DIARY

[IGNATIUS' MYSTICAL JOURNEY AS RECORDED IN HIS *SPIRITUAL DIARY*

PART I, The First Copybook.

THE PROCEDURES OF ELECTION.
February 2 to March 12, 1544.]

[STAGE I. HE CONSIDERS THE PROS AND CONS OF HIS ELECTION AND OFFERS IT TO GOD FOR APPROVAL. FEBRUARY 2–12.

Segment 1. He examines the options (1–6).]

[1]—[The Mass of] † Our Lady.[1]
C[hapter] 1.[2] Saturday [February 2, 1544].[3]
Abundance of devotion[4] during Mass, with tears,[5] with increased confidence in Our Lady, and with greater inclination to have no fixed income,[6] then, and throughout the day.

[2]—[Chapter] 2.[7] Sunday [February 3. Fourth Sunday after Epiphany].
The same, and with greater inclination to have no fixed income, then, and throughout the day.

[3]—Our Lady.
C[hapter] 3. Monday [February 4].
The same, and with other sentiments;[8] and I was more inclined throughout the day to have no fixed income. In the evening, a coming close to Our Lady with much affection and much confidence.

238

[4]—Our Lady.

C[hapter] 4. Tuesday [February 5].

Vision

=//=

Before, during, and after Mass I had an abundance of devotion and many tears which pained my eyes; a vision of the Mother and the Son as being favorably disposed to intercede with the Father ‖.[9] Then and throughout the day I was inclined and moved more toward no fixed income. In the afternoon, it was as if I felt or saw that Our Lady was favorably disposed to intercede.

[5]—Our Lady.

5. Wednesday [February 6].

Before and during Mass, with devotion and tears, and more disposed toward no fixed income. Then it seemed to me, with sufficient clarity, in a way different from the ordinary, that to have fixed income in part would generate confusion, to have it in whole would be a scandal and would contribute to depreciating the poverty which God our Lord praised so highly.

[6]—The Trinity.

6. Thursday [February 7].

Before Mass I had great abundance of devotion and tears, and throughout the whole day I experienced a warmth and notable devotion. I was always more inclined and moved toward no fixed income. At the time of Mass it appeared to me there was a notable approach to the Father, with much devotion and interior motion to ask him. It seemed to me that the two mediators had interceded, and I had some sign of seeing them.

[2. He offers his tentative conclusion to God (7–14).]

[7]—The Name of Jesus.

7. Friday [February 8].

After notable devotion and tears during prayer, from the preparation for Mass and during it, much abundance of devotion and tears also. I refrained from speech when I could, and stood fast in the intention of no fixed income.

[8]—Then, after Mass with devotion and not without tears, I went over the elections[10] for an hour and a half or more, reflecting on that which appeared to me to have the stronger reasons and that to which my

will was more moved, that is, not to have any fixed income. Wishing to present this to the Father[11] through the mediation and prayers of the Mother and the Son, and first praying to her to help me in approaching her Son and the Father, and then praying to the Son to help me in approaching the Father in the company of the Mother,[12] I felt in myself a motion toward the Father or that I was being lifted up before him. As I advanced the hairs on my head stood up and I experienced a movement like an extraordinary warmth[13] in my whole body. Following this, tears and very intense devotion ‖.

[9]—Reading this later on and judging that it was well thought out, I experienced fresh devotion not without my eyes filling with tears[14] ‖; then, remembering[15] these graces I had received, a fresh devotion.

[10]—In the afternoon for an hour and a half or more, I went through the elections[16] in the same way. I made the election to have no fixed income and found myself experiencing devotion and a certain elevation of spirit, with great tranquility and without any contradictory thought of possessing anything. I no longer desired to continue the deliberations for as long as I had thought of doing a few days before.

[11]—Mass of the Annunciation.
8. Saturday [February 9].
The night before I was greatly weakened by poor sleep, but during my prayer I had tranquility of mind and sufficient devotion along with spiritual movement, warmth, and a tendency to tears.

. . .

As I read through the options again with much tranquility and devotion, it seemed to me throughout that it was better not to possess a fixed income in part, or in whole, and that the matter did not merit further consideration. I regarded the matter as finished, and thus with peace of mind I remained steadily determined to have no fixed income.

[12]—Mass of the Day [Septuagesima Sunday].
9. Sunday [February 10].
Reviewing the elections with much devotion and not without tears, I made the offering to have no fixed income. This I did first during my customary prayer. Before, during, and after Mass, with sufficient devotion and tears, I was always with the thought of no fixed income. I found repose in the offering made, after I had felt much light in reflecting.[17] Then I experienced certain sentiments toward the mediators. This was not without a vision ‖.

[13]—At night, going over the deliberations concerning fixed income in whole, in part, or none at all, I made the offering of having none, with much devotion, interior peace and tranquility of soul, with a certain security or conviction that it was a good election.[18]

[14]—The Holy Spirit.
10. Monday [February 11].
In the midst of my accustomed prayer, without deliberations, while offering or asking God our Lord that the oblation made be accepted by his Divine Majesty, I had abundant devotion and tears. Later, speaking with the Holy Spirit in view of saying his Mass, with the same devotion or tears I seemed to see him or perceive[19] him in dense brightness[20] or in the color of a flame of fire burning in an unusual way. Through all of this the election made was confirmed in me ||.

[3. He feels confirmed in his election according to the Third Time (15).]

[15]—Later in order to reflect on the elections and enter into them as I had determined, I picked up the reasons which I had in written form in order to examine them. I prayed to Our Lady, and then to the Son, and the Father to give me his Spirit to reason and discern,[21] even though I had already spoken of the matter as something finished. Feeling much devotion and certain insights with some clarity of vision, I sat down and in a general way I considered fixed income in whole, or in part, or none at all. I felt a desire to consider other insights which came to me, namely, how the Son first sent the apostles to preach in poverty; and then how the Holy Spirit, by communicating himself and the gift of tongues, confirmed them; and how thus, when the Father and the Son sent the Holy Spirit, all three Persons confirmed that mission.[22]

[4. He again offers the conclusion to God (16–18).]

[16]—At this point, greater devotion entered me, and every desire to consider the matter further left me. With weeping and sobbing, on my knees, I made my offering to the Father to have no fixed income. So numerous were the tears flowing down my face and the sobs while I made the offering and after it that I could hardly rise because of the sobbing and tears from the devotion and the grace which I had received. After I did rise, the devotion and sobs continued. They came after I had

made the offering to have no fixed income. I considered the offering ratified, validated, and so on.

[17]—A little later while I was walking and recalling to memory what had happened, I experienced a new interior impulse to devotion and tears ‖.

[18]—A little later still when I was about to leave for Mass, while giving myself to a short prayer, I experienced an intense devotion, and tears came over me as I somehow perceived interiorly or saw the Holy Spirit.[23] This, so to speak, made the election seem a finished matter. And yet I was unable to see either of the other two divine Persons.[24]

[5. He begins acts of thanksgiving (19–22).]

[19]—Then in chapel before Mass and during it I had an abundance of devotion and of tears. Later with great tranquility and security of soul, like a tired person taking a good rest and neither seeking nor desiring to search for anything further, I considered the matter finished—except for giving thanks and expressing devotion to the Father, and offering the Mass of the Trinity in accordance with the decision I had made to say it tomorrow, Tuesday.

[20]—About the Persons who were hiding themselves.

[21]—The Trinity.
11. Tuesday [February 12].
Praying after awakening, with insights and tears I kept on giving very intense thanks to God our Lord for the gift and clarity I had received, so great as to be beyond my power to explain.

[22]—After I arose the interior warmth and devotion I had lasted. While remembering the great good I had received,[25] I was moved to a new devotion and increased tears. That was also the case while I was going to Don Francesco,[26] while I was with him, and during my return. I did not lose the warmth and intense love.

⟨Later at about daybreak a point or temptation occurred to me, namely, to have a fixed income only for the church. But with much clarity and knowledge and deep devotion I desired totally to close the door on that point. In much peace and understanding and likewise with much devotion, I gave thanks to the Divine Persons. The occasion for this temptation was my getting up from prayer to see if I could quiet the noise coming from another room.[27] Afterward on my way to Mass and during it, it seemed to me that the warmth within was contending with the wind outside. I saw clearly the good within and the evil outside. Then in the middle of the Mass, with warmth and some devotion but no coldness, more disturbances arose from those in the room and from the one who was hearing the Mass. When I finished Mass I examined the matter, remaining seated with interior devotion.⟩

. . .

[STAGE II. HE REPEATS THE ELECTION, OFFERING, AND THANKSGIVING. FEBRUARY 13–18.

1. He again reviews the options (23–35).
2. He makes the offering a third time (36–38).
3. He gives thanks to God (39–43).]

[39]—16. Sunday [February 17. Sexagesima Sunday].
. . .

[41]—When Mass [on February 17] was ended, in the chapel and then in the room I was eager to give thanks on my knees for the great gifts and graces I had received. I lost all desire to reiterate the offering already made (although this was my customary practice, not without devotion). I considered the matter as settled. On the other hand the devotion I felt drew me to remain there, relishing the experience I was having.

[42]—Then wondering whether I would exit the election or not, with great peace I decided in the affirmative and felt special interior motions and tears. Although I thought I could linger in them for a while, I arose while they were still with me. I departed with the intention of concluding the election at least before dinner the next day; I also intended to give thanks, beg for strength, and repeat the previous offering out of devotion to the Holy Trinity, whose Mass I would say.

[43]—The Holy Trinity. The End.[28]
17. Monday [February 18].
Shortly before I went to bed last night I experienced some warmth, devotion, and great confidence that by concluding I would find the Divine Persons, or grace in them. After lying down I felt special consolation in thinking of these Persons. I crossed my arms on my breast with deep recollection in my soul.

[4. Instead of confirmation, he experiences aridity and loss of confidence (44).]

[44]—I slept but awoke in the morning before daybreak. I found myself very sluggish and deprived of all spiritual things. For about the first half of my usual prayer there was no relish or very little; and with that I had no confidence of finding grace in the Most Holy Trinity. I resumed my prayer and it seems that I made the rest of it with much devotion, sweetness, and spiritual relish.

[STAGE III. HE RENEWS HIS OFFERING AND GIVES THANKSGIVING. FEBRUARY 18–22.

1. Through his mediators he approaches the Trinity and begs to renew his offering (45–46).]

[45]—Then, desiring to get up, I had the thought of delaying my meal and of taking care not to be disturbed until I found what I desired.[29] I felt a new warmth and devotion toward weeping. I dressed with the thought of abstaining from food for three days to find that which I desired. Knowing that this thought too was from God, I found new strength, warmth, and spiritual devotion, and I was moved even more toward weeping.

[46]—A little later, wondering where to begin and remembering that it might be with all the saints, I commended myself to them so that they would ask Our Lady and her Son to be my intercessors with the Holy Trinity. I did this with much devotion and earnestness and found myself covered with tears. In this way I sought for confirmation of my past offerings by many petitions. I took the angels, the holy fathers, the apostles and disciples, all the saints, and so on, as intercessors with Our Lady and her Son. Again I asked and begged them with long supplications to see to it that my last confirmation and thanksgiving would arise before the throne of the Holy Trinity.

[2. He again feels confirmed and makes the offering a fourth time (47).]

[3. He begs its acceptance from God (48–50).]

[48]—Later[30] while I was preparing the altar and vesting, words came to me: "Eternal Father, confirm me! Eternal Son, confirm me.

Eternal Holy Spirit, confirm me. Holy Trinity, confirm me. My One and Only God, confirm me." I said this many times, with great vehemence, devotion, and tears; and I felt it very deeply. I also uttered, "Eternal Father, will you not confirm me?" as if I were sure of an affirmative reply. In a similar way I prayed to the Son and to the Holy Spirit.

[49]—While I said Mass without tears, yet the entire Mass was not altogether without them. Moreover, there was a certain warm devotion —bright red, so to speak—and many sighs of much devotion. Nevertheless at some times I did not feel these things in abundance and I wondered why no effusion or flood of tears poured out. These thoughts disturbed me, caused me to lose devotion, and made me discontented over this failure to find confirmation from this last Mass of the Trinity.

[50]—After Mass I quieted myself and compared my lowliness with the divine wisdom and greatness. I continued in this manner for some hours until a thought came that I should not trouble myself about saying more Masses. I grew indignant at the Most Holy Trinity.[31] I had no desire to determine anything farther.[32] I considered the past as something finished. Some small doubt came over me. But devotion did not leave me at any time during the day, even though this devotion was in some small way assailed and fearful of making some mistake.

[4. He decides to seek further (51).]

[51]—The Trinity. 1st.[33]
18. Tuesday [February 19].
. . . the intense love I felt toward the Holy Trinity . . . gave me confidence and I determined to say the Mass of the Holy Trinity, so as to see afterward what I would do. . . . Then with devotion and spiritual confidence, I decided to say successively six or more Masses of the Holy Trinity.

[5. Before, during, and after Mass he receives great insights into the Holy Trinity (52-64).]

[52]—On the way to Mass [that of the Holy Trinity, on Tuesday, February 19] and just before it, I was not without tears. During the Mass[34] there were many and very peaceful tears, and very many insights into the Holy Trinity. These enlightened my understanding to such a degree that it seemed to me I could not learn so much by hard study. Later when I reviewed the matter again I thought that I had understood

more in my experiencing or seeing than I would even if I should study all my life.[35]

[53]—As soon as Mass was over I offered a short prayer with the words: "Eternal Father, confirm me; Son, and so on, confirm me." Tears streamed down my face, and my will to persevere in saying their Masses grew stronger (and I consented according to whatever number I would determine later). With much intense sobbing I drew much closer to his Divine Majesty and felt more assured in my increased love of him.

[54]—In general, during Mass and before it the insights were about the appropriation[36] of the prayers of the Mass when one is addressing God, or the Father, or the Son, and so on while attending to the operations of the Divine Persons and their processions,[37] more by experiencing with feeling or contemplating than by understanding. Since all these things corroborated what had been done, I was encouraged for the future.

[55]—On that same day, even when I was walking in the city with great interior joy and when I saw three rational creatures, or three animals, or three other things, and so forth, I saw them as images reminding me of the Holy Trinity.[38]

[56]—The Trinity. 2nd.
19. Wednesday [February 20].
Before starting my prayer I felt a devout eagerness to do so. After beginning, I experienced much warm or bright and mild devotion. I had no insights but was drawn rather to a confidence of soul which did not terminate in any one Divine Person.

[57]—Then, confirming myself about the past, I recognized the evil spirit there. That is to say, he was the one who wanted to make me doubt and become indignant against the Most Holy Trinity,[39] as was stated in chapter 17.

[58]—With this recognition I felt a new interior impulse to tears. Likewise later on, before and during Mass, I experienced a greatly increased, quiet, and tranquil devotion, along with tears and some insights.

[59]—I also felt or believed, both before and after Mass, that I should not continue further; or, the desire to proceed left me—espe-

cially after Mass because of that great peace or satisfaction of soul. For it seemed unnecessary to continue the Masses of the Most Holy Trinity, unless as a thanksgiving or fulfillment of my promise;[40] but not out of any need to confirm what had been decided.

[60]—The Trinity. 3rd.
20. Thursday [February 21].
Throughout the whole time of my prayer, I felt continual and very great devotion, warm brightness, and spiritual relish. I seemed somehow drawn partly upward.[41]

[61]—Then while I was making my preparation in my room, at the altar, and while vesting, there were some interior spiritual impulses drawing me to tears. In this state I finished Mass and remained in great spiritual repose.

[62]—Throughout Mass there were tears in greater abundance than the preceding day. Once or several times I was unable to speak, experiencing spiritual insights to such an extent that I seemed to understand that there was, so to speak, nothing more to be known about this matter of the Holy Trinity.

[63]—The reason for this is the following. Previously I had been trying to find devotion in the Trinity, and I neither desired nor adapted myself to seeking or finding the Trinity in prayers to the Father. For such prayers to the Father did not seem to me to be consolation or visitation pertaining to the Holy Trinity. But during this Mass I was knowing, or experiencing, or contemplating—the Lord[42] knows—that to speak to the Father was to recognize that he was one Person of that Holy Trinity. This brought me to love that Person's whole self; and that all the more because the other two Persons were by their very essence present in that One.[43] I experienced the same recognition about prayer to the Son, and again about prayer to the Holy Spirit. I rejoiced that when I perceived consolations from any One of them I recognized them with joy as coming from all Three. To have untied this knot, or whatever else it might be called, seemed so important to me that I kept on saying about myself: "And you, who are you? Where did you come from? How could you merit this? Or whence did this come to pass?" and the like.

[64]—The Trinity. 4th.

21. Friday [February 22].

During the whole of my usual prayer I experienced much help from grace that was warm and in part bright. There was much devotion, even though on my part I sometimes found it easy to fall into distractions. However, the assistance of the grace did not cease. Later while I was preparing the altar, there were certain motions toward tears, and I repeated often: "I am not worthy to call upon the name of the Holy Trinity." This thought and repetition moved me to greater interior devotion. While I was vesting, this consideration and others with it opened my soul still more to tears and sobs. I began Mass and continued to the Gospel,[44] which I read with much devotion and great assistance from warm grace. Later this grace seemed to struggle, like fire with water, with some thoughts ⟨about salvation, sometimes expelling and sometimes conserving them⟩.

[STAGE IV. BRILLIANT CLARITY THROUGH MEDIATION OF JESUS. FEBRUARY 23–MARCH 4.

1. He receives confirmation from Jesus in an unexpected way (65–70).]

[65]—The Trinity. 5th.

22. Saturday [February 23].

In my customary prayer I found nothing at its beginning,[45] but from the middle on there was much devotion and satisfaction of soul, with some manifestation of bright clarity.

[66]—While I was preparing the altar the thought of Jesus came to me, and an urge to follow him. Deeply in my soul I thought that since he is the head of the Society, that very fact is a greater argument for proceeding in total poverty than all the other human reasons—even though it also seemed that all the other reasons which I had considered in the deliberations favored the same conclusion. This thought moved me to devotion and to tears, and to such a firmness that even if I were not to find tears at Mass or in my Masses and the like, this sentiment seemed sufficient to make me remain firm in time of temptations or tribulations.

[67]—As I went to vest, these thoughts increased and appeared to be a confirmation, although I did not receive consolations in this regard. The fact that Jesus showed himself or made his presence felt seemed to

me to be in some way a work of the Most Holy Trinity; and I remembered the occasion when the Father placed me with the Son.[46]

[68]—As I finished vesting the name of Jesus imprinted itself so intensely within me and I was so fortified or seemingly confirmed for the future that tears and sobs came upon me with a new force. As I began Mass, ⟨overwhelming[47]⟩ motions of copious grace and devotion continued to help me, along with peaceful, continual tears. Even when Mass was finished, a great devotion and impulses to tears lasted until I had unvested.

[69]—During Mass I experienced diverse sentiments in confirmation of what has been stated. At the moment when I held the Blessed Sacrament in my hands, a voice and an intense emotion surged within me never to leave him for all heaven or all the world or the like. I felt new motions, devotion, and spiritual joy. I added "for my part, doing whatever was in my power." I made this addition because of my companions who had signed.[48]

[70]—Later during the day whenever I thought of Jesus or memory of him came to my mind, I had a certain deep perception or intellectual seeing which brought continual devotion and confirmation.

[2. He experiences, through Jesus, divine confirmation of that clarity (71–73).]

[71]—Mass of the Day [Quinquagesima Sunday].
23. Sunday [February 24].

In my customary prayer, from the beginning up to its very end, I experienced continual assistance from much internal, gentle grace and I was full of warm and very sweet devotion. While I was preparing the altar and vesting, the Name of Jesus was represented to me with much love and confirmation. Amid tears and sobs my will to follow him became stronger.

[72]—During the entire Mass I experienced continuous and very great devotion along with many tears, so that often I could not speak. All the devotions and sentiments terminated in Jesus.[49] Therefore I could not apply them to the other Persons except, so to speak, inasmuch as the First Person was the Father of such a Son. In regard to that, spiritual responses came to mind: "What a Father! And what a Son!"

[73]—After Mass, during prayer I experienced that same perception of the Son. Whereas I had sought confirmation from the Holy Trinity, I now perceived that it was being communicated to me by

Jesus, who was showing himself to me and giving me such interior strength and sure confirmation that I had no fear for the future. The thought came to me to beg Jesus to obtain pardon from the Holy Trinity for me.[50] Thereupon I had increased devotion along with tears and sobbing, and the hope of obtaining this grace. I found myself very strong and confirmed for the future.

[3. He clearly sees a past error (74–78).]

[74]—Then at the fire[51] a fresh representation of Jesus came to me along with great devotion and impulse to tears. Later as I was walking along the street Jesus represented himself to me and I experienced strong motions and tears. After I spoke to Carpi[52] and was returning home I similarly felt great devotion. After the meal, especially after I passed through the door of the vicar,[53] in the house of Trana,[54] while perceiving or seeing Jesus I experienced many interior motions amid many tears. I asked and begged Jesus to obtain for me pardon from the Most Holy Trinity, and all this time a feeling of great confidence remained in me that I would obtain it.

[75]—All through these hours I found in myself such intense love and such perception or seeing of Jesus that I thought that in the future nothing could come and separate me from him, or make me doubt about the graces or confirmation I had received.

[76]—St. Matthias.

24. Monday [February 25].

During the first prayer I had much devotion, and later even more with warmth and the assistance of copious grace. Yet on my side, because of some disturbances that I suffered from others, I found myself easily distracted. I did not ask or seek confirmation, but I desired reconciliation with the three Divine Persons. Then when I was vested to say Mass but did not know to whom to commend myself or where to begin, and while Jesus was communicating himself to me, this thought came to my mind: "I want to move forward and start the prayer 'I confess to God' (*Confiteor Deo*), just as Jesus said in the Gospel of the day [Matt. 11:25] 'I confess to you' (*Confiteor tibi*, and so on)."

[77]—Immediately I moved forward into that prayer of confession, with new devotion and not without impulses to shed tears. I entered into the Mass with great devotion, warmth, tears, and occasional loss of speech. In the prayers to the Father, it seemed to me that Jesus was presenting them, or that he was accompanying into the Fa-

ther's presence those which I was saying. I deeply perceived or saw this in a way that cannot be explained.

. . .

[4. Through prayer to Jesus he conforms to whatever spiritual way will be most pleasing to the Trinity (79–82).
5. The Mediation of Jesus and visions confirm him in this new attitude (83–91).]

[82]—The First Day of Lent [Ash Wednesday].
26. Wednesday [February 27].
. . .

[83]—Upon entering the chapel, during prayer I perceived deeply in my heart, or more precisely I saw beyond my natural powers, the Most Holy Trinity and Jesus. He was representing me, or placing me, or serving as my mediator with the Most Holy Trinity in order that intellectual vision might be granted to me. At this perception and sight I was covered with tears and love terminating chiefly on Jesus.[55] Toward the Trinity too I felt a respect of affectionate awe[56] closer to reverential love than to anything else.

[84]—Then when I thought of praying to the Father, with similar deep feeling I perceived Jesus exercising the same role. Deeply within myself it seemed that in the presence of the Father and the Holy Trinity Jesus was doing it all.

[85]—I began Mass with many tears and through the whole Mass I continually had much devotion and tears. Likewise at one moment I saw in a remarkable way the same vision of the Holy Trinity as at first.[57] All the while my love for the Divine Majesty was growing greater still. Several times I lost the power of speech.

[86]—When Mass was finished and I was in prayer and later near the fire, several times I experienced very intense devotion terminating in Jesus, and that not without special interior impulses to tears or something more.

[87]—In writing this I find my intellect being drawn to see the Holy Trinity in such a way that I seem to see the three Persons, though not distinctly as before. At the time of Mass, when saying "Lord Jesus Christ, Son of the Living God" and so on (*Domine Iesu Christe, fili Dei vivi*),[58] it seemed to me that in spirit I saw Jesus in the same way as I described the first time, as something white, that is, his humanity. But now in this second time, deeply in my soul I was seeing him in another

way, that is to say, I perceived not the humanity alone, but that in his whole self he is my God,[59] and so forth. There was a fresh outpouring of tears, great devotion, and the like.

[88]—The Trinity. 7th.
27. Thursday [February 28].
During the whole of my customary prayer there was much devotion and much helping grace, warm, bright, and loving. When I entered the chapel I felt a fresh devotion. After kneeling down I had a manifestation or vision of Jesus at the feet of the Most Holy Trinity and, with this, motions and tears. This vision was not as long or as clear as the past one on Wednesday, although it seemed to be of the same kind. Later during Mass there were tears, much devotion, and some profitable sentiments. After Mass I was not without tears.

[89]—Of the Wounds.
28. Friday [February 29].
During my customary prayer, from the beginning to its very end, there was very great and very bright devotion which covered my sins and would not allow me to think about them. Outside the house, in the church[60] before Mass, I had a vision of the heavenly fatherland or of its Lord, in the form of an insight into the Three Persons, and into the Second and Third Persons as being in the Father. During Mass at times there was much devotion, but without insights or any motions to tears. [90]—When Mass was finished I had the same vision of the fatherland or of its Lord without the distinction of Persons, but clearly, just as I did on many other occasions, sometimes more clearly and sometimes less. All day long there was special devotion.
. . .

[6. He leaves everything to the divine initiative (92–96).
7. Devotion and love toward the Trinity (97–102).
8. Intense love for the Holy Trinity (103–110).]

. . .

[104]—The Trinity. 9th.
32. Tuesday [March 4].
In my customary prayer I was much helped by grace and devotion which, if clear, was brighter, and had a sign of some warmth. On my

252

side, with this help I found it very easy to plunge myself into the thoughts which came to mind and to get up. After dressing I looked over the entrance antiphon of the Mass,[61] and I was totally moved to devotion and love ending in the Holy Trinity.

. . .

[109]—When I had finished Mass and unvested, during my prayer at the altar there was so much sobbing and effusion of tears, all terminating in the love of the Holy Trinity, that I seemed to have no desire to leave. For I was feeling so much love and so much spiritual sweetness.

[110]—Then several times near the fire I experienced interior love for the Holy Trinity and impulses to weep. Later, in the house of Burgos[62] and in the streets until half past three in the afternoon, whenever I remembered the Holy Trinity I felt an intense love and sometimes motions toward weeping. All these visitations terminated in the Name and Essence of the Holy Trinity. However, I did not clearly and deeply perceive or see distinct Persons in the way that I mentioned above at various times. All of these visitations were drawing me to greater confidence. I had no desire to say more Masses to reconcile myself farther but I wished to complete the number promised. I also hoped to have joy in Their Divine Majesty.[63]

. . .

[STAGE V. HE EXPERIENCES LUMINOUS AND WARM DEVOTION, FEELS RECONCILED, AND DECIDES. MARCH 5-12.

1. In humility he feels complete reconciliation with the Trinity (111-116).
2. He has rest after labor (117-120).
3. He perceives the Divine Essence and the Divine Persons amid Intense Brightness (121-126).]

. . .

[126]—The Trinity. 12th.
25. [bis]. Friday [March 7].
I began my customary prayer with much devotion. Although I desired ⟨to see again something which I saw yesterday,⟩ I did not receive increased devotion by looking above. From the middle of the prayer onward there was very much devotion. It was continuous and

accompanied by much bright, warm, and very gentle clarity. The same devotion lasted after the prayer.

[4. He looks below and sees the Divine Essence reflected in creatures (127–133).]

[127]—Then during the preparatory prayer and likewise in the chapel my mind was peaceful and recollected. While I was vesting a little later there were fresh motions toward weeping and conforming myself with the divine will so that it would guide me, carry me onward, and so forth. "I am a child" [Jer. 1:6] and so on. I began Mass with much devotion, interior reverence, and impulses to weep. As I pronounced the words "Blessed be the Holy Trinity"[64] and during the entire prayer, I experienced a new perception, a fresh and greater devotion and impulses toward weeping. I did not raise my understanding to consider the Divine Persons as distinct nor to distinguish them, nor did I lower my understanding to the letter.[65] Rather, this visitation seemed to me to be interior, midway between the Trinity's dwelling place above and the letter.[66]

[128]—And so as I went forward with many continuous tears I opined that I had no permission to look above. I looked not above but rather to the middle area, and that brought me an increase of intense devotion with profuse tears. I had an increasing affective awe and reverence for the visions from above, and there came to me a sure confidence that a permission would be given to me, or that I would receive a manifestation when the right time would arrive ⟨without any effort from myself to procure it⟩.

[129]—At these times I experienced the visitations as terminating in a variety of ways: sometimes in the Holy Trinity, sometimes in the Father, sometimes in the Son, sometimes in Our Lady, sometimes in the saints or in an individual saint.[67] I shed many tears, which then ceased at the middle or after the middle of the Mass, that is, near the prayer "This oblation, therefore" (*Hanc igitur oblationem*). Sometimes strong fire battled with water, because I could not find the Sacrament.[68]

. . .

*[5. He experiences devotion and contentment in this new
attitude of humble conformity to God's will (134–144).]*

[134]—The Trinity. 13th.
26 [bis]. Saturday [March 8].

In my customary prayer, from the beginning to the end, there was a
great and constantly growing help of grace, with devotion that was very
clear, bright, and warm. It resulted in much satisfaction and contentment, both in the preparatory prayer and in the chapel.

[135]—While vesting I experienced fresh motions which lasted to
the end, together with greater ones and with many tears. A very great
humility appeared within me, so that I could not look up to heaven. The
less I wanted to look above, wanting instead to humiliate and lower
myself, so much the more relish and spiritual visitation did I feel.[69]

[136]—At the beginning of Mass and all during it, there was much
interior devotion and spiritual warmth, not without tears. I had continual devotion and an inclination to weep. At intervals, although I was
willing not to lift the eyes of my understanding upward, but rather to
make myself content with everything; and although I even prayed, if it
were to God's equal glory, not to be visited with tears,[70] sometimes my
understanding unintentionally went upward and I seemed to see something of the Divine Being which at other times it is not in my power to
see even when I so desire.

[137]—Mass of the Day [The Second Sunday of Lent].
27 [bis]. Sunday [March 9].

My customary prayer was like that of former days. After vesting I
had during the preparatory prayer fresh devotion and motions toward
weeping. They terminated principally in the Holy Trinity and in Jesus.

[138]—As I entered the chapel, the motions and tears were greater.
All of them terminated in the Holy Trinity, and sometimes in Jesus,
sometimes in both of them together or almost together. This took place
in such a way that the termination in Jesus did not diminish devotion to
the Holy Trinity, and vice versa. This devotion lasted until I vested,
sometimes accompanied by tears.

[139]—Then during Mass there was an exterior warmth which
moved me to devotion and cheerfulness of mind, with a few impulses or
motions toward weeping. Yet I was more content without them than
when I had them, sometimes in abundance. Not feeling insights, vi-

sions, or tears in any way, I thought that God our Lord wanted to show me some way or manner of proceeding.[71]

[140]—I passed the whole day with much contentment of soul. At night I seemed to be disposing myself to a devotion which terminated in the Holy Trinity and in Jesus. This occurred in such a way that they showed themselves to my understanding, allowing themselves to be seen in a certain way. I wanted to dispose myself to the Father, to the Holy Spirit, and to Our Lady; but in this I found no devotion or any vision. For a moment, however, there was an insight into or vision of the Most Holy Trinity and of Jesus.

[141]—The Name of Jesus.
28 [bis]. Monday [March 10].
In my customary prayer there was much devotion, especially during the second half. Before the preparatory prayer there was fresh devotion, along with a thought or judgment that I ought to act or be like an angel during the ceremonies of saying Mass; and my eyes gently filled with tears.

[142]—Then in the chapel and during Mass I had devotion at the same thought. I conformed myself to what the Lord was ordaining and I thought that his Divine Majesty would provide, by arranging everything for the good, and so forth [Rom. 8:28]. During this time on occasions I saw in some way the Essence of the Father—that is, first the Essence and then the Father; in still other words, the devotion terminated first in the Essence and then in the Father, but sometimes in another way and without such clear distinction.

[143]—Our Lady.
29 [bis]. Tuesday [March 11].
During all of my customary prayer there was much devotion—clear, bright, and so to speak warm. In the chapel, at the altar, and later there were tears and my devotion terminated in Our Lady, although I did not see her. During the whole Mass the devotion remained and sometimes motions toward tears. After Mass too the devotion continued. During these periods I had many visions. At times I saw the Divine Essence and at times my attention terminated in the Father; that is, first I saw the Essence and then the Father. In the chapel before Mass it occurred to me, as if I had permission to look above,[72] that to look above was for me a remedy against distractions from things below. Immedi-

ately motions and tears surged up. Then I tried to look above, and both when I saw something and when I did not see anything I found devotion. I also found a remedy against so easily turning my attention away from what I ought to do throughout the whole of Mass.

[144]—The Holy Spirit.
30 [bis]. Wednesday [March 12].
During my customary prayer there was much devotion; and during the second half, much devotion that was clear, bright, and so to speak warm. In the chapel because of someone's coming down the stairs in haste I could not dispose myself for Mass. For my preparation I returned to my room and composed myself, amid tears. While I was going to the chapel, and later at the beginning of Mass and then during one part of it, I had much devotion and sometimes motions to weep. During the rest of Mass I struggled many times about what I should do to conclude the matter,[73] for I was not finding what I was looking for. During these periods there was no sign of visions or insights.

[6. In spiritual desolation, he submits to whatever is more pleasing to God and then receives spiritual consolation (145–149).]

[145]—When Mass was finished, and then in my room, I found myself totally deprived of any help and was unable to relish my mediators or the Divine Persons. I felt as remote and separated from them as if I had never felt anything in their regard, or would ever feel anything in the future. Instead thoughts came to me sometimes against Jesus, sometimes against another.[74] I was quite confused by various thoughts, now about leaving the house and renting a room to avoid noises, or about going without eating,[75] or whether I ought to begin a new series of Masses, or move the altar to a higher floor.[76] Nowhere did I find rest, although I desired to end[77] at a time when I would be in a state of consolation and totally satisfied.

[146]—Finally I examined whether I should proceed further, because on the one hand I seemed to be looking for too many signs, that is, for a length of time or a number of Masses celebrated. All of this was for my own satisfaction, since the matter was clear in itself. Hence I was seeking, not certitude about the matter, but rather an end of the whole process in a manner fitted to my own pleasure. On the other hand, I thought that if I should stop the whole process at a time when I was so distressed, I would not be content later on, and so forth.

[147]—Finally, since there was no difficulty in the matter itself, I considered that it would be more pleasing to God our Lord to conclude without waiting or seeking more proofs, and without saying more Masses to obtain them. As I began an election toward this purpose I felt it would please God our Lord more to conclude. I felt also that I had been wanting the Lord to condescend to my desire, that is to say, to my desire to finish at a time when I found myself much visited. When I became aware of this inclination of my own and the contrasting good pleasure of God our Lord, I began at once to understand and to desire to accede to the good pleasure of God our Lord.[78]

[148]—With this, the darkness gradually began to leave me and tears came. As they increased, my intention to say more Masses for this purpose faded away. A thought came to say three Masses of the Trinity in thanksgiving, but to me it seemed to come from the evil spirit. I decided to say none and my love of God increased much. Tears, sobs, and fortitude came in great abundance as I knelt for a long while and then paced back and forth. Again I fell on my knees, with many, varied, and diverse thoughts[79] amid profound interior satisfaction. Although this visitation was so great (that I experienced considerable pain in my eyes) and lasted more or less for the space of an hour, the tears finally ceased. I doubted whether I ought to conclude that night, if a similar outpouring should occur, or right away.

[149]—Even though the outpouring had ceased, it seemed to me better to end immediately; that to seek or to delay until evening would be a desire of further searching for which there was no reason. Thus, in the presence of God our Lord and all his court and so forth, I proposed to conclude the matter at this point and to proceed no further in this material. At this last proposal too interior motions, sobs, and tears surged up. Even though it was a time of great floods of tears, I considered everything as ended; furthermore that I ought not to seek for more Masses or some visitation, but to conclude on this very day.

[7. He definitively concludes and experiences God's full confirmation (150–153).]

[150]—Finished.[80]

[151]—It was after 1:30 P.M. when I sat down to eat. After a while, the tempter tried without success to make me show some sign of doubting. Instantaneously without any qualms I replied, as if to a temptation already overcome, "Go where you belong." I experienced a

confirmation, through tears and complete security about everything that had been determined.

[152]—A quarter of an hour later I awakened to a new understanding. I clearly saw that at the time when the tempter was enticing me to thoughts against the Divine Persons and the mediators, he was trying to stir up doubt about the matter itself. And I saw that, on the contrary, when I was experiencing visitations or visions from the Divine Persons and the mediators, I felt complete firmness and confirmation about that matter. This perception was accompanied by a spiritual relish. It was as if tears were coming to my eyes amid much security of soul.

[153]—During the grace at table I had a partial perception of the Father's Being and also of the Being of the Holy Trinity, and a certain spiritual motion impelled me toward devotion and to tears. Throughout the whole day I had neither experienced nor seen anything like it, although I had sought it many times. The great visitations of this day did not terminate in any distinct or particular Person, but in general in the Giver of graces.

[PART II, The Second Copybook.
A RECORD IN GRATITUDE FOR MYSTICAL FAVORS.
March 13, 1544 to February 27, 1545]

[STAGE VI. WALKING ALONG A NEW PATH: LOVING HUMILITY AND AFFECTIONATE AWE. March 13, 1544 to February 27, 1545.

1. Contentment and peace of soul (154–155).

A TRANSITION: March 13–16, 1544.]

[154]—I took these four days to avoid examination of anything pertaining to the Constitutions.[81]

[155]—Mass of the Day.
1. Thursday [March 13].
⟨Before and⟩ during Mass I conformed myself to the divine will in regard to the absence of tears. For me this would be a kind of rest from work, a repose from searching, or from wondering whether to have or not to have.[82] Then during the whole day there I had contentment and complacency in my soul.

[2. Affectionate awe and reverence (156–160) March 14-16.]

[156]—The Holy Spirit.
2. a. 1. d.[83] Friday [March 14].

Before, all during, and after Mass there were many tears terminating sometimes in the Father, sometimes in the Son and so forth, even in the saints. However, there was no vision, except insofar as my devotion at intervals terminated sometimes in one, sometimes in another. During all these times before, during, and after Mass I had a steady thought which penetrated the depth of my soul: How great is the reverence and affectionate awe[84] with which I ought to pronounce the name of God our Lord, and so on; and further, that I ought to seek, not tears, but this affectionate awe and reverence.

[157]—To such an extent did I exercise myself in this affectionate awe before Mass in my room, in the chapel, and during the Mass that when tears came to me, I immediately repulsed them in order to attend to the affectionate awe. I thought that neither I nor anything of mine brought on this affectionate awe which kept on increasing my devotion and tears to a great extent. As a result I became convinced that this was the path which the Lord was seeking to point out to me, just as in those past days when I thought that he was seeking to show me something.[85] I became convinced of this: When saying Mass, for the spiritual profit of my soul I ought to attach a greater value to this grace and knowledge than to all the other past graces.

[158]—Our Lady.
3. Saturday [March 15].

During part of the Mass I had a certain interior affectionate awe and reverence; but during the greater part nothing which gave me the power to perceive interiorly either affectionate awe or reverence.

[159]—Mass of the Day [The Third Sunday of Lent].
4. a. 1. Sunday [March 16].

Before Mass and during all of it there were many tears, with the devotion and tears terminating now in one person, now in another; but there were no clear or distinct visions. Before Mass I prayed in my room that affectionate awe, reverence, and humility would be given me; also that visitations or tears would not be given me if that should be an equal service of the Divine Majesty; or else that I would enjoy his graces and visitations purely and without self-interest.

[160]—Thereupon all the later spiritual visitations brought me affectionate awe, not only toward the Divine Persons when I named or remembered them, but also when I reverenced the altar and the other things pertaining to the sacrifice.[86] When I happened to notice tears or visitations or to desire them,[87] I tried to repulse them; and thus when I attended first to the affectionate awe, the visitations came later. I judged that the contrary, namely, to attend first to the visitations and then to the affectionate awe, was wrong.[88] This seemed to confirm what I felt last Friday, ⟨that to walk along this path was to go straight ahead in the service of God our Lord, which I esteemed more important than anything else⟩.

[3. Confirming an election by the new way of affectionate awe and reverence (161–171). March 17–24.]

[161]—Here I began my preparations, considering first of all the material pertaining to the missions.[89]

[162]—Our Lady.
1. a. 1. Monday [March 17].
Before Mass, tears, and during Mass many tears, so many that several times I could not speak. This entire visitation terminated sometimes in one Person and sometimes in another, in the same way as on the preceding day and in the same manner, namely, in affectionate awe and reverence which confirmed all the past. I had found the way which was being pointed out to me. It seemed to be the best of all and the one I ought to follow always.

[163]—During some periods of time before saying Mass while recollecting myself in my room, I did not find any affectionate awe or reverence which brought noteworthy spiritual experience or interior relish. I seemed indeed to be powerless to find it, and yet I desired to have it or find it.

[164]—Then a little later in the chapel the divine will seemed to be for me to try to seek and find, even though it was not in my power to find. Then the Giver of graces provided such an outpouring of knowledge, visitation, and spiritual relish accompanied, as I mentioned, by such continual tears that I could not speak. It seemed that at every word by which God is named, such as Lord and the like, I was penetrated deeply by an affectionate awe and an admirable reverential humility which seem impossible to explain.

[165]—The Name of Jesus.
2. a— 1 d— Tuesday [March 18].
During Mass there were tears. Before and after Mass too I was not without them, and everything was directed toward affectionate awe and reverence.

[166]—The Trinity.
3. 1. d. Wednesday [March 19].
During Mass, the whole time, there was a great abundance of tears which continued also after Mass. During Mass I often lost the power of speech. The thrust of it all was toward affectionate awe and reverence and many other interior sentiments.

[167]—Our Lady.
4. a. 1— Thursday [March 20].
Before Mass and during it I was not without some tears, and I also had diverse interior motions terminating in affectionate awe.

[168]—The Name of Jesus.
5. a— 1— Friday [March 20].
Before Mass and during it I was not without some tears terminating in affectionate awe. I also experienced some interior motions.

[169]—The Holy Spirit.

6. 1. d. Saturday [March 22].
During the entire Mass there were many tears flowing gently, and after too. Before Mass they were accompanied by mo-

Vision
===/==

tions toward weeping and I perceived or saw the Holy Spirit himself. Everything was affectionate awe.[90]

[170]—Mass of the Day [The Fourth Sunday of Lent].
7. a. 1. Sunday [March 23].
Before and during Mass many intense tears, all terminating in affectionate awe.

[171]—The Trinity.

8. 1 Monday [March 24].

During Mass there were tears several times, terminating in affectionate awe.

[4. Visions and realization that affectionate awe is God's gift (172–176). March 25–29.]

[172]—Our Lady.

9. a 1 d Tuesday [March 25].

There were tears before and after Mass; during Mass there were
many tears, with a vision of the Divine Being. It termi-
Vision   nated in the Father, several times in the form of a circle;
═╫═   and all this was directed toward affectionate awe.[91]

[173]—The Name of Jesus.

10. a− 1 Wednesday [March 26].

During Mass there were tears at various times, and before Mass
motions toward them. Until the Secret Prayer[92] of the Mass, not only
was I unable to feel interior affectionate awe but I could not even find
any aptitude to help myself toward it. From this I concluded and saw
that I could not by my own power make any progress toward finding it.
At the Secret Prayer and afterward I did have a spiritual visitation which
terminated in affectionate awe.

. . .

[5. Reverence, affectionate awe, and the further gift of loving humility (177–182). March 30–April 1.]

[177]—Mass of the Day [Passion Sunday].

14. a. 1 d. Sunday [March 30].

Before Mass, in my room, in the chapel, and in my preparation
there were many tears. During the whole Mass, too, tears
Vision   were present in great abundance; and after Mass they
were very intense.

[178]—During this period of time I kept on thinking that humility,
reverence, and affectionate awe ought to be not fearful but loving. This
thought took root in my mind so deeply that I begged over and over
again:[93] "Give me loving humility, and with it reverence and affection-

ate awe." After these words I received new visitations. Moreover, I repulsed tears in order to attend to this loving humility and so forth.

[179]—Later during the day I experienced great joy in remembering this. It seemed to me that I ought not to stop there, but that the same would apply in relation to creatures; that is to say, loving humility and all it brings would so apply;[94]—except at those times when it would not contribute to the glorification of God our Lord; as today's Gospel states: it would be saying: "I would be like you, a liar."[95]

[180]—During these periods of time, on several occasions I had a vision of the divine Being in circular shape, as previously.

[181]—Mass of the Day [Monday of Passion Week].
15. 1. d. Monday [March 31].
During and after Mass there were tears, terminating in loving reverence, and so on. At times I judged that neither love nor reverence and the like were within my own power.

[182]—Mass of the Day [Tuesday of Passion Week].
16. 1. Tuesday [April 1].
During Mass there were many tears terminating in loving humility and so on. I thought that in order to find this during the sacrifice of the Mass I have to draw profit from it throughout the entire day and try not to yield to distractions.

. . .

[6. He understands the relation of these new gifts to his fidelity or infidelity (183–188). April 2–5.]

[183]—Mass of the Day [Wednesday of Passion Week].
17. a. 1. Wednesday [April 2].
During my customary prayer, later on in my room, then in the chapel, while I was vesting there were tears, and during
Vision   Mass a great abundance of them.[96] During these periods on several occasions I had a vision of the divine Being. Sometimes it terminated in the Father in the circular shape. This brought me many insights and interior understandings.

[184]—In times of greater knowledge or of greater visitations I thought that I ought to be content not to be visited with tears, and to

consider it better to be visited or not visited in accordance with what God our Lord is more pleased to do. During some times when I was not visited in this way I thought that this was perfection so great that I did not hope for this grace, or I feared that I could not obtain it.

[185]—Then at another time when I was having a visitation especially vivid I seemed to find satisfaction in considering it better not to be visited by God our Lord. For I received no visitation either because I did not dispose myself or make progress during the entire day, or because I gave way to some thoughts which distracted me from his words in the sacrifice of the Mass[97] and from his Divine Majesty. Therefore I thought it was better not to be visited during the time of my faults; and that God our Lord (who loves me more than I love myself) was arranging this for my greater spiritual profit. Hence to receive a visitation it was proper for me to press forward not only during the sacrifice of the Mass, but also during the entire day. This corresponded to what I understood on the preceding day from these and similar insights which are so great and so delicate that I can find neither memory nor understanding to explain or describe them.

[186]—Mass of the Day [Thursday of Passion Week].
18. Thursday [April 3].
There were no tears before, during, or after Mass. When Mass was over I found myself more content without tears but with affection. I judged that God our Lord was bringing about what was better for me.

[187]—Mass of the Day [Friday of Passion Week].
19. a. 1. Friday [April 4].
Before Mass I experienced tears, and during Mass a great abundance of them together with many insights and interior sentiments which I had experienced also before Mass. When we do not find reverence or affectionate awe full of love, we ought to seek the affectionate awe which springs from fear, meanwhile looking at our own faults. Our objective is to obtain the affectionate awe full of love.

[188]—Mass of the Day [Saturday of Passion Week].
20. a. 1. Saturday [April 5].
Before Mass, with tears and during Mass with many tears.

[7. In mystical prayer he conforms himself totally with God's will (189-190). April 6-7.]

[189]—Mass of the Day [Palm Sunday].
21. a. 1. d. Sunday [April 6].
Before Mass I had tears, and during Mass after the Passion[98] many continual tears. They were directed toward conformation of my will to the divine will. After Mass I had the same experience accompanied by tears.

[190]—Mass of the Day [Monday of Holy Week].
22. 1 Monday [April 7].
Throughout Mass there were many tears drawing me to conformity with the divine will.

[8. He lists instances of the infused gift of tears (191-220).]

[191]—Mass of the Day [Tuesday of Holy Week].
23. 1 Tuesday [April 8].
During Mass, with tears.

[192]—24. 1 Wednesday [April 9. Wednesday of Holy Week].
During Mass, with tears.

[193]—25. Thursday [April 10. Holy Thursday.]
Without tears.

---

[194]—26. [April 11. Good Friday].[99]

[195]—27. [April 12. Holy Saturday].

---

[196]—Mass of the Day [Easter Sunday].
28. 1. d. Easter Sunday [April 13].
During Mass, with many tears, and after Mass, with tears.
. . .

[219]—42. Wednesday [May 7].
43. Thursday [May 8]. } It seems to me, without tears.
44. Friday [May 9].

[220]—45. 1 Saturday [May 10]. With many tears during Mass.

[9. He receives a final mystical gift: loquela (221–240). May 11–28.]

[221]—46. a. l. Sunday [May 11. The Fourth Sunday after Easter].
I had tears before Mass and, during Mass too, continuous tears in great abundance. Along with them was an interior *loquela*[100] of the Mass which to a still greater extent seemed to be given by God. On that same day I had asked for it, because during the entire week I had sometimes found the exterior loquela and sometimes not. Still less had I found the interior *loquela*, although last Saturday I found [it][101] a little more purified.

[222]—Similarly during all the Masses of the week, although I was not visited so much by tears, I had throughout each Mass greater peace or contentment because of my relishing the *loquelas* with ⟨an interior⟩ devotion. This contentment was greater than at many other times when I had experienced tears during part of the Mass. The loquelas of this day seemed to me very noticeably different from all of those in the past. For they came so slowly, interiorly, gently, and without noise[102] or great motions that they seemed to arise so entirely from within that I do not know how to explain the matter. Throughout the entire duration of the interior and the exterior *loquela* everything was moving me toward divine love and the divinely granted gift of the *loquela*. Along with itself the interior *loquela* brought deep in my soul a harmony so great that I cannot express it.

[223] This Sunday before Mass I began and planned to go forward with the Constitutions.[103]

[224]—All Saints.
47. 1. d. Monday [May 12].
There were many tears during Mass and some after Mass, all of them like those of the preceding day and accompanied by an intense relish of the interior *loquela*. It seemed to resemble, or I seemed to remember, the *loquela* or heavenly music. I had growing devotion and tearful affection, for I felt that I was perceiving or learning from God.
. . .

[234]—[The Feast of] the Ascension.
57. a. 1. Thursday [May 22].

Before Mass in my room and in the chapel there were many tears. During much the greater part of the Mass itself I was without tears but experienced much *loquela*. However, this cessation of the spiritual visitations of tears stirred up doubts as to whether the enjoyment or sweetness of the *loquela* might be from the evil spirit. As I proceeded a bit farther, I thought I might be taking too much pleasure in the tone or sound of the *loquela* and was not paying enough attention to the meaning of its words. Immediately many tears flowed and I thought I was being taught[104] about the procedure I ought to follow, meanwhile hoping always for further instruction for the future.

[235]—[The Mass of] The Ascension.[105]
58. 1. Friday [May 23].
With tears.

[236]—The Holy Spirit.
59. Saturday [May 24].
Without tears.

[237]—40 [bis].   a. l. Sunday [May 25].

Before Mass, many tears in my room, tears in the chapel, and a great abundance of continual tears during Mass, with the two admirable *loquelas*.

[238]—Ascension.
41 [bis].   1. Monday [May 26].
During Mass, tears and interior *loquela*.

[239]—Ascension.
42 [bis].   a. l. Tuesday [May 27].
Before Mass, tears; during Mass many tears with an interior *loquela* which increased.

[240]—Ascension.
43 [bis].   .a 1 d. Wednesday [May 28].

Before and after Mass, tears; during Mass, many tears and an admirable interior *loquela*.

[10. He lists further occurrences of the gift of tears (241–490). May 29, 1544–February 27, 1545.]

[241]—Ascension.
44 [bis].   .a 1 d. Thursday [May 29].
Before, during, and after Mass, tears.

[242]—45 [bis]. Friday [May 30]. Without tears.

[243]—46 [bis]. 1 Saturday [May 31]. With tears.

[244]—47 [bis]. [Pentecost] Sunday [June 1]. With tears.
. . .

[365]— Here begin the dots; and those used before are no longer used.[106]

[366]—[October 1] 4. a. 1. d. Saturday, before Mass .O.C.Y. and during Mass a great abundance of them [tears]; also after Mass.

[367]—[Eighteenth Sunday after Pentecost, October 5].
5. ä 1. d. Sunday, before O.C.Y. and during Mass a great superabundance of continuous tears, many times with loss of the power of speech, and with fear of losing my sight; after Mass, tears.
. . .

[488]—[February 25].
25. ä 1 d Wednesday, O C Y tears during Mass; and after.

[489]—[February 26].
26. ä 1 d Thursday, O C Y during Mass in great abundance, and continuous; also after Mass.

[490]—[February 27].
27. ä 1 d Friday, O C Y during Mass in great abundance, and continuous; also after Mass.

END OF THE EXTANT FRAGMENT
OF THE *SPIRITUAL DIARY*

D. Selections from the

CONSTITUTIONS OF
THE SOCIETY OF JESUS

ABBREVIATED CONTENTS

1. INTRODUCTION

In Ignatius' *Autobiography*, *Exercises*, and *Spiritual Diary*, we have seen him chiefly as the person, saint, and mystic. In his *Constitutions* we shall view him as the founder, organizer, and animator of his apostolic religious order and of its members' life and work.

a. The Title and Structure

First of all we do best to attend to some technical terminology. After the jurist Gaius (ca. A.D. 180) the Latin word *constitutio* often meant a decree, statute, regulation, or ordinance. A collection of such statutes was entitled Constitutions (*Constitutiones*). In line with this usage, each statute in Ignatius' work is called a constitution, and the work as a whole is entitled *Constitutions of the Society of Jesus*. We should not think of these Constitutions as equivalent to the American Constitution, that is, as the foundational law of the Jesuit Order. In the Society of Jesus the fundamental law is the papal Formula of the Institute as now contained in the bull *Exposcit debitum* of 1550. The Jesuit *Constitutions* are statutes applying that fundamental law in greater detail.

Through a usage which dates back to 1558, the term *Constitutions* has been employed also in a comprehensive sense as the title of an entire collection: four separate treatises which Ignatius left in manuscript at his death.[1] First among them comes the *General Examen*, which, for the benefit of candidates and their examiners, explains the Society's institute, spirit, and manner of life. In this *Examen* were items which Ignatius deemed to require further explanation; and by a letter (such as A, B, or C) he referred readers to further explanations in the second treatise, entitled *Declarations on the Examen*, a collection of authoritative explanations of the related phrases or passages of the *Examen*. Next comes the central legislative treatise, entitled the *Constitutions of the Society of Jesus*. It likewise on occasions refers its readers to the fourth treatise, the *Declarations on the Constitutions*. All the single statutes in these four treatises have equal juridical value. In an edition in Rome in 1570 each declaration was placed immediately beneath the passage it explained. In this way the four treatises were interwoven and printed as one book, with the *Examen* ahead of the *Constitutions*.[2] That has been the usual practice ever since and is followed here. Each declaration is printed in italics and inserted within the *Examen* or *Constitutions* immediately following the statute which it explains. Until recently the system of references was cumbersome, for example: *Constitutions*, Part 4, ch. 13, no. 2, decl. A. All this can now be given simply as *Cons* [455], thanks to an edition at Rome in 1949. In it numbers enclosed in brackets were added to the statutes in Ignatius' text and have now become standard. Passages in the *Examen* are designated either as *Exam* [32] or as *Cons* [32].

Since the *Constitutions* were to be applied throughout the Society, Ignatius knew that they would have to be supplemented in future years by further determinations adapting them to new circumstances of times and places. Hence in [136] he provided for further decrees which he called ordinations or rules (*ordenanzas o reglas*). Many sets of such rules have arisen, such as the Rules of the Roman College, or rules for sacristans, cooks, or priests.[3] Further, since the *Constitutions* received their legislative binding force from the approval of the First General Congregation in 1558, subsequent general congregations have authority to interpret or change them, provided there is no conflict with papal law. To meet the needs and circumstances of successive centuries, many collections of decrees of general congregations and ordinances of superiors general have arisen and been printed in separate collections, but the text of Ignatius' own classic *Constitutions* has wisely been kept unchanged.

It is characteristic of Ignatius to set forth a clear and attractive end to be achieved and then to develop the means to attain it. A prime example is the *Exercises*. At their very beginning, in the Foundation ([23]) he states the end of human beings, salvation; and all the rest of the book offers means to attain it more richly. In the *Examen* he proceeds in the same way. Already in [3] he states the Society's end, to labor strenuously for personal sanctification and the spiritual welfare of the neighbor, and then he treats the means to attain it, such as the vows and training in piety. He calls this the "order of intention" ([135]).

In the *Constitutions*, however, he reverses this order and works from the means upward to the end in view, the fully constituted Society. He terms this procedure the "order of execution" ([135]), that is, of implementation. He divides his *Constitutions* into ten "Parts." In a loosely chronological order he treats first of the individual members: their admission, spiritual and intellectual formation, definitive incorporation into the Society, and application to its work (Parts I–VII). Then he writes of their relations among themselves and with their head or superior general (Part VIII), then of the general himself (IX), and lastly of the Society as a fully constituted whole and of its preservation and development (X).

This order was practical but it entailed overlapping and repetitions. For any given topic, such as prayer, he had a comprehensive concept in his conscious or subconscious mind; but from it he drew only what seemed most important for the occasion at hand. For example, he had a comprehensive concept of prayer, but in writing for novices in Part III of his *Constitutions* he focused on some aspects, and on others when writing for formed Jesuits in Part VI. In neither place was his thought complete. To interpret either passage correctly we must consult the other, and to get his whole concept we must draw from passages in his other writings where he treats the topic. In printings of the complete text abundant cross-references are given, usually in the margins. However, in this set of selections this seems impractical.

b. A Manual of Discernment

Ignatius could have made his *Constitutions* merely a dry collection of statutes, of do's and don'ts—as has been done in many codes ancient and modern. In contrast to that procedure, however, he skillfully wove into the legislative prescriptions the spiritual motivation for carrying them into practice. As a result, his book is a classic of spirituality as well as of religious legislation. The selections chosen for this book will be chiefly those of a spiritual nature.

The same spiritual ideas and principles which vivify the *Exercises* control everything in the *Constitutions*. These two books pertain respectively to the individual and social levels, and he regarded both of them as means and methods to bring greater service and glory to God, in time and eternity. The end of human persons expressed in the Principle and Foundation (*SpEx* [23]), "to praise, reverence, and serve God," reappears in other words when he states the end of the Society (*Cons* [3]). Ignatius envisaged all the procedures and structures treated in the *Constitutions* as means to that supreme end. The principle which concludes the Foundation, that one should choose what is more conducive to that supreme end, flowers in the *Constitutions* into the criterion guiding all choices treated. Throughout them Ignatius continually repeats the phrase "the greater glory" of God, or a similar phrase like "service" which implies it. At first appearance this constant recurrence may seem to be a mere repetition of a motto or cliché, but that is not true, for usually the phrase is functionally important in the immediate context. By inserting "the greater glory of God" Ignatius is usually reminding the reader of the proper criterion for deciding about options. Important examples can be seen in [618, 622a, d, e][4] below.

As a result, his *Constitutions* is not merely a set of precepts but also, perhaps more importantly, a manual of discernment toward helping superiors or members to discover the better choices in the opinions they meet: Which option is likely to result, in the long run, to lead to greater glory of the Divine Majesty?

c. Part IV as a Classic of Christian Educational Theory

Part IV of the *Constitutions* has a particular importance insofar as it presents the chief guiding principles which constitute Ignatius' theory of Christian education. By studying this part we can observe the process by which his worldview flowed into and shaped his newly discovered ministry of education. It thus gave rise to the whole system of Jesuit schools, which were a part of the Catholic Reformation and have been an important influence within the Church and society until the present day. Between 1547 and 1556 he himself opened thirty-three colleges and approved six more. Thus Part IV was composed contemporaneously with the infancy of the Jesuit system of colleges and universities and the Christian education imparted in them. Without awareness of that background of ongoing development our understanding of Part IV will be very imperfect. With it in mind, we see how Ignatius won a place among the great educators of history, and how this Part IV is rightly considered a classic of the theory of Christian education.

Education is here taken to mean the process by which the elders of society, especially the parents, educators, and officials both religious and civil, endeavor to transmit the ideals of their culture to the young. To them they want to impart their total way of thinking, living, and working, in order to lead them to a life adequately human, in order that the youths may take their places capably and effectively in the social, national, and religious life of their era. This wide concept of education

278

was called "discipline" by the Hebrews, *paideia* by the Greeks, *educatio*, *institutio*, *formatio*, or *humanitas* by the Romans, and "education," or "liberal education," or "education in the liberal arts" by later Europeans. From among these educators, too, sprang theoreticians who gave expression to the ideals of their culture, such as Plato or Quintilian. That was the tradition which Ignatius subconsciously absorbed in his sixteenth-century Europe.

In Part IV of the *Constitutions*, however, Ignatius was not aiming to write an orderly treatise on educational theory, as Plato did in his *Republic*. Instead he was composing practical statutes for organizing and managing Christian schools in the concrete circumstances of the Renaissance. However, while writing those statutes he was applying the background of all his thought, God's redemptive plan, to the day-by-day work of conducting Christian schools. Consequently his statutes and letters on education contain also his educational ideals, that is, his large guiding principles and objectives. They are always implicitly present, and as scattered occasions arise he often states them explicitly. Many of his statutes pertain to sixteenth-century circumstances which have passed away, but his large guiding principles have perennial value and can be applied, with appropriate adaptations, in any later eras. By study and analysis of Part IV and related letters we can discover those principles and spell them out in such a way that they form a comprehensive and orderly synthesis of his theory of Christian education.

d. Ignatius' Chief Educational Ideals

Some eleven of Ignatius' chief educational ideals and principles, along with their documentation in his *Constitutions* and letters, can be pointed out here as follows.[5]

1. The educator has the ultimate objective of stimulating the student to relate his activity to his or her final end: the knowledge and love of God in the joy of the beatific vision ([307, 351, 388, 440, 448, 813]).

2. The immediate objective of the teacher and the student is the student's deep penetration of his or her fields of study, both sacred and secular ([480]; see also [341, 355, 358, 381]). All this educational work should be ordered to the praise of God and the well-being of humankind here and hereafter (see also [307, 351, 381, 368, 400, 440, 448, 622]).

3. The Society of Jesus hopes by means of its educational work to send capable and zealous leaders into the social order, in numbers large

enough to leaven it effectively for good ([440, 622,e] and the letter to Araoz, no. 15, below on pages 361–365).

4. The branches of study should be so integrated that each makes its proper contribution toward the goal of the curriculum as a whole: a scientifically reasoned Christian outlook on life, a Christian worldview enabling the student to live well and meaningfully for this world and the next. The student should learn the philosophical and theological basis of his or her faith ([446–452]).[6]

5. Theology is the most important branch in the curriculum, since the light it offers is the chief means of gaining the Christian worldview, and of tying matters treated elsewhere into a unity by showing how all creation can be directed to God's greater glory ([446–452]) and greater self-fulfillment of human beings here and hereafter.

6. In a Jesuit university, any faculty can function as long as it contributes to the Society's general purpose (see [446–452], where Ignatius lists all the higher faculties of his era).

7. The formation offered should be both intellectual and moral, insofar as it provides, from Christian ethics, scientifically reasoned motives for moral living ([481]; see also [392, 395, 403]).

8. As far as possible, the professors should be personally interested in the students and their progress ([481]). This leads to a sense of helpful Christian presence and community.

9. Jesuit schools should transmit the cultural heritage of the past and also provide facilities for persons engaged in research or creative activity ([446; 653]).[7]

10. Jesuit schools should be alert to appropriate and adapt the best procedures emerging in other schools of the day—as Ignatius showed by his example and letters.[8]

11. Jesuit schools should continually adapt their procedures and pedagogical methods to circumstances of times, places, and persons ([455]; see also [385, 468]).

These and others similar were the principles operative in the Jesuit schools from 1547 to 1773. The Jesuit schools striving to implement them in practice numbered 372 by 1625 and 612 by 1710. Shortly before the suppression of the Society in 1773 the Jesuits were directing 15 universities and staffing 176 seminaries.[9] Ignatius' theory of Christian education gains reinforcement today from the statement of Vatican Council II, "On Christian Education," no. 1: "A true education aims at the formation of the human person with respect to his ultimate goal, and simultaneously with respect to the good of those societies of which, as a human being, he is a member."

In the fifteenth printing of his widely used book *The Doctrines of the Great Educators*,[10] Robert R. Rusk treats thirteen whose educational doctrines have made an outstanding impact on educational practice: Plato, Quintilian, Elyot, Ignatius, Comenius, Milton, Locke, Rousseau, Pestalozzi, Herbart, Froebel, Montessori, and Dewey. He rightly states on page 88 that Ignatius "is as worthy of a place amongst the great educators as amongst the saints."

Part IV of Ignatius' *Constitutions* clearly reveals his ideals of Christian education in their primary sources. These same ideals have been those of the subsequent Jesuit tradition of secondary and university institutions, in which they have been applied with adjustments to the continually changing cultural circumstances. Ignatius' same vision of education is also briefly synthesized in his letter of December 1, 1551 to Antonio de Araoz, pages 361–365 below.

e. The Plan of Presentation

Although Ignatius' *Constitutions* is too lengthy a book for presentation in its entirety here, we hope to present a comprehensive view of their four component treatises as one consecutive whole and thereby enable the reader to see the details in perspective. Our selections will be concerned chiefly with spirituality and will be made according to the following plan. We shall print the title of each Part, and under it the title of any chapter from which we draw one or more selections. Usually the selections themselves will be separate paragraphs which bring out highlights of Ignatius' apostolic spirituality, but to give also an idea of his style and manner of treatment, two unabridged units will be presented: (1) chapter 12 of Part IV, which shows the structure of a Jesuit university as he conceived it in his day; and (2) the whole of the summarizing Part X on the preservation and development of the fully constituted Society.

The selections are taken, with retouchings of some details, from this writer's earlier book: St. Ignatius of Loyola, *The Constitutions of the Society of Jesus: Translated, with an Introduction and a Commentary* (St. Louis, 1970), abbreviated as *ConsSJComm*. The notes too are usually abbreviated forms of more extensive treatments and references in that earlier book, but updated from various sources, especially from the recent work of Antonio M. de Aldama, S.J., of the Jesuit Historical Institute in Rome, *An Introductory Commentary on the Constitutions* (St. Louis, 1989), hereafter abbreviated as *AldamIntro*. It is the first volume to appear in a forthcoming series of Aldama's commentaries in English translations, respectively on the Formula of the Institute and on Parts VI, VII, VIII, and IX of the *Constitutions*.

Selections from the
CONSTITUTIONS OF THE
SOCIETY OF JESUS

I. THE GENERAL EXAMEN AND ITS DECLARATIONS: THE FIRST AND GENERAL EXAMEN WHICH SHOULD BE PROPOSED TO ALL WHO ASK FOR ADMISSION INTO THE SOCIETY OF JESUS

Chapter 1
THE INSTITUTE OF THE SOCIETY OF JESUS AND THE DIVERSITY OF ITS MEMBERS

[1]—1. This least congregation, which at its earliest foundation was named the Society of Jesus[1] by the Holy See, was first approved by Pope Paul III, of happy memory, in the year 1540.[2] Later it was confirmed by the same Holy Father in 1543 and by his successor Julius III in 1550.[3] On other occasions too it is mentioned in different briefs and apostolic letters which grant it various favors and thereby presuppose high approval and confirmation of it.

[2]—A. *This Examen is usually proposed to all after they enter the house[4] of the first probation.[5] Nevertheless, if in some particular case discretion should suggest that another and more summary examen be proposed, or that the present text be handed out to be read without asking for replies about its contents, or if the knowledge possessed about some candidate is already sufficient, it would not be necessary to conduct the examination by means of this present text. . . .*

[3]—2. The end of this Society is to devote itself with God's grace not only to the salvation and perfection of the members' own souls,[6] but

also with that same grace to labor strenuously in giving aid toward the salvation and perfection of the souls of their neighbors.[7]

[4]—3. To achieve this end more effectively, the three vows of obedience, poverty, and chastity are taken in the Society. Poverty[8] is understood to mean that in the Society no fixed revenues[9] may be sought or possessed for the Society's living expenses or for any other purposes. This holds true not only of the individual members but also of the churches or houses of the professed Society.[10] Neither may the members accept any stipend or alms for Masses, sermons, lectures, the administration of any of the sacraments, or for any other pious function among those which the Society may exercise in accordance with its institute (even though such acceptance would be permissible for others). Such stipends or alms are customarily given in recompense for the ministries mentioned; but the Society's members may not accept them from anyone other than God our Lord; and it is purely for his service that they ought to do all things.

[5]—4. Furthermore, although the Society owns colleges and houses of probation which have fixed revenues for the living expenses of the scholastics before they enter into the professed Society or its houses [B], nevertheless, in conformity with the bull which is explained in the Constitutions, the revenues of this kind may not be used for another purpose. Neither the houses of the professed nor anyone of the professed or their coadjutors may use these revenues for themselves.

[6]—B. *These houses of probation are in a way branches of the colleges; and in them those who will later be stationed in the colleges are received and tested for a time.*

[7]—5. In addition to the three vows mentioned, the professed Society also makes an explicit vow to the sovereign pontiff[11] as the present or future vicar of Christ our Lord. This is a vow to go anywhere his Holiness will order, whether among the faithful or the infidels, without pleading an excuse and without requesting any expenses for the journey, for the sake of matters pertaining to the worship of God and the welfare of the Christian religion.

[8]—6. In other respects, for sound reasons and with attention always paid to the greater service of God, in regard to what is exterior the manner of living is ordinary.[12] It does not contain any regular penances or austerities which are to be practiced through obligation. But those may be taken up which each one, with the superior's approval, thinks likely to be more helpful for his spiritual progress, as well as

those which the superiors have authority to impose upon the members for the same purpose.

. . .

[10]—7. The persons who are received into this Society of Jesus, considered as a whole, are of four classes,[13] in view of the end which the Society pursues. . . .

. . .

Chapter 4
SOME OBSERVANCES WITHIN THE SOCIETY WHICH ARE MORE IMPORTANT FOR THE CANDIDATE TO KNOW

[53]—1. The intention of the first men who bound themselves together in this Society should be explained to the candidates. Those founders' mind was that those received into it should be persons already detached from the world and determined to serve God totally, whether in one religious institute or another; and further, in conformity with this, that all those who seek admission into the Society should, before they begin to live under obedience in any house or college belonging to it, distribute all the temporal goods they might have, and renounce and dispose of those they might expect to receive. . . .

. . .

[81]—26. If he is pleased to remain in the Society, his food, drink, clothing, shoes, and lodging will be what is characteristic of the poor; and he should persuade himself that it will be what is worst in the house, for his greater abnegation and spiritual progress and for reaching a certain equality and common norm among all. For where the Society's first members have passed through these necessities and greater bodily wants, the others who come to it should endeavor, as far as they can, to reach the same point as the earlier ones, or to go farther in our Lord.

. . .

[98]—41. A candidate who thinks that God our Lord gives him courage and strength in regard to all that has been said, and who judges his incorporation into this Society to be conducive to greater divine glory and more salutary for his own conscience, ought to see the bulls and Constitutions and all the rest which pertain to the Society's Institute, in the beginning and afterward every six months, as was stated above ([18]). In addition to this it is expedient for him to make a general

confession of his whole past life to a priest whom the superior appoints for him, because of the many benefits which this entails. . . .

When he has fulfilled the two years of probation, and shown himself always obedient and edifying in his association with others and in various tests, and has with great humility performed the penances which will be imposed on him for his errors and negligences or defects; and when he and the Society or the superior of the house are content, he will be eligible to be incorporated into the Society[14] . . . for greater divine glory and greater profit of his own soul.

. . .

[101]—44. It is . . . highly important[15] to bring this to the mind of those who are being examined (through their esteeming it highly and pondering it in the sight of our Creator and Lord), to how great a degree it helps and profits one in the spiritual life to abhor in its totality and not in part whatever the world loves and embraces, and to accept and desire with all possible energy whatever Christ our Lord has loved and embraced. Just as the men of the world who follow the world love and seek with such great diligence honors, fame, and esteem for a great name on earth, as the world teaches them, so those who are progressing in the spiritual life and truly following Christ our Lord love and intensely desire everything opposite. That is to say, they desire to clothe themselves with the same clothing and uniform of their Lord because of the love and reverence which he deserves, to such an extent that where there would be no offense to his Divine Majesty and no imputation of sin to the neighbor, they would wish to suffer injuries, false accusations, and affronts, and to be held and esteemed as fools (but without their giving any occasion for this), because of their desire to resemble and imitate in some manner our Creator and Lord Jesus Christ, by putting on his clothing and uniform, since it was for our spiritual profit that he clothed himself as he did. For he gave us an example that in all things possible to us we might seek, through the aid of his grace, to imitate and follow him, since he is the way which leads people to life. Therefore the candidate should be asked whether he finds himself in a state of desires like these which are so salutary and fruitful for the perfection of his soul.

[102]—45. In a case where through human weakness and personal misery the candidate does not experience in himself such ardent desires in our Lord,[16] he should be asked whether he has any desires to experience them. If he answers affirmatively that he does wish to have holy desires of this kind, then, that he may the better reach them in fact, he

should be questioned further: Is he determined and ready to accept and suffer with patience, through the help of God's grace, any such injuries, mockeries, and affronts entailed by the wearing of this uniform of Christ our Lord, and any other affronts offered him, whether by someone inside the house or the Society (where he desires to obey, be humiliated, and gain eternal life) or outside it by any persons whatsoever on earth, while returning them not evil for evil but good for evil?

. . .

II. THE CONSTITUTIONS OF THE SOCIETY OF JESUS AND THEIR DECLARATIONS

Preamble to the Constitutions

[134]—1. Although it must be the Supreme Wisdom and Goodness of God our Creator and Lord which will preserve, direct, and carry forward in his divine service this least Society of Jesus, just as he deigned to begin it; and although what helps most on our own part toward this end must be, more than any exterior constitution, the interior law of charity and love which the Holy Spirit writes and engraves upon hearts;[17] nevertheless, since the gentle arrangement of Divine Providence requires cooperation from his creatures, and since too the vicar of Christ our Lord has ordered this, and since the examples given by the saints and reason itself teach us so in our Lord, we think it necessary that constitutions should be written to aid us to proceed better, in conformity with our Institute, along the path of divine service on which we have entered.

[135]—2. In the order of our intention, the consideration which comes first and has more weight is that about the body of the Society taken as a whole; for its union, good government, and preservation in well-being for greater divine glory are what is chiefly sought. Nevertheless, this body is composed of its members; and in the order of execution, that which takes place first is what pertains to the individual members, in the sequence of admitting them, fostering their progress, and distributing them in the vineyard of the Lord. Therefore, our treatise will deal first[18] with these individual members, through the aid which the Eternal Light will deign to communicate to us for his own honor and praise.

[136]—The purpose of the Constitutions is to aid the body of the Society as a whole and also its individual members toward their preservation and development for the divine glory and the good of the universal Church . . .

But in addition to them [the Constitutions], we have thought it wise in our Lord to compose also these Declarations and Annotations. They possess the same binding force as the other Constitutions, and can be instructive in greater detail to those who have charge of the other members about some matters which the brevity and universality of the other Constitutions left less clear. The Constitutions and the Declarations both treat of matters which are unchangeable and ought to be observed universally; but they must be supplemented by some other ordinances which can be adapted to the times, places, and persons in different houses, colleges, and employments of the Society, although uniformity ought to be retained among all the members as far as possible. . . .

. . .

PART I. THE ADMISSION TO PROBATION

Chapter 1
THE PERSON WHO ADMITS

[138]—1. The authority to admit to probation will belong to those whom the superior general of the Society thinks fit, and to the extent he thinks good. In communicating this authority he will look to what is conducive to greater service to God our Lord. . . .

. . .

[142]—3. It is highly important for the divine service to make a proper selection of those who are admitted and to take care to know their abilities and vocation well. . . .

. . .

Chapter 2
THE CANDIDATES WHO SHOULD BE ADMITTED

[147]—1. To speak in general of those who should be admitted, the greater the number of natural and infused gifts someone has from God our Lord which are useful for what the Society aims at in his divine service, and the more experience the candidate has in the use of these gifts, the more suitable will he be for reception into the Society.

. . .

PART II. THE DISMISSAL OF THOSE WHO WERE ADMITTED
BUT DID NOT PROVE THEMSELVES FIT

Chapter 1
WHO CAN BE DISMISSED, AND BY WHOM

[204]—1. Just as it is proper, for the sake of the end sought in this Society, the service of God our Lord by helping souls who are his, to preserve and multiply the workers who are found fit and useful for carrying this work forward, so is it also expedient to dismiss those who are found unsuitable, and who as time passes make it evident that this is not their vocation or that their remaining in the Society does not advance the common good. However, just as excessive readiness should not be had in admitting candidates, so ought it to be used even less in dismissing them; instead, one ought to proceed with much consideration and weighing in our Lord. The more fully one has been incorporated into the Society, the more serious ought the reasons to be. Nevertheless, no matter how advanced the incorporation may be, in some cases anyone can and should be separated from the Society. . . .

. . .

PART III. THE PRESERVATION AND PROGRESS
OF THOSE WHO ARE IN PROBATION[19]

Chapter 1
PRESERVATION PERTAINING TO THE SOUL
AND TO PROGRESS IN VIRTUES

[243]—1. The considerations previously expounded, dealing with the admission of those to whom God our Lord gives a call to our Institute and suitable ability for it, and with the dismissal of those who through lack of such ability reveal that they have not been called by his Divine Wisdom, are necessary. In similar manner, due consideration and prudent care should be employed toward preserving in their vocation those who are being kept and tested in the houses or colleges, and toward enabling them to make progress, both in spirit and in virtues along the path of the divine service, in such a manner that there is also proper care for the health and bodily strength necessary to labor in the

Lord's vineyard. Therefore what pertains to the soul will be treated first and then what pertains to the body ([292]).

. . .

[250]—4. All should take special care to guard with great diligence the gates of their senses (especially the eyes, ears, and tongue) from all disorder, to preserve themselves in peace and true humility of their souls, and to give an indication of it by silence when it should be kept and, when they must speak, by the discretion and edification of their words, the modesty of their countenance, the maturity of their walk, and all their movements, without giving any sign of impatience or pride. In everything they should try and desire to give the advantage to the others, esteeming them all in their hearts as better than themselves [Phil. 2:3] and showing exteriorly, in an unassuming and simple religious manner, the respect and reverence befitting each one's state, in such a way that by observing one another they grow in devotion[20] and praise God our Lord, whom each one should endeavor to recognize in his neighbor as in His image.

. . .

[282]—22. It will be very specially helpful to perform with all possible devotion the tasks in which humility and charity are practiced more; and, to speak in general, the more one binds himself to God our Lord and shows himself more generous toward his Divine Majesty [T], the more will he find God more generous toward himself and the more disposed will he be to receive graces and spiritual gifts which are greater each day.

[283]—T. *To bind oneself more to God our Lord and to show oneself generous toward him is to consecrate oneself completely and irrevocably to his service,[21] as those do who dedicate themselves to him by vow. But although this is a great help toward receiving more abundant grace, no one ought to be commanded or in any way constrained to do it within the first two years. . . .*

[284]—23. To make progress, it is very expedient and highly necessary that all should devote themselves to complete obedience,[22] by recognizing the superior, whoever he is, as being in the place of Christ our Lord and by maintaining interior reverence and love for him. They should obey entirely and promptly, not only by exterior execution of what the superior commands, with becoming energy and humility, and without excuses and murmurings even though things are commanded

which are difficult and repugnant to sensitive nature; but they should try to maintain in their inmost souls genuine resignation and true abnegation of their own wills and judgments, by bringing their wills and judgments wholly into conformity with what the superior wills and judges, in all things in which no sin is seen, and by regarding the superior's will and judgment as the rule of their own, in order to conform themselves more completely to the first and supreme rule of all good will and judgment, which is the Eternal Goodness and Wisdom.

. . .

[287]—25. All should love poverty as a mother, and according to the measure of holy discretion all should, when occasions arise, feel some effects of it. Further, as is stated in the Examen [53–59], after the first year they should be ready, each one, to dispose of their temporal goods whenever the superior may command it, in the manner which was explained to them in the aforementioned Examen.

[288]—26. All should make diligent efforts to keep their intention right,[23] not only in regard to their state of life but also in all particular details. In these they should always aim at serving and pleasing the Divine Goodness for its own sake and because of the incomparable love and benefits with which God has anticipated us, rather than for fear of punishments or hope of rewards, although they ought to draw help also from them. Further, they should often be exhorted to seek God our Lord in all things,[24] stripping off from themselves the love of creatures to the extent that this is possible, in order to turn their love upon the Creator of them, by loving him in all creatures and all of them in him, in conformity with his holy and divine will.

. . .

Chapter 2
THE PRESERVATION OF THE BODY

[292]—1. Just as an excessive preoccupation over the needs of the body is blameworthy, so too a proper concern about the preservation of one's health and bodily strength for the divine service is praiseworthy, and all should exercise it. . . .

. . .

PART IV. THE INSTRUCTION OF THOSE WHO ARE RETAINED IN
THE SOCIETY, IN LEARNING AND IN OTHER MEANS OF
HELPING THEIR NEIGHBOR[25]

PREAMBLE

[307]—1. The aim which the Society of Jesus directly seeks is to
aid its own members and their neighbors to attain the ultimate end for
which they were created.[26] To achieve this purpose, in addition to the
example of one's life, learning and a method of expounding it are also
necessary. Therefore, after the proper foundation of abnegation of
themselves is seen to be present in those who were admitted and also
the required progress in virtues, it will be necessary to provide for the
edifice of their learning and the manner of employing it, that these may
be aids toward better knowledge and service of God, our Creator and
Lord. Toward achieving this purpose the Society takes charge of the
colleges and also of some universities, that in them those who prove
themselves worthy in the houses but have entered the Society un-
equipped with the necessary learning may receive instruction in it and
in the other means of helping souls. Therefore with the favor of the
Divine and Eternal Wisdom and for his greater glory and praise, we
shall treat first of what pertains to the colleges and then of the universities.

. . .

Chapter 4
THE CARE AND WELFARE OF THE
SCHOLASTICS[27] ADMITTED

[339]—1. What was stated in Part III [292–306] will suffice about
the care and welfare, in regard to the body and external matters, of those
who live in the colleges. . . .

[340]—2. In regard to spiritual matters, . . . While they [the
scholastics] are applying themselves to their studies, just as care must be
taken that through fervor in study they do not grow cool in their love of
true virtues and of religious life, so also during that time there will not
be much place for mortifications and long prayers and meditations.[28]
For their devoting themselves to learning, which they acquire with a
pure intention[29] of serving God and which in a certain way requires the

whole person, will be not less but rather more pleasing[30] to God our Lord during this time of study.

. . .

[342]—3. Consequently, in addition to confession and Communion, which they will frequent every eight[31] days, and Mass which they will hear every day, they will have one hour. During it, they will recite the Hours of Our Lady,[32] and examine their consciences twice each day, and add other prayers according to the devotion of each one until the aforementioned hour is completed, in case it has not yet run its course. They will do all this according to the arrangements and judgment of their superiors, whom they oblige themselves to obey in place of Christ our Lord.

. . .

Chapter 5
THE MATTERS WHICH THE SCHOLASTICS
OF THE SOCIETY SHOULD STUDY

[351]—1. Since the end of the learning which is acquired in this Society is with God's favor to help the souls of its own members and those of their neighbors,[33] it is by this norm that the decision will be made, both in general and in the case of individual persons, as to what branches ours ought to learn, and how far they ought to advance in them. And since, generally speaking, help is derived from the humane letters of different languages [A], logic, natural and moral philosophy, metaphysics, scholastic and positive theology, and Sacred Scripture, these are the branches[34] which those who are sent to the colleges should study. . . .

. . .

Chapter 6
MEANS BY WHICH THE SCHOLASTICS WILL
PROGRESS TOWARD LEARNING THE
AFOREMENTIONED BRANCHES WELL

[360]—1. In order to make great progress in these branches,[35] the scholastics should strive first of all to keep their souls pure and their intention in studying right,[36] by seeking in their studies nothing except

the glory of God and the good of souls. Moreover, they should frequently beg in prayer for grace to make progress in learning for the sake of this end.

[361]—2. Furthermore, they should keep their resolution firm to be thoroughly genuine and earnest students, by persuading themselves that while they are in the colleges they cannot do anything more pleasing to God our Lord than to study with the intention mentioned above; likewise, that even if they never have occasion to employ the matter studied, their very labor in studying, taken up as it ought to be because of charity and obedience, is itself work highly meritorious in the sight of the Divine and Supreme Majesty.[37]

[362]—3. The impediments which distract from study should also be removed, both those arising from devotions and mortifications which are too numerous or without proper order and also those springing from their cares and exterior occupations whether in duties inside the house or outside it in conversations, confessions, and other activities with one's neighbors, as far as it is possible in our Lord to excuse oneself from them. For in order that the scholastics may be able to help their neighbors better later on by what they have learned, it is wise to postpone exercises such as these, pious though they are, until after the years of study, since there will be others to attend to them in the meantime. All this should be done with a greater intention of service and divine glory.

. . .

[366]—4. An order should be observed in pursuing the branches of knowledge. The scholastics should acquire a good foundation in Latin before they attend lectures on the arts;[38] and in the arts before they pass on to scholastic theology; and in it before they study positive theology.[39] Scripture may be studied either concomitantly or later on.

. . .

Chapter 7
THE CLASSES HELD IN COLLEGES OF THE SOCIETY

[392]—1. To take care that in our colleges not only our own scholastics may be helped in learning, but also those from outside in both learning and good habits of conduct, where classes [open to the public][40] can be conveniently held, they should be established at least in

humane letters, and in more advanced subjects in accordance with the possibilities[41] existing in the regions where such colleges are situated. The greater service of God our Lord is always to be kept in view.

. . .

Chapter 8
THE INSTRUCTION OF THE SCHOLASTICS IN THE MEANS OF HELPING THEIR NEIGHBOR

[400]—1. In view of the objective which the Society seeks by means of its studies, toward the end of them it is good for the scholastics to begin to accustom themselves to the spiritual arms which they must employ in aiding their neighbor; and this work can be begun in the colleges, even though it is more properly and extensively done in the houses.

. . .

[402]—3. Similarly, they will exercise themselves in preaching and in delivering sacred lectures in a manner suitable for the edification of the people, which is different from the scholastic manner. . . .

. . .

[406]—4. They should also practice themselves in the administration of the sacraments of confession and Communion, by keeping fresh in mind and endeavoring to put into practice not merely what pertains to themselves, but also what pertains to the penitents and communicants, that they may receive and frequent these sacraments well and fruitfully for divine glory.

. . .

[408]—5. After they have had experience of the Spiritual Exercises in their own selves, they should acquire experience in giving them to others. Each one should know how to give an explanation of them and how to employ this spiritual weapon, since it is obvious that God our Lord has made it so effective for His service.

. . .

THE UNIVERSITIES OF THE SOCIETY

Chapter 11
THE ACCEPTANCE OF UNIVERSITIES

[440]—1. Through a motive of charity colleges are accepted and classes open to the public are maintained in them for the improvement in learning and in living not only of our own members but even more especially of those from outside the Society. Through this same motive the Society can extend itself to undertaking the work of universities, that through them this fruit sought in the colleges may be spread more universally through the branches which are taught, the number of persons attending, and the degrees which are conferred in order that the recipients may be able to teach with authority elsewhere what they have learned well in these universities of the Society for the glory of God our Lord.[42]

. . .

Chapter 12
THE BRANCHES TO BE TAUGHT[43] IN THE UNIVERSITIES OF THE SOCIETY

[446]—1. Since the end of the Society and of its studies is to aid our fellowmen to the knowledge and love of God and to the salvation of their souls, and since the branch of theology is the means most suitable to this end, in the universities of the Society the principal emphasis ought to be put upon it.[44] Thus diligent treatment by highly capable professors should be given to what pertains to scholastic doctrine and Sacred Scripture, and also to the part of positive theology which is conducive to the aforementioned end, without entering into the part of the canons which is directed toward trials in court.

[447]—2. Moreover, since both the learning of theology and the use of it require (especially in these times) knowledge of humane letters [A] and of the Latin, Greek, and Hebrew languages, there should be capable professors of these languages, and that in sufficient number. Furthermore, there may also be teachers of other languages such as Chaldaic, Arabic, and Indian, where these are necessary or useful for the end stated, with attention given to the diversities of place and reasons which may move us to teach them [B].

297

The Organizational Framework in 1556

Approximate
age of pupil

Elementary

5 to 7 — *Elementary Education:* begun
6
7
8
9

Elementary Education: begun (but ordinarily not in Jesuit schools).

Elementary education comprised: how to converse in Latin, how to read it, and how to write it. Generally there was no formal instruction in or about the vernacular.

The *University* is entered at about the age of ten.

Secondary

10
11
12
13

Humane letters begun, in the *Faculty of Languages*, especially of Latin and Greek.

For able pupils, about six months each in four classes of grammar. They studied the grammar of Latin, which they previously knew how to speak. The highest class of grammar was often completed by the age of twelve.

Next came two years of rhetoric, poetry, and history. In them, the objective was complete facility in the art of speaking, reading, and writing Latin, with elegance when possible, before beginning the study of philosophy and the other arts (for which Latin was still an indispensable tool).

Higher

14
15
16

Philosphy and the other arts begun, in the *Faculty of Arts*.

Chairs of logic, physics, metaphysics, moral science, and mathematics.

After three years was conferred the degree of Bachelor of Arts; and on many, after six months more, of Master of Arts.

17
18
19
20

Theology begun, in the *Faculty of Theology;*
or entry to *Faculty of Law,*
or, to *Faculty of Medicine*

Theology was the most important subject; was open to externs.

Chairs of scholastic theology, positive theology, canon law, scripture.

There was a four-year cycle of the fundamental courses, after which the ordinary course of theology was completed. Ordination might occur at about the age of twenty-one.

21
22
23

There were two years more of acts and exercises for those who desired the Degree of Doctor of Theology.

Chart 1. Schematic Outline:
A University as Conceived by St. Ignatius

Reproduced, with permission, from George E. Ganss, S.J., *St. Ignatius' Idea of a Jesuit University* (Milwaukee: Marquette University Press, 1954), page 45.

[448]—A. *Under the heading of humane letters is understood, in addition to grammar, what pertains to rhetoric, poetry, and history.*[45]

[449]—B. *When a plan is being worked out in some college or university to prepare persons to go among the Moors or Turks, Arabic or Chaldaic would be expedient; and Indian would be proper for those about to go among the Indians; and the same holds true for similar reasons in regard to other languages which could have greater utility in other regions.*

[450]—3. Likewise, since the arts or natural sciences dispose the intellectual powers for theology, and are useful for the perfect understanding and use of it,[46] and also by their own nature help toward the same ends, they should be treated with fitting diligence and by learned professors. In all this the honor and glory of God our Lord should be sincerely sought [C].

[451]—C. *Logic, physics, metaphysics, and moral philosophy should be treated, and also mathematics in the measure appropriate to secure the end which is being sought.*

To teach how to read and write would also be a work of charity if the Society had enough members to be able to attend to everything.[47] *But because of the lack of members these elementary branches are not ordinarily taught.*

[452]—4. The study of medicine and laws, being more remote from our Institute, will not be treated in the universities of the Society, or at least the Society will not undertake this teaching through its own members.[48]

Chapter 13
THE METHOD AND ORDER OF TREATING THE AFOREMENTIONED BRANCHES

[453]—1. To give such treatment of both the lower branches and also of theology, there should be a suitable arrangement and order both for the morning and the afternoon.

[454]—2. And although the order and hours which are spent in these studies may vary according to the regions and seasons, there should be such conformity that in every region that is done which is there judged to be most conducive to greater progress in learning [A].

[455]—A. *Concerning the hours of the lectures, their order, and their method, and concerning the exercises both in compositions, which ought to be corrected by the teachers, and in disputations within all the faculties, and in*

delivering orations and reading verses in public—all this will be treated in detail in a separate treatise⁴⁹ [approved by the general].⁵⁰ This present constitution refers the reader to it, with the remark that it ought to be adapted to places, times, and persons, even though it would be desirable to reach that order as far as this is possible.

. . .

Chapter 14
THE BOOKS WHICH SHOULD BE EXPOUNDED

[464]—1. In general, as was stated in the treatise on the colleges [358], in each branch those books will be lectured on which are found to contain more solid and safe doctrine; and those which are suspect, or whose authors are suspect, will not be taken up. But in each university these should be individually designated.

In theology there should be lectures on the Old and New Testaments and on the scholastic doctrine of St. Thomas⁵¹ [B]; and in positive theology those authors should be selected who are more suitable for our end.

. . .

[466]—B. *The Master of the Sentences will also be lectured on. But if in time it seems that the students will draw more help from another author, as would be the case through the writing of some compendium or book of scholastic theology that seems better adapted to these times of ours, it will be permitted to make this book the subject of the lectures. . . .*

. . .

Chapter 15
THE TERMS AND DEGREES

. . .

[478]—4. In the matter of the degrees, both of master of arts and of doctor of theology, three things should be observed. First, no one, whether a member of the Society or an extern, should be promoted to a degree unless he has been carefully and publicly examined by persons deputed for this office, which they should perform well, and unless he has been found fit to lecture in that faculty. Second, the door to ambition should be closed by giving no fixed places to those who receive degrees; rather, they should "anticipate one another with honor" [Rom. 12:10], without observing any distinction which arises from places.

Third, just as the Society teaches altogether gratis,[52] so should it confer the degrees completely free, and only a very small expenditure, even though it is voluntary, should be allowed to the extern students, that the custom may not come to have the force of law and that excess in this matter may not creep in with time. The rector should also take care not to permit any of the teachers or other members of the Society to accept money or gifts, either for themselves or for the college, from any person for anything he has done to help him. For according to our Institute, our reward should be only Christ our Lord, who is "our reward exceedingly great" [Gen. 15:1].

. . .

Chapter 16
WHAT PERTAINS TO GOOD MORAL HABITS

[481]—1. Very special care should be taken that those who come to the universities of the Society to obtain knowledge should acquire along with it good and Christian moral habits. It will help much toward this if all go to confession at least once every month, hear Mass every day and a sermon every feast day when one is given. The teachers will take care of this, each one with his own students.

. . .

Chapter 17
THE OFFICIALS OR MINISTERS OF THE UNIVERSITY

[490]—1. The complete charge, that is, the supervision and government of the university, will belong to the rector. . . . The rector will have four consultors or assistants who in general can aid him in matters pertaining to his office and with whom he discusses the matters of importance.[53]

. . .

[493]—2. There will also be a chancellor, a person distinguished for learning and great zeal who is able to judge wisely in the matters which will be entrusted to him. It is his duty to act as general representative of the rector in carefully organizing the studies, in directing the disputations in the public acts, and in judging the competence of those to be admitted to the acts and degrees. He himself will confer the degrees.

. . .

[498]—4. There will also be a notary to give public certification to the degrees and other matters which will occur; and two or three beadles, one in the faculty of languages, another in that of arts, and another in that of theology.

. . .

[501]—5. The university will be divided into these three faculties. In each one of them there will be a dean and two other representatives, chosen from among those who better understand the affairs of that faculty. When they are summoned by the rector they can tell him what they think would be advantageous for the welfare of their faculty. When they perceive something of this kind while conferring among themselves, they should inform the rector even though they have not been summoned.

. . .

PART V. ADMISSION OR INCORPORATION
INTO THE BODY OF THE SOCIETY

Chapter 1
ADMISSION, WHO SHOULD ADMIT, AND WHEN

[510]—1. Those who have been sufficiently tested in the Society, and for a time long enough that both parties may know whether their remaining in it is conducive to greater service and glory to God our Lord, ought to be admitted . . . in a more intrinsic manner[54] as members of one same body of the Society. . . .

. . .

Chapter 2
THE QUALITIES OF THOSE TO BE ADMITTED

[516]—1. Since no one should be admitted into any of the aforementioned categories[55] unless he has been judged fit in our Lord, those persons will be judged worthy for admission to profession whose life is well known through long and thorough probations and is approved by the superior general. . . . For this purpose, after those who were sent to studies have achieved the diligent and careful formation of the intellect by learning, they will find it helpful during the period of the last probation to apply themselves in the school of the heart,[56] by exercising themselves in spiritual and corporal pursuits which can engender in

them greater humility, abnegation of all sensual love and will and judgment of their own, and also greater knowledge and love of God our Lord; that when they themselves have made progress they can better help others to progress for glory to God our Lord.

. . .

PART VI. THE PERSONAL LIFE OF THOSE ALREADY ADMITTED OR INCORPORATED INTO THE SOCIETY

Chapter 1
WHAT PERTAINS TO OBEDIENCE

[547]—1. In order that those already admitted to profession or to membership among the formed coadjutors may be able to apply themselves more fruitfully according to our Institute in the service of God and the aid of their neighbors, they themselves ought to observe certain things. Although the most important of these are reduced to their vows which they offer to God our Creator and Lord in conformity with the apostolic letters, nevertheless, in order that these points may be further explained and commended, they will be treated in this present Part VI.

What pertains to the vow of chastity does not require explanation,[57] since it is evident how perfectly it should be preserved through the endeavor in this matter to imitate the angelic purity[58] by the purity of the body and mind. Therefore, with this presupposed, we shall now treat of holy obedience.

All should keep their resolution firm to observe obedience[59] and to distinguish themselves in it, not only in the matters of obligation but also in the others, even though nothing else is perceived except the indication of the superior's will without an expressed command. They should keep in view God our Creator and Lord, for whom such obedience is practiced, and they should endeavor to proceed in a spirit of love and not as men troubled by fear. Hence all of us should exert ourselves not to miss any point of perfection which we can with God's grace attain in the observance of all the Constitutions and in our manner of proceeding in our Lord, by applying all our energies with very special care to the virtue of obedience shown first to the sovereign pontiff and then to the superiors of the Society.

Consequently, in all the things into which obedience can with charity be extended [B], we should be ready to receive its command just as if it were coming from Christ our Savior, since we are practicing the obedience to one in his place[60] and because of love and reverence for him. Therefore we should be ready to leave unfinished any letter[61] or anything else of ours which has been begun and to apply our whole mind and all the energy we have in the Lord of all that our obedience may be perfect in every detail[62] [C], in regard to the execution, the willing, and the understanding. We should perform with great alacrity, spiritual joy, and perseverance whatever has been commanded to us, persuading ourselves that everything is just and renouncing with blind obedience[63] any contrary opinion and judgment of our own in all things which the superior commands and in which (as was stated [264]) some species of sin cannot be judged to be present. We ought to be firmly convinced that everyone of those who live under obedience ought to allow himself to be carried and directed by Divine Providence through the agency of the superior as if he were a lifeless body which allows itself to be carried to any place and to be treated in any manner desired, or as if he were an old man's staff[64] which serves in any place and in any manner whatsoever in which the holder wishes to use it. For in this way the obedient man ought joyfully to devote himself to any task whatsoever in which the superior desires to employ him to aid the whole body of the religious Institute; and he ought to hold it as certain that by this procedure he is conforming himself with the divine will more than by anything else he could do while following his own will and different judgment.

. . .

[549]—B. *Such things are all those in which some sin is not manifest.*

[550]—C. *The command of obedience is fulfilled in regard to the execution when the thing commanded is done; in regard to the willing when the one who obeys wills the same thing as the one who commands; in regard to the understanding when he forms the same judgment as the one commanding and regards what he is commanded as good. And that obedience is imperfect in which there does not exist, in addition to the execution, also that agreement in willing and judging between him who commands and him who obeys.*[65]

[551]—2. Likewise, it should be strongly recommended to all that they should have and show great reverence, especially interior reverence, for their superiors, by considering and reverencing Jesus Christ in them; and from their hearts they should warmly love their superiors as fathers[66] in him. Thus in everything they should proceed in a spirit of charity. . . .

. . .

Chapter 2
WHAT PERTAINS TO POVERTY
AND ITS CONSEQUENCES

[553]—1. Poverty,[67] as the strong wall of the religious life, should be loved and preserved in its integrity as far as this is possible with God's grace. The enemy of the human race generally tries to weaken this defense and rampart which God our Lord inspired religious institutes to raise against him and the other adversaries of their perfection.
. . .

. . .

[555]—2. In the houses or churches[68] which the Society accepts to aid souls, it should not be licit to have any fixed revenue, even for the sacristy or building or anything else, in such a manner that any administration of this revenue is in the control of the Society. But the Society, relying on God our Lord whom it serves with the aid of his divine grace, should trust that without its having fixed revenue he will cause everything to be provided which can be expedient for his greater praise and glory.
. . .

Chapter 3
THE OCCUPATIONS WHICH THOSE IN THE
SOCIETY SHOULD UNDERTAKE AND THOSE WHICH
THEY SHOULD AVOID

[582]—1. In view of the time and approval of their life through which those wait before being admitted among the professed and even among the formed coadjutors, it is presupposed that they will be men who are spiritual and sufficiently advanced to run in the path of Christ our Lord to the extent that their bodily strength and the exterior occupations undertaken through charity and obedience allow. Therefore, in what pertains to prayer, meditation, and study and also in regard to the bodily practices of fasts, vigils, and other austerities or penances, it does not seem expedient to give them any other rule[69] than that which discreet charity[70] dictates to them, provided that the confessor should always be informed and also, when a doubt about expediency arises, the superior. The following statement is the only one which will be made in general. On the one hand, the members should keep themselves alert that the excessive use of these practices may not weaken the bodily

energies and consume time to such an extent that these energies are insufficient for the spiritual help of one's neighbor according to our Institute; and on the other hand, they should be vigilant that these practices may not be relaxed to such an extent that the spirit grows cold and the human and lower passions grow warm.

. . .

[586]—4. Because the occupations which are undertaken for the aid of souls are of great importance, proper to our Institute, and very frequent; and because, on the other hand, our residence in one place or another is so highly uncertain, our members will not regularly hold choir for the canonical hours or sing Masses and offices. For one who experiences devotion in listening to those chanted services will suffer no lack of places where he can find his satisfaction; and it is expedient that our members should apply their efforts to the pursuits that are more proper to our vocation, for glory to God our Lord.[71]

. . .

PART VII. THE DISTRIBUTION OF THE INCORPORATED
MEMBERS IN CHRIST'S VINEYARD AND THEIR RELATIONS THERE
WITH THEIR NEIGHBOR

Chapter 1
MISSIONS[72] FROM THE HOLY FATHER

[603]—1. Just as Part VI treats of the duties which each member of the Society has in regard to himself, so Part VII deals with the members' duties toward their neighbor (which is an end eminently characteristic of our Institute) when these members are dispersed to any part of Christ's vineyard, to labor in that part of it and in that work which have been entrusted to them. They may be sent to some places or others by the supreme vicar of Christ our Lord, or by the superiors of the Society, who for them are similarly in the place of his Divine Majesty; or they themselves may choose where and in what work they will labor, when they have been commissioned to travel to any place where they judge that greater service of God and the good of souls will follow; or they may carry on their labor, not by traveling but by residing steadily and continually in certain places where much fruit of glory and service to God is expected.

Since one's being sent on a mission of His Holiness will be treated first, as being most important, it should be observed that the vow which the Society made to obey him as the supreme vicar of Christ without any excuse, meant that the members were to go to any place whatsoever where he judges it expedient to send them for the greater glory of God and the good of souls, whether among the faithful or the infidels. The Society did not mean any particular place, but rather that it was to be distributed into diverse regions and places throughout the world, and it desired to proceed more correctly in this matter by leaving the distribution of its members to the sovereign pontiff.

. . .

Chapter 2
THE MISSIONS RECEIVED FROM THE SUPERIOR OF THE SOCIETY

[618]—1. To be able to meet the spiritual needs of souls in many regions with greater facility and with greater security for those who go among them for this purpose, the superiors of the Society, according to the faculty granted by the sovereign pontiff, will have authority to send any of the Society's members whomsoever to whatsoever place these superiors think it more expedient to send them, although these members, wherever they are, will always be at the disposition of His Holiness.

However, there are many who request help while considering more their own spiritual obligations to their flocks, or other advantages not so immediately their own, rather than the common or universal benefits. Therefore the superior general, or whoever holds this authority from him, ought to bestow much careful thought on missions of this kind in order that, when he sends subjects to one region rather than to another [D], or for one purpose rather than for another [E], or one particular person rather than another or several of them [F], in this manner or in that, for a greater or lesser time, that procedure may always be used which is conducive to the greater service of God and the universal good.

. . .

[622,a]—*D. To proceed more successfully in this sending of subjects to one place or another, one should keep the greater service of God and the more universal good before his eyes as the norm to hold oneself on the right course.*[73] *It appears that in the vineyard of the Lord, which is so extensive, the following procedure of selection ought to be used. When other considerations are equal (and this should be understood in everything that follows),*

that part of the vineyard ought to be chosen which has greater need, because of the lack of other workers or because of the misery and weakness of one's fellowmen in it and the danger of their eternal condemnation.

. . .

[d]. *The more universal the good is, the more is it divine. Therefore preference ought to be given to those persons and places which, through their own improvement, become a cause which can spread the good accomplished to many others who are under their influence or take guidance from them.*

[e]. *For that reason, the spiritual aid which is given to important and public persons ought to be regarded as more important, since it is a more universal good. This is true whether these persons are laymen such as princes, lords, magistrates, or ministers of justice, or whether they are clerics such as prelates. The same also holds true of the spiritual aid which is given to persons distinguished for learning and authority, because of that reason of its being the more universal good. For that same reason, too, preference ought to be shown to the aid which is given to the great nations such as the Indies, or to important cities, or to universities, which are generally attended by numerous persons who by being aided themselves can become laborers for the help of others.*

[f]. *Similarly, the Society ought to labor more intensely in those places where the enemy of Christ our Lord has sown cockle [Matt. 13:24–30], and especially where he has spread bad opinion about the Society or stirred up ill will against it so as to impede the fruit which the Society could produce. This is especially to be observed if the place is an important one of which account should be taken, by sending there, if possible, persons such that by their life and learning they may undo the evil opinion founded on false reports.*

. . .

Chapter 4
WAYS IN WHICH THE HOUSES AND COLLEGES CAN HELP THEIR NEIGHBOR

[636]—1. Since the Society endeavors to aid its neighbor not merely by traveling through diverse regions but also by residing continually in some places, for example, in the houses and colleges, it is important to have learned the means in which souls can be helped in those places, in order to use that selection of these means which is possible for the glory of God our Lord.

. . .

PART VIII. HELPS TOWARD UNITING THE DISTANT MEMBERS
WITH THEIR HEAD AND AMONG THEMSELVES

Chapter 1
AIDS TOWARD THE UNION OF HEARTS

[655]—1. The more difficult it is for the members of this congregation to be united with their head[74] and among themselves, since they are so scattered among the faithful and among the unbelievers in diverse regions of the world, the more ought means to be sought for that union. For the Society cannot be preserved, or governed, or, consequently, attain the end it seeks for the greater glory of God unless its members are united among themselves and with their head. Therefore the present treatise will deal first with what can aid the union of hearts[75] and later with helps toward the union of persons in congregations or chapters. With respect to the union of hearts, some of the helpful means lie on the side of the subjects, others on the side of the superiors, and others on both sides.

. . .

[659]—3. Since this union is produced in great part by the bond of obedience, this virtue should always be maintained in its vigor; and those who are sent out from the houses to labor in the Lord's field should as far as possible be persons practiced in this virtue. . . .

. . .

[662]—4. To this same virtue of obedience is related the properly observed subordination of the superiors, one to another, and of the subjects to the superiors, in such wise that the individuals dwelling in some house or college have recourse to their local superior or rector and are governed by him in every respect. Those who are distributed throughout the province refer to the provincial or some other local superior who is closer, according to the orders they received; and all the local superiors or rectors should communicate often with the provincial and thus too be directed by him in everything; and the provincials in their turn will deal in the same way with the general. For this subordination, when well observed in this manner, will preserve the union[76] which is attained chiefly through it, with the help of the grace of God our Lord.

. . .

[666]—6. On the side of the superior general, that which will aid toward this union of hearts consists in the qualities of his person [G].

They will be treated in Part IX [723–725]. With them he will carry on his office, which is to be for all the members a head from whom descends to all of them the impulse necessary for the end which the Society seeks. Thus it is that from the general as the head flows all the authority of the provincials, and from the provincials that of the local superiors, and from that of these local superiors that of the individual members. Thus too from that same head come the assignments to missions; or at least they come by his mandate and approval. The same should be understood about the communication of the graces of the Society; for the more the subjects are dependent upon their superiors, the better will the love, obedience, and union among them be preserved.

[667]—G. *Among other qualities, his good reputation and prestige among his subjects will be very specially helpful; and so will his having and manifesting love and concern for them, in such a way that the subjects hold the opinion that their superior has the knowledge, desire, and ability to rule them well in our Lord. For this and many other matters he will find it profitable to have with him persons able to give good counsel, as will be stated in Part IX [803, 804], whose help he can use in what he must order for the Society's good manner of proceeding in diverse regions, unto divine glory.*

Further help will be found in his having his method of commanding well thought out and organized,[77] through his endeavoring to maintain obedience in the subjects in such a manner that the superior on his part uses all the love and modesty and charity possible in our Lord, so that the subjects can dispose themselves to have always toward their superiors greater love than fear, even though both are useful at times. He can also do this by referring some matters to them when it appears probable that they will be helped by this; and at other times, by going along with them to some extent and sympathizing with them when this, it seems, could be more expedient.

. . .

[671]—8. The chief bond to cement the union of the members among themselves and with their head is, on both sides, the love of God our Lord. For when the superior and the subjects are closely united to his Divine and Supreme Goodness, they will very easily be united among themselves, through that same love which will descend from the Divine Goodness and spread to all other human beings, and particularly into the body of the Society. Thus from both sides charity will come to further this union between superiors and subjects, and in general all goodness and virtues through which one proceeds in conformity with the spirit. Consequently there will also come total contempt of temporal

things, in regard to which self-love, the chief enemy of this union and universal good, frequently induces disorder.

Still another great help can be found in uniformity, both interior uniformity of doctrine, judgments, and wills, as far as this is possible, and exterior uniformity in respect to clothing, ceremonies of the Mass, and other such matters, to the extent that the different qualities of persons, places, and the like, permit.

. . .

[673]—9. Still another very special help will be found in the exchange of letters between the subjects and the superiors, through which they learn about one another frequently and hear the news and reports which come from the various regions. The superiors, especially the general and the provincials, will take charge of this, by providing an arrangement through which each region can learn from the others whatever promotes mutual consolation and edification in our Lord.[78]

. . .

Chapter 2
THE OCCASIONS FOR HOLDING A GENERAL CONGREGATION

[677]—1. In the treatment of the union of persons which takes place in congregations of the Society, various points must be considered: the occasions when the persons should assemble, who should meet, and by whom they should be summoned; also where, when, and in what manner they ought to come together; and the determination of the material to be treated in the congregation.

To begin with the explanation of the first point, the occasions on which the congregation and general chapter[79] should take place: It is presupposed that for the present it does not seem good in our Lord that such a congregation should be held at definite intervals or very often; for the superior general, through the communication which he has with the whole Society and through the help he gets from those near him, can spare the Society as a whole from that work and distraction as far as possible. Yet on some occasions a general congregation will be necessary, for example, for the election of a general, whether it be because of the death of the preceding general or because of any of the reasons for which a general may relinquish that office and which will be treated further on [774, 782].

. . .

[680]—2. The second occasion arises when it is necessary to deal with long-lasting and important matters, as would be the suppression or transference of houses or colleges; or with other very difficult matters pertaining to the whole body of the Society or its manner of proceeding, for greater service to God our Lord.

. . .

PART IX. THE SOCIETY'S HEAD, AND THE GOVERNMENT DESCENDING FROM HIM

Chapter 1
THE NEED OF A SUPERIOR GENERAL AND HIS LIFELONG TERM OF OFFICE

[719]—In all well-organized communities or congregations there must be, besides the persons who take care of the particular goals, one or several whose proper duty is to attend to the universal good. So too in this Society, in addition to those who have charge of its single houses or colleges and of its single provinces where it has those houses or colleges, there must be someone who holds that charge of the entire body of the Society, one whose duty is the good government, preservation, and development of the whole body of the Society; and this person is the superior general. There is a possibility of electing him in either of two ways, namely, for a determined period or for his whole life. But since his experience and practice of government, his knowledge of the individual members, and the prestige he has with them are a great aid in performing this office well, his election will be for life[80] and not for a determined period. Thus too the Society, being universally occupied with important matters in the divine service, will be less disturbed and distracted by general congregations.

. . .

Chapter 2
THE KIND OF PERSON THE SUPERIOR GENERAL SHOULD BE

[723]—1. In regard to the qualities which are desirable in the superior general[81] [A], the first is that he should be closely united with God our Lord and intimate with him in prayer and all his actions, that from God, the fountain of all good, the general may so much the better

obtain for the whole body of the Society a large share of his gifts and graces, and also great power and efficacy for all the means which will be used for the help of souls.

. . .

[724]—A. *The six qualities treated in this chapter are the most important, and all the rest are reduced to them. For they include the general's perfection in relation to God; further, what perfects his heart,*[82] *understanding, and execution; and further still, those qualities of body and those extrinsic goods which help him. Moreover, the importance of these six qualities is indicated by the order in which they are placed.*

[725]—2. The second quality is that he should be a person whose example in the practice of all virtues is a help to the other members of the Society. Charity should be especially resplendent in him, toward all his neighbors, and above all toward the members of the Society; and genuine humility too should shine forth, that these characteristics may make him highly lovable to God our Lord and to men.

[726]—3. He ought also to be independent of all passions, by his keeping them controlled and mortified, so that in his interior they may not disturb the judgment of his intellect and in his exterior he may be so composed, particularly so self-controlled when speaking, that no one, either a member of the Society who should regard him as a mirror and model, or an extern, may observe in him any thing or word which does not edify.

[727]—4. However, he should know how to mingle rectitude and necessary severity with kindness and gentleness, to such an extent that he neither allows himself to swerve from what he judges to be more pleasing to God our Lord nor ceases to have proper sympathy for his sons. Thus although they are being reprimanded or punished, they will recognize that in what he does he is proceeding rightly in our Lord and with charity, even though it is against their liking according to the lower man.

[728]—5. Magnanimity and fortitude of soul are likewise highly necessary for him to bear the weaknesses of many, to initiate great undertakings in the service of God our Lord, and to persevere in them with constancy when it is called for, without losing courage in the face of the contradictions (even though they come from persons of high rank and power), and without allowing himself to be moved by their entreaties or threats from what reason and the divine service require. He should be superior to all eventualities, without letting himself be exalted

by those which succeed or depressed by those which go poorly, being altogether ready to receive death, if necessary, for the good of the Society in the service of Jesus Christ, God and our Lord.

[729]—6. The third quality is that he ought to be endowed with great understanding and judgment, in order that this talent may not fail him in either the speculative or the practical matters which may arise. And although learning is highly necessary for one who will have so many learned men in his charge, still more necessary is prudence along with experience in spiritual and interior matters, that he may be able to discern the various spirits and to give counsel and remedies to so many who will have spiritual necessities.

He also needs discretion in exterior matters and a manner of handling such diverse affairs as well as of conversing with such various persons from within and without the Society.

[730]—7. The fourth quality, one highly necessary for the execution of business, is that he should be vigilant and solicitous to undertake enterprises as well as energetic in carrying them through to their completion and perfection, rather than careless and remiss in such a way that he leaves them begun but not finished.

[731]—8. The fifth quality has reference to the body. In regard to health, appearance, and age, on the one hand account should be taken of propriety and prestige, and on the other hand of the physical energies which his charge requires [B], that in it he may be able to fulfill his office to the glory of God our Lord.

[732]—B. *Thus it seems that he ought to be neither very old, since such a one is generally not fit for the labors and cares of such a charge, nor very young, since a young man generally lacks the proper prestige and experience.*

[733]—9. The sixth quality pertains to extrinsic endowments [C]. Among these, preference ought to be given to those which help more toward edification and the service of God in such a charge. Examples are generally found in reputation, high esteem, and whatever else aids toward prestige with those within and without.

[734]—C. *Nobility, wealth which was possessed in the world, reputation, and the like, are extrinsic endowments. Other things being equal, these are worthy of some consideration; but even if they are lacking, there are other things more important which could suffice for election.*

[735]—10. Finally, he ought to be one of those who are most outstanding in every virtue, most deserving in the Society, and known as such for a considerable time. If any of the aforementioned qualities

should be wanting, there should at least be no lack of great probity and of love for the Society, nor of good judgment accompanied by sound learning. For in regard to other things, the aids which he will have (and which will be treated below [789–808]) could through God's help and favor supply to a great extent for many deficiencies.

. . .

Chapter 4
THE AUTHORITY OR PROVIDENT CARE WHICH THE SOCIETY SHOULD EXERCISE IN REGARD TO THE SUPERIOR GENERAL

[766]—1. The authority or provident care[83] which the Society will have in regard to the general, always for the sake of the universal good and greater edification, will lie in six concerns which can help toward glory to God our Lord [A].

[767]—A. *The Society will exercise this authority through the assistants, who will be described later* [779].

[768]—2. The first concern has reference to external things such as clothes, food, and any expenditures touching upon the general's person. In this area the Society will be able to make extensions or restrictions in accordance with what it judges to be fitting for the general and the Society and to be conducive to greater service to God. The general in turn ought to be content with what is provided.

[769]—3. The second concern pertains to the care of his body, that he may not go beyond measure in labors or excessive severity. The superior in turn will consent to be controlled and will be satisfied with what the Society orders.

[770]—4. The third concern pertains to his soul in relation to his person and office, since even in perfect men there could be some need of this concern. The Society should have with the superior general (and the same practice can be employed with subjects) some person who has the following obligation. After he has had recourse to God in prayer and has asked light from his Divine Goodness, if he judges it right he should, with proper modesty and humility, admonish the general about anything in him which he thinks will be more conducive to greater service and glory to God. This person could be the general's confessor or someone else appointed by the Society who seems suitable for this purpose.

Chapter 6
AIDS TO THE SUPERIOR GENERAL FOR THE GOOD PERFORMANCE OF HIS OFFICE

[789]—1. The proper function of the general is not to preach, hear confessions, and perform other similar ministries (though as a private person he will see what he can do in these ministries when the occupations proper to his office leave him opportunity, but under no other circumstances). Instead, his office is to govern the whole body of the Society in such a manner that through the divine grace it may be preserved and developed in its well-being and manner of proceeding for glory to God our Lord [A], by employing his authority as is expedient for that end.

[790]—A. *He will achieve this kind of government primarily by the influence and example of his life, by his charity and love of the Society in Christ our Lord, by his prayer which is assiduous and full of desires and by his sacrifices, to obtain the grace of the aforementioned preservation and development. On his own part he should hold these means in high esteem and have great confidence in our Lord, since these are the most efficacious means of gaining grace from his Divine Majesty, the Source of what is longed for. Especially should the general do this as necessities occur.*

Next, he will achieve this kind of government by his solicitude to maintain the observance of the Constitutions, by keeping himself frequently informed by the provincials of what is occurring in all the provinces and by writing to the provincials his opinion about the matters which they communicate to him, and by so acting that provision is made where it is proper, either through himself or through the ministers who will be described later.

[791]—2. When those qualities of his intense spiritual life and great virtues which are treated above in Chapter 2 [725–728] are presupposed, he still has need of good ministers for the more detailed affairs. For although he himself sometimes treats of them directly, he cannot escape the need of lower superiors, who ought to be selected men, to whom he can give much authority and ordinarily refer those particular matters. More generally, his own dealing among these lower superiors will be with the provincials, just as the provincials' dealing will be with the rectors and local superiors, that the proper subordination may be the better preserved. But sometimes, in order to have more information about all things and because of other cases which commonly occur, the general will deal with the rectors or local superiors and also with individual persons. He will endeavor to help them with

counsel, reprimand, and correction, if necessary. For it pertains to him to supply for the defects of the lower superiors and, with the divine favor and aid, to bring toward perfection what has been imperfect in them.

. . .

PART X.
HOW THE WHOLE BODY OF THE SOCIETY CAN BE PRESERVED AND DEVELOPED IN ITS WELL-BEING[84]

[812]—1. The Society was not instituted by human means; and neither is it through them that it can be preserved and developed, but through the omnipotent hand of Christ, God and our Lord. Therefore in him alone must be placed the hope that he will preserve and carry forward what he deigned to begin for his service and praise and for the aid of souls. In conformity with this hope, the first and best proportioned means will be the prayers and Masses which ought to be offered for this holy intention through their being ordered for it every week, month, and year in all the regions where the Society resides.

[813]—2. For the preservation and development not only of the body or exterior of the Society but also of its spirit, and for the attainment of the objective it seeks, which is to aid souls to reach their ultimate and supernatural end, the means which unite the human instrument with God[85] and so dispose it that it may be wielded dexterously by his divine hand are more effective than those which equip it in relation to human beings. Such means are, for example, goodness and virtue, and especially charity, and a pure intention of the divine service, and familiarity with God our Lord in spiritual exercises of devotion, and sincere zeal for souls for the sake of the glory of him who created and redeemed them and not for any other benefit.[86] Thus it appears that care should be taken in general that all the members of the Society may devote themselves to the solid and perfect virtues and to spiritual pursuits, and attach greater importance to them than to learning and other natural and human gifts. For they are the interior gifts which make those exterior means effective toward the end which is sought.

[814]—3. When based upon this foundation, the natural means[87] which equip the human instrument of God our Lord to deal with his fellow human beings will all be helps toward the preservation and development of this whole body, provided they are acquired and exercised for the divine service alone; employed, indeed, not that we may

put our confidence in them, but that we may cooperate with the divine grace according to the arrangement of the sovereign providence of God our Lord. For he desires to be glorified both through the natural means, which he gives as Creator, and through the supernatural means, which he gives as the Author of grace.[88] Therefore the human or acquired means ought to be sought with diligence, especially well-grounded and solid learning, and a method of proposing it to the people by means of sermons, lectures, and the art of dealing and conversing with others.

[815]—4. In similar manner, great help will be derived from maintaining the colleges in their good state and discipline, by having the superintendency over them exercised by those who cannot receive any temporal gain, such as members of the professed Society, which will take care that those who possess the talent for it may receive formation in life and learning worthy of a Christian. For these students will be a seedbed[89] for the professed Society and its coadjutors. Furthermore, if universities over which the Society exercises superintendency are added to the colleges, they too will aid toward the same end, as long as the method of procedure described in Part IV [440–509] is preserved.

[816]—5. Since poverty is like a bulwark of religious institutes which preserves them in their existence and discipline and defends them from many enemies; and since the devil uses corresponding effort to destroy this bulwark in one way or another, it will be highly important for the preservation and development of this whole body that every appearance of avarice should be banished afar, through the Society's abstention from accepting fixed income, or any possessions, or salaries for preaching, or lecturing, or Masses, or administration of sacraments, or spiritual things, as is stated in Part VI [565], and also through its avoidance of converting the fixed revenue of the colleges to its own utility.

[817]—6. It will also be of the highest importance toward perpetuating the Society's well-being to use great diligence in precluding from it ambition, the mother of all evils in any community or congregation whatsoever. This will be accomplished by closing the door against seeking, directly or indirectly, any dignity or prelacy[90] within the Society, in such a way that all the professed should promise to God our Lord never to seek one and to expose anyone whom they observe trying to obtain one; also in such a way that one who can be proved to have sought such a prelacy becomes ineligible and disqualified for any office.

The professed should similarly promise to God our Lord not to seek any prelacy or dignity outside the Society, and, as far as in them lies, not to consent to being chosen for a similar charge unless they are compelled by an order from him who can command them under pain of sin. Each one should desire to serve souls in conformity with our profession of humility and lowliness, and to avoid having the Society deprived of the men who are necessary for its purpose.[91]

Each one should further promise to God our Lord that if some prelacy outside the Society is accepted through the aforementioned manner of compulsion, he will at any time whatsoever later on listen to the counsel of him who is the general of the Society, or of someone else whom the general substitutes for himself; and that if he judges what has been counseled to him to be the better thing, he will carry it out [A]. He will do this, not because he, being a prelate, has any member of the Society as a superior, but because he desires to oblige himself voluntarily before God our Lord to do that which he finds to be better for his divine service, and to be happy to have someone who presents it to him with charity and Christian freedom, to the glory of God our Lord.

[818]—A. *After observing the pressure which has been exerted in so many ways to bring members of the Society to accept bishoprics; and after resisting in many cases;[92] and after being unable to resist in accepting the patriarchate and bishopric of Ethiopia, we bestowed thought upon this aid for this latter undertaking and for other similar ones when resistance may be impossible. However, the Society does not oblige itself to undertake this helpful activity each time one of its individual members must accept some bishopric, but it remains free to omit this activity or to take it up where it is judged to be of great importance for the divine service. Moreover, after the profession is made, this simple vow will be taken along with the other vows which have been mentioned.*

[819]—7. Much aid is given toward perpetuating the well-being of this whole body by what was said in Part I [142–144], Part II [204], and Part V [516–523] about avoiding the admission of a crowd, or of persons unsuitable for our Institute, even to probation, and about dismissals during the time of probation when it is found that some persons do not turn out to be suitable. Much less ought those to be retained who are addicted to vice or are incorrigible. But even greater strictness should be shown in admitting persons among the approved scholastics and formed coadjutors, and strictness far greater still in regard to admission to profession. This profession should be made only by persons who are selected for their spirit[93] and learning, thoroughly and lengthily tested, and known with edification and satisfaction to all after various proofs of virtue and abnegation of themselves. This procedure is used

that, even though the numbers are multiplied, the spirit may not be diminished or weakened, when those who are incorporated into the Society are such as have been described.

[820]—8. Since the well-being or illness of the head has its consequences in the whole body, it is supremely important that the election of the superior general be carried out as directed in Part IX [723–735]. Next in importance is the choice of the lower superiors in the provinces, colleges, and houses of the Society. For in a general way, the subjects will be what these superiors are.

It is also highly important that, in addition to that choice, the individual superiors should have much authority over the subjects, and the general over the individual superiors; and, on the other hand, that the Society have much authority in regard to the general, as is explained in Part IX [736, 757, 759, 766–788]. This arrangement is made that all may have full power for good and that, if they do poorly, they may be kept under complete control.

It is similarly important that the superiors have suitable ministers, as was said in the same Part [798–810], for the organization and execution of the affairs pertaining to their office.

[821]—9. Whatever helps toward the union of the members of this Society among themselves and with their head will also help much toward preserving the well-being of the Society. This is especially the case with the bond of wills, which is the mutual charity and love they have for one another. This bond is strengthened by their getting information and news from one another and having much intercommunication, by their following one same doctrine, and by their being uniform in everything as far as possible, and above all by the link of obedience, which unites the individuals with their superiors, and the local superiors among themselves and with the provincials, and both the local superiors and provincials with the general, in such a way that the subordination of some to others is diligently preserved.

[822]—10. Temperate restraint in spiritual and bodily labors and similar moderation in relation to the Constitutions, which do not lean toward an extreme of rigor or toward excessive laxity (and thus they can be better observed), will help this entire body to persevere in its good state and to be maintained in it.

[823]—11. Toward the same purpose it is helpful in general to strive to retain the good will and charity of all, even of those outside the Society, and especially of those whose favorable or unfavorable attitude toward it is of great importance for opening or closing the gate leading

to the service of God and the good of souls [B]. It is also helpful that in the Society there should neither be nor be seen partiality to one side or another among Christian princes or rulers, but in its stead a universal love which embraces in our Lord all parties (even though they are adversaries to one another).

[824]—B. *First of all an effort should be made to retain the benevolence of the Apostolic See, which the Society should especially serve; and then that of the temporal rulers and noble and powerful persons whose favor or disfavor does much toward opening or closing the gate to the service of God and the good of souls. Similarly, when an unfavorable attitude is perceived in some persons, especially in persons of importance, prayer ought to be offered for them and the suitable means should be employed to bring them to friendship, or at least to keep them from being hostile. This is done, not because contradiction and ill-treatment are feared, but that God our Lord may be more served and glorified in all things through the benevolence of all these persons.*

[825]—12. Help will also be found in a discreet and moderate use of the favors granted by the Apostolic See, by seeking with all sincerity nothing else than the aid of souls. For through this God our Lord will carry forward what he has begun; and the fragrance [2 Cor. 2:15] arising from the genuineness of the good works will increase the benevolent desire of others to avail themselves of the Society's aid and to help the Society for the end which it seeks, the glory and service of his Divine Majesty.

[826]—13. It will also be helpful that attention should be devoted to the preservation of the health of the individual members [C], as was stated in Part III [292–306]; and finally, that all should apply themselves to the observance of the Constitutions. For this purpose they must know them, at least those which pertain to each one. Therefore each one should read or hear them every month.

[827]—C. *For this purpose it is expedient that attention should be given to having the houses and colleges in healthy locations with pure air and not in those characterized by the opposite.*

THE END

E. SELECTED LETTERS

CONTENTS

INTRODUCTION

In the line of books, Ignatius composed only the four represented above; but as a writer of letters he was prolific. Most of these remained unpublished until rather recent times. A collection of 97 of them, published by R. Menchaca in 1804, excited others to ransack archives and other sources for more. By 1889, 802 letters in Spanish and a few more in Italian were available in the six volumes of *Cartas de San Ignacio* published in Madrid.[1] Then came the master edition printed from 1903 to 1911, also in Madrid, by the Historical Institute of the Society of Jesus. It bears the title "Letters and Instructions of St. Ignatius" (*Sti. Ignatii de Loyola Epistolae et Instructiones*). This series, 12 volumes of about 800 pages each, contains Ignatius' letters and instructions numbered from 1 to 6,742, presented in chronological order, critically edited, and to some extent analyzed and annotated. In Volume 12 are 74 additional letters, discovered too late to be placed in their proper sequence. This collection gives Ignatius a high rank among important persons of his century whose correspondence has been published. For example, we know of about 500 letters of St. Teresa, 2,040 of Erasmus, 3,426 of Luther, and 4,271 of Calvin.[2]

Ignatius' letters range over the whole gamut of things religious and secular which came to the attention of the general of a worldwide religious order. Addressed to kings and emperors, popes, cardinals, and bishops, lay men and women, saints and sinners, they have furnished immense information about Ignatius which was unavailable to earlier biographers and historians. Naturally, too, they reveal many new aspects of his rich personality, such as his human warmth, his interest in men and women with their joys and hopes, plans and frustrations. His sympathetic understanding reached into all the circumstances of their daily lives, but always with a consciousness that all their affairs ought to be related to their eternal interests. He is always trying to see things from God's point of view, and to help his correspondents to fit their lives and affairs cooperatively into God's plan of salvation for those who use their freedom wisely. Consequently in his letters we see him applying his spiritual principles to the multifaceted situations of men and women as they were trying to play their own roles in the complicated historical circumstances of their day.

Able to give here only a few samples of this extensive correspondence, we have chosen ten letters which exemplify that application of his spiritual principles in practice. The translations, by Martin E. Palmer, S.J., are made from the texts in the twelve volumes in the Monumenta Historica Societatis Iesu, *Sancti Ignatii de Loyola: Epistolae et Instructiones* (Madrid, 1903–1911).

* * *

1. To Inés Pascual
A Letter of Spiritual Direction
The Original is in *EppIgn*, I:71–72

Inés Pascual was a pious widow whom Ignatius met in Barcelona when he came there from Manresa in March, 1522. Struck with admiration of his manifest holiness, she became his benefactress. When he returned from the Holy Land in early 1523 to study in Barcelona, he resided chiefly in her house while he studied Latin under Master Ardèvol. From spring of 1523 to summer of 1525 he shared a room with Isabel's son Juan, to whom he became a close friend.

This is the earliest of Ignatius' extant letters. At the time he wrote it, Inés was depressed because a lady companion whose name remains unknown had died, and because disparaging remarks were being made about other ladies who like herself had been associating with Ignatius. Hence Ignatius wrote this friendly letter. He encourages her to continue the practice of virtue in spite of the present difficulties and to serve the Lord in joy while taking proper care of her health.

Barcelona, December 6, 1524

I have decided to write you this because of the desires to serve the Lord that I have seen in you. I can well believe that at the present time, because of your missing the blessed servant whom the Lord has been pleased to take to himself, because of the many enemies and difficulties you meet with in God's service where you are, and also because of the enemy of human nature and his incessant temptations, you are feeling overwhelmed. For the love of God our Lord try to keep going forward. Always avoid whatever things are harmful. If you avoid them, temptation will have no power against you. This is what you should be doing always, placing the Lord's praise ahead of everything else.

All the more so since the Lord does not require you to do anything exhausting or harmful to your person. He wants you to live taking joy in him and granting the body whatever it needs. Let all your words, thoughts, and behavior be in him, and attend to your bodily necessities for his sake, always placing the observance of God's commandments first. This is what he wants and what he commands us. And anyone who gives careful thought to this will find that there is more trouble and pain in this life . . . [four or five words missing].

A pilgrim named Calixto[3] is now staying there; I would very much like you to talk with him about your affairs. Indeed, you may well discover in him more than appears on the surface.

And so, for the love of our Lord let us make every effort in him, since we owe him so much. For we tire of receiving his gifts much sooner than he tires of giving.

May Our Lady intercede between us poor sinners and her Son and Lord; may she obtain for us the grace that, with the cooperation of our own toil and effort, our weak and sorry spirits may be made strong and joyful in his praise.

The poor pilgrim
Iñigo

2. To Isabel Roser.
Consolation, the Bearing of Insults,
the Third Way of Being Humble
I:83–89

Isabel Roser, née Ferrer, a noble lady of Barcelona, and her husband Juan, a businessman, led lives of piety and charity. One day, while listening to a sermon in the church of Santa María del Mar, she observed Ignatius with rapt attention, seated amid children on the altar steps. Deeply impressed, she described his whole demeanor to her husband and they invited him to their house. After dinner they asked Ignatius to speak about the things of God. His fervent reply initiated a lifelong spiritual friendship. She became so fond of Ignatius that she offered to defray the expenses of his studies and thus became his chief benefactress through his years in Barcelona, Paris, and Venice. On occasions, however, she showed signs of nervous disorders which Ignatius sympathetically understood.[4]

In the present letter Ignatius replies from Paris to three letters from Isabel which expressed complaints about various sufferings which had come upon her. He encourages her to draw spiritual profit from the vexations, and he thanks her for her gift of money. By now in 1532 his Exercises were almost in their final form, and his advice manifestly springs from their Foundation and his concept of the Three Ways of Being Humble.

Paris, November 10, 1532

May the grace and love of Christ our Lord be with us.

Along with Doctor Benet I received three letters from your hand, together with twenty ducats. May God our Lord will to credit them to you on the day of judgment; and may he repay you through me. I am confident that in his divine goodness he will repay you in his own good and sound currency, and also that he will not let me incur the guilt of ingratitude—supposing that he eventually makes me worthy in some respects to afford service and praise to his Divine Majesty.

You speak in your letter of God's will being fulfilled in la Canilla's[5] banishment and departure from this life. In reality, I cannot feel sorrow for her, but only for ourselves who abide in this place of immense weariness, pains, and calamities. Having known how in this life she was loved and cherished by her Creator and Lord, I can readily believe that she will be well received and welcomed and will not miss the palaces, pomps, riches, and vanities of this world.

You also write me about the apologies of our sisters in Christ our Lord. They owe me nothing; it is I who am eternally indebted to them. If they employ their means elsewhere for the service of God our Lord, we should be glad. And if they do not or cannot, I truly wish I had something I could give to them so that they could do much for the service and glory of God our Lord. As long as I live I cannot help being their debtor, but I think that after we have left this life they will be well repaid by me.

In your second letter you tell me of the long ailment and illness you have gone through, and of the severe stomach pains you still have. Truly, when I think of your present ill-health and pains I cannot help feeling it in my own soul, since I desire for you every imaginable well-being and prosperity which could help you for the glory and service of God our Lord. However, when I reflect that these infirmities and other temporal deprivations are often from the hand of God our Lord to help us know ourselves better and be more thoroughly rid of the love of created things and more fully aware of the brevity of this life of ours so that we will furnish ourselves for the other life which will last forever, and when I reflect that he visits with these afflictions those for whom he has great love, then I can feel no sadness or pain. For I think that through an illness a servant of God ends up with half a doctorate in how to direct and order his or her life to the glory and service of God our Lord.

Likewise, you ask my pardon if you fail to supply me with more funds, since you have many obligations to fulfill and insufficient resources. There is no reason to speak of pardon. It is about pardon for myself that I am concerned—for I fear that, if I fail to fulfill the obligations toward all my benefactors laid on me by God our Lord, his divine and righteous justice will not pardon me—all the more so in view of what I owe to you personally. In the end, if I prove unable to fulfill my responsibilities in this regard, my only hope is that, taking into account whatever merits I shall gain before the Divine Majesty (obtained through his grace, of course), the Lord himself will distribute them to those to whom I am indebted, to each person according as he has helped me in his service, and above all to you, to whom I owe a greater debt than to anyone else I know in this world. I am fully aware of this debt, and I trust in God our Lord that I will constantly deepen and increase my awareness of it.

And so be sure that from now on I will receive your wholesome and sincere concern for me with as much satisfaction and spiritual gladness as I would any amount of money you could send me. God our Lord requires that we have greater regard and love for the giver than for the gift, keeping the person always before our eyes and in our soul and in our heart.

You also ask whether I would think it advisable to write to our other sisters and benefactresses in Christ for help in the future. In this I would rather be guided by your judgment than by my own. Even though in her letter la Cepilla offers and shows a willingness to help me, I do not think for the present that I will write her for help in my studies. We have no assurance of reaching another year; and if we do, I trust that God our Lord will give us insight and judgment so as to serve him best and always correctly discern his will and desire.

In the third letter you speak of the spitefulness, intrigues, and untruths which have surrounded you on every side. I am not at all surprised at this, no matter how much worse it might be. On the day you decide, resolve, and bend every effort to work for the glory, honor, and

service of God our Lord, at that moment you join battle with the world
and raise your standard against it. You undertake to cast down what is
lofty and embrace what is lowly, resolving to accept equally exaltation
or humiliation, honor or dishonor, wealth or poverty, affection or
hatred, welcome or repulse—in short, the world's glory or all its insults.

We cannot give much importance to insults in this life when they
are only words. All the words in the world will never hurt a hair of our
heads. Malicious, vile, and wounding words cause us pain or contentment only through our own desires in their regard. If our desire is to
possess the unconditional honor and esteem of our neighbors, we will
never be solidly rooted in God our Lord, or remain unscathed when we
meet with affronts.

Thus, to the very extent that I once took satisfaction at the world's
offering you insults, I was pained to hear that your adversities, suffering, and hardships have driven you to have recourse to medicines. May
it please the Mother of God that—so long as you maintain complete
patience and steadfastness by considering the greater insults and affronts undergone for our sakes by Christ our Lord, and so long as there
is no sin on the part of others—you might meet with even worse
affronts so that you may merit more and more. If we fail to attain this
patience, we have greater cause to complain of our own sensuality and
flesh, and of our own failure to be as mortified and dead to worldly
things as we ought, than of the persons who affront us. The latter are
giving us an opportunity for greater profits than anyone can earn in this
life, and greater wealth than anyone can amass in this world—as was the
case with a person in the monastery of St. Francis here in Paris. This is
what happened.[6]

There was a house where Franciscan friars often visited. Their
demeanor being very holy and religious, a grown-up young girl living in
the house formed a great love for the monastery and house of St.
Francis—so great in fact that one day she dressed as a boy and went to
the monastery of St. Francis and asked the guardian to let "him" take
the habit because "he" had a deep desire to serve not only God our Lord
and St. Francis but also all the religious of that house. He spoke so
appealingly that they immediately gave him the habit.

While he was living thus in the monastery a life of great recollection and consolation, it happened that, on a trip made with their superior's permission, this friar and another companion once stayed over-
night in a certain house. In the house there was a young woman who

became enamored of this good friar. Consequently (or rather, because the devil entered her) she decided to accost the good friar while he was sleeping and get him to have relations with her. When the good friar awoke and threw her off, she was so infuriated that she began scheming how to do the good friar as much harm as she could.

Accordingly, some days later this wicked girl went to speak with the guardian, demanding justice and claiming that, among other things, she was pregnant by the good friar of his house. And so the guardian seized the good friar and decided (since the matter had become notorious in the city) to put him bound in the street at the monastery doors so that everyone could see the justice inflicted upon the good friar.

He spent many days in this condition, rejoicing in the injuries, insults, and obscene words he heard uttered against himself. He made no self-defense to anyone, but within his soul conversed with his Creator and Lord, since he was being given an opporunity for such great merit in the eyes of his Divine Majesty.

After a period of time spent in this spectacle, when everybody had seen how great was his patience, they all begged the guardian to forgive the past and restore him to his love and to his house. The guardian, himself already moved to pity, received him back.

The good friar lived many years in the house, until God our Lord's will for him came to fulfillment. Upon undressing him for burial after his death, they discovered that he was not a man but a woman, and consequently that he had been the victim of a terrible calumny. Amazed, all the friars had praise for his innocence and holiness that exceeded their curses against his wickedness. However, even today there are many who remember this friar—or nun—better than anyone else who lived in the house over a long period of time.

And so I would be more attentive to a single shortcoming of my own than to all the evil that people might say of me.

May the most holy Trinity grant you, in all trials of this life and in everything else in which you can serve him, the same degree of grace that I desire for myself. May he grant me nothing more than what I desire for you.

Please commend me most sincerely to Mosén Roser, and to any who you think will be really pleased to hear from me.

Poor in goodness,
Iñigo

[Postscript:] In Arteaga as well as several persons from Alcalá and Salamanca I see much steadfastness in the service and glory of God our Lord. For this, infinite thanks be to God.

As you direct, I am writing to la Gralla about the reconciliation; the letter is going with that of [Inés] Pascual; also to la Cepilla.

3. To Teresa Rejadell.
On Discernment of Spirits
I:99–107

Teresa Rejadell, a friend of Isabel Roser, was a holy Benedictine nun in the convent of Santa Clara, Barcelona. While Ignatius was study-ing Latin in Barcelona from 1523 to 1525 she sought spiritual direction from him. He, always eager to speak about God with kindred souls, willingly gave it. This spiritual friendship led to an interchange of letters which lasted almost until her death in 1553.[7] Considerable worldliness existed in that convent, and Teresa was the leader of a small group which hoped to bring about reform.

This is his first extant letter to her, the longest spiritual document he wrote to her. It was sent from Venice on June 18, 1536, and is a reply to a letter of hers now lost. It offers spiritual direction which gives us a window into the content of the hours of spiritual conversations which she and he had held in Barcelona. It reflects Ignatius' fundamen-tal experiences at Loyola and Manresa and contains much of his basic spiritual teaching, especially on discernment of spirits. It is often called a commentary on his Rules in SpEx [313–336]. We provide an outline by inserting headings into the text.

Venice, June 18, 1536

May the grace and love of Christ our Lord be always our protec-tion and help.

Your letter, which I received some days back, has caused me much joy in the Lord whom you serve and wish to serve even more, and to whom we must ascribe everything good that we see in a creature.

You wrote that Cáceres[8] would inform me at length about your concerns. He not only did so but also informed me about the advice or opinion he gave you on each of them. Reading over what he tells me, I find nothing to add, although I would prefer to have the information in a letter from you, since no one can explain another person's interior experiences as well as the person who is undergoing them.

[1. Her Request for Spiritual Direction]

You ask me for the love of God our Lord to undertake the care of your soul. It is true that, without my deserving it, his Divine Majesty has for many years now given me the desire to give as much satisfaction as I can to all, men and women, who walk in the way of his will, and also to serve those who labor in the service owed to him. And since I have no doubt that you are one of these persons, I long to be where I could demonstrate what I say through deeds.

You also earnestly beg me to write you what our Lord tells me and to let you know definitely what I think. I will be very glad to tell you my definite opinion in the Lord. If on a given point I seem severe, it will be less against yourself than against the one who is trying to upset you.

There are two matters about which the enemy is causing you confusion, not so as to make you fall into any sin that could separate you from your God and Lord, but in such a way that he does confuse you and draw you away from his greater service and your own greater peace of mind. First, he is persuading you to have a false humility. Second, he is causing in you an excessive fear of God, which you dwell upon and occupy yourself with too much.

[2. The Enemy's Tactics with Beginners: He Tempts Sometimes to False Humility, Sometimes to Pride and Vainglory]

As for the first: The enemy's general practice with persons who desire and are beginning to serve God our Lord is to throw up obstacles and impediments. This is the first weapon with which he strives to harm them. He says, for example: "How are you going to live a whole lifetime of such penance, with no pleasure from friends, relatives, or possessions, leading such a lonely a life, with no respite? After all, you can save your soul in other ways and without such hazards." He tells us we will have to live a longer life than any human being ever lived amid the hardships he pictures to us. He refrains from telling us about the great comfort and consolation which our Lord is accustomed to give to such souls when the new servant of the Lord breaks through all these obstacles and chooses to suffer along with his Creator and Lord.

Then the enemy tries his second weapon: pride and vainglory. He tells the person that he possesses much goodness and holiness, and exalts him higher than he deserves.

If the servant of God resists these arrows by humbling and abasing himself and refusing to consent to the enemy's suggestions, the enemy comes with his third weapon. This is a false humility. When he sees how good and humble the Lord's servant is, how even while fulfilling all that the Lord commands he still thinks it is worthless and focuses on his own weakness and has no thought of self-glorification, the enemy then injects the suggestion that, if the person adverts to anything that God our Lord has given him by way of deeds or resolves and desire, he sins through another species of vainglory because he speaks approvingly of himself.

In this way the enemy tries to get the person not to talk about the good things he has received from his Lord, so that he will not produce fruit in others or in himself. For to cultivate awareness of what one has already received is always a help toward even greater things. (Of course speaking about such things must be done with great moderation and only with the motive of benefiting people, that is, oneself or other persons whom one sees to be disposed for it and likely to give the speaker credence and be benefited.) Thus, when we humble ourselves, the enemy tries to draw us on to a false humility, that is, to a humility that is excessive and perverted.

What you say aptly demonstrates this. After recounting your weaknesses and fears, which are very much to the point, you say, "I am a poor religious; I think I desire to serve Christ our Lord." You lack the courage to say, "I desire to serve to Christ our Lord," or, "The Lord gives me desires to serve him." Instead you say "I think I desire to serve him."

If you reflect, you will realize that these desires to serve Christ our Lord do not come from yourself but are given to you by the Lord. And so when you say, "The Lord gives me strong desires to serve him," it is the Lord himself you are praising by making known his gift; it is he and not yourself in whom you boast, since you do not attribute the grace to yourself.

[3. Tactics for Ourselves: When the Devil Exalts Us, Humble Ourselves. When He discourages Us, Foster Our Faith and Hope]

Hence we must reflect carefully. If the enemy lifts us up, we must put ourselves down by counting our sins and miseries. If he casts us down and depresses us, we should raise ourselves up in genuine faith and hope in the Lord by calling to mind the blessings we have received and the great love and concern with which he is waiting to save us. We must remember that the enemy does not care whether he tells a truth or a lie so long as he besets us.

Reflect how the martyrs, when haled before idolatrous magistrates, professed themselves servants of Christ. So, when you are haled before the enemy of all humanity to be tried by him in this way, and he attempts to rob you of the strength given you by our Lord and to weaken and intimidate you with his tricks and deceits, you will have the courage, not to say that you desire to serve our Lord, but to proclaim without fear that you are his servant and would rather die than leave his service. If the enemy makes me think of justice, I will immediately think of mercy; if he makes me think of mercy, I will counter by thinking of justice.

This is how we have to proceed so as to avoid being troubled and so as to outwit our deluder. We should rely on the Scripture text which states, "Beware of being so humble that you fall into folly" [see Sir. 13:10].

Now to the second point. When the enemy has produced in us a fear through a semblance of humility (a humility that is spurious), and has gotten us not to speak even of things that are good, holy, and profitable, he then inspires an even worse fear, namely, that we are separated, estranged, and alienated from our Lord. This fear results largely from what has gone before. After conquering us in the matter of the prior fear, the enemy finds us easier to tempt with the subsequent one.

To make this somewhat clearer, I will mention a further procedure of the enemy's. If he finds a person who has an easygoing conscience and who lets sins go by without weighing their gravity, he does his best to make the person think venial sins no sins at all, mortal sins venial, and very serious mortal sins of little consequence. Thus he exploits the failing he perceives in us, in this case the overly lax conscience.

[5. Lessons from the Lord: During Consolation, We Should
Humble Ourselves; and during Desolation, Counterattack against It]

On the other hand, when he encounters a person who has a delicate
conscience (no fault in itself) and sees that the person not only repulses
mortal sins, and venial sin so far as he can (for they are not all in our
power), but even tries to repel every semblance of slight sin, imperfection, or defect, then the enemy attempts to throw this excellent conscience into turmoil by charging sin where there is none and defect
where there is perfection, so that he can confound and distress us.
Often, when he cannot get a person to sin and has no prospect of doing
so, he will at least try to torment the person.

To make it somewhat clearer how this fear is produced, I will
mention, although briefly, two lessons which our Lord either gives or
permits (giving the first and permitting the second).

The lesson which he gives is interior consolation; this dispels all
confusion and draws a person to every form of love of the Lord. In this
consolation to some persons he gives light, and to others he reveals
many secrets, and so forth. In a word, with this divine consolation all
hardships are a pleasure and all labors repose. For a person going forward with this fervor and warmth and interior consolation, the heaviest
burden seems light and the harshest penance or labor very sweet. This
consolation points out and opens for us the path we should follow and
the contrary path we should avoid. This consolation does not dwell in
us uninterruptedly but always follows its definite periods as has been
ordained, all for our own progress.

Then, when we are left without this consolation, the other lesson
comes. That is, our ancient enemy sets up every possible obstacle to
turn us aside from what we have begun. He sorely afflicts us in ways
completely contrary to the first lesson. He frequently causes us to be sad
without our knowing why we are sad. We cannot pray with devotion,
cannot contemplate, cannot even speak or hear of the things of God our
Lord with any interior taste or relish. Not only this, but if the enemy
sees us weakened and downcast by these accursed thoughts, he suggests
that we are utterly forgotten by God our Lord. We begin to think we
are totally separated from our Lord, and that all we have done and all we
desire to do is worthless. He thus strives to reduce us to total discouragement.

Thus we can see that what causes all our fear and weakness is dwelling excessively at such times on our miseries and submitting so abjectly to his lying suggestions.

And so we must observe which is on the offensive. If it is consolation, we must abase and humble ourselves and remember that the trial of temptation will soon come. And if temptation, darkness, or sadness comes, we must oppose it without letting it affect us, waiting patiently for the consolation of the Lord, which will disperse all confusion and outer darkness.

[6. God's Loftiest Activities in the Soul, and the Subtle Deceits of the Devil Connected with Them]

We still have to discuss how we should understand impressions we have received from God our Lord, and, having understood them, make use of them. It often happens that our Lord moves and compels our soul to a particular course of action. He opens up our soul; that is, he speaks inside the soul without the din of words, raising it up wholly to his divine love,[9] so that we are incapable—even if we wanted to—of resisting his intention. This intention of his which we make our own is necessarily in conformity with the commandments, the precepts of the Church, and obedience to our superiors; it will be utterly humble, for the same divine Spirit is present in all.

But the way we can often deceive ourselves is this: In the time which follows such a consolation or inspiration, while the soul is still full of joy, the enemy approaches and, under cover of and on the pretext of this joy, attempts to make us add something to what we have received from God our Lord, so as to bring us to disorder and total confusion. At other times he gets us to retrench from the message we have received, by throwing up obstacles and difficulties to prevent us from fully carrying out what has been shown to us.

Here more than anywhere else is where we need caution. Sometimes we inhibit our enthusiasm for speaking of the things of God our Lord; at other times we say things that go beyond the enthusiasm or movement that accompanies us. For, when the enemy tries in this way to make us exaggerate or diminish the communication received, we must look more to the good of other persons than to our own desires. We must move cautiously for the purpose of helping others, as one does when fording a river. If I find a good footing or path, or prospect of producing some good, I go forward. But if the ford is rough and there is danger that my good words may produce scandal, I will always rein in and look for a better time or occasion to speak.

We have brought up topics that cannot be handled in a letter, at least without very extensive treatment. Even then there would be matters that are more readily experienced than explained, particularly in writing. Our Lord willing, I hope to see you there soon, and then we can go more deeply into some matters. In the meantime, since you have Castro[10] closer at hand I suggest you correspond with him. No harm can come of it, and possibly some good. And since you ask me to write just what I think in the Lord, I say this: Blessed will you be if you can hold fast to what you have.

I close, praying that the most holy Trinity by its infinite and supreme goodness may bestow upon all of us plentiful grace to know its most holy will and perfectly to fulfill it.

Poor in goodness,
Iñigo

4. To Magdalena de Loyola y Araoz.
A Letter of Consolation and a Request
I:151–152

Ignatius' devout mother Marína Sanchez de Licona died before 1498, the year in which Magdalena de Araoz married Ignatius' brother Martín García and thus came to the castle of Loyola as the bride of its new lord. Hence she is the one by whom Ignatius was brought up from the age of seven onward. She had been a maid of honor to Queen Isabella the Catholic in the devout atmosphere of the court of Castile. After his wounding at Pamplona she was his nurse during his recuperation. There is likelihood that the volumes which led to Ignatius' conversion, Ludolph's Life of Christ *and Jacobus'* Golden Legend, *were gifts to her from Isabella which she brought to Loyola and then in 1521 handed to Ignatius during his convalescence.*

Ignatius felt great esteem for Magdalena and her deep, prudent piety. After his brother Martín died he wrote her the following letter, to console her and request her to influence her son Beltrán, the new lord of Loyola, to carry forward the reform of the local clergy which Ignatius had already urged upon him.[11]

Rome, September 24, 1539

The grace and love of Christ our Lord be always our protection and our help.

Upon learning that the good pleasure of God our Lord had been fulfilled by removing from these present sufferings the companion he gave you for a certain time in this life, I immediately did the best thing I could do for any person: I said Mass for his soul at an altar where every time Mass is celebrated a soul is delivered from purgatory.

We should not weep while he rejoices, or grieve while he is glad. Instead we should look to ourselves—for we will come to the same point as he—and live in such a way during this life that we may live forever in the other. Of course I am altogether certain that you are fully convinced of this, since I have always known you to be a woman who fears God our Lord.

Now it remains for me to ask you, for the service of God our Lord, to assist us with your good works and prayers in a project we have undertaken for God's glory, and which, worthless as we are, we have carried forward. For details I refer you to my letter to your son Beltrán. I hope that he will in all things let himself be guided by you—even though I am confident that he who at another time knew how to squander both what he had and what he did not have will now act generously (if he is at all able) in a matter as devout, righteous, and holy as this.

I conclude, praying his Divine Majesty to dispose of us and of everyone in the way we may best serve him in all things and in all things give thanks forever and ever.

Poor in goodness,
Iñigo

5. To Teresa Rejadell.
Consolation, Counsel on Difficulties, and on Frequent Communion
I:274–276

An understandable lull occurred in the correspondence with Teresa during the first years when Ignatius was busy with the founding of the Society. However, occasional news about him reached her through visits from Father Antonio de Araoz, whom he asked to visit her on his journeys to Spain. Considerable need of canonical and other reform still existed in the convent of Santa Clara. It had begun as a convent of Franciscans and was changed to the Benedictine rule in one effort to

solve difficulties, and now it was unclear which rule was being more
followed in fact. The present letter is a reply to two which she wrote to
him. Although they no longer exist, in them she no doubt told him about
the death of her friend Sister Luisa, a fellow member of the group
seeking reform, about the continuing troubles in the convent, and about
criticism which other nuns were voicing against herself and a few of
her companions who were receiving the Eucharist weekly and some-
times daily.

Ignatius himself is the person who had counseled this practice.
Throughout all his years of apostolic activity a few leaders in the
Church were cautiously trying to promote reception of Communion
more frequently than the few times a year then customary. Ignatius
constantly did all he could to further that movement. The present letter
gives us a sample of the reasons and procedures he employed in this
apostolate.[12]

Rome, November 15, 1543

May the sovereign grace and love of Christ our Lord be always our
continual protection and help.

1. Having learned that God's will has been fulfilled in withdrawing from the present trials of this life your sister (and our own in our
Lord) Luisa, I have many grounds and indications to assure me that she
is now in the other life, full of glory forever and ever. From there, just
as we remember her in our poor and unworthy prayers, I am confident
she will favor and repay us with holy interest. And so if I were to go on
at length with words of consolation I would feel I was insulting you,
since I am sure that you conform yourself as you ought to the perfect
and everlasting providence which solely looks to our greater glory.

2. As to the problem of the habit and observance: where you have
received a judgment in your favor, and even if you had not but have
confirmation by the Apostolic See, you should have no doubts. You are
certainly in conformity with the service and will of God.[13] For the rule
of any blessed saint can oblige under sin insofar as it is approved by the
vicar of Christ our Lord or by another with his authority. Thus the
rules of St. Benedict, St. Francis, or St. Jerome possess no force of
themselves to oblige under sin, but possess such force when they have
the confirmation and authorization of the Apostolic See, because of the
divine authority which the latter confers upon the rule.

3. Regarding daily Communion, we should recall that in the early
Church everybody received daily, and that since that time there has

been no ordinance or document of our Holy Mother the Church or of the holy doctors, either positive or scholastic, against a person's being able to receive Communion daily if so moved by devotion. And while St. Augustine[14] did say that he neither praised nor blamed the daily reception of Communion (although elsewhere he exhorted all to receive every Sunday), he states later on, speaking of Christ our Lord's most sacred body, "This is our daily bread; therefore live in such a way that you can receive it every day."

This being the case, even in the absence of so many good indications or salutary motions we can rely upon the good and solid witness of our own conscience. That is, given that all things are lawful for you in our Lord, if—barring obvious mortal sin or anything you can deem to be such—you judge that your soul derives more help and is more inflamed with love for our Creator and Lord, and if you receive Communion with this intention, having found by experience that this spiritual food offers you sustenance, peace, and tranquility, preserving and advancing you in his greater service, praise, and glory, so that you have no doubt about this, then it is licit, and indeed would be better, for you to receive Communion every day.[15]

On this point and on some others I have spoken at length with Araoz, who will deliver this letter. Referring you to him in our Lord regarding all matters, I close, praying God our Lord by his infinite clemency to guide you and govern you in all things through his infinite and supreme goodness.

Poor in Goodness,
Iñigo

6. To the Fathers and Brothers of Coimbra.
On Discretion, and Obedience as a Means to It
I:687–693

The Society developed rapidly in Portugal, where Ignatius' companion Simao Rodrigues was provincial, but deviations arose, especially in the College of Coimbra, toward opposite extremes: excesses by some in penances such as public flagellations and by others toward a lax and too comfortable life. By failing to apply proper remedies Rodrigues was risking some of the key principles of Ignatius' spirituality, especially discretion. Hence the general sent to the Jesuits in Portugal a long letter of May 27, 1544. which recommended discretion and obedience as a means to it.[16] Possibly his addressing it to the whole community was a delicate attempt to influence Rodrigues without direct reprimand. In any case, eight months later Ignatius found it expedient to write the present letter of 1548 on obedience. Its contents are similar to his compact treatment in Constitutions [547–552]. However, any success it achieved was only temporary. Disorders in Portugal persisted. Consequently seven years later Ignatius composed his classic letter of March 26, 1553, on obedience (too long for use here), in which his teaching on the topic is developed far more amply than anywhere else in his writings.[17] For over four centuries it was read at table every month in all Jesuit communities. In many other religious institutes too it was regarded as the best treatise on obedience and was probably the most widely read of his letters. It is in LettersIgn, pp. 287–295.

In March, 1547, Ignatius appointed Polanco as his secretary. Hence in the present letter of 1548 to Portugal we find new traits of orderly, flowing, periodic style which came from the new secretary. Ignatius probably outlined the letter, entrusted the writing to Polanco (whose learning appears in the numerous quotations), and then corrected the draft in detail.

Rome, January 14, 1548

May the grace and peace of Jesus Christ our God and Lord be felt always and increase in our souls. Amen.

What I am writing to Master Simão[18] would suffice for essential matters, and my own poor health and heavy business would readily excuse me from nonessential ones. However, the great love with which Jesus Christ our Lord has placed you within my soul prevents me from taking advantage of any excuse, knowing as I do that because of the devotion of your obedience you derive consolation in our Lord from letters which are written to you from here, just as I and all of us here are greatly consoled in the same Lord by the good news we receive here of your spiritual progress in learning and virtue.

I trust in God our Creator and Lord that this joy of ours will daily increase as the occasions for it increase, rather than be diminished by any diminishment of its occasions, and that you will be among those spoken of by the Wise Man in Proverbs: "The path of the just, as a shining light, goes forward and increases even to perfect day" [Prov. 4:18].

And so I beg of him who is the author of this day, as the sun of wisdom and justice, to bring to perfection in his mercy what he has begun in you, until he allows you to find him and know "where he feeds, where he lies at midday" [Song 1:6], glorifying himself in you all and displaying the riches of his almighty hand and infinite magnificence in his spiritual gifts in your souls, and through you in the souls of many others.

Moreover, dearest brothers in Jesus Christ our God and Lord, I also beseech you by the same Lord to make yourselves able to receive his visitation and spiritual treasures by purity of heart and genuine humility, by your all having the same thought and the same desire, and by that outward and inward peace which houses in the soul and enthrones there as king him who is called the Prince of Peace [Isa. 9:6]—in a word, by your all being made completely one in our Lord Jesus Christ.

And since such a unity among many cannot be maintained without order, nor order without the due bond of obedience between inferiors and superiors (as the whole of physical nature, the angelic hierarchies, and well-regulated states among human beings teach us, all of which are united, preserved, and governed by subordination), I emphatically recommend to you this holy obedience. It should be observed by each individual toward his superiors at whatever level they are his superiors, such as toward those with jobs in the house as regards their own bailiwicks, confessors in matters of conscience, and the rector in all things. Similarly the rector, just as everyone else, should be subject in everything to the provincial,[19] particularly since God our Lord employed him as his instrument for starting his work there. The provincial, in turn, will be obedient to whomever God our Lord may give him as superior general, just as the general will be to him who is supreme over all. Moreover, without distinction of persons we must recognize in every superior Jesus Christ our Lord since it is to him and for his sake that all obedience should be given, no matter to whom it is given.

Now for this obedience to bring about and preserve unity it must affect not only outward but also interior actions such as those of the will. For no one reaches the lowest rung of obedience, as Bernard says,[20] who does not make the will of the superior his own—and the superior's understanding as well, for unity of wills cannot be maintained if a person holds on to dissenting views and, even though he does and wills what the superior orders, holds a contrary opinion and places his own judgment above that of the superior. It is quite certain that, where there is no question of a thing's being sinful or so obviously wrong that it constrains the intellect, genuine obedience subjects to the superior not merely the work but also the will, and not merely the will but the judgment as well. Then unity is rendered firm and lasting, and under this holy and sweet yoke peace and tranquility become in a certain sense (so far as our present wretched state allows) unshakable.

From this, people who do things contrary to the superior's intention can see that, even though they perform actions which would be good and commendable in themselves, such as mortifications, contemplations, and so forth, these persons hardly have part in obedience since they do the contrary of what they are commanded, follow their own wishes in opposition to their superior's, and prefer their own judgment to the judgment of the one who governs them.

How far from making a pleasing sacrifice to God is anyone who offers God a nonobligatory action, even an action which is of itself more perfect, against the mind of his superior! Such people should understand, as Bernard says, that a person makes no offering acceptable to the Holy Spirit if he fails to perform his particular obligations, such as a subject's obeying his superior, about whom almighty God declares, "Whoever hears you hears me; whoever despises you despises me" [Luke 10:16].

This seems to have been the sort of sacrifice that Saul offered in disobedience to what God our Lord commanded him through the prophet Samuel: "The people have spared the best of the sheep and of the herds so that they might be sacrificed to the Lord your God" [1 Sam. 15:15]. And how did the prophet answer him? "Why have you not listened to the voice of the Lord, and have done evil in the eyes of the Lord?" [1 Sam. 15:19]. Afterward, when Saul appealed to his sacrifices, he replied: "Does the Lord desire holocausts and victims, and not rather that the voice of the Lord should be obeyed? For obedience is better than sacrifices, and to hearken rather than to offer the fat of rams. For it is like the sin of witchcraft to rebel, and like the crime of idolatry to refuse to obey" [1 Sam. 15:22f].

Similarly, Cain's sacrifice of the fruits of the earth was valueless and unworthy of being looked upon by God, for such are any toils and sufferings of body and even of soul, or any other work whatever, when offered without the required obedience and charity. On the contrary, "the Lord had respect to Abel, and to his offerings," for he "offered of the firstlings of his flock and of their fat" [Gen. 4:4]. Such is the noble sacrifice of one's own will and understanding, presented with the devotion of obedience to the Divine Majesty through his ministers in an odor of sweetness.

Whoever offers his body in affliction or in any other way against obedience is missing the salt which Leviticus says must be offered with every sacrifice. This is not that living and reasonable sacrifice acceptable to God our Creator and Lord that St. Paul commends [Rom. 12:1]. I wish the truth spoken by St. Bernard were thoroughly understood and retained in memory: "Anything done without the will and approval of the spiritual father will be booked to vainglory and not to one's credit."[21] And how much more so, if it is done in contravention of his will! What greater pride is possible than to place one's own will and judgment above that of the person we have acknowledged as superior in the place of Jesus Christ our Lord? And in fact experience shows that such persons usually are proud, and consequently have themselves to blame if even medicines and remedies—such as would be the mortifications mentioned when practiced with the approval of the superior and in accordance with reason—should for them prove poisonous and lethal.

Great is the glee of the enemy of our nature when he sees a soul traveling, even on ways that are lofty and sublime, without caution and without the bridle of someone able to rule and govern, for he has all the more reason to anticipate its fall and plunge to ruin. And zeal, which under the direction of obedience would be holy, becomes a powerful weapon and instrument of the devil for robbing the heart of true charity and hence of spiritual life.

Recall how the children of Israel were defeated by their enemies when against obedience they still wished to enter the promised land, so that you may beware of transgressing against obedience still more in highly spiritual matters. Recall that, though few in number, they defeated hosts of enemies when acting through obedience; whereas many succumbed to a few when acting against it.

Since, as you know, everything is written for our instruction and edification [Rom. 15:4], you should be glad to be ruled as far as possible by this holy and safe counsel of obedience. You should be convinced in the Lord that you are walking straight ahead and conforming yourselves to God's will when you trample your own will underfoot and hold above your head and before your eyes the will of your superiors, believing that Divine Providence will by this means guide and rule you so that you will arrive at your own greater perfection and the help of your neighbor.

And may it please his Divine Majesty to do this, so that in all things greater honor and glory may be given to his holy name forever.

Yours in our Lord,
Ignacio

7. To Francis Borgia.
Counsels on Prayer, Penances, Discretion, and Mystic Favors
II:233–237

Francis Borgia, born October 28, 1510, was a trusted advisor of Emperor Charles V in Spain, and his wife, Leonor de Castro, was a lady-in-waiting to Charles' wife, the Empress Isabella. From 1539 to 1543 Francis was viceroy of Catalonia. When his father died in late 1542 he inherited the dukedom of Gandía. In Barcelona he came to admire the Jesuits Antonio de Araoz and Pierre Favre and determined to build a college for the Society in Gandía. On May 6, 1546, Favre laid the cornerstone for this, the Society's first college for extern students. After Francis' wife Leonor died suddenly in 1546, with Ignatius' permission he took the first vows of the Society on February 1, 1548. However, he maintained secrecy about this until he could complete arrangements for his children and settle his estates. He was a very prayerful person leading an interior life of penances and mystic prayer even while engaged in administrative business.[22]

In a now-lost letter to Ignatius earlier in 1548, Francis explained his practices of prayer and penances and requested direction about them. Ignatius, no doubt mindful of his own indiscretions at Manresa shortly after his own conversion and now appraising them from the perspective of his later experience, composed the present letter of September 20, 1548. Its style is typically rough and complicated, but the advice he gives is full of wisdom, experience, charity, and discretion. This is one of his most beautiful letters of spiritual direction—counsel from one canonized saint to another. The mystic of Manresa was communicating to a kindred soul, the novice mystic of Gandía.

Rome, September 20, 1548
May the supreme grace and eternal love of Christ our Lord be always our continual protection and help.

As I learned of your excellent method and procedure in spiritual as well as corporal matters having to do with your own spiritual progress, I have certainly derived from them fresh reason for great joy in our Lord. I give thanks to his Eternal Majesty for this, and can only ascribe it to his divine goodness, from which all that is good derives.

And yet, since I also realize in our Lord that we may need particular spiritual or corporal exercises at one time and different ones at another, and inasmuch as those that have been good for us at one time are not continuously so at another, I will tell you in his Divine Majesty what occurs to me on this subject, since your lordship bids me state what I think.

My first thought, then, would be to cut in half the total time allotted to these interior and exterior exercises. The reason is this. When and to the degree that we have thoughts—stemming from ourselves or from our enemy—which lead us to think and reflect about irrelevant, useless, or illicit matters, and we wish to keep the will from delighting in these or yielding them consent, to that same degree we should ordinarily increase our interior and exterior exercises, depending upon individual persons and the different sorts of thoughts or temptations, adapting the exercises to the individual in order to overcome them. On the other hand, the more such thoughts weaken and die, the more there arise good thoughts and holy inspirations to which we should give unreserved admission, wholly opening the doors of our soul. Hence, with fewer arms being needed to overcome the enemies, from what I can tell in our Lord of your lordship's case I would judge it preferable to convert half of your time into study (since not only infused but also acquired knowledge will always be quite necessary or advantageous in the future), to administration of your estates, and to spiritual conversations—always endeavoring to keep your soul in peace, quiet, and readiness for whenever our Lord wishes to work in it. For it is without doubt a higher virtue of the soul and a greater grace to be able to enjoy one's Lord in a variety of duties and places rather than in one only. We should make a great effort in his divine Goodness to obtain this.

As for the second point, regarding fasts and abstinences, my thought would be that for our Lord's sake you ought to protect and strengthen your stomach and other physical faculties, not weaken them. My reason is that, when a soul, first, is disposed and resolved rather to lose its temporal life altogether than offend the Divine Majesty by even the slightest deliberate sin; and, second, is not being plagued by particular temptations of the enemy, the world, or the flesh—and since I am convinced that by God's grace both of these are true of your lordship —I very much desire that your lordship impress upon your soul that, since both soul and body belong to your Creator and Lord, you must give him a good accounting of both. You must not let the bodily nature become weakened, for if it does the inward nature will no longer be able to function properly.

Hence, while for a certain period I highly praised fasts, rigorous abstinence, and retrenchment from ordinary food, and derived joy from them, I can no longer do so now that I see that these fasts and abstinences keep the stomach from functioning naturally or digesting ordinary meats or other foods which supply proper sustenance to the body. My thought would rather be that you should pursue every means to strengthen the body, eating whatever foods are permitted you and with whatever frequency you find helpful (barring offense to the neighbor). For we ought to render the body goodwill and love in the measure that it obeys and serves the soul, and that the latter, with the body's help and obedience, becomes better disposed for the service and praise of our Creator and Lord.

Regarding the third point, that is, inflicting hurt upon the body for our Lord's sake, my thought would be to abandon any practice that could draw even a drop of blood. And if his Divine Majesty has given you the grace for this, and for all that I have mentioned (as I am convinced in his Divine Goodness that he has), for the future it would be better—without giving reasons or arguments for it—to relinquish this practice and, rather than trying to draw blood, to seek the Lord of all in a more immediate way, that is, his most holy gifts—for example, an influx or drops of tears at (1) our own or others' sins, (2) the mysteries of Christ our Lord's life here on earth or in heaven, or (3) consideration and love of the Divine Persons. The tears have greater value and worth the higher are the thoughts and considerations that prompt them. However, while in themselves the third kind of consideration is more perfect than the second, and the second than the first, still for a given person the best is the one where God our Lord most communicates himself through a manifestation of his holy graces and spiritual gifts. For he sees and knows what is best for you; knowing all things, he points out the path for you. And in order for us to discover this path with the help of his grace it is very helpful to make a variety of trials and experiments so as to travel along the path which it becomes clearest to you is the happiest and most blessed in this life and entirely directed and ordered to that other life without end—with ourselves being embraced and made one with these most holy gifts.

By these gifts I mean those that are not in our own power to summon at will but rather are sheerly given by him who gives and can accomplish all that is good. Such are (with his Divine Majesty as their goal and scope) intensity of faith, of hope, of charity; spiritual joy and repose, tears, intense consolation; elevation of mind, divine impressions and illuminations—along with all other experiences of spiritual relish and feeling which are ordered to these gifts, with humility and reverence toward our Holy Mother the Church and her established leaders and teachers.[23]

Any of these most holy gifts should be preferred to all acts affecting the body, which have value only so far as they contribute toward obtaining these gifts or part of them. I do not mean that we should seek these gifts solely for the satisfaction or delight they give us. Rather, our intention should be that our thoughts, words, and actions, which we know from personal experience to be tainted, cold, and troubled when these gifts are absent, may be ardent, clear, and right for God's greater service. Thus we desire such spiritual gifts—or part of them—and graces insofar as they can help us toward God's greater glory.

Hence, when the body has endangered itself through excessive hardships, the soundest thing is to pursue these gifts through acts of the understanding and other moderate practices. Thus not the soul alone will be healthy: With a healthy mind in a healthy body the whole will be healthier and more apt for God's greater service.

As to how you should act in more particular matters I do not think it advisable in our Lord to speak. I am confident that the same Divine Spirit that has hitherto guided your lordship will continue to guide and rule you for the future, to the greater glory of his Divine Majesty.

8. To Antonio Brandão.
Replies to Sixteen Questions of Antonio Brandão
III:506–513

The Portuguese Jesuit Antonio Brandão, ordained but technically still a scholastic because he had not yet pronounced his final vows (Cons [511]), had accompanied Simão Rodrigues on a journey from Portugal to Rome. There he requested Polanco to obtain Ignatius' opinions on a list of sixteen questions which he submitted. They pertained to a wide range of practical problems in the spiritual life which are met by a Jesuit during his period of studies. Ignatius complied. His answers, written by Polanco, are an authentic commentary illuminating his concept of apostolic spirituality[24] and its application to problems arising in daily life. In reading the answers, however, we should remember that many of the practices discussed pertain to social situations in a former era of religious life. Details of the applications would be different today and discretion is required, but the opinions given contain a tenor of thought as valid for today as for the 1500s.

Rome, June 1, 1551

Instructions that are given by our Father Ignatius, or at his direction, to those living outside Rome, and other notable matters that should not be forgotten.

For Portugal

These are the points on which a scholastic of the Society [Brandão] desires to have information according to our Father's mind:

1. How much time should someone studying in a college devote to prayer and to conversing with his brethren, supposing the rector sets no limits to these two occupations?

2. Should he omit Mass on some days or say it daily even if it were to impede his studies somewhat?

3. After finishing philosophy, which branch of theology, speculative or moral, should he concentrate on more—assuming that one cannot devote himself fully to both in the college?

4. What should he do if he finds himself sometimes having inordinate desires for learning?

5. Should he offer himself for a particular task without the superior's having asked him, or leave the whole matter in the superior's hands?

6. What subjects of meditation should he use that would be most in keeping with our vocation?

7. In confession, should a person list his imperfections in minute detail or mention only the larger ones so as to keep the confession short?

8. In hearing the confession of members of the community, should he question them even about matters not related to sin? In these cases,

should he ask the penitent's permission to tell the superior about what was said in confession?

9. How should he deal with the superior regarding the temptations experienced by others? Should he report them in full even if some of them may be over and done with?

10. Should one correct an imperfection noticed in a member of the Society, or allow the individual to be deluded into thinking it is no imperfection?

11. If before God one believes that his superior—say, the rector —is wrong about something, ought he to inform the provincial (and similarly with other subordinate superiors) or ought he to blind his own judgment in the matter?

12. What rule should one follow as regards writing to externs or members of the Society not because of need or a command of obedience but merely out of charity or courtesy?

13. In dealing with externs or members of the Society, should one use language they will find ingratiating or instead employ a certain religious forthrightness?

14. What should be done in the matter of giving someone information about the Society, and how should this be gone about?

15. In dealing with people outside the Society, may one advise them to enter a particular religious order? And is it proper to counsel an extern, or someone in the house without vows, to take vows?

[16]. What should they do about using or not using a privilege of the Society in dealing with a penitent?

Ignatius' Replies, Given through Polanco
[Reply to Question 1]. The first question has two parts. The answer to the first part is to remember that the purpose of a scholastic at his studies in the college is to acquire knowledge with which to serve God for his greater glory by helping his neighbor. Now this task demands the entire person, and he would not be devoting himself completely to his studies if he gave himself to lengthy periods of prayer.

Hence, in the case of scholastics who are not priests (except in cases of interior disturbance or exceptional devotion), one hour over and above Mass is all that is needed. During Mass he can make some meditation while the priest is saying the silent parts. During the allotted hour he may as a general rule recite the office of Our Lady or some other prayer, or else meditate, depending upon the rector's decision.

For a priest scholastic all that is needed[25] are the obligatory office of the hours, Mass, and the examens. He could take an additional half hour in case of exceptional devotion.

The second part of the question will be answered by considering the purpose of conversing with others, which is to influence for good those we converse with. This purpose is frustrated by talking either too little or too much. Hence one should avoid the extremes and try to strike a mean.

In connection with this second part, our reverend Father spoke of the great importance we should give to obedience. His wish was this: Just as individual saints have outstanding characteristics that are not possessed by others, and just as the same is true of one religious order in relation to another, so he desired that the Society should have one outstanding characteristic that would put it on a par with any other religious order, even though other orders might have excellences that our institute cannot have (though in some things—say, poverty—we might well be able to equal them). Our reverend Father said that he wanted our outstanding feature to be obedience. He said that we have a greater obligation in this regard because of the fathers' extra vow of obedience to the sovereign pontiff and because they are not allowed to plead any excuse against carrying out what obedience commands. He also said that this obedience cannot be perfect unless the subject's understanding is completely conformed to that of the superior. Without this, the subject's life will be a continual purgatory, with little hope of perseverance.

[Reply to Question 2]. To the second question our reverend Father answered that, considering the purpose of the studies of one of our men, in cases where (1) obedience, (2) the common good, or (3) exceptional devotion do not dictate otherwise, it suffices to say two Masses a week, besides Sundays and feast days.

[To 3]. As to the third question, preference should be given to speculative theology, since he will be forced to spend time on moral theology once he has left the college, needing it for his talks and other activities, whereas speculative theology is more properly studied in the schools where truths and their underlying grounds are examined.

[To 4]. The fourth question will be answered with the sixth.

[To 5]. The fifth. It is good for a person to place himself once and for all at the superior's disposal for our Lord's greater glory, leaving all concern about it to him as one who holds the place of Christ our Lord on earth, not making frequent representations to him—unless something occurs that might especially move one to do so.

[To 6]. The sixth. In view of the end of our studies, the scholastics cannot engage in long meditations. Over and above the exercises for growth in virtue (daily Mass, an hour for vocal prayer and examen of conscience, weekly confession and Communion), they can practice seeking the presence of our Lord in everything: their dealing with other people, their walking, seeing, tasting, hearing, understanding, and all our activities. For his Divine Majesty is truly in everything by his presence, power, and essence.

This kind of meditation—finding God our Lord in everything—is easier than lifting ourselves up and laboriously making ourselves present to more abstract divine realities. Moreover, by making us properly disposed, this excellent exercise will bring great visitations of our Lord even in short prayers.[26]

In addition, the scholastics can practice frequently offering to God our Lord their studies together with the effort that these demand, recalling that we undertake them for his love and setting aside our personal tastes so as to render some service to his Divine Majesty by helping those for whose life he died. We could also make these two practices the matter of our examen.

To these exercises may be added that of preaching in the colleges. For, after the example of a good life, one of the things most helpful to the neighbor (and one the Society is especially oriented to) is preaching. Our reverend Father was of the opinion that considerable fruit could be gathered from the scholastics' getting practice in preaching. He thought they should preach on Sundays on a subject of their own choosing, and that by way of practice, so as not to lose study time, two or three of them could declaim at supper the formula of the "tones"[27] that they had been taught. At first they could declaim the formula we use here at Rome. After working through that one, it would be easier for them to go on to another, adding to or subtracting from the Roman formula to fit in with the custom of the region. The advantages of this fine exercise are very great, but are omitted here for brevity's sake.

[To 7]. The seventh [on confessing imperfections]. To avoid being deluded, we should notice from which side the enemy attacks and tries to make us offend our Lord God. If he is making the way to mortal sin easy, a person should strive to weigh even the least imperfections in that area and confess them. If the person finds himself being drawn to mental perturbation by making sin out of what is not sin, he should avoid going into minute details and mention only his venial sins—and only the more important of these. And if by God's grace the person has reached peace with our Lord, he should confess his sins briefly, omitting the details but striving to feel confusion for his sins in God's presence. He should reflect that the one against whom venial sins are committed is infinite, a fact which imparts infinite gravity to the sins themselves, but that by God our Lord's sovereign goodness they are venial and can be forgiven by using holy water, striking one's breast, grieving over them, and so forth.

[To 8]. As to the first part of the eighth question: the confessor sometimes may and should ask questions about venial faults, for this can help uncover mortal sins and get the penitent to manifest his conscience more fully and so obtain greater help.

The second part of the eighth question. For greater clarity, our Father insisted on the importance of the superior's being aware of whatever his subjects are going through so that he can provide for each according to his needs. In this way, the superior will avoid placing someone experiencing temptations of the flesh next to the fire, by assigning him, say, to hear women's confessions, and so forth; he will avoid entrusting government to someone who is lacking in obedience. To prevent such things happening, our Father makes a practice of reserving certain cases to himself: all mortal sins and strong temptations against the Society's institute or against its head, and against perseverance.

In view of this, the confessor, discreetly and taking into account the matter and particular circumstances, may ask permission to tell the matter to the superior, from whom there is reason to believe the person will receive more help in the Lord than from any other source.

[To 9]. The ninth. The answer to the ninth may be gathered from the preceding, and it is that the superior should be wholly informed about everything, even of things over and done with (assuming that one does this without ill will and with concern for the due observance of charity toward the neighbor).

[To 10]. The first part of the tenth question concerns the correction of another. An important factor in doing this successfully is the authority enjoyed by the person giving the correction, or his love—and this love must be perceived. Lacking either of these, the correction will be ineffective; there will be no amendment. Hence, correcting others is not for everyone.

Moreover, no matter how one makes an admonition (after having judged that it will lead to the person's amendment), he should not state things too forthrightly, but along with some commendation and in a roundabout way. For one sin can bring another in its train: The sin already committed may dispose a person to take the bestowal of correction badly.

As to the second part of the tenth question—on whether a person ought to leave someone else under the false impression that something is not an imperfection—our reverend Father said that for the first person's own progress it would be better to do this: the more attention one pays to others' faults the less he will dwell within himself and see his own faults, and the less progress he himself will make. However, in a case where a person is advancing in perfection and has his own passions under control and in good order, and our Lord expands his heart so that he may be a help to others as well as to himself, that person may well correct someone who does wrong, keeping to the procedure discussed in number 11 immediately below.

[To 11]. In reply to the eleventh question, our Father recounted what he had said to the other first fathers after six of them had made their profession together; namely, that there were two ways they could help him perfect his own soul: first, by their own perfection; and, secondly, by their calling to his attention anything they judged was not according to God. However, he wanted them to follow this procedure: Before admonishing him they should have recourse to prayer, and then, if they still thought and judged the same in the presence of the Lord, they were to tell him privately—a procedure he himself follows now.

For doing this well, our reverend Father said that it would be a great help if the superior entrusted this duty to some of his subjects— priests, for example, and persons who give edification. A person concerned only to benefit himself would do well to blind the eyes of his judgment. If a person is under obligation to express his opinion, he should be careful first to place himself in the presence of our Lord so as to know and decide what he ought to do. Second, he should find some good way of telling the person if he thinks he will profit by it; otherwise, he should tell the person's superior.

Here our Father mentioned that it was a great advantage to have a syndic to report things to the superior. Also, to have one or two men as vice-rectors, one subordinate to the other, to assist the rector. In this way the rector can be of much greater help to different persons and enjoy greater love from his subjects, acting as their refuge if in some matter they find themselves dealt with harshly by the vice-rectors.

[To 13]. Our Father's reply to the thirteenth seemed rather striking to me—namely, that in dealing with another we should take a cue from the enemy who wishes to draw a person to evil. He goes in by the way of the one he wishes to tempt but comes out by his own way. Thus we may adapt ourselves to the inclinations of the person we are dealing with, adapting ourselves in our Lord to everything, only to come out later with the good we were laboring for.

Our Father made another remark on how to break free from someone there was no prospect of helping. He suggests talking to him emphatically about hell, judgment, and the like. The person will then not come back—or, if he does, it will probably be because he has felt himself touched in some way by the Lord.

The third thing he mentioned was that one should adapt oneself to the temperament of the person being dealt with—whether phlegmatic, or choleric, and so forth. But this should be done with moderation.

The remaining questions depend more on individual circumstances which are not indicated.

9. To Jean Pelletier.
5. The Apostolic Ministries in a College
III:542–550

Father Jean Pelletier was the first rector of the Roman College when it opened on February 22, 1551. Ignatius hoped that its procedures would be imitated in other colleges which he rapidly established. When he opened a college at Ferrara in June, 1551, he appointed Pelletier its rector. As Ignatius sent men to staff these colleges he thought not only of the teaching which Jesuits would do there but also of the wide range of ministries which they would exercise among the citizens of the region. In his mind a typical staff would consist of priests (some as teachers, some for other ministries), scholastics (some as teachers and some as students), and lay brothers. For example, in 1556 the college at Palermo had 6 priests (2 of whom were teachers), 7 scholastics (3 of them as teachers and 4 as students), 9 lay brothers, and

10 scholastic novices.[28] *The present letter, a circular letter meant with small adaptations also for other communities, was one of the most complete of such letters. We provide an outline in three parts by inserting headings into the text.*

AN INSTRUCTION ON THE MANNER OF PROCEEDING,
sent to Ferrara,
and in about the same tenor of thought
also to Florence, Naples, and Modena.

Rome, June 13, 1551

There are three objectives you should keep in mind. One is the preservation and increase in spirit,[29] learning, and numbers of the members of the Society. The second is the edification and spiritual advancement of the city. The third is the consolidation and increase of the temporalities of the new college, so that the Lord may be better served in the first and second objectives.

PART I. [The Conservation and Development of the Society, by Means Such as Right Intention, Obedience, Studies, and the Like]

The first objective, regarding the members of the Society, provides the basis for the others. For the better the men themselves are, the greater also will be their suitability to be accepted by God as instruments for the edification of externs and the permanence of the foundation.

1. Therefore all should strive to have a right intention,[30] so that they will seek entirely "not the things that are their own but the things that are Jesus Christ's" [Phil. 2:21]. They should endeavor to conceive great resolves and desires to be true and faithful servants of God and to render a good account of themselves in whatever responsibilities they are given, with a genuine abnegation of their own will and judgment and a total submission of themselves to God's government of them by means of holy obedience—and this whether they are employed in high or lowly tasks. They should offer the most fervent prayers they can for obtaining this grace from the Giver of every good. Moreover, the superior should occasionally remind them of this.

2. As far as possible, the order and method of the college here [in

Rome] should be followed, especially in the matter of weekly confession and Communion, the daily examination of conscience and hearing of Mass in the house, the practice of obedience, and the avoidance of dealings[31] with externs except as the rector shall direct. The latter will determine how far each man may be entrusted with responsibility for the edification of others without danger to himself.

3. Within the house they should practice preaching daily during dinner and supper, a different man on each day of the week. This should be extempore, or with at most an hour's preparation for these sermons in the refectory. In addition, some times during the week there should be further exercises in preaching in the vernacular or in Latin, with a subject being proposed for them to speak on unexpectedly; there should be sermons in Greek also, and the "tones"[32] may be used (this latter may be varied according to the capacity of the student).

4. Each one should strive to make progress in learning and in helping others, studying and teaching what is assigned him by the rector. Care must be taken that the lessons are accommodated to the students and that the latter get a thorough grounding in grammar along with training in composition, with careful corrections by the masters. They should engage in discussions and debates.

5. Through academic and spiritual conversations they should strive to draw others to the way of perfection.[33] With their younger pupils, however, this should be done only with the greatest tact; and not even older students may be received [into the Society] without their parents' permission. If it is deemed proper to receive an older student into the house (when he has made this decision for himself), or to send him off to Rome or some other place, this may be done. However, discretion and the anointing of the Holy Spirit will point out the best course. In case of doubt one should write to the provincial or to Rome just to be sure.

6. For the better attainment of these ends, it will be useful to have some of the more advanced students carefully compose Latin discourses on the Christian virtues and pronounce them publicly in the presence of all every week or every other week on Sundays and feast days. To these talks they should invite young men and others, especially those who seem to have some aptitude for the religious life. This is a good means to create in those whom the Lord may call a disposition to take the path of perfection. At the least, the speaker will make a good impression and give edification, and those in the house will be advanced in literary practice and in the virtues.

PART II. [Means of Reaping Spiritual Fruit: Various Ministries to Others]

Regarding the second objective, that of working for the edification and spiritual profit of the city (over and above helping outsiders by means of prayer):

1. They[34] provide an education in Latin and Greek to all comers, according to their ability, by giving class lectures and having the students practice debate and composition.

2. They take care to teach the catechism to children on all Sundays and feast days, or on a weekday. On another day they have them memorize some little bit according to the program of the Roman College or however they think best. This is done in the house or in their own church or in any suitable place nearby that they think most appropriate. This practice could well produce more spiritual benefit than preaching.

3. Care should be taken that the pupils form good habits, having them hear Mass daily if possible, attend the sermons held on feast days, go to confession once a month, and give up blaspheming, swearing, and using indecent language.

4. Thought should be given to having sermons preached on Sundays and feast days; or only having one of the men teach catechism classes in the church or in a public place; or having some men practice preaching in the monasteries.

5. Thought should be given to holding lectures on Holy Scripture or scholastic theology for priests—for example, something on the sacraments or cases of conscience.

6. They should give special attention to heretical teachings, and be properly equipped against those professing them. They should know by heart the topics controverted with the heretics and attentively try to uncover and cure their infections; or, if this is not possible, to controvert their false doctrines—but tactfully, not antagonizing these persons but trying to rescue them with love.

7. They should draw people to the sacraments of penance and Communion, and be prepared for administering them.

8. Through spiritual conversation they can be of help to everyone they deal with, particularly when they find in them some disposition to be benefited. The Exercises of the First Week could be given to large numbers, but the following weeks only to those who show suitability for the state of perfection, are very well disposed to be helped, and give themselves totally to the Exercises.

9. Where there is time, they should take care to assist prisoners, by visiting the jail if possible, having one of the men preach there, urging them to make their confession and turn to God, and hearing the prisoners' confessions if they have the opportunity and can do this without detriment to tasks that are more pressing and pleasing to God.

10. They should also remember the hospitals—if, as I say, they occasionally have time left over. They should try to console and give spiritual help to the poor as far as they can. Here also occasional exhortations will be profitable, unless circumstances indicate otherwise.

11. In general they should try to be aware of the pious works in the city where they reside, and do what they can to further them either by their own efforts or through others. Moreover, they should show diligence and charity in starting new works that do not exist.

12. While numerous means of helping the neighbor and numerous pious works are suggested, discretion will be their guide in making a choice among them, since they cannot undertake them all. They should keep their eyes always on the greater service of God, the common good, and the Society's good reputation, along with the interests of the college and the characteristic concerns of the Society.

PART III. [Means to Win the Good Will of Important Persons, Secure Proper Endowment and Site for the College, and the Like]

The third objective consists in skillfully striving to consolidate and increase the temporal goods of the new college. Over and above the sacrifices and prayers to be offered by all in the house for this intention insofar as it is for God's glory, the observance of what was mentioned in the first and second objectives will be more effective than any other means we could devise. But to touch on a few means special to this third objective, the following will be helpful:

1. They should work to preserve and increase the goodwill of those in authority, complying with their wishes wherever this is possible according to God and serving them in the pious works they are especially interested in promoting where this offers no prejudice to God's greater service. They should also be careful to preserve their own good reputation and authority with these persons, and speak so as to convince them of the Society's commitment to expand its work even though it ordinarily begins in a small way so that it may then grow rather than diminish.

2. They should also work to win over private citizens and benefactors, and engage them in talk about spiritual matters. To devote
special care to helping these persons is something quite appropriate and
quite acceptable to God, whose affairs are being carried forward.

3. The better to preserve their own authority in spiritual things,
they should try if possible to have requests made and temporal affairs
handled by their friends rather than by themselves. At least this should
be done in such a way that there is no appearance of greed. To avoid all
such concern, it would be better if they could settle on a fixed amount
for their support, although this should not be stated except in a way and
at a time that is right.

4. If it has not already been done, they should give special attention to the eventual acquisition of a good and sufficiently large property,
or one capable of enlargement so as to suffice for house, church, and
school; if possible, it should not be too far away from the activity of
the city.

5. There should be weekly correspondence with us so that they
can receive assistance and guidance in various matters.

10. To Antonio de Araoz.
On the Ministry of Christian Education
IV:5–9

*Antonio de Araoz, a nephew of Ignatius, joined the group of com-
panions in Rome in 1539. From then to 1543 he made three journeys to
Spain and worked in various cities there. In Lent of 1544 he transmitted
to Ignatius the offer of Francis Borgia to found a Jesuit college at
Gandía and witnessed its opening to extern students in 1546. In 1547
he was named the first provincial of the province of Spain. After the
successes of the colleges at Gandía and Messina, Ignatius was enthusiastically establishing colleges, especially in Italy, many of which were
planned to grow into universities by the addition of faculties of philosophy and theology. Hence he commissioned Polanco to write to Araoz as
provincial the following letter detailing possible procedures and urging
him to establish such colleges.*

*This letter is a synthesis of Ignatius' early ideas on the ministry and
apostolate of Christian education. Many of its ideas reappear in more
developed form in his chief educational document, Part IV of the Constitutions, which he left in manuscript at his death in 1556. This letter*

of 1551 also shows his thinking, planning, and procedures from which the entire system of Jesuit schools grew. As we saw above on page 48, by 1556 he himself opened 33 such colleges and approved 6 more. By 1710 they numbered 612. We provide an outline below by inserting headings into the text.

Rome, December 1, 1551

The Peace of Christ. Seeing that God our Lord is moving his servants in your region as well as here to start a number of colleges of this Society, our Father has thought it good to provide counsel about the procedure and advantages which have been learned through experience regarding the colleges here (for those of the colleges there are already well known). He wants this to be fully studied, so that, as far as the matter is in our hand, nothing may be left undone for God's greater service and the aid of our neighbors.

[1. The Procedure for Founding and Endowing a College]

The manner or method employed in founding a college is this. A city (like Messina and Palermo in Sicily), or a ruler (like the king of the Romans and the dukes of Ferrara and Florence), a private individual (like the prior of the Trinità in Venice and Padua), or a group of persons (as in Naples, Bologna, and elsewhere) provide an annual sum of money—some of them in perpetuity from the beginning, others not until they can test and verify the value of this work.

A suitable building is procured, two or three priests of very solid doctrine are sent, along with some of our own students,[35] who, in addition to pursuing their own education, can aid that of other students and, through their good example, personal contact, and learning, help them in virtue and spiritual progress.

[2. The Steps in Opening a College]

The procedure in such places is this. At the beginning three or four teachers in humane letters are appointed. One of the teachers starts off with elementary grammar, accommodating himself to beginners; another is assigned to those on an intermediate level, another for those more advanced in grammar. A different teacher is assigned to the students of the humanities who are further along in the Latin, Greek, and—if there is an inclination for it—Hebrew languages.

When the school has been advertised, all who wish are admitted free and without receipt of any money or gratuity—that is, all who know how to read and write and are beginners in [Latin] grammar. However, being young boys,[36] they must have the approval of their parents or guardians and observe certain conditions, as follows.

They must be under obedience to their teachers regarding which subjects they study and for how long.

They must go to confession at least once a month.

Every Sunday they must attend the class on Christian doctrine given in the college, as well as the sermon when one is delivered in the church.

They must be well-behaved in their speech and in all other matters, and be orderly. Where they fail in this or in their duties, in the case of young boys for whom words do not suffice, there should be a hired extern corrector to chastise them and keep them in awe; none of our men is to lay his hand on anyone.

The names of all these pupils are registered. Care is taken not only to provide class instruction but also to have them do exercises in debating, in written composition, and in speaking Latin all the time, in such a way that they will make great progress in letters and virtues alike.

When there is a fair number of students who have acquired a grounding in humane letters, a person is appointed to inaugurate the course in the arts [i.e., philosophy]; and when there are a number of students well grounded in arts, a lecturer is appointed to teach theology—following the method of Paris, with frequent exercises.[37] From that point on, this whole arrangement is continued. For experience shows that it is inadvisable to begin by teaching arts or theology: lacking a foundation, the students make no progress. (This plan applies to places where there is a readiness for something more than humane letters—a readiness that does not always exist. In other places it is sufficient to teach languages and humane letters.)

Beyond this, the priests in the colleges will aid in hearing confessions, preaching, and all other spiritual ministrations. In this work the young men sometimes have grace that equals or exceeds that of the priests, God our Lord being greatly served thereby.

[3. The Accruing Benefits of Christian Education]

So much for the method. Now I shall mention the advantages which experience has shown to accrue from colleges of this type for the

Society itself, for the extern students, and for the people or region where the college is situated (although this can in part be gathered from what has already been said).

[a. For the Jesuits who Study or Teach in a Such a College]

The advantages for our own men are these.

1. First of all, those who give classes make progress themselves and learn a great deal by teaching others, acquiring greater confidence and mastery in their learning.

2. Our own scholastics who attend the lectures will benefit from the care, persistence, and diligence which the teachers devote to their office.

3. They not only advance in learning but also acquire facility in preaching and teaching catechism, get practice in the other means they will later use to help their neighbors, and grow in confidence at seeing the fruit which God our Lord allows them to see.

4. Although no one may urge the students to enter the Society, particularly when they are young boys, nevertheless through good example and personal contact, as well as the Latin declamations on the virtues held on Sundays, young men are spontaneously attracted, and many laborers can be won for the vineyard of Christ our Lord.[38]

So much for the advantages for the Society itself.

[b. For the Extern Students]

For the extern students who come to take advantage of the classes the benefits are the following.

5. They are given a quite adequate education. Care is taken to ensure that everyone learns, by means of classes, debates, and compositions, so that they make great progress in learning.

6. The poor who lack the means to pay the ordinary teachers or private tutors at home here obtain gratis an education which they could hardly procure at great expense.

7. They profit in spiritual matters through learning Christian doctrine and grasping from the sermons and regular exhortations what they need for their eternal salvation.

8. They make progress in purity of conscience—and consequently in all virtue—through the monthly confessions and the care taken to see that they are decent in their speech and virtuous in their entire lives.

9. They draw much greater merit and fruit from their studies, since they learn from the very beginning to make a practice of directing all their studies to the service of God, as they are taught to do.

[c. For the Country or Region]

For the inhabitants of the country or region where these colleges are established there are in addition the following benefits.

10. Financially, parents are relieved of the expense of having teachers to instruct their children in letters and virtue.

11. Parents fulfill their duty in conscience regarding their children's formation. Persons who would have difficulty finding even for pay teachers to whom they could entrust their children will find them in these colleges with complete security.

12. Apart from the schooling, they also have in the colleges persons who can give sermons to the people and in monasteries and help people through administration of the sacraments, to quite visible good effect.

13. The inhabitants themselves and the members of their households will be drawn to spiritual concerns by the good example of their children, and will be attracted to going more often to confession and living Christian lives.

14. The inhabitants of the region will have in our men persons to inspire and aid them in undertaking good works such as hospitals, houses for reformed women, and the like, for which charity also impels our men to have a concern.

15. From among those who are at present merely students, in time some will emerge to play diverse roles—some to preach and carry on the care of souls, others to the government of the land and the administration of justice, and others to other responsible occupations. In short, since the children of today become the adults of tomorrow, their good formation in life and learning will benefit many others, with the fruit expanding more widely every day.

I could elaborate this further. But this will suffice to explain our thinking here about colleges of this kind.

May Christ, our eternal salvation, guide us all to serve him better. Amen.

END OF THE SELECTED LETTERS

NOTES

NOTES

KEY TO THE ABBREVIATIONS

AHSJ	*Archivum Historicum Societatis Iesu.* Periodical, Rome
AldamIntro	Aldama, A. M. de, *An Introductory Commentary on the Constitutions* (St. Louis, 1989)
Autobiog	The *Autobiography* of St. Ignatius
BibThSpEx	Cusson, G., *Biblical Theology and the Spiritual Exercises* (St.Louis, 1988)
Cons	*The Constitutions of the Society of Jesus*, by St. Ignatius, in any text
*Cons*MHSJ	*Constitutiones et Regulae Societatis Iesu*, 4 vols, the critically edited texts in the series Monumenta Historica Societatis Iesu (Rome, 1934–1948)
ConsSJComm	*The Constitutions of the Society of Jesus.* Translated, with an Introduction and a Commentary, by G. E. Ganss, S.J. (St. Louis, 1970)
DalmIgn	Dalmases, C. de, *Ignatius of Loyola: Founder of the Jesuits. His Life and Work* (St. Louis, 1985)
DalmMan	Dalmases, *Ejercicios Espirituales. Introducción, texto, notas y vocabulario* por Cándido de Dalmases (1987). The critically edited Spanish text in the form of a manual for practical use
DeGuiJes	De Guibert, J. *The Jesuits: Their Spiritual Doctrine and Practice* (St. Louis, 1986)
Directory	*Directory to the Spiritual Exercises of . . . Ignatius* (London, 1925). The official Directory issued by Aquaviva in 1599
DirSpEx	*Directoria Exercitiorum Spiritualium (1540-1599)* (Rome, 1955)
DSpir	*Dictionnaire de spiritualité* (Paris, 1937–)
Dudon	Dudon, *Saint Ignatius of Loyola* (Milwaukee, 1949)
EppIgn	*S. Ignatii Epistolae et Instructiones*, 12 volumes in MHSJ (Rome, 1903–1911)
FN	*Fontes Narrativi*, 4 volumes in MHSJ (Rome, 1923–1960)

KEY TO THE ABBREVIATIONS

IdeaJesUn	G. E. Ganss, *St. Ignatius' Idea of a Jesuit University* (Milwaukee, 1956)
InstSJ	*Institutum Societatis Iesu.* 3 volumes (Florence, 1892–1893)
LettersIgn	*Letters of St. Ignatius,* translated by W. J. Young (Chicago, 1959)
LeturEstud	Leturia, P. de, *Estudios Ignacianos,* 2 volumes (Rome, 1957)
LeturIñg	Leturia, *Iñigo de Loyola* (Chicago, 1965)
MHSJ	Monumenta Historica Societatis Iesu, the series of critically edited historical sources of the Jesuits, 124 volumes
MonNad	*Epistolae et Monumenta Patris H. Nadal.* 6 vols in MHSJ
MonPaed	*Monumenta Paedagogica.* 5 volumes in MHSJ
n or nn	note(s), or footnote(s), or endnote(s)
no or nos	number(s)
NCathEnc	The *New Catholic Encyclopedia* (New York, 1967)
NDicTh	*The New Dictionary of Theology* (Wilmington, 1987)
Obrascompl	*Obras completas de San Ignacio,* 4th ed. (Madrid, 1982)
OxDCCh	*Oxford Dictionary of the Christian Church* (1974)
PG	Patrologia Graeca, ed. Migne
PL	Patrologia Latina, ed. Migne
SpDiar	The *Spiritual Diary of St. Ignatius,* 1544–1545
SpEx	The *Spiritual Exercises* of St. Ignatius, in any text
*SpEx*MHSJ	*Exercitia Spiritualia S. Ignatii . . . et Eorum Directoria* (1919), in MHSJ
*SpEx*MHSJ*Te*	*Sti. Ignatii . . . Exercitia Spiritualia. Textuum antiquissimorum nova editio,* (Rome, 1969). The critical text of the *Exercises,* edited by C. de Dalmases as volume 100 in the series MHSJ. It is a revision of *SpEx*MHSJ (1919).
ST	*Summa theologiae* of St. Thomas Aquinas

NOTES ON THE GENERAL
INTRODUCTION

1. See esp. Rom. 16:25–26; Ephes. 1:9–10, 3:1–20; Col. 2:2. For a collection of Scripture texts which briefly give a bird's-eye view of the chief steps in God's evolving plan of creation, redemption, and final glorification, see G. Cusson, *Biblical Theology and the Spiritual Exercises* (St. Louis, 1988), pp. 342–344.

2. Pastor, *History of the Popes* (St. Louis, 1924) 13:194–195.

3. Jacob Burckhardt, *The Civilization of the Renaissance in Italy* (New York, 1904), p. 76; see also George E. Ganss, *St. Ignatius' Idea of a Jesuit University* (Milwaukee, 1956), pp, 164–166, 323.

4. Joseph de Guibert, *The Jesuits: Their Spiritual Doctrine and Practice* (St. Louis, 1972), p. 84.

5. To solve the editorial problems arising from these two terms, we use *Exercises* (in italic type) when the term clearly refers to the published book, and Exercises (in roman type) when the term refers to Ignatius' still unpublished manuscript, or to the activities of an exercitant guided by the book. Since the uses often overlap, the decisions are sometimes arbitrary. Similarly, we shall use *Constitutions*, a collection of statutes, in italics, when the term refers to Ignatius' published book, and Constitutions (in roman type) when it refers to his manuscript, or to one or a few of its component statutes.

To make references easier, in editions since 1928 a number in square brackets has been added to each section of Ignatius' text of his *Exercises*, *Constitutions*, and *Spiritual Diary*, e.g., [21].

When references which could be footnotes are run into our text, e.g., as he states (*SpEx*, [91])," the parentheses ( ) indicate that the numbers are equivalently a footnote run into our own text, and the square brackets [ ] that the numbers themselves are a modern editorial addition to Ignatius' text. Works cited in abbreviated form following first mention are identified in Key to the Abbreviations. pp. 369–370.

6. *DeGuiJes*, pp. 70, 178.

7. See Pedro de Leturia, *Iñigo de Loyola*, 2d ed. (Chicago, 1965), p.

43. Leturia is excellent on Ignatius' Basque background.

8. *Fontes Narrativi de S. Ignatio et de Societatis Iesu Initiis*, 4 vols. (Rome, 1943–1965) I:154; see also Cándido de Dalmases, *Ignatius of Loyola, Founder of the Jesuits: His Life and Work* (St. Louis, 1985), p. 33; *Scripta de S. Ignatio* (Rome, 1904) I: 587; John Wickham, "The Worldly Ideal of Ignatius," *Thought* 29 (1954): 209–236.

9. *The Golden Legend of Jacobus de Voragine*, trans. and adapted from the Latin by G. Ryan and H. Ripperger (New York, 1941) 1:597–599.

10. Ibid. 2:413–416.

11. Ibid. 2:494–495. For Augustine's statement see *The City of God*, Book 14, ch. 8.

12. *Exhortationes*, in *FN* I:306–307.

13. *DalmIgn*, p. 43; *LeturIñg*, pp. 84, 114, 115.

14. Ludolphus de Saxonia, *Vita Christi, ex Evangelio et approbatis ab Ecclesia catholica doctoribus sedule collecta*, ed. L. M. Rigollot (Paris, 1878), 4 vols.; see the tables of contents for each volume. The English translations below are mine.

15. *Dios nuestro Señor*, "God our Lord": In the *Exercises* alone this reverential phrase occurs 58 times, and "Christ our Lord" 72 times (*DalmMan*, pp. 193, s.v. *Criador, Dios*). He also calls Christ the "eternal Lord of all things" ([98]), the Creator who became also a human being ([53]), "our Creator and Redeemer" ([229]), and in *Cons* [728] he writes "Jesus Christ, God and our Lord." In letters too he writes of "Christ, our Creator, Redeemer, and Lord" and "our Creator and Lord" (*Letters of St. Ignatius of Loyola*, tr. W. J. Young [Chicago, 1959], pp. 29, 85; see also Deliberation on Poverty, no. 13). For extensive references see Hugo Rahner, *Ignatius the Theologian* (New York, 1968), pp. 9, 15–16; and Harvey D. Egan, *Ignatius Loyola the Mystic* (Wilmington, 1987), p. 96; *BibThSpEx*, p. 57; *The New Dictionary of Theology* (Wilmington, 1987), p. 213. See also n. 15 on *SpEx* [23] below.

16. *Exhortationes in Hispania*, in *FN* I:305.

17. *LeturIñg*, pp. 87–96; *DeGuiJes*, p. 25.

18. Codina, in *Exercitia Spiritualia S. Ignatii . . . et eorum Directoria* (Madrid, 1919), pp. 57–94; Leturia in *LeturIñg*, p. 112. There are, of course, paragraphs where dependence of *thought* on Ludolph's *Vita* is manifest—a topic concretely expounded by Raitz von Frentz in *Revue d'ascétique et de mystique* 25 (1949): 375–388. On the deep influence of Ludolph on Ignatius, see *BibThSpEx*, pp. 8–22, esp. p. 10.

19. *NCathEnc* 2:483.

20. *DalmIgn*, p. 57; *FN* I:29*, with the footnotes.

21. Câmara, in *FN* II:584, 659; *DeGuiJes*, pp. 155–157.

22. Some examples are Hugo Rahner (1935 and 1949), Joseph de Guibert (1935 and 1953), Adolf Haas (1953), Roger Cantin (1955), Victoriano Larrañaga (1947 and 1956), Gilles Cusson (1966), and Ignacio Iparraguirre (1967). Harvey D. Egan, in *Ignatius Loyola the Mystic*, presents a competent study which takes account of and adds to virtually all the previous ones.

23. See *DeGuiJes*, pp. 60–61, 608; also 55, 58–59, 73. Mystics find great difficulty in recounting their sublime experiences, and theologians find similar difficulty in interpreting what the mystics have written. An early example is found in Augustine's classic work, *The Literal Meaning of Genesis: An Unfinished Book*, trans. and annotated by J. H. Taylor (Ramsey, N.J., 1982). In Book 12, trying to explain St. Paul's rapture to the third heaven (2 Cor. 12:2–4), he states in ch. 6: "When we read one commandment, 'you shall love your neighbor as yourself,' we experience three kinds of vision: one through the eyes by which we see the letters; a second through the spirit [the soul], by which we think of our neighbor even when he is absent; and a third through an intuition of the mind, by which we see and understand love itself." In chs. 6 through 10 he humbly labors to explain these kinds of vision further. See St. Augustine, *The Literal Meaning of Genesis*, 2:185, 303.

24. E.g., *DeGuiJes*, pp. 606–607, with the references in nn. 5 and 6. Here too the terminology stems at least from Book 12, ch. 11 of Augustine's classic treatise on the problem, in *The Literal Meaning of Genesis*, p. 191: "These three kinds of vision, therefore, namely corporeal, spiritual, and intellectual, must be considered separately, so that reason may ascend from the lower to the higher."

25. *DeGuiJes*, p. 40. Laínez' statement is in *FN* I:140.

26. Câmara, *Memoriale*, no. 137, in *FN* I:610; *DalmIgn*, p. 63.

27. Nadal in *FN* II:252, no. 17.

28. Doc. 2 of 1548, on pp. 52–53 of Leturia, "Genesis de los Ejercicios de san Ignacio y su influjo en la fundación de la Compañía de Jesús," *Estudios Ignacianos* (Rome, 1957) 2:3–55. His Doc. 12 (1574), ibid., 52–53, cited from *FN* II:526–527, is similar. Nadal too makes similar statements, *FN* I:306–307.

29. Leturia, *Estudios* 2:14.

30. See p. 24, with n. 16.

31. See *DalmIgn*, pp. 65–66; *SpEx*MHSJ*Te*, pp. 31–32; Leturia, *Estudios* 2:21–23.

32. *FN* I:84.

33. Laínez in *FN* I:100; Ignatius in *EppIgn* I:119.

34. Leturia, *Estudios* 2:23–24; *DalmIgn*, p. 122.

35. Book I, ch. 1, no. 2, in *Petri Lombardi Sententiarum libri quattuor* (Paris: Migne, 1853), col. 13. In Ignatius' comparable view, all things created are means to salvation, and should be used or discarded insofar as they are helps or hindrances to it (*SpEx*, [23]); on the hierarchy of beings, see, e.g., *Cons* [666]; on purity of intention, *Cons* [288, 340, 360].

36. See, e.g., *Cons* [307, 446–452, 671].

37. *Petri Lombardi Sententiarum libri quattuor*, ed. Migne (Paris, 1853), col. 143. For Ignatius' comparable thought see the Foundation, *SpEx* [23].

38. For a diagrammatic presentation of the structure of the *Summa theologiae*, see *The Catholic Encyclopedia* (1912) 12:669.

39. *Summa theologiae* 2–2, 132, 1, ad 1.

40. *ST* 3, 26–49.

41. *ST* 1–2, 114, 4 and 8. For a theological study on God's purpose in creation, see Philip J. Donnelly, "St. Thomas and the Ultimate Purpose of Creation," *Theological Studies* 2 (1941): 53–83; also, "The Doctrine of the Vatican Council on the End of Creation," ibid. 4 (1943): 3–33.

42. *FN* II:198; see also *DalmIgn*, p. 123, on Ignatius' competence in theology and the remark of Dr. Martial Mazurier at Paris.

43. *LettersIgn*, pp. 9–11 and 5–8; see also *DeGuiJes*, p. 35.

44. Their ages were: Ignatius, 46; Bobadilla, 30; Codure, 29; Xavier, 31; Laínez, 35; Rodrigues, probably about 30; Salmerón, 21. Hence he received the diaconate on June 24, but priesthood only in October, when he was 22.

45. *FN* II:133. Ignatius' contemporaries constantly translated *Compagnia di Gesu* or *Compañía de Jesús* as Societas. This shows what the term *Compañía* meant to them.

46. *Regimini* [3]; *Exposcit*, [4] (English in *ConsSJComm*), p. 68; *Cons* [7, 527, 529, 612].

47. *FN* I:140.

48. *MonNad* IV:461; V:162 [15]. *DeGuiJes*, p. 45. For the relation of this characteristic to his theory of apostolic spirituality, see n. 30 on *Cons* [430] below.

49. *FN* III:327; *DalmIgn*, p.163. Possibly, however, Paul III made this remark during an earlier interview with the companions. See also

André Ravier, *Ignatius of Loyola and the Founding of the Society of Jesus* (San Francisco, 1988), p. 33. In regard to most items connected with the founding of the Society of Jesus, wherever we give a reference to *DalmIgn*, supplementary information can be found in this excellent book of Ravier. The French original appeared in 1973.

50. The text in English is in J. C. Futrell, *Making an Apostolic Community of Love* (St. Louis, 1970), pp. 187–194.

51. Text in *Cons*MHSJ I:16.

52. *DalmIgn*, pp. 298–304.

53. *DalmIgn*, pp. 220, 223–234; W. V. Bangert, *A History of the Society of Jesus* (St. Louis, 1986), pp. 33, 37–39.

54. *EppIgn* IV, 5–9; English above, pp. 361–365 and in *IdeaJesUn*, pp. 25–27.

55. The list is in Allan P. Farrell, *The Jesuit Code of Liberal Education* (Milwaukee, 1938), pp. 431–435.

56. Martin P. Harney, *The Jesuits in History* (New York, 1940), pp. 201–202. On the historical background of the Jesuit educational tradition, see John W. O'Malley, "The Jesuit Educational Enterprise in Historical Perspective," in *Jesuit Higher Education. Essays on an American Tradition of Excellence*, ed. Rolando E. Bonachea (Pittsburgh, 1989), pp. 10–25.

57. See *Obras completas de San Ignacio*, ed. I. Iparraguirre and C. de Dalmases, 4th ed. (Madrid: Biblioteca de Autores Cristianos, 1982), pp. 53–55.

58. *Obrascompl*, p. 225.

59. *FN* II:494, no. 83; see also *DalmIgn*, p. 281.

60. See, e.g., the samples in *DeGuiJes*, pp. 35, 83–84.

61. In his day "fixed revenue" (*renta*) meant the reception of revenues at regularly recurring intervals. Such revenues came from what we might call invested capital and often it would be a fixed annual income from the ownership of land.

62. On the authorship, see Codina, in *Cons*MHSJ I:ccvi; for the text of the Formula of 1539, see *Cons*MHSJ I, 14–21; English in Georg Schurhammer, *Francis Xavier: His Life, His Times* (Rome, 1973) 1:462. It reappeared with slight revisions in *Regimini* of 1540. After ten years of experience Ignatius suggested further slight revisions to Pope Julius III, who approved them in a new bull, *Exposcit debitum* of July 21, 1550. This remains the definitive Rule currently in force. The English text is in *ConsSJComm*, pp. 63–73.

63. *Cons*MHSJ II:clxiv.

64. Preface of Nadal, no. 1, in *Obrascompl*, p. 85.

65. Preface of Câmara, no. 1, ibid., p. 87.

66. *FN* II:121; see also *FN* IV:144–146; *MonNad* IV:662.

67. On Ignatius' style, see *Obrascompl*, pp. 53–57; *DeGuiJes*, pp. 70–71, 147–148.

68. For examples of this classical terminology, see, e.g., *DeGuiJes*, pp. 605–609; De Guibert, *The Theology of the Spiritual Life*, nos. 2–20, 231–250, 381–422; Tanquerey, *The Spiritual Life*, pp. 323–340, 454–471, 602-608; 649–715; *Oxford Dictionary of the Christian Church*, s.v. Ascetical Theology, Asceticism, Mystical Theology, and Mysticism.

69. For examples of the developing and still fluidly diverse terminology see, e.g., *NDicTh*, s.v. "Asceticism," "Mysticism," "Mystical Theology," "Spirituality"; Harvey D. Egan, *Christian Mysticism: The Future of a Tradition* (New York, 1984), pp. 1–29; *Ignatius Loyola the Mystic*, pp. 20–31; *Christian Spirituality: Origins to the Twelfth Century*, ed. Bernard McGinn and John Meyendorff (New York, 1985), pp. xii–xvii; Sandra M. Schneiders, "Spirituality in the Academy," *Theological Studies* 50 (1989): 676–697.

THE AUTOBIOGRAPHY

INTRODUCTION

1. Cited by Dalmases in *Obrascompl*, p. 75, from *MonNad* III:540.
2. *FN* I:338–339.
3. *Obrascompl*, p. 77, n. 51.

Ch. 1. Pamplona and Loyola

1. The most probable date of Ignatius' birth, based esp. on the testimony of his nurse, is 1491. Hence his statements in the *Autobiography* have greatly puzzled historians. If he was 26 at Pamplona in May 1523 (as he states here), his birth would be in 1495; and if he was 62 in 1555 (as he states below in no. 30), his birth would be in 1493. Perhaps he simply erred; or, thinking the matter relatively unimportant in his context, he may have meant his statements as mere approximations. In his era many people were far less concerned about the year of their birth than we are today. See *DalmIgn*, pp. 24–25; *FN* I:4*–24*.

2. Confession to a lay person when no priest was available was a common practice in the Middle Ages and was recommended in prayer books in the 1500s. It manifested contrition, but was not obligatory.

3. Respectively the *Life of Christ* by Ludolph of Saxony and *The Golden Legend* by Jacobus de Voragine, in Spanish translations. See above, General Introduction, pp. 15 and 19.

4. We do not know who this lady was. One guess, typical of the rest, is the princess Catalina, younger sister of Emperor Charles V, who in 1525 married King John III of Portugal.

5. Ignatius' companions had shown eagerness to learn how he came to write the *Exercises*. Here he begins to tell of the experiences which were in time to result in the section on discernment of spirits (*SpEx* [313–336]). In Ignatius' terminology, to discern is to see deeply with a view to recognizing and distinguishing. Hence, in this case he observed that his thoughts about worldly things pleased him but left him dissatisfied later, while the thoughts about holy things both consoled him when present and left him joyful also afterward. He concluded that

the thoughts of the first kind came from the devil and those of the second from God. One thought which gave him such joy, that about the pilgrimage to Jerusalem, probably arose from the praise which Ludolph gave it in his Prologue.

Ch. 2. Road to Montserrat

6. Ignatius' confessor was Dom Jean Chanones, who, to help him prepare for a general confession, handed him a copy of the *Book of Exercises for the Spiritual Life* (*Ejercitatorio de la vida espiritual*) by García Jiménes de Cisneros, O.S.B. Some items of the First Week and the Examinations of Conscience in Ignatius' later *Exercises* may well have arisen from its influence (*LeturIñg*, pp. 149–150). The shrine mentioned was that of the Black Virgin in the Benedictine monastery at Montserrat. It was and is a much frequented place of pilgrimage.

Ch. 3. Sojourn at Manresa

7. The serpent pleases at first but later brings depressing temptations. From this effect Ignatius discerns that the serpent is the devil (see *Autobiog*, 31 below). This serpent will again appear to Ignatius in Paris and Rome.

8. Here we learn that Ignatius' practice of weekly confession and communion, of which he was later a great promotor, began already at Manresa. In the sixteenth century the practice was unusual.

9. In the second period of his stay at Manresa, perhaps in late May or early June, his struggle with scruples and desolation begins. It will last until late July.

10. The anxiety caused by the scruples tended toward abandonment of practices pleasing to God, and the false consolations led to loss of sleep necessary to serve him. From these bad effects Ignatius recognized them as temptations coming from a devil. His ability to discern is growing. This knowledge will eventually grow into his Rules for the Discernment of Spirits now in *SpEx* [313–336].

11. Ignatius now begins to treat the third period of his stay in Manresa, that of divine illuminations. On these five mystical experiences in *Autobiog*, 29–30, see the General Introduction, above, pp. 28–33. Notice the rather abrupt transition into the second paragraph of no. 27. Ignatius was here resuming his narrations to Câmara in March, 1555, after a seventeen-month interruption because of other business.

The first narrations had been in August–September, 1553; the third took place October 20–22, 1555 (*Obrascompl*, pp. 70, 106).

12. *Teclas*: keys as on a piano. Each produces its own sound, but the three sounds together are one harmony. On similar mystical experiences which made him talkative and joyful for the rest of the day, see, e.g., *SpDiar* [53–55] and the comments above in the Introduction, pp. 28–33.

13. Ignatius' interests, we observe, are shifting toward apostolic activity as well as personal sanctification.

14. Similar visions of Christ are recounted below in *Autobiog*, 41, 44, 48, 96, 99.

15. This is the "outstanding illumination" (*eximia ilustración*) which had immense transforming effect on him at this time of his life. On it see above, Introduction, pp. 28–33. Since 1940 it has been extensively discussed by writers such as De Guibert, Leturia, Haas, Cantin, Cusson, Egan, and others.

16. On the strong arguments that Ignatius was focusing here more on the intensive quality of his experiences than on their quantity, see Introduction, pp. 31–32 above.

17. See also above in ch. 3, nn. 7 and 10. Now, after some four months, Ignatius at last recognizes clearly that the serpent who brought thoughts seemingly holy at first but leading to a bad result was in reality the devil. Ignatius will later point out this deception in his Rules for Discernment more appropriate for the Second Week (*SpEx* [328–336]); see esp. [334] on the recognition of the enemy "by his serpent's tail and the bad end to which he leads." For Ignatius, genuine discernment was often a lengthy process requiring much patience.

18. A *blanca* is a copper coin of little value; a penny.

Ch. 4. Pilgrimage to Jerusalem

19. Ignatius sailed from Venice on July 14, 1523, in a ship named the *Negrona*, disembarked in Jaffa on August 31, and entered Jerusalem on Friday September 4. From diaries kept by two of his fellow pilgrims, Swiss Peter Füssly and Philip Hagen of Strasbourg, we learn many details of his pilgrimage. See, e.g., *DalmIgn*, pp. 78–79.

20. On September 5, Ignatius and his group visited Mount Sion, the Cenacle, the Church of the Dormition of Mary, and the Holy Sepulchre. On the 6th they walked the Way of the Cross from the Tower

Antonia to Calvary; on the 7th they visited Bethany and the Mount of Olives; on the 8th and 9th, Bethlehem; on the 10th and 11th, Jehosaphat and Gethsemane. After some rest, they went on the 14th to Jericho and the Jordan. They spent September 16–22 in Jerusalem. On October 3 he sailed from Jaffa. See *DalmIgn*, pp. 78–79.

21. By now apostolic service has been added to his original aim, personal sanctification by prayer and penance.

22. Early in his converted life he manifests his respect for the Holy See and its authority.

23. A name given to the Syrian Christians who worked in the Franciscan monastery of Mt. Sion in Jerusalem and wore a girdle, presumably for identification.

Ch. 5. The Return Voyage

24. A legend has it that St. James' body was miraculously transported to Santiago de Compostela in Spain.

25. A *marchetto* was a small coin worth a few cents, and the *quatrini* and *giulii* were smaller still.

26. King Francis I and Emperor Charles V were at war about possession of the duchy of Milan.

27. Ignatius uses *tu*, the pronoun of familiar address, instead of the more formal *usted*, your honor.

28. Andrea Doria, a Genoese admiral, transferred his allegiance from Francis I to Charles V in 1528.

Ch. 6. Barcelona and Alcalá

29. Ignatius met Isabel Roser in Barcelona in late February or early March of 1523. She remained his spiritual daughter and generous benefactor throughout his studies, which continued through 1536. They remained friends until her death in 1554. There was, however, one stormy period in their relations. On it see n. 4 on Ignatius' letter to her of Nov. 10, 1532, above.

30. Hitherto Ignatius knew no Latin. Isabel Roser introduced him to Ardèvol, who admitted him to his classes. Ignatius, thirty-four, sat on the benches with the small boys (*niños*) to learn the fundamentals of Latin.

31. All this experience will be reflected in his Rules for Discernment, *SpEx* [326, 332]. See above, *Autobiog*, 8, 19, and 26.

32. Their names were Calixto de Sa, Lope de Cáceres, and Juan de Arteaga. Ignatius was beginning to seek companions for his apostolic way of living.

33. The "logic of Soto" was perhaps an early manuscript of his *Summulae*, printed in 1524. St. Albert the Great's *Physicorum libri VIII* was a commentary on Aristotle's natural philosophy. Peter Lombard's *Sententiarum libri quattuor* (1157) was a widely used systematic presentation of scholastic theology.

34. Previously he had told us of his spiritual conversations at Manresa (*Autobiog*, 34) and Barcelona (37). Now for the first time in the *Autobiography* he uses the terms "giving spiritual exercises" (*en dar ejercicios espirituales*).

35. In ch. 6 Câmara's three marginal notes are unclear and unhelpful to us.

36. Diego de Guía (Eguía) entered the Society in 1540 and was for a time Ignatius' confessor.

37. "Wearers of sackcloth." The companions were all dressed in the same way but were not priests or religious. This generated suspicion that they were some new sect—and further, perhaps Alumbrados.

38. The Alumbrados or Illuminati were a loosely knit group of spiritual persons in sixteenth-century Spain. Some were saintly; but others, unbalanced, claimed doubtful visions and revelations and were treated severely by the Inquisition. In 1526 the Inquisition of Toledo condemned 48 propositions of the Alumbrados. Suspicion was widespread while Ignatius was in Alcalá.

39. Vicar general of the archbishop of Toledo.

40. The young Juan Renalde had joined Ignatius' group in Alcalá.

41. The two women were María del Vado and her daughter Luisa Velázquez. Against Ignatius' advice they made a pilgrimage to the shrine of the Holy Face at Jaen in southern Spain.

Ch. 7. Troubles at Salamanca

42. Ignatius saw the trap in this leading question. If he answered "the Holy Spirit" he might be charged with Illuminism.

43. Erasmus, the famous humanist, had many admirers and many adversaries who found his satires on abuses in the Church disrespectful of the Church itself or even heretical. While Ignatius was in Salamanca some Franciscans and Dominicans were among those hostile to Erasmus and an atmosphere of suspicion was rife.

44. Probably a certain Francisco de Frias, otherwise unknown.

45. This is the first occasion in the *Autobiography* when Ignatius speaks of the Exercises as something written.

46. A real or fictitious problem case to test Ignatius' knowledge of canon law.

Ch. 8. At the University of Paris

47. He arrived in Paris on February 2, 1528 (*EppIgn* I:74).

48. Ignatius, now thirty-seven, again sat with small boys (*niños*). He also began his experience of "the order and method of Paris." This consisted of a well planned and organized sequence of studies with much self-activity (*exercicio*) of the students, in contrast to the haphazard procedures common elsewhere. Later Ignatius will insist on this "order and method of Paris" for his own schools (*Cons* [366]; see *ConsSJComm*, p. 191, n. 6). On the College of Montaigu, see Dudon, *St. Ignatius of Loyola* (Milwaukee, 1949), pp. 135–138.

49. His trips occurred in 1529, 1530, and 1531. In 1529 he met the famous humanist and educational reformer Luis Vives.

50. These exercises transformed their lives, in a way that the other students regarded as foolishness for which Ignatius was responsible. Peralta later became a canon of the Cathedral of Toledo and Castro a Carthusian.

51. In mid-79 Câmara's text abandons Spanish and continues in Italian because, dictating in Genoa, he had no Spanish amanuensis.

52. Doña Leonor Mascarenhas, a noble Portuguese who came to Spain with Isabella when Isabella married Emperor Charles V in 1526. Doña Leonor ever remained a great benefactor of the Society of Jesus.

53. *Comendador*: a commander, i.e., a rank in an order of knighthood.

54. On the feast of St. Remy, October 1, 1529, Ignatius planned to transfer to the College of Sainte-Barbe to begin his studies in "the arts," that is, the course in philosophy. In the first two years of the arts the students studied logic, and in the third, Aristotle's Physics, Metaphysics, and Ethics. A good idea of the material studied can be gained from Pierre Tartaret, *In Aristotelis philosophiam* (Venice, 1592), a typical textbook used at Paris. Of its 389 pages, it devotes 139 to Aristotle's *Physics*, 59 to *On the Soul*, 20 to the *Metaphysics*, and 68 to the *Ethics*. On it see W. Ong, *Ramus, Method, and the Decay of Dialogue* (Cambridge, 1958), pp. 136–144, esp. 141; also, *ConsSJComm*, p. 188.

55. Notice the same procedure here as at Barcelona. By discernment Ignatius recognized the experience as a temptation, and he disclosed it to a prudent counselor. See *Autobiog*, 55 above, with n. 4.

56. Francisco de Javier from Navarre and Pierre Favre (Petrus Faber) from Savoy. They were to become the first of his permanent followers. In Paris he won also other permanent associates: Simão Rodrigues, a Portuguese, who became friendly with him in 1532, Diego Laínez and Alfonso Salmerón, Spanish students who learned about him in Alcalá and came to Paris in 1533 to find him, and then became his followers; and Nicolás Bobadilla, another Spaniard, who came also in 1533. However, while narrating to Câmara on this particular day, Ignatius here mentioned only these two, perhaps because they had died —Favre in 1546 and Xavier in 1552. In 1534 Ignatius gave the Exercises to all of them: to Favre in January, to Laínez and Salmerón in spring, to Rodrigues and Bobadilla a little later, and to Xavier in September, after he had taken the vow along with the others at Montmartre on August 15.

57. The precise meaning of the expression is unknown. It seems that at some universities the students, to show humility, sat on a stone while answering their examiners. In the qualifying examination Ignatius ranked 30th in a class of 100. On March 13, 1533, he passed the more difficult final examination and, at considerable expense, received the Licentiate in Arts. This degree permitted him to teach at Paris or anywhere in the world. A year later, on March 14, 1534, he received the degree of Master of Arts, the equivalent of a doctorate (*DalmIgn*, pp. 115–117; *Obrascompl*, p. 144, n. 25).

58. Why did he doubt? He has not told us. Possibly because taking the degree would be seeking an honor; or because he thought that paying the necessary fee would be inconsistent with his determination to live poorly.

59. Ignatius suffered stomach pains for the rest of his life. An autopsy in 1556 revealed the cause as gallstones with referred pains to the stomach. See *DalmIgn*, pp. 126, 288–289.

60. In April 1534 he began to study theology in the Dominican convent of Sainte-Jacques and in the Franciscan convent nearby. He continued until he left Paris in April, 1535, and later for the year of 1536 in Venice.

61. This is the substance of the vow which the seven "friends in the Lord" took at Montmartre, on August 15, 1534. Its precise formula is unknown. After Ignatius' departure for Spain in April 1535, the re-

maining six renewed the vow on August 15, 1535, and in it were joined by three more friends, Claude Jay from Savoy, and from France Jean Codure and Paschase Broët. These ten were to become the founding members of the Society of Jesus.

62. Ignatius had also another motive, to repair the bad example of his youthful escapades, as Polanco tells us (*FN* II:568).

63. Valentín Liévin, a priest.

Ch. 9. Farewell to Spain

64. The Province of Gupúzcoa.

65. In *Autobiog*, 33.

66. Ignatius intended to continue his theological studies in Bologna, but he found the climate undesirable and went to Venice, where he studied theology from early January, 1536, until Lent, 1537. In Venice he stayed with a good and learned man whose excellent library he used. This man was probably Andrea Lippomani, prior of the monastery of La Trinità, a future benefactor of the Society.

Ch. 10. Venice and Vicenza

67. Pietro Contarini, a noble Venetian cleric who later became bishop of Cyprus, was from a family different from that of Cardinal Gasparo Contarini, who greatly aided Ignatius in Rome. Gasparo de' Dotti was the vicar of the papal nuncio to Venice. Rozas remains unidentified. Diego de Hoces was a native of Málaga, who died early in 1538 in Padua.

68. Doctor Pedro Ortiz, professor of Scripture from Salamanca, was vexed with Ignatius only temporarily about Castro and Peralta (see *Autobiog*, 77). Later he was to be immensely friendly and helpful to the Society. See *Autobiog*, 96, and *DalmIgn*, p. 144 and Index, s.v. Ortiz. Gian-Pietro Caraffa became a cardinal in 1536 and pope as Paul IV on May 23, 1555. Ignatius had disagreements with him in Venice and fears about him later on in Rome (*DalmIgn*, pp. 141, 185–187).

69. On June 24, 1537, Ignatius, Xavier, Laínez, Rodrigues, Bobadilla, and Codure were ordained priests. Ignatius was forty-six years old. The nuncio granted them faculties throughout the Republic of Venice. Salmerón was still too young to be ordained.

70. "Under the title of poverty." This technical canonical term pertains to assurance that an ordinand would have material support

sufficient for his future food and lodging. For secular priests this title might be the local church they would serve, or a benefice, or their patrimony; and for religious, their profession was called "the title of poverty" (*NCathEnc* 10:726). The companions' vows of poverty and chastity and their sufficient learning were the titles under which Bishop Vincenzo Nigusanti ordained them (see in MHSJ, *Fontes documentales*, p. 529; *DalmIgn*, p. 146).

71. For Ignatius, intensive spiritual experiences like those at Manresa are back. See Introduction, p. 41 above. Hugo Rahner, De Guibert, and others see in Ignatius' spiritual experiences at Vicenza the possible germ of his ideas for the Jesuit "third year of probation" or "tertianship," which he prescribed in *Cons* [516]. After the years of intellectual training the scholastics should have another year in "the school of the heart" to cultivate virtues such as greater humility, love of God, and apostolic zeal. See *DeGuiJes*, p. 37, n. 40; *ConsSJComm*, p. 233, n. 4.

72. The ill person was Rodrigues.

73. "The two" were Dr. Pedro Ortiz and Cardinal Gian Pietro Caraffa. See nn. 67 and 68 above.

74. At La Storta, eight miles from Rome, in mid-November 1537. On the importance of this mystical vision for Ignatius at this turning point in his life, and for its influence on his contemporary Jesuits, see Introduction, pp. 41–42 above.

75. In Rome the three soon engaged in preaching, works of charity, and giving the Exercises. Favre lectured on Scripture and Laínez on scholastic theology in the University of Rome, La Sapienza. On occasion Pope Paul III invited them to participate with other theologians in theological disputations during his meals. Shortly after Easter, April 21, 1538, the rest of the ten "friends of the Lord" arrived in Rome.

Ch. 11. The First Year in Rome

76. This theologian and professor of Scripture was by now an influential person in the papal curia and a permanent friend of the group. Ignatius knew far less theology than he, but Ortiz stated that from Ignatius he learned a new theology different from what one learns from books: a theology to be put into practice. See *DalmIgn*, pp. 154–155. Another to whom Ignatius gave the Exercises was Cardinal Gasparo Contarini, president of the pontifical commission for the reform of the Church.

NOTES

77. Francisco Estrada shortly later entered the Society.

78. Ignatius regarded these as perhaps the most severe persecutions he endured. Agostini Mainardi, an Augustinian preacher who soon became a Lutheran, his friend Mudarra, along with Miguel Landívar and Barreda, two others who had grievances against Ignatius, spread calumnious lies that Ignatius and his friends were immoral persons preaching doctrinal errors. Many were influenced, including Cardinal de Cupis. Probably by now Ignatius and his group were thinking at least dimly that it might be wise for them to become a religious order, for which a good reputation and papal approval would be necessary. Ignatius, seeing that this defamation might spoil all his future work, felt that public and juridical approbation was necessary. He had a two-hour interview with Cardinal de Cupis and another for an hour with Pope Paul III, who were both impressed by his sincerity and zeal. The pope ordered a juridical trial to be held, and a sentence favorable to Ignatius came on November 18, 1538. See *DalmIgn*, pp. 157–162.

79. On Ignatius' work for the orphans, see *DalmIgn*, pp. 184–185.

80. Time was pressing; Câmara was to depart for Portugal on October 23, and with him Nadal enroute to Spain. So Ignatius tells Câmara he can learn the rest of the account from Nadal on their journey, but Câmara, aware that other Jesuits were eager to know more details about the writing of the Exercises and Constitutions, pressed Ignatius by his question. Ignatius complied.

81. In this last interview Ignatius returns to his interior life and the many graces God has given him. They included the mystical favors which often brought him confirmation about practical agenda, especially while he was composing the Constitutions. Concrete examples of what these favors were are recorded in his *Spiritual Diary*, e.g. [83–91].

82. His *Spiritual Diary*, of which we have only a part. In its present size it could hardly be the "rather large bundle" mentioned here.

83. *Renta*: This Spanish word means, not receipts of any kind, but fixed or regularly recurring revenues. A technical point of canon and religious law is involved here. See pp. 219–220 above, with n. 10.

THE *SPIRITUAL EXERCISES*

1. INTRODUCTION

1. S. Ignatii de Loyola, *Exercitia Spiritualia: Textuum antiquissimorum nova editio*, Monumenta Historica Societatis Iesu (Rome, 1969).

2. These are now referred to as the Autograph Directory (in *Obrascompl*, pp. 295–298), and as Dictated Directories (of which examples can be seen ibid., pp. 299–303).

3. This Directory is contained in *Directoria Exercitiorum Spiritualium (1540–1599)* (Rome, 1955), pp. 569–751. Two English translations exist: *Directory of the Spiritual Exercises of Our Holy Father Ignatius: Authorized Translation* (London: Manresa Press, 1925), and in *The Spiritual Exercises of Saint Ignatius of Loyola*, trans. W. H. Longridge (London, 1919), pp. 271–278. For the history of the Directories see *DeGuiJes*, pp. 243–247.

4. *SpEx* [2].

5. See *BibThSpEx*, pp. 39–43; 219–233, (particularly 220 and 224), 278–279; 296–301; also *DeGuiJes*, pp. 539–543; 564.

2. THE EXERCISES
The Introductory Explanations

1. *Anotaciones*: This word means, in Spanish as in English, a jotting or note added by way of commentary or explanation, such as a marginal note. In Ignatius' *Exercises*, however, these notes are explanations which serve as his introductory chapter; hence we turn the word by the more descriptive term "introductory explanations." The Exercises properly so called begin only at [21] below. These introductory explanations explain the nature and purpose of the Exercises ([1]); the procedure in general ([2–3]); their division and duration ([4]); the basic dispositions required in the exercitant ([5]); the director's dealings with the exercitant in his or her most vital experiences ([6–17]); the adaptations of the Exercises to different classes of retreatants ([18–20]).

Explanations 3, 5, 11, 12, 13, 16, and 20 deal with the exercitant's dispositions, and 1, 2, 4, 6–10, 14, 15, 17, 18, and 19 are addressed chiefly to directors (see Iparraguirre in *Obrascompl*, 4th ed. [1982], p. 15).

Originally these twenty sections were probably mere notes which Ignatius jotted down while his experience with the Exercises was growing. In time he gathered them together at the beginning of the *Exercises*, without troubling himself to find a more descriptive title.

2. Inclinations, attachments, tendencies, etc., which are not in conformity with the principles which will be given below in the Foundation ([23]).

3. The good spirits may be God or an angel, the evil spirits are devils. For Ignatius these spirits are always persons, intelligent beings. Discernment of spirits is a means to discernment of the will of God, on which see n. 144 on [336] below. For Ignatius' experiences and reflections from which his teachings on discernment of spirits ([313–336]) evolved, see, *Autobiog*, esp. 8, 19–20, 26.

4. *Mociones*: "Motions" is here Ignatius' technical term, taken from scholasticism, to designate the interior experiences, such as thoughts, impulses, inclinations, urges, moods, consolations, desolations, and the like. For further explanations see nn. 92 on [182] and 131 on [313] below.

5. Ignatius' mention of the purgative and illuminative "life" (*vida*) clearly refers to the classic doctrine of the three ways (*viae*) or stages of growth in the spiritual life. Early Directories too apply that doctrine to the *Exercises*—e.g., González Dávila, and the official *Directory* of 1599, ch. 11, nos. 2, 3; 18, no. 3; 37, no. 1; 39. Ignatius could have learned this doctrine already at Montserrat from Cisneros' *Ejercitatorio*, or from other books during his studies. Only here does he himself mention this doctrine in the *Exercises*.

6. The term *benefice* originally meant a grant of land for life as a reward (*beneficium*) for services. As canon law developed, the term came to imply an ecclesiastical office which prescribed certain spiritual duties or conditions ("spiritualities") for the due discharge of which it awarded regularly recurring revenues ("temporalities"). See *OxDCCh*, p. 156; *NCathEnc* 2:305. The system was obviously subject to abuses of neglecting the spiritual ministration, but Ignatius regarded benefices as such as good, objects about which one should be indifferent, i.e., impartial ([16, 169, 171, 178, 171]).

7. In [18, 19, and 20] Ignatius indicates the chief manners in which the Exercises can be adapted to various classes and circumstances

of people. The principles enshrined in the *Exercises* can be communicated through a great variety of ways and means. Hence many forms of retreats naturally evolved. The ideal, the closed retreat of thirty days is treated in [20]; the "Exercises in Everyday Life," an open retreat near to that ideal, in [19]; and in [18] a retreat either closed or open which aims at whatever is possible in the circumstances.

8. Ignatius' term *pecados mortales* is here translated "capital sins" because it refers to the traditional teaching on seven capital vices, commonly listed (with variations) as pride, anger, avarice, gluttony, lust, envy, and sloth. They are sources (*capita*) from which other sins easily flow. In Ignatius' day (as in ours) they were often called "mortal" or "deadly" sins, although this terminology is rather inaccurate because in concrete instances they may be mortal or venial sin or no sin at all. Ignatius uses *pecados mortales* to mean the capital sins in [18, 238, 244, and 245], and to mean mortal sins which bring eternal damnation in [33, 44, 48, 52, 57, 165, 314, 370], where we translate the phrase by "mortal sins" (see *DalmMan*, p. 200).

9. G. Cusson, *The Spiritual Exercises Made in Everyday Life: A Method and a Biblical Interpretation* (St. Louis, 1989), is a directory which sprang from his extensive experience in the practice of the Exercises according to "Annotation 19." Materials arranged for giving or making such retreats can be found in Joseph A. Tetlow, *Choosing Christ in the World: Directing the Spiritual Exercises according to Annotations Eighteen and Nineteen. A Handbook* (St. Louis, 1989).

THE FIRST WEEK
The Purpose of the Exercises

10. To "overcome oneself" is the "negative" purpose of the Exercises—a preliminary removal of obstacles, such as sin or disordered inclinations to it. This is often a first step indispensable to spiritual progress.

11. In Ignatius' way of thinking, to "order one's life" is to bring its details into accordance with the Principle and Foundation about to be given in [23]. To the previously mentioned negative end he now succinctly adds the genuine, positive, and inspirational aim of the Exercise, eternal salvation. New and enriching aspects of this goal, especially the supernatural aspects taught by Christ, emerge as the exercitant goes through the Exercises, and even subsequently as he or she goes through life in the light of them.

Yet what is the essential end of the Exercises? This topic has been immensely discussed. With some oversimplication to get to the heart of the matter, the chief writers can be divided into two schools, "electionists" (e.g., L. de Grandmaison) and "perfectionists" (e.g., L. Peeters). De Grandmaison maintained in 1921: The end is to prepare a spiritually minded person to make a wise election of a state of life in which he or she can serve God best. The text as it stands is clearly directed to that end. Peeters objected in 1931: The end and culminating point of the Exercises can only be a union with God which is most intimate and total. An answer to these two extremes was written by Joseph de Guibert shortly before his death in 1942 and posthumously published in 1953: Those two ends are complementary, not mutually exclusive. If we consider Ignatius' printed text of 1548 and his process in writing it while winning companions from 1534 onward, the end expressed *in his text* is to facilitate a good election; and that is the supposition which best enables us to interpret the wording of Ignatius' text itself. However, if we consider the uses which he himself made of his text, we see that he gave the exercises to persons whose election was already made (e.g., Xavier, Favre), and that his objective was to lead them to intensive union with God. He found the principles in the text leading to an election to be equally suitable for guiding exercitants to lofty union with God, but he did not trouble himself to state this explicitly by stylistic revisions in the text itself. He left it to directors to adjust the text and its principles flexibly to the personalities and needs of each exercitant. On this discussion, see *DeGuiJes*, pp. 122–132, esp. 126; also, ch. 13, esp. 531–532; on its extent and history, see Cusson, in *BibThSpEx*, pp. 80–93.

12. That is, to avoid coming to a decision through attachments, inclinations, likes or dislikes which are not in accord with the norms for the proper use of creatures in [23].

13. Or, "the other person may be saved" [from error or blame]. The Spanish text is ambiguous and can be translated either way.

To profit from the Exercises, an exercitant must be reasonably open to their content and to the director. A retreatant who is suspicious or hostile and searching for heresy or Illuminism would lack the desirable openness. Ignatius is here asking for fairness. If something is unclear, let the exercitant ask about it. On the historical situation behind this presupposition, see Hervé Coathalem, *Ignatian Insights: A Guide to the Complete Spiritual Exercises* (Taichung [Taiwan], 1971), p. 57.

The Foundation

14. Should the Foundation be considered as a part of the First Week which, Ignatius stated in [4] above, is devoted to the consideration of sins? In answer to this controverted question, yes, for these reasons. In about 1536 at the time of Helyar's retreat, the Foundation seemingly was still among the Introductory Explanations (*anotaciónes*) used to prepare exercitants for the retreat before it began. It was merely recalled by a brief explanation on the morning of the first day, on which the exercise on sin was to begin in the afternoon. But this Foundation contained a vision which focused the exercitant's attention on God's whole plan of creation and salvation as it was evolving in history, and it also presented the vital principle of indifference, the hinge on which the election depends. Hence it was gradually made a part within the retreat itself. In his Dictated Directory Ignatius himself advised keeping the exercitant "on the consideration of the Foundation and on the particular and general examens for three or four days or even more" (*SpEx*MHSJ, p. 791). Thus it began to be divided into points and became a part of the First Week, even though the announced topic of that Week had been the "sins" ([4]). See *BibThSpEx*, pp. 47–51. Furthermore, in the manuscript of *A*, the Autograph text, as also in *P¹*, the First Latin Version, the title *primera semana* is found above [21–22]. By 1556 the Foundation was the first exercise within the retreat itself, and hence with Dalmases (*DalmMan*, p. 55) we place this title immediately before [23]. See *BibThSpEx*, pp. 47–51.

15. *Dios nuestro Señor*, "God our Lord," is Ignatius' oft-recurring expression of deep reverence for God (see n. 15 above on the Introduction). Since he is a Christian writing his Exercises for Christian exercitants in his own culture, he meant the triune God of revelation. He had no reason to prescind from it and operate by natural reason alone like a teacher of philosophy today. Moreover, he often calls Christ "our Creator" and uses "God our Lord" when he is thinking chiefly of Christ (Aldama, *An Introductory Commentary on the Constitutions*, p. 272; J. Solano, "Cristología de las Constituciones," in *Ejercicios-Constituciones: unidad vital* [Bilbao, 1975], pp. 207–208). Ignatius' terseness makes us unable to be certain whether his thought here is directly about the Trinity or Christ, but in either case Christ is included within the phrase "God Our Lord" in [23] (Solano, in *Miscelanea Comillas* 26 [1956], 173). The thought he expressed in the Foundation pertains to the supernatural level of divine revelation and is not con-

fined to the level of reason alone (see M. A. Fiorito, "Cristocentrismo del 'Principio y Fundamento' de San Ignacio," *Ciencia y Fe* 17 [1961]: 3–42). For Ignatius, of course, honor or appropriation of creation to Christ is implicitly given equally to the Father and the Holy Spirit.

Although the Foundation is explicitly Christian, however, it is not exclusively such. Its wording, when taken apart from the context of Christian culture in which it was written, is applicable to the end of humankind as known by reason alone, e.g, by Plato or Aristotle. Hence non-Christians too can with profit apply its truths to themselves in their own way.

16. *Salvar su ánima*, to save one's soul: i.e., to save one's whole self into the eternal life (John 17:3) of the beatific vision (1 Cor. 13:12; 1 John 3:2). *Anima*, a Latinism constantly used by Ignatius instead of *alma*, means the rational soul (*DalmMan*, p. 190). However, very often (as here) Ignatius uses *ánima* to mean the person, the whole self considered as a compound of body and soul. This sense of *anima* occurred in classical Latin (e.g., *Aeneid* xi:24; Horace, *Satires* i, 5, 41), the Latin Vulgate (e.g., Gen. 2:7, Matt. 16:26, 1 Cor. 15:45), and subsequently with great frequency in all the languages of Christian Europe throughout the Middle Ages to and including the present (see, e.g., Blaise, *Dictionnaire des auteurs chrétiens*, s.v. *"anima,"* 4; *Webster's Ninth New Collegiate Dictionary* (1986), s.v. "soul," 3, "a person's total self"). Throughout Christianity this has been the figure of synecdoche by which Christians named the part (soul, *anima*) to express the whole self, the living human being (*homo*). Simultaneously by reciting the creed they were professing their belief in the resurrection of the body. Their outlook was therefore manifestly a Christian dualism or anthropology and not the viewpoint of some Neoplatonists or others who depreciated the body as evil or as "the tomb of the soul." Awareness of this usage is a key necessary for accurate interpretation of virtually all Christian writers on spirituality.

17. "Indifferent": undetermined to one thing or option rather than another; impartial; unbiased; with decision suspended; undecided. It implies interior freedom from disordered inclinations. Variously nuanced by contexts, it is a key technical term of Ignatius' spirituality and very frequent throughout all his writings. In no way does it mean unconcerned or unimportant. To Ignatius' examples of indifference it is often wise to add some which are fully under the control of our free will, such as: whether to become a physician or a banker; whether to

read a book or go to a lecture. Ignatius' own examples are often outside our power to choose.

18. This Principle and Foundation is both the starting point of the Exercises and a premise from which flow conclusions of the greatest importance for the spiritual life. It orients us toward viewing God's plan of salvation as one extensive whole and toward fitting ourselves into our proper role within it as it evolves. It briefly presents God's plan in creating human beings for their spiritual growth and eternal self-fulfillment: their being happy by glorifying him both on earth and in the beatific vision. Thus it sketches the worldview of Christian faith as the background against which everything else in the *Exercises* and in life should be viewed. Further, the official *Directory* of 1599 regards it as "the basis of the whole moral and spiritual edifice" (ch. 12, no. 1). It has long been admired as a compressed summary of the chief principles of Ignatius' spirituality. The principles enunciated here, and also their implications, underlie and govern all his thought not only later in the *Exercises*, especially in the directives for an election ([169–189]) but also in his *Constitutions* (see, e.g., [622,a; also 616, 633]), *Spiritual Diary*, and letters, where they reoccur constantly as occasions for their application arise. Dalmases aptly quotes the great expert Luis de la Palma's *Camino espiritual . . . de los Ejercicios* (1626): "It is called a *principle* because in it are contained all the conclusions which are later explained and specifically expounded; and it is called a *foundation* because it is the support of the whole edifice of the spiritual life" (*DalmMan*, p. 57).

We can with profit elaborate La Palma's metaphor of the "whole edifice of the spiritual life." If we consider Ignatius' spiritual doctrine in the *Exercises* as a Gothic cathedral, this Principle and Foundation comprises four pillars supporting all their thought content, particularly that in the Election and the Rules for Discernment. These pillars are (1) a goal which attracts and inspires an exercitant toward making her or his life meaningful: salvation, the beatific vision, a goal which is objectively coextensive with St. John's eternal life (10:10; 17:3) or St. Paul's "mystery of Christ" (Ephes. 3:4–21); (2), the means to this goal, creatures rightly and wisely used; (3) a vital preliminary attitude: keeping oneself "indifferent," that is, with decision or choice suspended until the true reasons for a wise choice appear; and (4) the norm for choice among the options one faces: that which is likely to result in greater glory or praise to God (which entails one's own greater self-fulfillment and happiness). This result, the praise of God both on earth and in the beatific vision, is Ignatius' supreme end, and therefore the keystone of the arch which all the four pillars support.

Each of these four principles is made more meaningful as the Exercises proceed. For example, the end of human beings, baldly called "salvation" here, is formulated as "to praise God and save one's soul" in [169, 177, 179, 181]; "the praise and glory of God" in [167, 179, 180, 189, 240]; and "to arrive at perfection" in [135]. In all these cases the end about which Ignatius is writing is the beatific vision, the supernatural end of human beings, although in his culture he did not think it necessary to state this adjective when he wrote [23]. But he did state it specifically when he wrote in *Cons* [813] that the objective which the Society seeks is "to aid souls to reach their ultimate and supernatural end." It is practical and wise to ponder this end in the full light of modern biblical theology (see *BibThSpEx*, pp. 47–80, 98, 135, 138–139).

In his *Powers of Imagining: Ignatius de Loyola* (Albany, 1986), pp. 101–103, Professor Antonio T. de Nicolas maintains that *principio* in the Foundation cannot be correctly translated as "principle" but should be turned by "origin," for "origins have nothing to do with cognition and cognitive skills"; that therefore, since English translations other than his own use the word Principle, "they share a cognitive bias absent in the saint" and are "totally wrong." He supports his opinion by his theory on use of imagination in Ignatius, but not by study of the structure and coherence of Ignatius' thought. This writer finds the reasons advanced unconvincing and disagrees with his opinion. It ignores the conclusions which Ignatius continually draws from the Principle and Foundation throughout the *Exercises* (esp., e.g., in the election [169–189]), in the *Constitutions*, and in the Deliberation on Poverty, the close reasoning which Ignatius so carefully reviewed during the eminent affective and mystical experiences recorded in his *Spiritual Diary*. That opinion attributes error not only to the English translations but also to the best versions in French and German, and it sets itself in opposition to the tradition (mentioned above) of Spanish interpreters of the Foundation from La Palma to Dalmases. Close reasoning is characteristic of all Ignatius' writings, and to make the Exercises according to his directions requires a well-balanced union of logical reasoning, imagination, affectivity, and decisions.

The Examinations of Conscience

19. These examinations of conscience ([24–44]) represent instructions which, adjusted to personal needs, were to be given to exercitants early in the retreat. Examinations of conscience had forerunners among the Pythagoreans and Stoics and were practiced in the Christian tradition from early times. Ignatius practiced reflective self-examination to an extraordinary degree (see *DeGuiJes*, pp. 39–40, 66–68). In his *Exercises* he gave the practice two structures and methods which were original and have been widely used ever since. The Particular Examination ([24–31]) is concentrated on a single objective, such as correcting a sin, or one's predominant fault, or a group of nonsinful defects. Thus during the Exercises it can well be focused on the failings or negligences connected with the periods of prayer or the Additional Directives, etc. The General Examination ([32–44]) and its method ([43]) are aimed at self-purification and also at preparation for confession. On the General Examination see *DSpir* 4, cols. 1789–1837; on the Particular Examination, cols. 1838–1849.

20. In Ignatius' day breakfast was very light and was not taken by all. In summer the main meal (*comida*, dinner) was taken at 10:00 A.M. and supper (*cena*) at 6:00 P.M.; in winter at 11:00 and 7:00 (*DalmIgn*, p. 267).

21. The G probably means the first letter of the Italian *giorno*, day. The seven letters "g" indicate the days of the week. To count the faults, dots are entered for each day, on the top line for the morning and on the bottom line for the evening.

22. In the 1500s the ordinary faithful confessed only once a year, but in an extraordinarily detailed manner. Penitents prepared themselves, sometimes for several days, by reading books called "confessionals," which had long lists of sins. Their use entailed a review of the catechism and much moral theology. The accusation of sins was unusually long, went into more details and circumstances than necessary, and was sometimes made in writing. Ignatius' own confession at Montserrat is an example. It was made in writing and lasted three days (*Autobiog*, 17). In [32–44] he gives aids to help exercitants prepare for confession.

23. Cassian made virtually this same observation in his Conference 2 on Discretion of Spirits: "There are three sources of our thoughts. They come from God, the devil, and ourselves" (PL 49, col. 508). However, the source from which Ignatius drew his own statement is unknown.

24. The Latin Vulgate translation adds this clarification: "with evil intention or serious harm to the person's reputation" (*DalmMan*, p. 65).

25. Here too the Vulgate adds: "Among sins of speech could be listed those of ridiculing, insulting, and the like, which the giver of the exercises can develop as he deems necessary" (ibid.).

26. *Conciencia* can mean consciousness as well as conscience. An insightful and widely used article on this exercise is George A. Aschenbrenner, "Consciousness Examen," *Review for Religious* 31 (1972): 13-21.

The Meditations of the First Week

27. Here begin the exercises properly so called of the First Week. This week engages the exercitant in the purification of the soul from sin and inclinations to it. Sin is the attempt to frustrate God's plan of creation which has been pondered in the Principle and Foundation. Ignatius presents a global view of sin, its history, our role in that history, and Christ's role in it (see [53]; also *BibThSpEx*, pp. 136-165). Ignatius starts with the sins of the angels and of our first parents and comes down to the exercitant's own personal sins. Thus he induces the retreatant into viewing his or her sins and future role against that background of God's plan of salvation unfolding in the history of salvation. He or she learns how evil functions in its effort to impede the divine salvific plan, and how to cope with evil in one's own life.

In this first meditation, too, Ignatius explains in detail "meditation," the first of his two chief methods of prayer which he teaches in the *Exercises*. It is discursive mental prayer especially suited to "beginners" (*incipientes*) in the purgative way or stage of spiritual growth, who usually need to reason out principles and form basic convictions. He shows them how to proceed by using their mental powers of memory, intellect, and will. He will similarly teach his second fundamental method, "contemplation" as he uses the term, early in the Second Week in [101-117] below.

28. The preparatory prayer and preludes, each lasting a minute or so at the beginning of a prayer period, are means of recollecting oneself and performing the prayer in a better, reverential manner. Throughout the *Exercises* Ignatius considers them to be of great importance.

29. Intention is the directing of the will to an end. "Actions and operations" here is probably hendiadys, a frequent trait of Ignatius'

style. However, "actions" can be understood as exterior activities, and "operations" as interior (*DalmMan*, p. 69). Taken together these three words amount to "all my physical and mental efforts during this prayer period." Ignatius prescribes this prayer before all the remaining prayer periods.

30. *Composición*, used 13 times in the *Exercises*, means for Ignatius the mental act of putting things together. This act is done by the exercitant in order to put herself or himself into the right disposition for praying. The manner of doing this and the things to be put together vary according to context and often involve use of the imagination. In *SpDiar* [144], after struggling with distractions Ignatius wrote "I composed myself" for Mass. This chance remark has turned out to be a commentary which clearly shows the purpose of his *composición*.

31. *Todo el composito*: The description of human beings as composed of body and soul was commonplace terminology of the scholasticism which Ignatius studied at Paris for three and one-half years, and philosophers and preachers alike often spoke of the "corruptible body." Mark 1:13 states that Christ was in the desert for forty days, tempted by Satan "among the beasts." It is easy to see how these ideas, so commonplace in his day, had a direct influence on Ignatius. In his search for a vivid image to make the abstract thought of this prelude more concrete and by it to stir up the shame and confusion he counsels the retreatant to pray for in the second prelude immediately below, he imaginatively combined the above notions, probably without reflecting where he first learned them. His image was effective for his purpose.

However, it has also led some persons to find in his image a Neoplatonic or other exaggerated dualism which regarded the separate existence of the soul as the ideal and the body as a prison of the soul. If such influences existed, they were far weaker than those from the Bible and scholasticism. On them see W. Ong, "St. Ignatius' Prison Cage and the Existentialist Situation," *The Barbarian Within* (New York, 1954), pp. 242-259. See also n. 16 on [23] above.

32. "What I want and desire": In this Prelude the retreatant focuses on what he or she hopes to obtain in the prayer period, and asks God for what he genuinely wants (see, e. g., [48, 55, 65, etc.]). Throughout the Exercises Ignatius brings in this prayer of desire in the second or third prelude. Genuine desire is of great importance in his spirituality. On it see E. E. Kinerk, "Eliciting Great Desires: Their Place in the Spirituality of the Society of Jesus," *Studies in the Spirituality of Jesuits* 16 (Nov. 1984); also *BibThSpEx*, Index II, p. 375, s.v. "Desire." On the preludes,

see A. Brou, *Ignatian Methods of Prayer* (Milwaukee, 1949), pp. 94–108.

33. On this method of meditation or discursive mental prayer, see Brou, *Ignatian Methods*, pp. 109–122; L. Classen, "The Exercise with the Three Powers of the Soul," in *Ignatius, His Personality and Spiritual Heritage*, ed. F. Wulf (St. Louis, 1977), pp. 237–271; J. de Guibert, *The Theology of the Spiritual Life* (New York, 1953), pp. 195–197; A. Tanquerey, *The Spiritual Life* (Baltimore, 1930), pp. 319–315. Other Exercises which are meditations begin in [45, 55, 65, 136].

34. Ignatius took this statement from Ludolph's *Vita Jesu Christi*, I, ch. 2, no. 3, which states: "Adam was formed in the area of Damascus near Hebron." Hebron is twenty miles south of Jerusalem, in a valley named Damascus. On the theological doctrine expressed through the story of Adam and Eve see John L. McKenzie, *Dictionary of the Bible* (Milwaukee, 1965), s.v. "fall" and "sin," esp. on original sin, pp. 818–821; also, *NDicTh*, s.v. "original sin."

35. The colloquy is another constant element in Ignatian methods of prayer. On it see Brou, *Ignatian Methods*, pp. 119–121. Although it is especially fitting as the conclusion of prayer, it may be made at any time during it. See the *Directory* of 1599, ch. 15, no. 5.

36. In this colloquy the exercitant is led directly to Christ, whose presence is supposed throughout the entire First Week. The exercitant may turn to him at any time. On the Christology of the First Week, see *BibThSpEx*, pp. 161–163; H. Rahner, *Ignatius the Theologian* (New York, 1965), pp. 53–93.

37. The preceding meditation showed the exercitant the whole history of sin, from the angels to some soul lost forever; this second exercise shows to the retreatant her or his own place, actual and potential, in that history. Ignatius did not use "one's own" in his title, but that is clearly what he meant. It is attested by the whole context and by the many times he uses the first person throughout this exercise, e.g., *mis* in the second prelude, *he habitado* in [56], *yo* and *me* in [58].

38. *Proceso*, literally, a trial in court or its record. Ignatius' figure is that of an arraignment in a law court, when the list of charges against the accused is read. He further develops this figure in [74] below.

39. The descriptions given here and in [63] make clear that the repetitions are not a mere reviewing of the preceding meditation or contemplation, but rather an affective assimilation, a deepening personalization of one's previous interior experiences.

40. *Mundo.* Three meanings of world occur in the *Exercises*: (1) the inhabited earth; (2) all human beings; (3) any person or thing hindering one's advance to God, as here in [63] (*DalmMan*, p. 201).

41. These three petitions are a résumé of the fruit of the meditation, now reviewed in intimate conversations with Mary, Jesus, and the Father.

42. The prayer Soul of Christ (*Anima Christi*), found in a manuscript of about 1370, was widely known in the sixteenth century and Ignatius presupposes its text as known. Its author is unknown. In missals it has long been printed in the thanksgiving after Communion, until recently with the title "The Prayer of St. Ignatius." This description probably arose because he popularized the prayer through his *Exercises* (*DSpir* 1, cols. 670–671).

43. To [71] the Latin Vulgate translation adds: "If the director thinks it expedient for the exercitant's spiritual profit, other meditations can be added here, for example, on death, other penalties of sin, judgment, and the like, one should not think them forbidden, even though they are not listed here." To give them has been customary in and since Ignatius' day, especially after the development of retreats preached to groups. Their use is not equally frequent today.

44. *Adiciones,* literally "Additions." To bring out what they clearly are in this context, we translate this vague term by "additional directives." They inculcate practices, an environment, and a mental attitude to enable the exercitant to keep his or her attention focused undistractedly on the effort to commune intimately with God and to find what is being sought. However, they are means rather than ends and should be varied and adapted to circumstances and personalities.

45. This is another key principle of greatest importance in all Ignatian methods of prayer. On it see also [2, 12, 18, 209]; Coathalem, pp. 120–121; and esp. W. Longridge, *The Spiritual Exercises . . . with a Commentary* (London, 1919), pp. 71–72. 258–271. Through its prudent application any portion of an Ignatian prayer period may, with God's grace, lead to increasingly simplified prayer. For example, the satisfying pause in a contemplation (according to Ignatius' meaning in [101–109]) may, in the terminology explained on p. 67 above, become the gateway into acquired contemplation and even into infused contemplation if God should grant it. All of Ignatius' statements on the repetitions and application of the senses are relevant here, as also his letters of Sept. 20, 1548, to Borgia (*LettersIgn*, pp. 180–181), and of

Sept. 11, 1536, to Teresa Rejadell (ibid., p. 24). The psychological wellspring motivating use of this key principle is genuine desire, on which see n. 32 on [48] above.

46. *Partes inferiores*: E.g., the sensory appetites. In scholastic terminology, the one soul has three powers: intellective, sensitive, and vegetative. The "inferior parts" of the soul are those faculties or powers in regard to which the soul depends directly on the bodily senses for their operation. See St. Thomas, *ST* 3, 14, 1; 46, 7; also *DalmMan*, p. 204; and n. 54 on *sensualidad* in [97] below. Christ in his passion experienced pain in the "inferior parts" or faculties of his human soul. The "higher parts" or faculties are the intellect and will.

THE SECOND WEEK
The King

47. In the Second Week the exercitant will engage in exercises characteristic of the illuminative way or stage of spiritual development, especially by contemplating Christ, the Divine Light who has come into the world. Ignatius' introduction to all the remaining weeks is his classic contemplation on "The Kingdom" (an apt, descriptive, and frequent abbreviation of his own title, used already in the *Directory* of 1599, ch. 19, no. 1). This exercise presents a bird's-eye view of the Savior and his mission as they will be contemplated in detail through the remainder of the Exercises. It presents Christ as the realization of the ideal of the Principle and Foundation and is often called a Second Foundation for the rest of the *Exercises* (*Directory*, ibid.), to which it gives an explicit Christological orientation. Its aim is to stir up enthusiasm and desire to follow Christ in love and to accept his invitation to share in his saving mission. The thrust of this exercise toward enthusiastic generosity becomes especially clear in the suggested offering to which it leads: "Eternal Lord, I offer myself to labor with you in your mission, no matter what the cost."

48. This is an echo of Matt. 9:35 and 10:5. The word *castles* is an anachronism. Those which Ignatius saw were built by the crusaders. However, Christ did see Herod's grandiose constructions.

49. This parable ([32–34]) is merely an aid to the reality in the Second Part and should be meditated with relative brevity. There have been many interpretations of it and many comparisons with other leaders. Cusson aptly views the parable as a résumé of Ignatius' own experience with its fantasies and dreams. Before his conversion he

eagerly pursued worldly glory by serving dukes and Charles V, but he transferred his enthusiastic loyalty to the Eternal King (*BibThSpEx*, pp. 180–181). Similarly, an exercitant can take his or her past life with its dreams and fantasies and think of dedicating them to Christ by answering his call.

50. This meditation has a coloring of crusader mentality which is easily seen in the parable. On crusade spirituality in Ignatius, see Hans Wolter in *Ignatius, His Personality*, ed. Wulf, pp. 97–134.

51. This announced parallel is not fully carried out. In Part I, the parable, we have (1) the king, (2) his call, and (3) the response. In the more important application in Part II, the corresponding points are: (1) the King *and* his call, (2) the first response of the wholeheartedly dutiful, and (3) a second response which includes the first and raises it to greater heights: that of those eagerly generous to give distinguished service. As the second prelude makes clear, the chief focus of this contemplation is on these two degrees of generosity in the responses to Christ's call. The states of life are not explicitly treated until [135], although they are foreshadowed along the way, as can be seen in the offering in [98].

52. This is an invitation from Christ to accept a role with himself in his saving mission, the spreading of his Kingdom—which in its concrete reality is exercised through his Church, his Kingdom, and his Mystical Body (1 Cor. 12:11–31; Ephes. 1:23; Col. 1:18). See *BibTh-SpEx*, pp. 205–213. Especially in Matthew's Gospel, the "reign of God" (*regnum*) is shown to subsist in an organized society, *ekklesia* (16:18, 18:17), whose nature is further described by parables (13:24–30, 36–43, 47–50). See McKenzie, *Dictionary of the Bible*, s.v. "kingdom," p. 480, and s.v. "Matthew," p. 556.

53. This is an example of the Ignatian principle of counterattack (*agere contra*), inculcated also in [13, 97, 325, 350, 351]. On it, see Jules Toner, *A Commentary on St. Ignatius' Rules for the Discernment of Spirits* (St. Louis, 1982), pp. 160–162; 198–199.

54. *Sensualidad* is a term of scholasticism, meaning the appetitive faculty of the sensitive part of the soul, i.e., the soul as operating through the senses (see n. 46 on [87]). Aquinas states that "the motion of sensuality is a certain inclination of the bodily senses, since we desire things which are apprehended through the bodily senses" (*ST* 1, 81, 1, ad 1). Hence by *sensualidad* Ignatius means basically the sense appetites, and in this context one's sensitivities or sensibilities. Though the term is sometimes applied to excess in food, drink, or sex, it does not of itself

imply excess. It easily comes to mean the likes and dislikes of our human nature, which are often emotional. In [87] and here in [97] it refers to our human nature with its emotions, e.g., attachments, longings, inclinations, etc. They may be rightly ordered in accordance with the Principle and Foundation, or they may be ill-ordered by being opposed to greater good or by being sinful. For many a retreatant the sensitivities will be repugnances.

55. Actual poverty is the lack of material goods; spiritual poverty is detachment from them whether one has them or not. It also includes our emptiness before God and need of him for spiritual progress. For details, see n. 65 on [146] below. To reason them out is more appropriate there in the discursive meditation rather than in the colloquy here.

The Contemplations

56. A slavishly literal translation, "The First Day *and* First Contemplation," is misleading and misses what Ignatius really means. The first day also includes the Nativity in [110, 118, 120, 121].

In this and the following exercise on the Nativity Ignatius gives his most detailed explanation of "contemplation" as he uses this term in the *Exercises*. It is his second basic method of mental prayer and consists in attending to the persons, their words, and their actions, largely by use of the imagination. In general, contemplation is viewing or gazing and it stimulates reflections and emotions. Since this method leads to reflections it can be and often is discursive mental prayer. Ordinarily, however, it is an easier and more affective kind of prayer, especially suitable for the contemplation of scenes from the Gospels. On it see Brou, *Ignatian Methods*, pp. 130–145; *DeGuiJes*, pp. 133–137, 548, 607; Tanquerey, *The Spiritual Life*, no. 991, pp. 467–468; Longridge, pp. 257–262. Contemplation in this sense prepares for but is somewhat different from what many writers on ascetical or mystical theology term "acquired contemplation" or "infused contemplation." See the General Introduction above, pp. 61–63.

57. After viewing the fall of Adam and his descendants in the First Week, Ignatius here moves into the next great stage in the history of salvation: the Incarnation, Nativity, and subsequent hidden life.

At this point it is important for those reading or studying the *Exercises* to attend to the structure which he prescribed for the exercises performed within the remainder of the Second Week. His text itself, though applicable to persons in any state, in its structure directly envisages the ideal case of a generous exercitant who is deliberating about the choice of a state of life. For such a one the coming exercises will be divided into three time periods, all of them preparatory to the election or decision likely to come in the third. The first period, with five contemplations a day, will consist of three days devoted to contemplations on the Incarnation and hidden life, to bring the exercitant to growing affective attachment to Christ in his poverty and humility. The second period will consist of one day, the fourth. It starts with the brief Introduction to the Consideration of States of Life ([135]), followed by the discursive and other mental prayer in the Two Standards and Three Classes of Persons ([135–157]). These meditations aim to make sure of the attitude proper for a sound election, especially the indifference in case it has been weakened by subtle temptations or self-deceit. The third group consists of days 5 to 8 or up to day 12, devoted to contemplation on the life of Christ and simultaneous considerations on the election. See n. 76 below on [158].

58. *Historia*: In the 1500s this word meant "a narration and exposition of past events" to which an author sometimes added his own explanations or comments (Covarrubias, *Tesoro* [1611], p. 692). For Ignatius it means "the authentic basis" of the history ([2]), and often it is the preliminary explanation of a topic—given here in [102] by use of the imagination. His usage of the word is nuanced according to contexts.

59. The application of the senses is another method of mental prayer. It has a long previous history but is described here for the first time in the *Exercises*. In it there is less reasoning and drawing of conclusions, and a more restful manner of absorbing in an affective and more passive way the fruit of the previous contemplations of the day. It is "not discursive, but merely rests in the sensible qualities of things, such as the sights, sounds, and the like, and finds in them enjoyment, delight, and spiritual profit" (*Directory* of 1599, ch. 20, no. 3). Not all exercitants find themselves suited to it, but many, coming from the previous contemplations with warm devotion, find their love nourished by these sensible objects (ibid., no. 4). This method is less fatiguing than meditation or contemplation, and is therefore done in the evening when the exercitant is presumably tired. In his letter of Sept. 11, 1536, to Teresa Rejadell Ignatius makes observations applicable here (*Letters-Ign*, p. 24).

In points 1 and 2 Ignatius writes of the imaginative senses, sight and hearing, not exclusively but as joined to the intellect and will. In point 3 he passes on to the "spiritual senses," the intellect and will as functioning especially through their intuitive activities by which they discover features roughly similar to those perceived by the imaginative senses. On this topic see Coathalem, pp. 153–158; *DeGuiJes*, p. 246; Brou, *Ignatian Methods*, pp. 146–167; H. Rahner, *Ignatius the Theologian* (New York, 1968), pp. 181–213; *DSpir* I, cols. 810–828; other references in *Obrascompl*, p. 236.

60. This brief introduction is the transition to the second period of the Second Week, ordinarily occurring on its fourth day. Attention is now turned to the election expected to come some days later, probably near the end of the third period (days 5 to 8, but perhaps up to day 12 [161]). During those deliberations the exercitant is likely to experience subtle temptations, both from the devil with his deceits and from his or her own human weakness, likes, dislikes, or self-deceit. Here much reasoning becomes necessary. To help the retreatant to the right dispositions for making a sound choice of a state of life or for serious pursuit of spiritual progress in whatever state one will be in, on day 4 Ignatius presents two exercises consisting of discursive mental prayer: the Two Standards ([136]) and the Three Classes of Persons ([149]).

61. The states of life have been divided in many ways. In [134 and 135] Ignatius uses only two states, the observance of the commandments and of evangelical perfection, life in the world and religious life. That division, used by Christ with the rich young man (Mark 1:17–27), was common almost till the present time and was practical for the ideal retreatant whom Ignatius' text envisaged. In modern times, however, many have found those two categories unsatisfactory, and a gradually growing opinion found expression in Vatican Council II: "All Christians in any state or walk of life are called to the fullness of Christian life and to the perfection of love" (On the Church, no. 40). This more comprehensive teaching updates Ignatius' views but does not conflict with them. In fact, he equivalently states the new doctrine at the end of [135], "to come to perfection in whatsoever state of life God may grant us to elect." One practical division for retreatants deliberating about a state of life today is: the states of 1, marriage; 2, single persons in the world; 3, diocesan priesthood; 4, religious life as a priest, brother, or sister.

The Two Standards

62. *Banderas*, "standards" in the sense of flags or banners around which the followers of the respective leaders rally. This justly famous meditation, to which Ignatius attached great importance, is very imaginatively presented. It seems to be original with Ignatius, though the theme of opposition between the forces of good and evil is frequent throughout the centuries. St. Paul counseled: "Put on the armor of God so that you may be able to stand firm against the tactics of the devil. For our struggle is not with flesh and blood but with the principalities, . . . the evil spirits in the heavens" (Ephes. 6:11). Augustine viewed history as a struggle between the City of God, the sum total of human beings and angels who are living according to God's directing laws, and the City of This World, the sum total of human beings and angels who live according to their own desires rather than his. In the Lives of the Saints which Ignatius read at Loyola in 1521, Jacobus de Voragine wrote a paragraph (quoted above on p. 18 describing Augustine's City of God: "He also treats of the two cities, Jerusalem and Babylon, and their kings," Christ and the devil. Jacobus' paragraph and Ignatius' Two Standards have much the same tenor of thought. It is at least possible that Ignatius read that paragraph and found in it the germ of his Two Standards. As we saw above (ibid.), both the Kingdom and the Two Standards were part of the nucleus of the primitive *Exercises*.

63. The aim of this meditation, as the third prelude clearly shows, is to study the tactics of the two leaders, Christ and Lucifer.

64. Pride, the capital "sin," is a source of myriad other offenses (see note 8 on [18] above). These steps in [146] are examples of the devil's tactics, particularly suited for tempting one deliberating about self-dedication to God. Satan also has innumerable other tactics, and each exercitant does well to think of those which might be used against himself or herself. With obvious changes the same holds true of the tactics of Christ in [146] below.

65. *Pobreza actual*, actual poverty, is that really existing, and not merely potential (*DalmMan*, pp. 189, 202)—the actual lack of material goods. *Pobreza spiritual*, spiritual poverty, is that of the "poor in spirit" of the beatitude (Matt. 5:3). Des Freux's Latin translation of [98] in the Vulgate, "with poverty of spirit as well as of things" (*cum paupertate tum spiritus tum rerum*), makes clear Ignatius' meaning in both these terms, so important for his spirituality.

In Old and New Testament times the vast majority of people were poor and had a very low standard of living. Only a few were rich and there was virtually no middle class. Christ wanted his followers to have poverty of spirit, that is, interior detachment from material goods, whether they possessed them or not, so that they might have heavenly riches (Matt. 6:19-21; 13:22). He also spoke of the religious value of the actual poverty of the devout poor and taught them how to view it, e.g., in his discourse on Providence (Matt. 6:25-33). Such actual poverty (today termed also real, material, or effective) can be a sign and means of interior detachment when it is inspired by trust in God. What matters above all, Christ concludes, is to seek to cooperate with God's plan of salvation: "Seek first the kingdom of God and his righteousness, and all these things will be given you besides" (Matt. 6:33). (See Léon-Dufour, *Dictionary of Biblical Theology*, p. 437).

The term actual poverty can also mean the vowed poverty of a religious institute. In [147] Des Freux translates *pobreza actual* by "divestment of one's goods" (*in rerum expoliatione*); and in [157] by "the renouncing of one's goods" (*in rerum abdicatione*), a canonical term for vowed poverty. Hence for one deliberating about entering religious life there is in [146 and 147] at least a hint or connotation of canonical poverty. Ignatius left it to the exercitant to take whichever meaning was more useful to him or her at the time.

To learn the full profound scope of what poverty means for Ignatius, however, we must go beyond the Exercises and consider his use of *pobreza* in his *Constitutions*, letters, and other writings. Then we see it as the profoundly humble attitude of a person who "has emptied his or her self of the love of earthly things" and "filled that self with God and his gifts" (*EppIgn* I:575, cited in Iparraguirre, *Vocabulario de Ejercicios Espirituales: Ensayo de Hermenéutica Ignaciana*, p. 183). Iparraguirre treats this at length, largely by citations from Ignatius (ibid., pp. 184-190). Cusson writes of the "absolute poverty of our spiritual condition" (*BibThSpEx*, p. 215; see also the Index, s.v. "Poverty"). To sum up, in its profound sense for Ignatius, poverty is our total emptiness before God and need of him for any and all spiritual progress.

66. Humility is the opposite of pride, hence characteristic of Christ as the opposite of Satan. Further, humility is a first step toward any and all virtues. Ignatius will soon develop this traditional teaching further in his three ways of being humble ([165-168]).

The Three Classes of Persons

67. This meditation is about three classes or groups of persons, all of whom are endeavoring to discard an affection for something which, though legitimate, is an obstacle to a greater good and therefore disordered. The classes are 1, the postponers; 2, the compromisers; and 3, the wholeheartedly indifferent, those open to whatever option God will in time show to be better. The aim of the meditation is to bring the exercitant to firm up the indifference acquired in the Foundation and, aided by this indifference, to become disposed to know and embrace whatever will be discovered to be more to God's glory, as the title and second prelude explicitly indicate. This is the disposition necessary for a sound election which is expected to come, not in this meditation, but a few days later, i.e., during or after the deliberations treated in [169–189].

Unfortunately, however, Ignatius' Spanish text of this meditation, overly terse and using a puzzling vocabulary, is a prime example of his unpolished style. It has been a source of disagreement among linguists and a cross to translators who time after time must choose one of several possible meanings. Moreover, there is great danger that a retreatant will be distracted by devoting more time and energy in efforts to figure out precisely what Ignatius means than in grasping and applying the spiritual principles presented in this meditation. These principles of indifference and choice are reasonably clear, being already known from the Foundation ([23]). Our translation hopes at least to minimize this unfortunate danger.

68. The first such difficulty occurs already in [149], which serves as the title in the Autograph text, *A*. It has *Tres binarios de hombres*, which means literally "Three binaries of persons," i.e., "three pairs"; and in [153] it has *primo binario*, "the first pair." What did Ignatius really mean by *binario* here? For clues we turn to the early translations. In the Latin version used in Paris in the 1530s, the translator (probably Ignatius himself) also has in the title, [149], "meditation on the three pairs of persons" (*meditatio trium binariorum hominum*) and in the first point, [153], "the first pair" (*primus binarius*). In the Latin Vulgate of 1548, translated under Ignatius' eyes and approved by his continual use, Des Freux translated *binario* in the title by the collective noun *classis*: "on the three classes of persons, that is, how they differ" (*de tribus hominum classibus seu differentiis*). In the points [153–155] he uses "the first class" (*prima classis*). All this evidence shows that Ignatius' thought

is manifestly about groups of persons, each of whom has the characteristics common to its class or group and is typical of it.

Here we should take into account Ignatius' environmental background at the University of Paris. In the fifteenth and sixteenth centuries the moralists, in solving their cases of conscience, used fictitious typical persons and called them a "pair" (*binarius*, Spanish *binario*); e.g., Titius and Bertha in a marriage case, or Titius and Caius in one about justice (*DalmMan*, p. 191). The Spanish *binario* or the Latin *binarius* might mean one typical person (e.g., Titius) or a pair of them (e.g., Titius and Bertha). In either case Ignatius was writing here about persons each of whom is typical of a class or category. Just as moralists set up their fictitious cases of conscience to exemplify the application of their principles, so is Ignatius in this meditation setting up a case in spirituality to exemplify his spiritual principles. Against this background, we translate *binarios* in [149] as "classes of persons," and in [153] as "persons typical of the first class."

When Ignatius is writing about the exercitant in the second and third preludes and in the note after the meditation, he uses the first person: "that I may desire and know" ([151]), "I will ask for the grace" ([152]), "when we feel an inclination against actual poverty" ([157]). However, even within the same sentence in [157] he changes the first personal pronouns from plural to singular, "we" to "him or her" (*nosotros* to *le*). But when he is writing about the typical persons in the points ([153–155]), he uses the third person (*el primo binario, primus binarius*), probably because the exercitant can more easily reason objectively about some person than oneself. More probably, this translator thinks, by *binario* Ignatius meant one person typical of the rest in the group. Gueydan and his team of experts also interpret *binario* as singular. In [149] he translates the title by "*méditation des trois hommes*," and in [153] *el primer binario* by "*le premier homme*." A *binario* means a person typical of a class. In English, however, to translate *binario* in the singular collides, especially in the pronoun-laden third point, with the lack in English of a pronoun of common gender in the third person. We think that by changing person to persons we can remain faithful to Ignatius' thought and also make clear the spiritual principles he wishes to present in this meditation.

69. *Historia*: Here the history is an exposition which sets up the case about the typical persons. See n. 58 on [102] above.

70. I.e., although it is licit to keep the money, the motive for retaining it is mingled with an attachment or inclination prompted by

self-love rather than the love of God. Therefore this attachment is not yet ordered according to the principles of indifference and choice contained in the Foundation ([23]). This lack of indifference, though not sinful, is a danger or impediment to a greater good.

71. "What is better" (in [149]), "more pleasing to his Divine Goodness" (in [151]), "what is more to the glory of his Divine Majesty and the salvation of my soul" here in ([152]), and "to serve God our Lord better" in ([155]) are all variant expressions equivalent to Ignatius' norm of choice in the Foundation ([23]), "what is more conducive to the end for which we are created." Similar variations of that principle and norm will occur throughout his treatment of the election below in [170–189].

72. *Afecto*: affection or attachment. In [153, 154, and 157] it means also an inclination or propensity (*DalmMan*, p. 189) and could be so translated. Gueydan, *Exercices*, pp. 97–98, translates it by the synonym *"inclination."*

73. Notice the future tense. Ignatius is preparing the retreatant's dispositions for the coming election, for which the deliberations will take place from day five onward. He or she is not expected to conclude the election in this meditation. Notice also that this person is not depending on human willpower alone; there is question of the mysterious interplay of human freedom and divine grace.

74. *In afecto*, in affection or desire: I.e., one is, on one's own part, disposed or willing to relinquish the affection or attachment (*DalmMan*, p. 103).

75. Notice that persons of this third class are perfect examples of the indifference of the Foundation. That, too, is the grace begged in the third prelude ([152]): "to choose what is more to the glory of God."

The Third Period of the Second Week

76. Here on day 5 the third period of the Second Week begins and runs flexibly through days 5 to 7 or up to day 12 (see n. 57 on [101] above). During this period there will be two parallel and interacting series of exercises: (1) contemplations on the public life of Christ, merely mentioned in [161–164] but with their details presented in [273–287]; and (2) considerations on the directives and methods of making an election ([169–189]). Early in the period the director will explain the Three Ways of Being Humble ([165–168]), and more gradually the principles and methods for making a sound election ([169–

189]). Thus the affective spirit of the contemplations and the colloquies on the Three Ways will provide the atmosphere for the deliberations about the election.

77. Notice that although there are four or five prayer periods per day, on days 5 to 7 or up to day 12 Ignatius assigns for each day only one Gospel topic—probably to avoid too great a multiplicity of thoughts while the exercitant is deliberating about the election.

Three Ways of Being Humble

78. *Maneras*, manners or ways, could be translated also as kinds, or modes, or degrees, or species, as will be explained just below. Ignatius' concept of the Three Ways of Being Humble is an important characteristic of his spirituality. He presents it, not in the form of a meditation or contemplation, but as a consideration which is to pervade the exercises, and also the time between them, on all the coming days devoted to election. His aim is to bring the exercitant to great openness to God and to a loving desire to be as like to Christ as possible. He also wants to induce the retreatant to review the principles of the Foundation from the new viewpoint of her or his love for God which has been growing through the contemplations. Here too, as in the Three Classes above, his severely terse style and his terminology have led to interpretations of his doctrine too numerous to be given in detail. A glance at the historical background of the topic and the terms he and his associates used in discussing it is a great help toward discovery of his genuine meaning.

St. Benedict in his *Rule* explained humility as the opposite of pride (*RB 1980: The Rule of St. Benedict in Latin and English with Notes*, ed T. Fry [Collegeville, 1981], pp. 191–201; ch. 7:1, 2). To reach the summit of humility a monk, knowing himself to be lowly, must climb Jacob's ladder and by twelve steps (*gradus*) arrive at the top, step twelve, by which he attains to perfect *love* of God (ibid., 67). St. Bernard praised this teaching, wrote his own book on *The Steps of Humility*, and in his Sermon 26 (PL 183, col. 610) observed that humility consists in subjection of our will to that of God. St. Thomas Aquinas too praised Benedict's doctrine, but remarked that the degrees (*gradus*) of humility are variously enumerated by different authors, some having three (*ST* 2-2, 161, 6). For Thomas too humility consists in the subjection of the person to God (ibid., 162, 5). Ignatius is clearly writing in this same tradition of thought and terminology, but we do not know the immediate sources from which he derived his terse treatment here in [165–168], seemingly his own formulation for his own purposes.

In the Autograph text, *A*, Ignatius used in [164] *tres maneras de humildad*, "three kinds" or "manners" of humility, or "three ways of being humble." The Latin version used in Paris in 1534 calls them *tres species humilitatis*, "three species of humility," and the Vulgate of 1548 *tres modos*, "kinds" or "sorts" of humility. Another interpretative key of great value comes to us from Pedro Ortiz, the doctor of Scripture and ambassador to the papal court who in 1538 made the Exercises for forty days under Ignatius' personal direction at Monte Cassino. In his notes, which no doubt reflect his conversations with Ignatius about the topic, he terms them degrees: "Three kinds and degrees *of love* of God and desire to obey and imitate and serve His Divine Majesty" (tres maneras y grados *de amor* de Dios y deseos de obedecer y imitar y servir a su Divina Majestad) (quoted in *Obrascompl*, p. 243; *BibThSpEx*, pp. 264–265; emphasis added).

All this put together indicates clearly that Ignatius is dealing successively with *three ways or manners of being lovingly humble*. They can be accurately called kinds, or modes, or species, or degrees. Particularly his third degree, like Benedict's twelfth step, is a humility permeated with great love, an *amorosa humildad*. Ignatius' first and second degrees are concerned with obedience to God's laws. The third degree moves beyond the law to love. (A climactic importance of this loving humility in Ignatius' own life will appear in his *Spiritual Diary* [154–490]. See Introduction to the *Diary* above, pp. 232–234, and *SpDiar*, 178–182.)

79. I.e., on each day throughout the remaining days of the Second Week. This protracted pondering will tend to put the retreatant's heart into the indifference which was intellectually perceived in the Foundation and Three Classes, and to keep him or her from shrinking back if he comes face to face with a choice of something for which repugnance is felt. The love for Christ will be so strong that it will outweigh the repugnance (*Obrascompl*, p. 243).

80. A person whose attitude is that of the second way of being humble has the indifference of the Foundation and is speaking the language of right reasoning.

81. A person whose attitude is that of the third way of being humble has indifference and is speaking the language of love. His or her attitude is: "I love Christ and want to be as like to him as possible, no matter

what the cost." This too is what she or he has been praying for in the third preludes of the contemplations on the mysteries of Christ, e.g., in [104, 113]. Lovers are willing and sometimes even desire to labor or suffer for the beloved, because by such labor or suffering they manifest their love, or increase it, or prove it. They choose the suffering, not as if it were a good or end in itself, but as a means to a higher good. See also note 15 on *Cons* [101].

The Election

82. *Elección*: The English word *election*, in its basic meaning of an act or process of electing, choosing, or selecting (*Webster's New International Dictionary*, unabridged, [1976]), accurately translates Ignatius' Spanish term. Among its synonyms, "election implies an end or purpose which requires exercise of judgment" (*Webster's Ninth Collegiate Dictionary* [1986], p. 692). The synonyms "choice" or "selection" could also be used here, but the term "election" so permeates all the literature on Ignatian spirituality from his day till now that we think it better to retain this traditional term.

83. Ignatius' characteristic insistence on clarity about ends and means is prominent in this section and clearly reminds a retreatant of the Foundation ([23]). Clarity about the end is the indispensable hinge on which a sound election turns.

84. This word *consideration* is taken from text P^1. P^2 uses "Note," and V "Introduction." A has nothing. The deliberations envisaged in [170–178] are expected to take place outside the prayer periods but also to be carried into them.

85. Although the main structure of Ignatius' text chiefly concerns a person deliberating about election of a state of life (see *DeGuiJes*, p. 126), here in [170] (as also in [178 and 189] below) he broadens the horizon of his text itself and states that the principles for an election may be applied to anything important to the spiritual life and not sinful. As Polanco wrote, "it may be made about a state of life or any other matters" (*SpEx*MHSJ, p. 30; quoted in *BibThSpEx*, p. 90).

86. The three favorable "Times" are occasions of spiritual experiences. The call mentioned in the First Time, precisely as it is described here, is rare in practice, but experiences more or less similar to it do occur and bring to a person a great peace of soul along with a sense of God's presence and illumination.

87. In the Second Time the retreatant reflects on the "motions" experienced in his or her soul and tries to learn, by applying the rules for the discernment of spirits ([313–336]) and perhaps from counsel of a director, which motions come from God, or a good angel, or an evil spirit. One may be stirred by strong experiences of consolation or desolation which manifest the trend of God's call, but there is some danger of illusion or self-deception; hence the need of discernment. Furthermore, in these experiences the will often precedes the intellect. Consequently it is prudent to supplement it by the reasoning in the third time, when the intellect is operating in tranquility under the influence of ordinary grace. On the three times, see Coathalem, pp. 187–190; also, the *Directory*, chs. 26 and 27. The deliberations for the election are ordinarily carried on outside the prayer periods, but also within them where they are made the object of prayer and colloquies. Hence the director should take care not to overburden the retreatant engaged in an election with too many prayer periods (see *Directory*, ch. 31, no. 2).

88. In this third time the exercitant considers the pros and cons which the question has in regard to attainment of her or his end, the greater service of God. Ordinarily the role of the will and affections is more predominant in the second time, and the intellect in the third time. The two procedures supplement each other. Ignatius in his own practice combined the activities of the second and third times, as his *Spiritual Diary* abundantly shows. See also *DeGuiJes*, Index, s.v. "Election," p. 644.

89. In the Foundation ([23]), Ignatius stated "I must *make* myself indifferent," i.e., acquire indifference; but here he writes "I must *find* myself indifferent," i.e., ask "Have I retained the indifference I established in the Foundation and Three Classes?"

90. A prime example of Ignatius' own use of this procedure is found in his Deliberation on Poverty (above, pp. 222–226). By putting the pros and cons on paper a person gains clarity of formulation and readier perception of the cumulative weight of each group.

91. *Deliberación* is here used by Ignatius in the sense of *determinación*, conclusion (*DalmMan*, p. 193). The Vulgate translates this passage by "conclude the election" (*electionem concludere*).

92. *Moción racional*: Here in [182], as also in [316 and 317], *moción* means a change in the soul arising from its own intellectual activity; and in the contrasting *moción sensual* it means an experience in the soul arising from sensitive human nature (*DalmMan*, pp. 200, 204). This meaning of *moción* should be carefully distinguished from its other

meaning in [227, 229, 330]: an experience in the soul caused by God, an angel, or a devil (see also n. 131 on [313] below).

93. The Second Method calls the affections and imagination into play more than the first, in which the stress is on reasoning.

94. *Forma y medida*: Our translation interprets *forma* here as a manner of doing something, hence, a procedure; and *medida* (basically "a measuring rod") as a norm. In the *Exercises*, *forma* sometimes means the scholastic "form" as distinct from "matter," and at other times "a manner of proceeding," a method, or a means. Both *forma* and *medida* have many meanings, and translators have understood them differently in many instances. See Gueydan, *Exercices*, pp. 82 and 143; also nn. 115 and 117 on [238] below.

95. The suggestions and spirit of this section are especially applicable to those who make annual retreats and aim at spiritual renewal rather than an election of a state of life or another matter of similar importance.

96. To understand this terse directive, stated in a somber negative manner, we must view it against the background from which it springs: Ignatius' desire to bring as much glory and service to God as possible. Rightly ordered self-love, self-will, and self-interest are good qualities, gifts of God which are often obligatory. Hence we should have, recognize, and esteem these gifts, since humility should be based on truth. However, they tend to excess and hence must be continually reexamined and readjusted according to the principles of the Foundation; else they lead to sin or at least hinder greater good. By now a generous retreatant will want to bring God as much glory as possible, and the divestment advised is a means to that end and an attack on the excess. It is a positive procedure.

THE THIRD WEEK

97. In the view of many commentators, after the election or reformation of life has been concluded, the purpose of the last two weeks is to confirm the exercitant by contemplation of Christ's sufferings in the Third Week and his joy in the Fourth (see, e.g., the *Directory* of 1599, ch. 35, no. 1). Other writers from the time of La Palma (1611) onward find this true but incomplete. Hitherto Ignatius has had the exercitant contemplating God's plan of salvation unfolding in history through the Incarnation, Nativity, and public life. That plan reaches its high point

on earth in Christ's redemptive death and Resurrection, and the aim of the last two weeks is the exercitant's profound and intimate association with Christ as he goes through suffering and death into the joy and glory of the risen life (Rom. 6:3–11; Col. 3:1, 2). In this interpretation the Third and Fourth Weeks pick up and develop Christ's call in the Kingdom ([95]): The disciple "must labor with me, so that through following me in the pain he or she may follow me also in the glory." The retreatant's inspiring task is participation in the whole of the paschal mystery, as described by Vatican Council II: "the work of Christ our Lord in redeeming mankind and giving perfect glory to God. He achieved this task principally by the paschal mystery of his blessed passion, resurrection from the dead, and glorious ascension" ("On the Liturgy," nos. 5, 6). For more on this view see, e.g., Coathalem, pp. 194–197, 209–212; and esp. Cusson, *BibThSpEx*, pp. 219–222, 233–235, 278–279, 287–292. Ignatius did not use the term *paschal mystery*, but the reality it expresses is manifestly the very substance of what he proposes for contemplation in the Third and Fourth Weeks.

98. Points 4, 5, and 6 are not necessarily successive new points, but rather viewpoints which can be brought into play on any of the contemplations previously indicated in points 1, 2, and 3.

For some personalities, to spend two full weeks merely contemplating the persons, their words, and actions begets fatigue and desolation. One important solution to this problem, to which these points 4, 5, and 6 ([196–198 and 223–224 below]) open the way, is to go through the Passion in empathy with Christ not only in regard to its physical activities but also in connection with their significance in God's redemptive plan. That plan is the preeminent message by which the exercitant should be guided during the Exercises; it shines through all the single events suggested for contemplation, and Ignatius wants the retreatant prayerfully to penetrate it as deeply as possible. We today, profiting by modern discoveries in theology, Scriptural exegesis, spirituality, and the like, can often see features of that plan not known to him. Just as he used the best sources he could in his day, however, our using those of our day is fully in accord with his own example and practice. The subject of our prayer can be not only the Gospel events of the Passion and risen life, but also their good effects in our own soul and in the history of salvation. This approach is discussed at length in Cusson's *BibThSpEx*, esp. pp. 278–281; see also pp. 39–43, 219–233 (esp. 220 and 224), 296–301; *DeGuiJes*, pp. 539–543, 564; David Stanley, *A*

Modern Scriptural Approach to the Spiritual Exercises, and his *"I En-countered God!" The Spiritual Exercises with the Gospel of St. John* (St. Louis, 1986) and many other writers.

99. Text *A* has "Two Classes," an error which is corrected by the "Three" in *V*.

100. *Reglas*. This is the first of five sets of such directives which Ignatius terms "Rules" in the *Exercises*: those on eating ([210–217]), on discernment of spirits I ([313–317]) and II ([328–336]), on distributing alms ([337–344]), and on maintaining a genuine filial attitude in the Church ([352–370]). Each set of these rules was given, not to all re-treatants, but according to the needs and desires of individuals (*Directory*, ch. 38, no. 1). In all these cases it is important to attend to what he means by "rules." The classical Latin *regula* has many meanings: (1) a measuring rod and then (2) a pattern, model, example, measure of right and wrong, and hence sometimes (3) an obligation or law. In ecclesiastical Latin *regula* (and the Spanish *regla*) often meant a rule imposing an obligation. However, by "rules" in the five sets just mentioned, Ignatius cannot mean rules imposing an obligation, since an exercitant has no obligation even to make the Exercises. Therefore he has other meanings according to contexts, such as directives, guidelines, norms, suggestions, or models, as when he wrote that Christ is "our model and rule" (*dechado y regla nuestra*, [344]).

101. By this time the exercitant, growing in eagerness to serve God well, is aware that the human appetites for food and drink are good but tend toward excess, a disorder that must be controlled by the virtue of temperance. Appropriately Ignatius offers directives for an examination of one's situation, correction of possible disorders, and formulation of a plan for the better use of these appetites. His suggestions should be properly adapted to the needs and circumstances of each person, and to modern knowledge of nutritious diet. Rules 1 through 4 deal with what one eats or drinks; rules 5 through 8 suggest ways of drawing greater spiritual profit from eating or drinking.

The structural connection of these rules with the Third Week is not readily apparent; they apply about equally well, with appropriate changes, to all Four Weeks. Why, commentators wonder, did Ignatius place them here? Perhaps, as the *Directory* indicates (ch. 35, no. 13), because there was room for them here; the First and Second Weeks were already crowded with new instructions which the exercitant had to learn. Others think that they were placed here because of the connection with the Last Supper ([191–198]) and to encourage mortification during the atmosphere of the contemplations on Christ's Passion. Another possible reason is: The readjustment of one's manner of living can begin immediately, within the context of the Exercises.

102. On May 12, 1556, two months before Ignatius died, he wrote to A. Adrianssens a letter of prudent advice on eating and drinking for the preservation of health (*LettersIgn*, p. 421). It serves as an excellent commentary on these rules, bringing out the spirit from which they sprang.

THE FOURTH WEEK

103. Ignatius now takes up the risen life, the next stage of the paschal mystery. Already in [4] above he stated that the Fourth Week was to be about the "Resurrection and Ascension." Rather surprisingly, however, he does not use the title "The Resurrection" for his first contemplation. Nevertheless that is the topic he has in mind, as is clear from [299] below in the Mysteries of Christ's Life, to which he refers us. There he describes this same contemplation by a more accurate title: "The Resurrection of Christ Our Lord. His First Apparition"—as he states also here in the first prelude ([219]). The appearance to Mary is a part of the Resurrection, and because of his tender love of her it is the first point which occurs to his mind to contemplate. This is another example of Ignatius' unconcern for stylistic niceties. In general, during this week he focuses, not on the Resurrection itself, but on the apparitions of the risen Christ communicating his joy as well as his graces and spiritual consolations to humankind now redeemed. The exercitant too shares abundantly in the graces of Christ's life-giving Resurrection.

104. *Infierno*, i.e., as in the Apostles' Creed: "He descended into hell" and probably associated with the Hebrew notion of sheol, the abode of the dead. See 1 Peter 3:19, 4:6.

105. Christ's apparition to Mary is not found in Scripture, but it is an opinion prominent in a long tradition of Christian writers. It is found in ch. 70 of the Life of Christ by Ludolph, and Ignatius may have accepted it from him. Ludolph cites testimony from Sts. Ambrose, Anselm, and Ignatius of Antioch. Cusson lists some twenty writers who held this opinion, including Sedulius, Paulinus of Nola, Albert the Great, Bernardino da Siena, Maldonatus, and Pope Benedict XIV (*BibThSpEx*, pp. 303–304).

106. The third prelude, the grace to be prayed for, also gives a clue to one important purpose of the Fourth Week: intimate association with

Christ in his joy. Virtually all commentators hold that the week pertains chiefly to the unitive way. Beyond that, however, they divide along the same lines as in the Third Week (see n. 91 above). One group, including the *Directory* of 1599 (ch. 36, no. 1), affirms confirmation of resolutions and union with Christ in his joy. Another group adds also a sharing as great as possible in the fruits of his life-giving Resurrection (see *BibThSpEx*, pp. 309–311).

107. This justly renowned contemplation, directed toward increasing the exercitant's love of God, is the conclusion and apt climax of the spiritual experience of the Exercises. Love of God is the greatest of the virtues (1 Cor. 13:13); and one who thinks he loves God but does not love his neighbor is in error (1 John 4:20). Early commentators Miró and Hoffaeus thought that this Contemplation to Attain Love could well be given in the Third, or Second, or even the First Week. Their opinion was short-lived; although this would bring some profit, it would not be fulfilling the function of this contemplation which Ignatius intended in the structure of the *Exercises*. Consensus soon arose that this contemplation pertains to the unitive way and is part of the Fourth Week, though it may be either spread through the other mysteries of the week or made as the last Exercise of the retreat (Polanco in *SpEx*MHSJ, p. 825, Nadal, González Dávila, and the *Directory* of 1599 [ch. 36, no. 2]; see *BibThSpEx*, pp. 312–314).

108. This is typical of Ignatius' practicality. He in no way depreciates affective love of another person with its warmth and consolation, but further points out the necessity of effective love, doing what is pleasing to the other. The effective love remains even when the affective love is difficult or absent (as in desolation). Moreover, affective love not carried into practice by effective love easily degenerates into self-interest or self-deceit.

109. This wise observation sets the stage for the movement of the thought throughout the contemplation. Love ordinarily arises from gratitude. The lover gives to the beloved and the beloved, recognizing the giver's goodness, experiences gratitude and increased love for the giver. Through their mutual love their friendship is deepened.

110. This prelude shows both the purpose of the contemplation and its function in the structure of the *Exercises* as a whole. The phrase "to love Christ more" in the Second and Third Weeks now becomes to love God more "in all things"—reminiscent of Ignatius' constant concern to "find God in all things" of ordinary everyday life. Another

important function of this contemplation is to build a bridge for intensive spiritual living in everyday life after the Exercises have ended (*Obrascompl*, p. 327; *BibThSpEx*, pp. 326–332).

111. The four points overlap somewhat; they view the gifts of God from many angles rather than in a logical order. Some find it helpful to contemplate God in point 1 as the giver of all gifts; in 2, as present in all the creatures and conserving their existence; in 3, as cooperating in their activities; and in 4, as the preeminent Source of all the good present in creatures. This offering, the "Take and Receive" (*Suscipe*), is one of the most famous of Ignatius' prayers and one regularly associated with him.

112. Notice the totality of this offering: The exercitant, in deep fervor from the month of spiritual experience and moved by profound gratitude to increased effective love, offers his or her whole self back to God, to be guided henceforth by his good pleasure through the rest of life.

113. God's immanence in all the created world, which the résumé in point 4 brings out, is an expression of his benevolent love for us. Awareness of this ignites in the human heart gratitude, adoration, and a loving application of one's whole self to serving him as well as possible. As the Exercises close, the exercitant—like Ignatius himself—has viewed the grandeur of the created universe: its origin from God ([23]), and its being destined to return to him (by contributing to his glorification through the joyful praise of those who have cooperated with his plan of creation and redemption). By starting with a love that descends from God above, the retreatants will view all created reality as being on its way to God through his being praised by those who are saved. These exercitants will find God in all things, and by means of them. They will resonate with words which Ignatius wrote on many other occasions: "May our Lord give us the light of his holy discretion, that we may know how to make use of creatures in the light of the Creator" (*LettersIgn*, p. 421); "All the good which is looked for in creatures exists with greater perfection in God who created them" (*EppIgn* 5:488; see also *LettersIgn*, pp. 18, 309); "May his holy name be praised . . . , he who has ordained and created them for this end [his own glorification] which is so proper" (*LettersIgn*, p. 83). The whole doctrine is summed up by St. Paul: "For from him and through him and for him all things are. To him be glory forever. Amen" (Rom. 11:36). See *BibThSpEx*, pp. 317–319, 326–332.

APPENDICES
Three Methods of Praying

114. The main course of Ignatius' Exercises for thirty days is now complete. The rest of his book consists of Appendices intended to be helpful both for cases which may arise during the retreat and also for carrying its fruits into persevering practice after the Exercises. The first of these appendices is the present one on the Three Methods of Praying. Beyond the basic methods of meditation and contemplation in his book he also teaches other methods, surprisingly many. His effort is to find some method suitable for any personality. In [18] above, Ignatius described this First Method of Praying as a "light exercise" which can be given to simple and illiterate persons who are unqualified for the full Exercises. In his *Constitutions* too he states ([649]) about these three methods that "anyone who has good will seems to be capable of these exercises." The *Directory*, however, points out that although these methods are suitable for beginners, they are also useful for persons very advanced (ch. 37, no. 1). For detailed commentary on these methods see Coathalem, *Ignatian Insights*, pp. 232–238; *Directory*, ch. 37.

115. *Forma, modo y ejercicios*: See n. 94 on [186] above and n. 117 just below. By *forma* Ignatius often means a manner of proceeding (see *forma de proceder* in [204]), and that can be its meaning in both instances here in [238]. See Gueydan, *Exercices*, pp. 82 and 143.

116. *Acepta*, i.e, agreeable, a pleasant experience. However, in the Latin Vulgate De Freux translates this word as "acceptable to God." This is possible but in the context it seems less probable as Ignatius' meaning.

117. Probably Ignatius means here the manner of proceeding (*forma*), that is, the method (*modo*) of meditation and contemplation properly so called which he explained above respectively in [45–53] and [101–117]. See also n. 94 on [186] and n. 115 above.

118. In text *A* this heading is part of the title in [238] above. We transfer it here where it is more functional in making the thought easier to grasp. The commandments are the first of four subjects suggested under the First Method.

119. Ignatius' manuscript, text *A*, has *tercera adición*, a manifest error for Fifth Note (*quinta nota* [131]) of the Second Week. This note adapts the Third Additional Directive of the First Week ([75]) to the Second Week.

120. *Pecados mortales, the capital sins*: See n. 8 above at [18] and the list of the capital sins there. The opposite virtues are humility, patience, generosity, temperance, chastity, neighborly love, and diligence.

121. Powers: the faculties of memory, intellect, and will, as in [45–52].

122. The Second Method is similar to the ancient tradition of "prayerful reading" (*lectio divina*) of which St. Benedict wrote in his *Rule*, ch. 48. On *Lectio divina* see D. M. Stanley, *The Exercises with . . . St. John*, pp. 311–327.

123. Ignatius' method of praying according to a rhythmic measure has noteworthy similarity to the "Jesus prayer" which with varying formulations was practiced and taught especially among Greek Fathers such as Diadochus of Photice (d. before 486), Hesychius of Jerusalem, St. John Climacus (d. 649), and others. A short formula such as "Jesus Christ, Son of God, have mercy on me" was recited with every breath to bring about an absorption in the presence of God. A documented history of the spread of this prayer, which had widespread popularity in the fourteenth century and its apogee in the seventeenth, is in I. Hausherr, *The Name of Jesus* (Kalamazoo, 1978), pp. 241–347. Particularly interesting are the citations from St. Francis Xavier (p. 343) and the Jesuit general Claudio Aquaviva (p. 334). See also *Westminster Dictionary of Christian Spirituality*, p. 223; *NCathEnc* 7:971; *DSpir* 8: cols. 1126–1150.

The Mysteries of the Life of Christ

124. "Mysteries" (*misterios*) here means the events or episodes in the life of Christ, the medieval sense of the word as found in the "mystery plays." Some of these events are also mysteries in the theological sense, "a religious truth revealed by God that human beings cannot know by reason alone," e.g., the Eucharist in [289]. Most of them are not mysteries in this strict theological sense. However, since they involve the actions of the God-Man and build up to his Passion and Resurrection, they implicate the great mysteries strictly so called, such as the Trinity, Incarnation, and Redemption (*NCathEnc* 10:148). Ignatius aims to furnish a series of topics for contemplation during the retreat and also, as [162] indicates, to help exercitants to continue such contemplations after the retreat.

Ignatius presents 51 mysteries from which a director may choose. All are from Scripture, except Christ's appearance first to Mary ([296]) and to Joseph of Aramathea ([310]). Almost all of Ignatius' topics are also in Ludolph's Life of Christ and in the same sequence as in Ludolph. This suggests that already at Manresa he drew up at least a preliminary list of these topics from the copybook of his readings at Loyola. However, the present form of these mysteries comes from his years in Paris. His quotations from Scripture are his own Spanish translations from the Latin Vulgate. At Manresa he did not yet know Latin, and Spanish translations of the New Testament were very rare before 1569. The first printed Spanish translation was the Protestant edition at Antwerp in 1543, after Ignatius' revisions of the Exercises. See *SpEx*MHSJ*Te*, p. 55; *DalmMan*, p. 142; Introduction above, pp. 12–13, 19–20.

125. The manuscript has parentheses (*parentesis*), the sixteenth-century usage which modern editions replace by quotation marks.

126. The manuscript has *Lucas en el primero capitolo, littera c*. This too is now replaced by the clearer citations of chapters and verses, the system of Estienne introduced in 1551. Ignatius compressed the sentences of Scripture which he translated from the Vulgate, but he kept the sense unaltered. The present English translation is made from Ignatius' Spanish.

127. In these points Ignatius presents for imaginative and reverent contemplation what he regards as the "history" (see n. 53 on [102]), the "authentic foundation" ([4]) which he wished to be the basis of the exercitant's reflections and applications. He obviously meant the *historia* insofar as he was able to know it from theological, devotional, and scriptural writings of his day. Since then, however, the historical character of Christ's words and deeds has been immensely nuanced by modern discoveries in all these fields. If knowledge of these developments does not shine through a modern director's presentation, he or she is likely to receive complaints from retreatants. Many problems are connected with this situation. In *BibThSpEx* Cusson sets them up well on pp. 39–43, 220, and 224 and discusses them on pp. 223–242, 278–279, 296–301; and on pp. 351–364 he gives an extended bibliography of articles and books on each of Ignatius' mysteries. Ordinarily, the more theological and scriptural knowledge a director or an exercitant brings to the contemplation of these mysteries, the more fruitful and solidly based will her or his spirituality be. See also pp. 59–60 above in "Keys to Interpretation," and Stanley, *The Spiritual Exercises with . . . St. John*, pp. xi–xii, xv–xvi.

128. Ignatius did not include Pentecost among these mysteries, possibly because it did not come under their title, "The Mysteries of the

Life of Christ our Lord." That he was not opposed to including it appears from this statement of Polanco, who knew his mind so well. He states that the Contemplation to Attain Love can be proposed after the first or second day of the Fourth Week and adds "but under the heading Resurrection include also the mysteries of the Ascension and Pentecost" (cited in *BibThSpEx*, p. 314, from *SpEx*MHSJ, p. 825).

Rules for the Discernment of Spirits

129. This short title, not in Ignatius' text, is an editorial addition by which his rules have been commonly known throughout their influential history. It has been added in many editions because Ignatius' own title is so long, compact, and unwieldy. It is a slightly free translation of the abbreviated title (probably Ignatius' own) in the First Latin Version before 1534, *P¹*: "Some rules toward discerning various spirits moving the soul" (*aliquot regulae ad discernendos varios spiritus animam agitantes*). However, the abbreviated English heading, although accurate, omits many important ideas from his own lengthy but terse and precise title which demands careful study.

The history of discernment of spirits, the subtle topic and art which Ignatius takes up here, extends from the Bible to the present time (see *DSpir* 3, cols. 1222–1291; translation by Innocentia Richards, in *Discernment of Spirits* [Collegeville, 1970]). However, Ignatius' well-known rules are based chiefly on his own experiences and his reflections upon them, as we learn from Câmara's note on *Autobiog*, 8, and also from ibid., 9, 20–22, 25–26, 54–55, 99–101. A short commentary in English is found in Coathalem, pp. 243–278. Toner's *Commentary* of 352 pages, mentioned just above, presents a deep and excellent analysis of these rules. Another excellent article is Michael J. Buckley, "Rules for the Discernment of Spirits," *The Way*, Supplement 20 (Autumn 1973): 19–37. Ignatius' letters of June 18 and Sept. 11, 1536, to Sister Teresa Rejadell, and of 1545 to St. Francis Borgia (*LettersIgn*, pp. 18–24, 24–25, 83–86) show how he applied his principles in practice and are also considered a commentary on these rules.

For this topic of discernment it is of great importance to understand Ignatius' terminology with precision. In his usage, to discern is to see deeply in order recognize and separate; in other words, to identify and distinguish the good spirits from the bad. The Spanish *discernir* (from Latin *discerno, discrevi, discretum*, to sever, separate) means to know, judge, comprehend, distinguish, or discriminate. For the substantive form of *discernir* Ignatius uses *discreción* ([176, 325]) in the sense of *discernimiento* (*DalmMan*, p. 194), that is, discernment, insight, discrimination. "Keenness of insight" and "skill in discerning or discriminating" (*Webster's Seventh New Collegiate Dictionary* [Merriam-Webster, 1967] are the meanings of the English word *discernment* which are most relevant for accurate understanding of Ignatius' thought here. See J. Toner, *Commentary*, pp. 18–19.

130. *Sentir y conocer*: These words reflect Ignatius' own experiences with discernment of spirits (see *Autobiog*, 7–8 above). First he noticed that spirits were affecting his soul, and little by little came to understand them. Some were good and moved him toward good, others bad. Then through many years of practice he gradually developed his experience into a refined art. This skill, he well knew, takes years to acquire. Here he is primarily helping directors to know what to watch for and say in dealing with retreatants, but through the directors he is also introducing exercitants in the First Week to their first acquaintance with this complex art of interpreting their interior experiences. Such exercitants can hope to understand these "motions" or tactics only to some extent (*en alguna manera*). It is wise for them to seek further help from a director.

131. *Mociones*, motions. In Ignatius' usage this word usually has a technical meaning: the interior experiences in the soul. They can be acts of the intellect (e.g., thoughts, lines of reasonings, imaginings, etc.); or of the will (such as love, hate, desire, fear, etc.); or of affective feelings, impulses, inclinations, or urges (such as peace, warmth, coldness, consolation, desolation, etc.). These can come (1) from ourselves under some control of our free will ([32]); or (2) from a good spirit (God or an angel); or (3) from an evil spirit.

132. "Are caused": In these present Rules Ignatius is directly treating only the last two categories just mentioned, the motions caused by good or evil spirits for their respective ends. Indirectly, however, the first category, motions arising from ourselves ([35]), can fall within the scope of his rules, insofar as the good or evil spirits can take these emotions and work on them for their respective ends. See Toner, *Commentary*, pp. 37–38. Ignatius clearly believed in the existence of angels and devils, and for him the spirits, whether good or evil, are always persons, intelligent beings. A few writers have held that the word *spirit* can be replaced by the motions (see, e.g., Coathalem, p. 244). Sometimes their opinion has sprung from modern doubts about the existence of devils or angels—see Toner, *Commentary*, pp. 34–37,

260–270; also, Paul Quay, "Angels and Demons: the Teaching of IV Lateran," *Theological Studies* 42 (March 1981): 20–45.

133. *Anima*: soul, used by synecdoche to mean the person (see n. 16 on [23] above). However, because Ignatius' training in scholastic philosophy is reflected in his writing and helps toward its interpretation, we think it better to retain "soul" as the safer guide to his thought in this subtle material.

134. I.e., because cases where they are applicable are more likely to arise during the First Week, though they may arise at any other time. The rules for the First Week are concerned especially with the experience of spiritual desolation and ways of coping with it to avoid deviation from pursuit of the end, salvation. They are particularly applicable to the purgative way. An outline of the treatment in the rules for the First Week, based on Toner, *Commentary*, pp. vi–vii, can be given as follows:

I. Fundamental Principles for discerning spirits: the contrary actions of the good and evil spirits on regressing and progressing Christians (Rules 1–2)
   A. Spiritual consolation and desolation (R 3–14)
      1. Their nature (R 3–4)
   B. Responding to the Holy Spirit during desolation (R 5–6)
      1. Accepting the desolation as a test (R 7)
      2. Counterattack by patience (R 8)
      3. Examination of the causes (R 9)
      4. During consolation prepare for desolation (R 10–11)
      5. Style and strategy of the devil (R 12–14).

135. *Por el synderese*: *Synderesis* is a person's natural ability to judge rightly in moral matters (*DalmMan*, p. 167). See also *ST* 1, 79, 12; also 1–2, 94, 1 ad 2.

136. "Spiritual Consolation": Throughout these Rules, whenever Ignatius uses the term *consolation* he means spiritual consolation, and only it. There are also many experiences of consolation which are nonspiritual, e.g., some licit such as that arising from the anticipated pleasure of a good meal and some illicit, such as pleasure in expected sinful activity. To interpret these as spiritual consolation is erroneous self-deceit. Spiritual consolation always includes a tendency toward an increase of charity. However, it can have concomitant overflow or effect on the emotions and senses, e.g., joy. This is accidental, however—something that can be present or absent. Consolation purely

sensible is excluded. There is a misunderstanding of Ignatius' term *consolation* which arises rather frequently in practice, though it is not found in reputable authors. Any feeling of joy, satisfaction, or peace is taken too hastily as a good spirit's sign of approval for some option. This omits the distinction between spiritual and nonspiritual consolation and often leads to false discernment, selfishness, or rationalization of less good conduct. See Toner, *Commentary*, pp. 283–284.

137. The Third Rule is of great importance for judging problems connected with infused contemplation. On this see Coathalem, pp. 257–258, 279–283; for bibliography, *Obrascompl*, p. 279.

138. As with consolation, so too the desolation treated in the *Exercises* always pertains to spiritual desolation, with its possible overflow into the emotions and senses. To interpret nonspiritual desolation as spiritual desolation is to steer oneself into danger of errors, self-deceit, and rationalization.

139. *Por fuerza*: in regard to physical strength. *De grado*: in its meaning of "willingly" or "spontaneously." Other translations are possible. This statement is extremely terse and even the ancient Latin versions turned or paraphrased it differently. *P¹* (probably by Ignatius) uses: "The devil is weak in physical strength and strong of own accord, like a woman" (*debilis per vim et fortissimus sponte ac mulier*). Ignatius clarifies the statement by the context below it. The devil cannot work directly on our will, but only indirectly by tempting us through the imagination or senses. If we show ourselves strong, he weakens and retreats. If we show ourselves weak, he grows strong and furious. To expand Ignatius' comparison into a depreciation of women in general goes beyond his text and is also historically erroneous. The 352 pages of his correspondence with women, assembled in Hugo Rahner's *St. Ignatius Loyola: Letters to Women* (New York, 1960), reveal him as a zealous, prudent, and understanding spiritual director of women who highly esteemed them and was similarly esteemed by them in return.

140. This brief title, customary in many editions, is added to Ignatius' text to facilitate references. See n. 129 on [313] above.

141. That is, for cases more likely to arise during the Second Week, especially emotions caused by the evil spirit using his deceptive tactics during the time of the election. This set of rules is especially applicable to the illuminative and unitive ways, and deals chiefly with demonic deceptions during the journey to the goal, the greater glory of God. See n. 134 on [313] above; also Coathalem, pp. 247–248. An outline, based on Toner, *Commentary*, follows.

I. The evil spirit in time of spiritual consolation (R II: 1–8)
    A. Deception beginning during spiritual consolation (R 1–7)
        1. Characteristics of the good and evil spirits (R 1)
        2. Consolation without a preceding cause (R 2)
        3. Consolation with a preceding cause (R 3)
        4. Deception in consolation with a preceding cause (R 4)
        5. How to detect such demonic deception (R 5–6)
        6. Learning by reflection on experience (R 6)
        7. Assurance and explanation (R 7)
    B. Deception during the afterglow of consolation (R 8).

142. Consolation without a previous cause is an invasion of God into the soul without any previous use of its own intellectual, volitional, or sense faculties. It may have been involved in the call of St. Matthew or St. Paul ([175]), or be similar to what St. Teresa called "the prayer of union" (*Interior Castle*, Mansion V, chs. 1–2), or to the "substantial touch" of St. John of the Cross (Coathalem, pp. 271–272; see also 256–257). Since it comes from God, it obviously cannot contain error. However, if a person (or his or her director) is to be sure that an experience is a genuine case of consolation without antecedent cause, subtle and careful discernment is necessary, and even that may turn out to be inconclusive. Ignatius' remarks are too brief to enable us to know with precision what he truly means by this phrase, or to answer the numerous questions it raises. Many interpretations ancient and modern have arisen but so far no one of them has won general agreement. Four recent opinions of Karl Rahner, Harvey Egan, Hervé Coathalem, and Daniel Gil are discussed by Toner, *Commentary* (1982), pp. 291–313. Great uncertainty remains, in his opinion, about the nature of consolation without preceding cause, how frequently it occurs, and how it functions in discernment either of spirits or of God's will. Harvey Egan, basing his thought on Karl Rahner, views the matter differently and cites other authors in support of his opinion. See his *The Spiritual Exercises and the Ignatian Mystical Horizon* (St. Louis, 1976), pp. 31–65.

143. That is, by acts (of perception, understanding, or willing) antecedent to the consolation which are a means by which the experience is stimulated. Such stimulation might arise, e.g., from one's meditations, contemplations, or reflections, from a book, homily, picture, etc.

144. At the end of these rules we are in position to observe a matter of great importance. The *Exercises* present two distinct forms of discernment: (1) discernment of the will of God and (2) discernment of

spirits, which is a means to discerning God's will. The principles used in both forms are as useful outside a time of retreat as within. The first procedure is found chiefly in the directives for making an election ([135, 169–189]), the second principally in the rules toward discernment of spirits ([313–336]). There is some overlapping in the two procedures, insofar as the suggestions in one are usually applicable also in the other; but the main objective in each set remains distinct. In discerning the will of God, a person asks questions such as: "By which option am I, with my personality and in my circumstances, likely to bring greater glory to God?" or "to serve God better?" or "to increase my supernatural life more and thereby bring him proportionally greater praise through eternity?" While engaged in such deliberations, he or she is likely to receive thoughts and impulses from the good spirit and subtle temptations from the evil spirit. Here recourse to discernment of spirits is needed, and perhaps also consultation with a counselor. Toner's *Commentary* touches on this distinction (pp. 12–15) and gives great help toward acquiring the art of discerning spirits. Similar help toward the more important art of discerning the will of God is found in his later book: *Discerning God's Will: Ignatius Loyola's Teaching on Christian Decision Making* (St. Louis, 1990).

Rules for Distributing Alms

145. Ignatius' title suggests that these rules are addressed chiefly to ecclesiastical officeholders, e.g., those who possess a benefice or are seeking one, in which they are charged to superintend the distribution of alms. Notice the words "ministry" ([337, 343]), "the distribution" rather than merely "giving" ([338, 342]), "office of my administration" ([340]), "office and duty of my ministry" ([341; cf. 343]). With appropriate adaptations, however, these rules can also serve as guides to nonofficeholders, as Ignatius points out in the last rule ([341]). See *DalmMan*, p. 175; *Obrascompl*, p. 284.

146. That is, the ecclesiastical goods, capital, foundations, gifts, and so forth made to the Church. To confer the office on someone is to appoint him or her also to administer these goods.

147. These incidents, not in the Gospels, are in Ludolph's *Vita Jesu Christi*, Part I, ch. 2, no.7, from which Ignatius probably took them.

The Notes on Scruples

148. Ignatius' title indicates that these are not rules or directives giving norms of conduct; rather, they are simple "notes" toward helping persons who are troubled by scruples. They are also helps for directors or counselors. They manifestly reflect his own experiences with scruples at Manresa, as recounted in *Autobiog*, 22–25, and also his experience in counseling others. They were wise counsels for his day and remain so, but for modern times they are incomplete and need to be supplemented by the many discoveries which have been made in pastoral experience, psychology, psychiatry, and the like. In his day scruples were too readily seen chiefly as an affliction brought on by God or the devil for their respective purposes. For some further comments and references, see David L. Fleming, *The Spiritual Exercises: A Literal Translation and a Contemporary Reading* (St. Louis, 1978), pp. 227–229.

149. Letter 64, in PL 77, col. 1195.

150. Possibly Ignatius took this quotation from the Life of St. Bernard in the *Flos sanctorum*, the Spanish translation of the Lives of the Saints (*Flos sanctorum*) published in 1493 (*DalmMan*, p. 179).

Thinking, Judging, and Feeling with the Church

151. Rules, i.e., guidelines, directives, norms, or suggestions to be prudently applied; but not obligations. See n. 100 on [210] above.

152. This is an attempt (admittedly with limited success) to pack the meaning of Ignatius' lengthy title into a short one for handy reference. Longstanding endeavors in the same direction have been "Rules for Thinking with the Church" and "Rules of Orthodoxy." They are accurate but incomplete, for his lengthy title in [352] involves far more than the realm of thought or correct belief.

His own title is found in three formulations which illumine one another, in texts P^1, V, and A, printed in parallel columns in *SpEx*MHSJ*Te*, pp. 374–375. Of the three, that in the Autograph, A, best reveals his whole thought; but it receives clarifications from P^1 and V, as will be seen in the following nn. 153 and 154.

These well-known and influential rules were in the manuscript of the Exercises during their revision in Rome (1539–1541), and possibly already during Ignatius' stay in Paris (1528–1535). In either case they reflect the Church's stormy situation which he knew by experience in both periods. Many people were justly clamoring for the Church's reform. Some of them pointed out the abuses respectfully and properly, but others acted irreverently and dangerously. For example, one group, the Illuminati in Spain and others like them in Paris, was practicing a pseudo-mysticism which ignored doctrinal accuracy and scorned the precisions of scholastic theology. A second group consisted of those openly heretical, such as the "Lutheranizers" (*Lutherizantes*) in Paris. In a grey area in between these two groups was a third, disgruntled Catholics and humanists who often gave reason to doubt whether their faith was still genuinely Catholic. They were critical of the Church, frequently uncharitable, sarcastic, or ambiguous. Erasmus is an example, with his captivating but mordant satires and exaggerations mocking pope, bishops, theologians, priests, and nuns. Two years before Ignatius arrived in Paris an edition of 20,000 copies of his *Praise of Folly* was exhausted. In May 1526, the Sorbonne requested Parlement to condemn his *Colloquia*. In Rome Ignatius contended with the persecutions stirred up by Landívar and the disguised heretics Mainardi, Mudarra, and Barreda (*Autobiog*, 98).

Most of these practices went contrary to Ignatius' temperament and typical procedures. For him the Church was a mother and a divinely established institution, an embodiment of the Kingdom of Christ. Painfully aware of her defects, he loved her nonetheless and sought her renewal—but his tactics were quiet, positive, and constructive. They aimed chiefly at interior reform of individuals through conversations and his Exercises, and eventually they blossomed into his Society of Jesus with its educational system, foreign missions, and other ministries. He placed these rules about the Church at the very end of his *Exercises*, and in them he is not polemical or argumentative. He is content to give calm counsel. He intended the rules especially for an exercitant who for a month had been gazing in love on Christ, contemplating his calls for help in spreading his Kingdom and his example, and was now about to return to ordinary life, perhaps among heretics or weak Catholics. Polanco states in his Directory that these rules are given as antidotes "to those things which the heretics of our time, or those showing affinity to their doctrine, are prone to attack or scorn. . . . Moreover, they serve not only to keep such an exercitant from erring by speaking privately or writing publicly in a manner other than proper, but they also help him to discern whether the statements and writings of others are departing from the Catholic Church's manner of thinking and speaking, and to advise others to be on their guard" (*Di-*

rectorium Polanci, no. 112, in *DirSpEx* [Rome, 1955], p. 327). On this topic, see Leturia, "Sentido verdadero en la Iglesia militante," *Estudios* 2:149–174; also, based chiefly on it, Ganss, "Thinking with the Church: The Spirit of St. Ignatius' Rules," *The Way*, Supplement 20 (1973): 72–82; see also *Studies in the Spirituality of Jesuits* 7 (January 1975): 12–20.

Many of Ignatius' topics and details are as applicable in our day as in his, but many too are rather obsolete in our vastly changed circumstances. What is most important for any person now is to catch the underlying tenor of a loyal attitude which runs all through Ignatius' rules, devise a similar attitude of his or her own, and by it guide oneself and others to live and work in loving loyalty to the Church, Christ's spouse and our mother.

153. *Sentido*, sense, reason, feeling, and many other meanings, is often used by Ignatius with nuances of his own. Frequently, as here, it means cognition which is basically intellectual but is savored so repeatedly that it becomes also deeply emotional and "satisfies the soul" ([2]). Thus it becomes a habitual attitude of mind, a frame of reference instinctively used to guide one's life (Leturia, *Estudios* 2:153).

154. Militant, i.e., the Church on earth, with the human defects found in many of her popes, bishops, priests, and other members.

155. This rule is the fundamental principle underlying all the rest. It is developed by three groups of directives which follow, as nn. 156, 157, and 158 below will indicate. In no other one place in the *Exercises* does Ignatius so fully reveal his concept of the Church: true spouse of Christ, our mother, and hierarchical. But his concept is richer still. Elsewhere he describes her as Christ's Kingdom to be spread ([91–95]), the community of the faithful ([177]), Roman (*SpEx*, [353] in text *P¹*), and as Christ's Mystical Body governed on earth by his vicar (*Letters-Ign*, pp. 367–372), from whom all authority descends through hierarchically ordered superiors (*Cons* [7, 603, 666, 736]).

156. Group I, Rules 2–9, gives suggestions for establishing an attitude on the devotions and way of life of loyal Catholics.

157. Group II, Rules 10–12, builds an outlook in regard to superiors in the Church, respectively in regard to jurisdiction, learning, and sanctity. The fundamental principle of this group is in Rule 10: Be more inclined to praise than to blame.

158. *Mayores* means, here and in [45, 351, 362], our superiors, the officials or authorities both ecclesiastical and civil (*DalmMan*, p. 200; Leturia, *Estudios*, 2:164).

159. In the 1500s many humanists and reformers were reacting against the scholastic teachers and their methods, often with scorn, and putting more stress on Scripture, sometimes taken alone or sometimes along with the Fathers. They set scholastic and positive theology in opposition, but Ignatius saw the good in both and presented the two as complementary. Thus through his *Exercises* [363] and his colleges and universities as guided by his *Constitutions*, his attitude exerted for centuries a widespread influence on the teaching and study of theology. On scholastic and positive theology see n. 39 on *Cons* [366] below.

160. This is a caution against premature admiration of living persons even over canonized saints. In Ignatius' experience, e.g., with Landívar, Mudarra, and Barreda in Rome in 1538, some living preachers were highly esteemed for a while but were disguising their heresy.

161. Group III, rules 13–18, treats of doctrinal topics, some of them controverted often passionately, and a manner of expounding them in the troubled sixteenth century. Again, the group begins with the fundamental principle in rule 13, which is in substance a rephrasing of Rule 1 ([353]).

162. *Determina*: "determine," in the meaning of "decide." Texts *P¹* of about 1534 and the Vulgate, text *V*, use the phrase "defines it" (*definierit*). Notice that Ignatius does not state that we ought to believe that white is black. Instead, he writes that "what *I see*" (*que yo veo*) "as white, I would believe to be black"; and the Latin Vulgate in 1548 translated this by "what appears to my eyes as white." In other words, the error would be in my hasty subjective judgment and not in the Church, because the Church is governed by the Holy Spirit and cannot err in her solemn definitions. This statement seems to be an allusion to Erasmus, who had written: "Nor would black be white, if the Roman Pontiff should pronounce it so, a thing which I know he will never do" (*DalmMan*, p. 183, citing Erasmus *Opera* 9 [1706]: 517).

FOR THE DELIBERATION ON POVERTY AND SELECTIONS FROM THE *SPIRITUAL DIARY*

1. FOR THE INTRODUCTION TO THE DELIBERATION ON POVERTY

1. *Rule* of St. Benedict, ch. 58.

2. Vermeersch, in *Catholic Encyclopedia* (1911) 12:325; Aldama, *La Formula del Institut de la Compañía de Jesús* (Rome, 1981), pp. 92–93.

3. Codina, in *Cons*MHSJ I: 35.

4. Antonio de Aldama, *La Formula del Instituto* (Rome, 1981), pp. 92–93; *Cons*MHSJ I:13, no. 15.

5. *Cons*MHSJ I:29. In the bull, however, a line of the Sketch was inadvertently skipped by a copyist in the papal court. This created obscurities about the ownership of the goods the Jesuits were permitted to have. See Aldama, *La Formula*, pp. 94–95, 97 with the reference to *Cons* [561–563].

6. By 1548 experience revealed several difficulties in the practice of the poverty prescribed in *Regimini*. The problems were resolved in the new bull which Ignatius requested from the Julius III, *Exposcit debitum* of July 21, 1550. It stated that the members could not retain "any stable goods (except those which are proper for their own use and habitation)." In other words, the Society could now own its dwelling places. Its poverty, hitherto closer to that of the original Franciscans, was now more similar to that of the Dominicans. For the training of the scholastics the First Sketch of 1539 and the bulls of 1540 and 1550 all permitted colleges which could have endowments and fixed revenues (as will be further explained below in n. 4 on *Cons* [2], pp. 451–452).

7. *Cons*MHSJ I:35.

8. *Cons*MHSJ I:73.

9. Codina, ibid., I:36.

10. See Covarrubias, *Tesoro de la lengua Castellana* (1611), p. 904. In our day too the latest unabridged *Diccionario de la Lengua Española*, 20th ed. (Madrid: Real Academía Española, 1984), lists only this one meaning of *renta*: "From the Latin *reddita*. A utility or benefit which something yields annually, or the yield which is collected."

11. *Cons*MHSJ I:34–36.

12. Codina, *Cons*MHSJ I:35.

13. See also Iparraguirre's n. 2 on *SpDiar* [1], *Obrascompl*, p. 341.

14. It is based on Iparraguirre in *Obrascompl*, pp. 31–317.

15. *Cons*MHSJ I:86–158.

16. *Obrascompl* p. 339. Many will also find it wise to review the editorial policy described above in n. 5 on the General Introduction, p. 371 above.

2. FOR THE DELIBERATION ON POVERTY

1. Notice that these same words, advantages and disadvantages, occur above in *SpEx* [181], in the description of an election in the Third Time.

2. "In part," i.e., limited to the churches and their sacristies.

3. "In whole," i.e., unlimited. Note further it is fixed income without civil right, and therefore could be considered to be alms applicable to all three of the cases mentioned in the deliberations of March 4, 1541, namely, (1) the Society, (2) for all things necessary, and (3) the churches and sacristies. See pp. 218–219 of the Introduction to the Deliberation on Poverty above, and Codina in *Cons*MHSJ I:35–36.

4. Motions: e.g., impulses, interior disturbances, etc. On this technical term see n. 131 on *SpEx* [313] above.

5. This refers to the conclusions from the deliberations of March 4, 1541. The two mentioned were Ignatius and Codure. We do not know whether or how Ignatius voted. See Introduction, pp. 218–219.

6. E.g., a non-Jesuit administrator (such as was Father Pietro Codacio at the time when Paul III assigned the church of the Gesù to the Society), or a scholastic, or a little later a spiritual coadjutor. Even a professed could superintend those fixed revenues which were without civil right (Codina, *Cons*MHSJ I:35–36).

7. The "house" here means the sacristy, from which he would take altar bread, wine, and the like. See Codina, ibid.

8. In the manuscript this bracketed paragraph enclosed in angular brackets is crossed out, probably by Ignatius himself.

9. I.e., than a fixed income limited to the sacristy, or than one unlimited in its applicability.

10. Ignatius and his companions did not think that all fixed revenues for the Society's churches were forbidden by the bull of Sept. 27, 1540. Those without civil right could be accepted as alms. See Codina, *Cons*MHSJ I, n. 3, on pp. 35–36.

11. No. 16, in angular brackets, was crossed out in the manuscript, seemingly by Ignatius himself.

3. FOR THE INTRODUCTION TO THE *SPIRITUAL DIARY*

1. Juan de la Torre, *Constitutiones Societatis Jesu Latinae et Hispanicae cum earum Declarationibus* (Madrid, 1892), pp. 348–363.

2. Codina, in *Cons*MHSJ I:86–158.

3. *Revue d'Ascétique et de Mystique* 19 (1938): 3–22, 113–140. He incorporated its substance into his later book, *DeGuiJes*, pp. 42–66, of which the French original was composed shortly before his death in 1942.

4. Especially important examples, with the dates of their chief publications, are: J. de Guibert (1938); I. Iparraguirre in *Obrascompl* (1952); M. Giuliani (1959); A. Haas and P. Knauer (1961); H. D. Egan (1987), whose *Ignatius Loyola the Mystic* absorbs the chief features of his predecessors.

5. *DeGuiJes*, pp. 44–45, slightly revising the same thoughts from his "Mystique ignatienne" in 1938.

6. *DalmIgn*, pp. 269–271.

7. Iparraguirre, in *Obrascompl*, p. 326, with the documentation.

8. *MonNad* V:162 [15].

9. *DeGuiJes*, pp. 56–60, 176–181; Egan, *Ignatius Loyola the Mystic*, pp. 119–122.

10. "The Mysticism of St. Ignatius according to His Spiritual Diary," in *Ignatius of Loyola: His Spiritual Heritage and Personality*, ed. F. Wulf (St. Louis, 1977), pp. 164–199; see esp. pp. 170–175. See also *Obrascompl*, pp. 331–332.

11. *Obrascompl*, pp. 335–337.

12. Loving humility is also similar to the summit of humility by which, in St. Benedict's Rule (ch. 7:1, 2, 62), a monk attains to perfect love, the twelfth or top rung of the Jacob's ladder which he should climb (see n. 78 on *SpEx* [164] above).

If "loving humility" can be considered to be the summit of the spiritual experience narrated in the *Diary*, it can also be seen as a most appropriate phrase to synthesize the graces of the *Exercises*. See n. 78 on *SpEx* [164] above.

The Second Week of the *Exercises* consists in the contemplation of the life of Jesus and in making a deliberate choice of the way I shall follow him. The contemplation of the Incarnation ([101–109]) is normative for all the contemplations that follow. In this exercise we see the Eternal Word of God who humbles himself to become incarnate in Mary's womb, and we see Mary, the model of every Christian response to Jesus, "humbling herself and giving thanks to the Divine Majesty" (*SpEx* [108]). The key exercises of the Second Week designed to assist the process of the election, namely the Call of the King ([91–98]), the Two Standards ([136–148]), the Three Classes ([149–156]), and the Three Ways of Being Humble ([164–168]) all tend to lead us to prefer and to choose actual poverty and humiliations with Christ poor and humiliated, if God wishes to place us with Christ in this way. Finally, humility is joined to, suffused with, and transformed by love, the grace prayed for in the Contemplation to Attain Love ([230–237]).

4. FOR THE *SPIRITUAL DIARY*

1. Ignatius almost always indicates the theme of the Mass he celebrates, and he does so in a variety of ways. On those days when the liturgical calendar allowed a choice, he selected a theme in keeping with his devotional inclinations. Of the 116 Masses he mentions, 30 are of the Holy Trinity, 20 of the Name of Jesus, 16 of the Virgin Mary, and 9 of the Holy Spirit. Since the majority of his entries center on the Mass he celebrates, his mysticism is rightly called Eucharistic. See *DeGuiJes*, pp. 53–55; Iparraguirre, in *Obrascompl*, p. 341.

2. In the left margin of his text for the first three days, Ignatius placed a "C" followed by a number. The "C" means "chapter," as we know from [57] below where he spells it out: "en el capitulo 17." After the first three entries, he no longer employs the "C" but only a number. Later in the *Diary* he occasionally errs in numbering these chapters.

3. Throughout this translation we will place within square brackets those parts of the date of the entry not supplied by Ignatius.

4. In Ignatius' spiritual vocabulary *devoción* is a key word which appears frequently in all his works, often with connotations of his own. By it he meant especially his ease in finding God, a state of spiritual consolation which included his intimate union with God and his attitude of profound respect before God. It is an affection for God that is prompt, compliant, and warmly loving. It is intimately linked with other key phrases of the Ignatian vocabulary, such as union with God, consolation, familiarity with God, charity, discreet charity, finding God in all things, and the like. See A. de la Mora, *La devoción en el espíritu de San Ignacio* (Rome, 1960); on the rich meaning of "devotion" in his Letters see Dumeige, *Lettres* (Paris, 1958), p. 25.

5. The frequency and importance of tears in the experience of Ignatius is remarkable, even in the history of Christian spirituality, where this gift has always been esteemed. In the Part I of the *Diary* between Feb. 2 and March 12, tears are mentioned 175 times. In Part II from May 29, 1544, until the end of the diary nine months later on Feb. 27, 1545, virtually every entry refers to tears. On twenty-six occasions he tells us that sobs (*sollozos*) accompanied his tears. On fourteen occasions tears prevented him from speaking. Six times he experienced fear of losing his sight because of weeping. See *DeGuiJes*, pp. 62–66; H. Egan, *Ignatius the Mystic*, pp. iii–v; for the statistics, Codina in *Cons*MHSJ I, Index, 427–429, s.v. *facultas, loquela, singulti*, and the like. Ignatius himself treats the topic in at least two letters: Sept. 20, 1548, to Francis Borgia, and Nov. 22, 1553, to N. Gaudano, in *Letters-Ign*, pp. 179–182 and 311–312. The Fathers of the Christian East such as Cassian and St. John Climacus attached great importance to tears, especially of compunction (*DSpir* 9, cols. 290–295). Ignatius had some tears of compunction, but usually his were tears of joy over the magnitude of God's favors to him. E.g., in *SpDiar* [169] he tells of many tears and adds: "Everything was affectionate awe"; in [170] his intense tears all terminated in affectionate awe.

6. As explained in the Introduction above, the precise point on which Ignatius is making his election is: Shall we permit fixed income limited to the churches or sacristies attached to the Society's houses for its professed members? He uses three terms technically: "No fixed income" (*no tener nada*) means no regularly recurring revenues such as interest or annual produce; the religious must live only on alms. Fixed

income "in part" means that which would be limited to the churches or their sacristies; "in whole" means fixed income unlimited in its application. If this fixed income was "without civil right," it was in theory canonically permissible to use it for the professed members, their house, and its church or sacristy. However, in 1541 Ignatius and his companions still had authority to compose constitutions which would limit or even discard this right.

7. In the original, the page is torn at this place and so the "C" does not appear, but only the number.

8. In the *Diary* "sentiment" (*sentimiento*) usually means a deeply experienced understanding of realities perceived in faith. John Futrell calls it "felt-knowledge," i.e., knowledge which has been deeply or emotionally perceived. See his *Making an Apostolic Community of Love* (St. Louis, 1970), pp. 111–116, and his "Vocabulary of the Spiritual Diary," published as an appendix in Joseph A. Munitiz, *Inigo: Discernment Log-book. The Spiritual Diary of Saint Ignatius Loyola* (London, 1987), pp. 75–77. *Sentimiento* is closely related to *sentido*, cognition savored so often that it takes on emotional overtones (see n. 153 on *SpEx* [352] above) and to *sentir*, to perceive, experience (on which see n. 19 on [14] below).

9. By these two vertical lines in the text Ignatius seemingly indicates that he has had a vision; and beside it in the margin is another sign: ══#══.

Similar marks occur at Feb. 8, 10, and 11. On March 22 and 25 ([169, 172]) he will write "Vision" in the margin and a similar sign. On March 30 and April 2 ([177, 183]) he will write "Vision" in the margin but no sign. On many other days visions are mentioned but no signs are placed in the text or the margin. See the respective notes in *Obrascompl*, or in A. Haas and P. Knauer, *Das geistliche Tagebuch* (Freiburg, 1961), p. 237, n. 8.

10. This is a reference to the reasons pro and con in the Deliberation on Poverty. Here Ignatius, while proceeding according to the Second Time for making an election (*SpEx* [176]), is using also the Third Time ([177]), according to the First Method, which he explains in [178–183].

11. Through his mediators he offers his decision to God in order to obtain confirmation of it, as he recommends in *SpEx* [183].

12. This exemplifies the manner of praying which Ignatius advised in the "triple colloquy," first to Mary, then through her to Jesus, and

438

through Jesus and Mary to the Father, as he recommends often in the *Exercises*, e.g., in [62–64, 109, 147, 156, 159, 225].

13. Just as other mystics write of fervor or ardor, Ignatius uses warmth to describe his religious experience—at least 32 times in the *Diary*. See Munitiz, *Discernment Log-book*, pp. 84–85 and 101 in the Index, s.v. "warmth." This component of his experience illustrates his teaching on the "application of the senses" (*SpEx* [121–126]) as a method of prayer. It too is rooted in the biblical, patristic, and medieval tradition of the "spiritual senses." See n. 59 on *SpEx* [121].

14. In his attention to detail and precision, Ignatius, by using expressions like *no sin agoa a los ojos* as here and *alguna agua a los ojos* in [141], distinguishes between tears and moistened eyes which can be the precedent to or consequence of actual weeping.

15. A characteristic of Ignatius' spirituality is gratitude to God, nourished by specific methods of remembering his favors; see, e.g., *SpEx* [230–237, esp. 234 and 235]. See also point 1 of that way of prayer which he calls the General Examen (on which see n. 27 on *SpEx* [43] above). Ignatius' very example of keeping and using a diary of graces received teaches us another method.

16. *Elecciones*: Notice the plural, very apt here because the main election entails simultaneous choices of various pros or cons listed in the Deliberation on Poverty. *SpDiar* [10–13] exemplify unusually well the various phases of the decision-making processes which Ignatius engaged in and proposes to others in *SpEx* [169–189].

17. This reflecting (*discurriendo*) is far more than a merely intellectual act. It entails rumination with mind and heart, with all the connotations which Ignatius attaches to *discurrir* in *SpEx* [51] in his suggestions for an exercitant's colloquy with Christ on the cross.

18. *Buena elección* is the same phrase which forms the two titles of *SpEx* [175 and 178].

19. *Sentir*, to perceive or experience, to feel, like its parent Latin *sentire*, etymologically means to perceive through the senses and also through the mind. Beyond these and its many further senses, in Ignatius' works this word has many important meanings peculiarly his own which have been extensively studied. In the *Diary* it often means or connotes the experience of multiple sentiments which are bringing light about God's will or the good pleasure of the Trinity (Iparraguirre, *Vocabulario de los Ejercicios Espirituales* [Rome, 1966], p. 194). Particularly important is the sense pointed out by E. Hernández Gordils: to be

the passive recipient of an extraordinary supernatural or mystical experience which affects various faculties of the soul down to its very depths (*Que su santisima voluntad sintamos y enteramente la cumplamos* [Rome, 1966], pp. 46–59, esp. 58). In all these instances, to perceive is a common and basic meaning, but according to cases it must be clarified by qualifying words such as deeply, in spirit, in the heart, or the like. Closely allied is *sentido*, knowledge savored so repeatedly that it takes on emotional qualities (Leturia, *Estudios* II:153; see n. 153 on *SpEx* [345] above). Also related to *sentir* is Ignatius' use of *sentimiento*, on which see n. 8 above. In Ignatius' usage *sentir* virtually always implies an underlying intellectual cognition.

20. "Dense brightness" (*claridad espesa*), in which the density refers to the content (fundamental truths) of what he perceived enshrined in brightness.

21. "Reason and discern" (*discurrir y discernir*): Notice how the first word describes the activities of the Third Time (*SpEx* [177]) and the second those of the Second Time ([176]) for Making a Good Election. He is interweaving the two procedures. His reference to the Deliberation on Poverty indicates that by this date, February 11, it was a completed document.

22. Ignatius here views the descent of the Holy Spirit (Acts 2:14) as confirming Christ's sending the apostles to preach throughout the world (Matt. 25:19; Mark 16:15). This sentence implies an extensive theology of apostolic missions: (1) Christ sends the apostles; (2) the Holy Spirit confirms this and (3) through the gifts of Pentecost enables the apostles to spread the Gospel message throughout the world. Moreover, all this is the extension into the exterior world of the relations and processions in the Trinity.

23. For the first time in the *Diary* Ignatius has a vision of the Holy Spirit. As a result he felt at first that the election was confirmed.

24. His failure to perceive the Father and Son along with the Holy Spirit made him doubt that his election had been confirmed. He had been hoping for confirmation from the Trinity, but now two of the Persons, as he will write next day, "were hiding themselves" (Giuliani). Ignatius' deletions and insertions make this passage difficult and open to other interpretations.

25. Here we see Ignatius putting into practice the gratitude which he inculcated in the Contemplation to Attain Love, esp. in [233, 234].

26. He probably means Francesco Vanucci, who was almoner of Pope Paul III and helped Ignatius in his works of charity.

27. The small house was old and creaky so that noises spread easily. This distracted him; and he noticed that the temptation came during distraction.

28. This decision to end the election turned out to be temporary. On the very next day he experienced aridity and spiritual desolation which unsettled him and made him feel a need of further confirmation from God.

29. Perhaps he means a delay of an hour or so to finish the election that morning before dinner, as he had decided ([42]) the previous day; or he may be thinking of a fast as a means of obtaining a favor from God, as he recommends in (*SpEx* [57]).

30. Above [48] Ignatius drew firm double lines across the page. When he did this is unknown. Possibly it was on some later occasion when he reviewed his diary and with fresh perspective recognized these marked passages as important signs, factors, or turning points in his process of discernment.

In his Autograph Directory of the Exercises, ch. 3, no. 21 (*Obrascompl*, p. 298), Ignatius recommends offering one alternative of an election to God on one day and the other alternative on a different day, to see what signs God may give. In the *Diary*, by renewing his offering on different days he is following a roughly similar procedure.

31. Two days later ([53]) he will appraise this indignation as a temptation from the evil spirit.

32. Probably he means the whole process of discernment; or possibly determination of some number of Masses. His text lacks specification.

33. The first of the "six or more Masses of the Holy Trinity" which he promises to say, immediately below.

34. To indicate some passages of the *Diary* as especially meaningful to himself, Ignatius drew around them lines left open at the right. A manuscript exists in the National Library at Madrid which contains only these passages, transcribed by his own hand. His desire to have them on one separate sheet manifests their special importance to him. See *DeGuiJes*, p. 43.

35. In *Autobiog*, 30, he makes a similar remark about his outstanding illumination beside the Cardoner.

36. Appropriation: attributing to one Person what is common to the three. Already at Manresa he prayed to the Father, Son, Holy Spirit, and the whole Trinity, and then wondered for a moment: "Why four prayers to the Trinity?" (*Autobiog*, 28). Now after his theological studies he understands and appreciates the appropriations far more deeply.

37. Processions: The theological explanation that the Father produces the Son (who proceeds from him by generation from the divine intellect), and the Father and the Son produce the Holy Spirit (who is the act of love proceeding from the divine will). Ignatius contemplates these divine operations as they are in God.

38. In *Autobiog*, 28, to explain his vision of the Trinity he used the image of three musical keys. His procedure here is somewhat similar.

39. As mentioned in [50] above. On "*capitulo 17*" see n. 2 on [1] above.

40. The promise made in [51] above to say successively six or more Masses of the Trinity. On Feb. 19 and 20 ([51–59]) Ignatius seemingly felt confirmed in his election of no fixed revenue.

41. Probably elevation of spirit as in [9] above, but possibly a levitation.

42. See 2 Cor. 12:2. Ignatius, like Paul, is vainly struggling to find language to express his ineffable mystical experiences.

43. He had been seeking devotion centered on the Trinity, and not only on the Father, but now God reveals to him how through the circuminsessions all three Persons are in the Father, and consequently how devotion paid to the Father (or to either of the other Persons) is simultaneously given to all three Persons. Similarly, any operation proceeding outward from one Person proceeds also from the other two.

44. In the Gospel of the Mass of the Trinity were the words of Matt. 28:18–20: "Go, therefore, and make disciples of all nations, baptizing them in the name of the Father, and of the Son, and of the Holy Spirit."

45. In the margin here Ignatius wrote "Confirmation from Jesus."

46. He refers to his moving experience at La Storta (*Autobiog*, 96).

47. *Espesa*, literally dense, heavy. See n. 20 on [14] above.

48. I.e., in the deliberations of March 4, 1541, his six companions had signed the agreement that fixed revenues would be permitted to the sacristies (see above, p. 219). Ignatius now had the embarrassing task of opposing this decision, and he was firmly resolved to do so.

49. Ignatius again wrote in the margin here: "Confirmation from Jesus."

50. Probably he is asking pardon for his vexation with the Holy Trinity on February 18, in [50]. He will return to this search for reconciliation in the days ahead, esp. in [76, 78, 110, 112, 118]. He now sees that he yielded to a bad attitude.

51. I.e., near the fire-pan of burning coals which was in the room.

52. Cardinal Rudolfo Pio da Carpi, the Cardinal Protector of the Society.

53. The vicar-bishop of Rome, Filippo Achinto, an expert in canon law.

54. Cardinal Gian Domenico de Cupis, who was the protector of the house of the catechumens founded by Ignatius. He was archbishop of Trani, which led Ignatius to refer to him as "Trana."

55. In this dense and difficult passage we follow the interpretation and punctuation of Knauer and Iparraguirre.

56. *Acatamiento*, veneration, respect, honor, was a word especially rich in meaning for Ignatius. This is the first mention in the *Diary* of *acatamiento* and *reverencia*, both of which he will use frequently in the rest of his diary to express his attitude toward God. We translate *acatamiento* as "affectionate awe." *Acatamiento allegado a amor reverencial* is a phrase typically Ignatian in which each word clarifies the other. Both *acatamiento* and *reverencia* are prominent characteristics of his spirituality and mysticism; see, e.g., *SpEx* [23] in the very first line of the Foundation. On his use of *acatamiento*, see Charles. E. O'Neill, "*Acatamiento*: Ignatian Reverence in History and in Contemporary Culture," *Studies in the Spirituality of Jesuits* 8 (Jan. 1976): 3–8, esp. p. 8.

57. *Primero*: This probably means his first Trinitarian vision at Manresa (*Autobiog*, 28). This is the only passage which Ignatius enclosed on all four sides.

58. The prayer of the Missal, between the "Lamb of God" and the priest's Communion.

59. Here too is continuity with the visions at Manresa and later (e.g., *Autobiog*, 44), but there is a progression. At Manresa his attention was more on "the humanity of Christ" like a white body and small, and here on Christ as God and man. On the intellectual character of Ignatius' visions and the comparative poverty of his images, see *DeGuiJes*, pp. 60–61, 608.

60. No doubt, the church of Our Lady of the Way.

61. I.e., of the Holy Trinity, which begins: "Blessed be the Holy Trinity and undivided Unity."

62. Cardinal Juan Alvarez de Toledo, O.P. As inquisitor general he was appointed by Paul III to examine the Exercises and gave a favorable opinion.

63. Notice Ignatius' progression of thought: First he celebrated Masses to obtain confirmation from the Trinity ([51]). After receiving it he celebrated them, not to seek further confirmation, but only to reconcile himself to the Divine Persons for his fault ([78]). Now in [110] he wishes merely to fulfill the promised number of Masses and have the spiritual joy.

64. I.e., of the entrance antiphon of the Mass of the Trinity.

65. By "the letter" he is probably referring to the text in the missal from which he was reading the Mass of the Trinity. As we shall soon see, his attention shifts among three levels: above, the abode of the Trinity; below, the text of the missal. It is one of God's creatures, reflects God's attributes, and reminds Ignatius of other creatures, especially our Lady and the saints. They are in the middle area ([128]), and are Ignatius' mediators ([129]), who are mirrors reflecting God's glories. In that middle area his attention rests. In it he finds reflections of God, and he also sees the Church, which prolongs Jesus' life and work (Matt. 28:18–20).

66. From this passage Hugo Rahner took the triple level as the framework of his beautiful essay on the content, characteristics, and comprehensive sweep of Ignatius' mystical knowledge, in *Ignatius the Theologian* (New York, 1967; original German, 1959), pp. 1–31.

67. On this day a noteworthy process of descent begins in Ignatius' thought. He does not find devotion by looking above to the Trinity. Hence he tries to find God in the middle area ([128]), i.e., in a global view of his mediators beneath the Trinity, starting with Jesus and coming down to some one saint. Finally (in [137]) the more he will keep his attention on these mediators rather than on the Trinity, the more will he receive visitations of devotion.

68. Some interpret the fire as metaphor for consolation and the water for desolation over inability to find the Sacrament. This passage is obscure and the manuscript presents problems. Perhaps he means that he could not find the solution to his problem during Mass, or simply that the fire became too hot and he threw some water on it.

69. The less he sought, i.e., with disordered eagerness for what seemed holier to him (as he had described in [119]), the more divine visitations he received. By this God was indicating that he wanted Ignatius to look at creatures below.

70. Since Feb. 27 Ignatius has been aware that God has been leading him along a new path, that of visitations without the gift of tears ([119]). Despite his delight in the tears he has been growing more content to be without that gift. Here in the spirit of the Third Way of Being Humble (*SpEx* [167]) he even prays to be deprived of it (Giuliani).

71. What he suspects here but cannot identify will later turn out to be the infused gift of affectionate awe (*acatamiento*) and reverence ([156–157] below) which develops into loving humility ([161–190]), the path he should henceforth follow.

72. He is referring to his discarded eagerness to look above, as he described it in [136] above. See also above [127] with n. 65 and [128].

73. Ignatius' erasures in the manuscript reveal that his doubt was about whether he should say more Masses for the intentions mentioned above in [51] or consider those already celebrated to be enough.

74. His experience exemplifies the desolation he describes in *SpEx* [317].

75. He had the same reaction on Feb. 16 after a fault.

76. I.e., to avoid the distracting noises on the first floor.

77. I.e., to decide his election. This was the fortieth day he had devoted to it and he had hoped to end it in a time of consolation and general satisfaction. This disappointment increased his desolation. God saw fit to send this trial now.

78. By his desire of more and more signs he had become like a person typical of the second class in *SpEx* [154], who wants God to come to where he is, rather than to go to God on his terms. Ignatius now makes himself a person typical of the third class in [155]; and God soon sends the consolation.

79. In [148 and 149] Ignatius unwittingly teaches by example how a colloquy is made according to the description he gives in *SpEx* [54].

80. Ignatius left considerable space before and after the word *finido* in his manuscript (Codina, *Cons*MHSJ I:125). The word is like a decisive punctuation mark. The long process of election, now ended, has resulted not only in Ignatius' decision against all fixed income for his churches but also in a great change in his interior attitude. He has advanced from disordered attachment to the kind of conclusion he himself wanted and has opened himself completely to what God wants.

81. His reason was perhaps to take the time to reflect on the new graces he has received (as Giuliani suggests). Perhaps another reason was also present: to rest, and clear his mind from complicated reasoning processes, and thereby gain a fresh perspective.

82. The verbs "have or not to have" lack an object. Probably he meant "fixed income" (*renta*), or possibly "tears" (*lagrimas*).

83. Henceforth these symbols *a l d* occur with great frequency and in varying combinations. Codina has reasoned to the following meanings (*Cons*MHSJ I:cviii–cix, 126).

a, tears before (*antes*) Mass.

l, tears during Mass (*la Misa*).

d, tears after (*despues*) Mass.

The minus sign, −, means: tears in lesser abundance. Sometimes Ignatius places a period before or after one of the letters and sometimes not, in varying combinations. Probably these periods had a meaning to him to which we have no key. We reproduce his varying usage.

84. Henceforth throughout this Part II of the *Diary* the infused gifts of affectionate awe (*acatamiento*), reverence (*reverencia*), and humility (*humildad*) will take on increasing importance in Ignatius' life and record keeping. They comprise the new path God wished to show him. On them see *DeGuiJes*, pp. 57–58; Egan, *Ignatius Loyola the Mystic*, pp. 186–190.

85. He is referring to March 9 ([139]) when he thought that God wanted to show some "manner of proceeding."

86. Here for the first time in the *Diary* he calls the Mass "the sacrifice" instead of "the Mass." Perhaps this is a deeper insight brought by the gifts of affectionate awe, reverence, and humility (Giuliani, Iparraguirre).

87. Notice the sequence of his spiritual progress: At first he had been looking for visitations and because they did not come in the manner he wanted he did not conclude his election. Now he is content to be without the visitations and wants only whatever is more pleasing to God.

88. I.e., not properly ordered to what is "more conducive to the end," God's glory (*SpEx* [23]) and the Introduction to making a good election ([169]). By seeking the visitations in the manner he himself desired he had been "ordering or dragging the end" ([169]), what is more pleasing to God, into subjection to the means, the visitations he was himself hoping to experience. Henceforth the procedure properly ordered will be to attend first to the affectionate awe and then to the visitations only if God should will them.

89. I.e., the Constitutions about the Missions, a preliminary draft (text in *Cons*MHSJ I:159–164) which gradually evolved into [603–617]

of Part VII of the *Constitutions*. Here "mission" means the pope's or superior's act of sending a Jesuit wherever the former thinks proper.

90. Here Ignatius wrote in the margin the word *Vision* and the sign $=\neq=$, as he did at [4] above.

91. Here too in the margin are the word *Vision* and the sign $=\neq=$.

92. This is now called the Prayer over the Gifts.

93. *Fientadamente*, not a Spanish word, seems to be a slip of the pen for *frecuentadamente* (Codina).

94. I.e., loving humility and all the gifts it brings with itself should not be limited to his relations to God but should extend also to creatures, especially his fellow human beings. For all these are like a mirror which reflects God and his goodness to us (Iparraguirre, following Larrañaga).

95. John 8:55. It is in the Gospel of the Mass which Ignatius said on this day, Passion Sunday. Ignatius seems to mean that at times we must take a critical attitude toward our neighbor for the sake of the truth, as Jesus did in the Gospel passage cited.

96. Here he wrote the word *Vision* in the margin but no sign $=\neq=$.

97. This may mean a distraction from the words of the Missal which are read or heard at Mass; or perhaps it should be coupled with the following phrase and means distraction from hearing words from God.

98. I.e., the long Gospel of the Passion read in the Mass of Palm Sunday.

99. Ignatius drew these horizontal lines above and below the pair of days on which he did not say Mass, Good Friday and Holy Saturday.

100. Here for the first time in the *Diary* Ignatius mentions a new mystical phenomenon. He describes it, however, as a gift which he has experienced earlier. He calls it *loquela*, which is not a Spanish word but Latin or Italian which he does not translate into Spanish. However (perhaps forgetting it is Latin) he treats it as Spanish by using the Spanish article and plural, *las loquelas*. The Latin *loquela* can mean an act of speaking, the speech itself, language, discourse, or locution. Ignatius' *loquela* seems to be a special mystical phenomenon. He mentions most of its characteristics in [221 and 234]. There was an exterior loquela with a beautiful tone (possibly with words containing a divine message) which he heard, like heavenly music, and an interior *loquela*, which had meaning and produced an interior experience of harmony and delight. All this moved him toward intense devotion, relish, and spiritual con-

solation. On it see *DeGuiJes*, pp. 61–62; and esp. Egan, *Ignatius Loyola the Mystic*, pp. 193–196. Some authors use the term *locution* to describe this or a similar mystical phenomenon; e.g., De Guibert in his *Theology of the Spiritual Life* treats of locutions in the context of inspirations from the Holy Spirit, pp. 111–113, 355–357.

101. A conjecture for the missing object of the verb *find*. Another possible meaning is "I found myself somewhat more purified."

102. Ignatius is discerning by means of *SpEx* [335]: The good spirit touches those who are spiritually advancing "gently, lightly, like water going into a sponge," and the evil spirit touches them "with noise and disturbance."

103. He means perhaps continued work on the "missions" mentioned on March 17 ([161] above); or perhaps on some new point.

104. The procedure he was "being taught" was to walk in complete submission to the will of God, in loving humility and affectionate awe. That lesson from God was probably more important for his spiritual progress than his concluding his election by the decision to permit no fixed income for the Society's churches. It is interesting to notice that at the time of his mystical illuminations at Manresa he was similarly convinced that he was being taught by God (*Autobiog*, 27).

105. As the samples below indicate, the rest of the *Diary* ([395–490]) consists entirely of very brief entries and abbreviations.

106. On October 4 Ignatius begins to place dots above the letter *a* which he has used since March 14 (see [156], with n. 83 above); and further, also to use new letters *O, C, Y* with varying periods before or after them. These new letters are signs to designate each of the three prayer-periods into which he divided the mental prayer that he made each morning. The first was what he called his "first" (*primera*) or "customary" (*acostumbrada*) prayer. He made this as soon as he awoke (see *SpEx* [73, 74])—often while still in bed because of his poor health. The second was that made in his room after dressing. He regarded it as a preparation for Mass. The third period was the prayer which he made in the chapel (*yglesia*) located a few steps from his room. This was his immediate preparation to celebrate Mass. In the light of this the meaning of his letters from [366] through [490] is as follows.

O: his first or customary prayer (*oración primera o acostumbrada*).

C: his prayer in his room (*cámara*).

Y: his prayer in the church or chapel (*yglesia* or *capilla*).

a: before Mass (*antes de la misa*); i.e., the three prayer-periods taken as a unit. By the dots placed above the *a* he distinguishes the respective prayer periods above.

a with *no* dot: tears in *one* of the three prayer-periods.

ä with *two* dots: tears in *two* of the three prayer-periods.

ä̈ with *three* dots: tears in all *three* prayer-periods.

An exception: In [379] he places one dot over the à.

On this topic see Iparraguirre in *Obrascompl*, p. 404; Codina in *Cons*MHSJ I:cvi–cxii.

ON THE SELECTIONS FROM THE
CONSTITUTIONS

1. ON THE INTRODUCTION

1. *Cons*MHSJ I:viii.

2. *Cons*MHSJ I:xvii–xviii.

3. They are published in *Cons*MHSJ IV, *Regulae Societatis Iesu (1540–1556)* (Rome, 1948).

4. On the meaning of "for the greater glory of God" as a criterion, see Walter J. Ong, " 'A.M.D.G.': Dedication or Directive?" *Review for Religious* 11 (1952): 257–264.

5. Those ideals are discussed more extensively in ch. 9 of *IdeaJes-Un*, pp. 191–201, obviously with a coloring of circumstances of the 1950s, some of which have passed away. On the application of these ideals today, see Ganss, "St. Ignatius and Jesuit Higher Education," in *Jesuit Higher Education*, ed. R. E. Bonachea (1989), pp. 160–167. The concept used above of education as *paideia* owes much to the masterful work of Werner Jaeger, *Paideia: The Ideals of Greek Culture*, 3 vols. (New York, 1941–1945). See also *The Characteristics of Jesuit Education* (Washington: Jesuit Secondary Education Association, 1987).

6. See also *IdeaJesUn*, pp. 54–55, 177, 191, 271–272.

7. Also, see *IdeaJesUn*, pp. 52–53, 195, 264.

8. *Cons*MHSJ I:lxxi; *IdeaJesUn*, pp. 28–31, 38.

9. Harney, *The Jesuits in History* (New York, 1941), pp. 201–202.

10. Robert R. Rusk, *The Doctrines of the Great Educators*, 3rd ed. rev. (London, 1965). The first edition appeared in 1918.

2. ON THE *EXAMEN*

1. Sections [1–10] of the *Examen* give us much basic terminology necessary to understand the structure of Ignatius' Society as well as many features in his apostolic spirituality. The Formula of the Institute as contained in the papal bull *Regimini* of Sept. 27, 1540, established the

Society's essential structure and characteristics. Here in the *Examen* Ignatius, merely sketching these for the benefit of candidates and their examiners, indicates especially how they differ from those of other orders (*AldamIntro*, pp. 22, 24–25). He will develop them more fully in the *Constitutions*. He takes up first his cherished title, *Compañía de Jesús*, *Societas Iesu* in Polanco's Latin translation of 1558. Since this title and institute had novel and sometimes controverted features, here in [1] he assures the candidate that they have been approved by the Holy See. For Ignatius the basic meaning of *Compañía* and *Societas* was an organized group which has Jesus as its head and is completely at his service (see, e.g., *DalmIgn*, pp. 149–151; *DeGuiJes*, pp. 38, 42). For Ignatius the more important word in the title was Jesus. His own interpretation is given by Polanco: "It is not called Society of Jesus on the ground that we are making ourselves companions of Jesus, but in the same way that a society or cohort is named after its leader; and by our Institute we desire to follow Him" (*EppIgn* XII:615). Any military connotations were metaphorical; religious were commonly referred to as soldiers of Christ. However, in this title many, even among Ignatius' companions, have found other connotations and overtones. Hence it has received additional interpretations and emphases, supplementary rather than exclusive, and also misinterpretations from his opponents (see *ConsSJ-Comm*, pp. 76, 345–349). Nadal points out that the title stems from the meditations on the Kingdom and the Two Standards (*MonNad* V: 136 [5]).

2. In the bull *Regimini militantis Ecclesiae*, found in *ConsMHSJ* I:24–32.

3. In *Exposcit debitum*, ibid., pp. 373–383, currently in force. An English translation is in *ConsSJComm*, pp. 63–73.

4. In the *Constitutions* "houses" and "colleges" are technical terms. According to the Formula of the Institute approved by the pope in 1540, the professed members of the Society were to dwell in "houses" (*domus, casas*) dedicated to their priestly ministries rather than studies, and these professed members were to have no fixed or regularly recurring revenues but to live only on alms. However, to train young men who would later be incorporated into the Society and live in these houses, the Society was permitted to possess colleges dedicated to studies, i.e., domiciles like the colleges at the University of Paris, from which the Jesuit students, the "scholastics" (*scolares, scholastici*), would go to lectures in some nearby university. These colleges were permitted

to possess endowments and regularly recurring revenues for the support of these Jesuit "scholastics" (*Regimini* [6] in *Cons*MHSJ, I:29–30). "Houses of probation" were considered to be branches of a college ([6] below). Changes in the plans for colleges were to be made if experience revealed them to be useful in helping the Church (*Cons*MHSJ I:57, no. 13; Lukács in *Woodstock Letters* 91 [1960]: 128). Ignatius expected that most professed members of the Society would live in the houses, and that these "professed houses" would far outnumber the colleges. The colleges were to be seedbeds (*seminarios*) to supply men for the houses. In history, however, the exact opposite happened. The colleges multiplied rapidly, the houses did not. The legal concept of the house remained almost unchanged, but as the colleges evolved the term took on new meanings.

Gradually after 1547 classes were introduced into the colleges and then opened to extern students, whether clerical or lay, along with the Jesuit scholastics. Donors to establish professed houses for Jesuits alone were difficult to find, but there were many who were eager to establish colleges for Jesuits from which the lay youths of the region would also profit. At Ignatius' death in 1556 there were 2 professed houses (Rome and Coimbra) and 48 dwellings classified as colleges (see *DalmIgn*, pp. 301–302; Ganss, "The Origin of Jesuit Colleges and the Controversies about Their Poverty (1539–1608)," in *Woodstock Letters* 91 (1962): 126–137, 142–143, reprinted in T. Clancy, *An Introduction to Jesuit Life* (St. Louis, 1976), pp. 286–297, 302–303. This article is chiefly a digest in English of archival research which L. Lukács published in *AHSJ* 29 (1960): 189–245. See also n. 6 on p. 433 above.

5. After years of experimentation, in 1556 text *B* of the *Constitutions* divided the formation of the Society's scholastics into three periods of "probation," i.e., of training and testing. The first probation was to last 12 to 15 days, during which the candidate was a guest, examining the Society and being examined by it. The second probation was to consist of spiritual training (or noviceship) for two years. They led the candidates (1) to simple but perpetual vows of poverty, chastity, and obedience along with the vowed promise to enter the Society by final vows years later ([16, 336]), and then (2) to entrance into a college for the years of intellectual training as approved scholastics ([336]). This training is treated in Part IV ([307–509]) and is regarded as an extension of the second probation. The third probation, later termed the tertianship, was made after the completion of the studies. It was

another year of spiritual formation through prayer, abnegation, lowly apostolic work, and preaching. By all this the young priest proved his willingness and ability to do the Society's often humble work ([71, 516]).

6. On the word *soul* used by synecdoche for the whole self or person, see n. 16 on *SpEx* [23] above. *Cons* [3] summarizes in a theoretical way what is expressed concretely in the Formula of the Institute, I.

7. In the early monastic orders persons entered explicitly and chiefly to pursue their personal spiritual development, though apostolic work also gradually grew up. Ignatius naturally desires that indispensable goal of spiritual development, but he further stresses here that the personal development is to be directed toward apostolate. Thus there is one spirituality which is totally apostolic. At first sight he may seem to be proposing here two ends of the Society, the personal and the apostolic, but in his concept there is only one end, the greater glory of God sought by means of both personal sanctification and apostolic endeavor.

8. Of the three vows, Ignatius treats only poverty here because of details in his practice which differed from that in other orders.

9. *Rentas*: fixed or regularly recurring revenues to which one has a right as they come due periodically, such as annually.

10. In the ancient monastic orders, the individual monk or nun could not own property, but the monastery could possess it and the right to its income. In the mendicant orders neither the members nor their houses could own stable material goods; their financial support was to come from either begging or their own work. This is the form of canonical poverty which Ignatius and his companions chose by their "determination" on June 11, 1539. Ignatius' Institute also brought a new stress on gratuity of ministries (e.g., in [478, 816]). The legislation on poverty given so sketchily here for candidates is filled out later in Part VI ([553–581]).

11. "Vow to the sovereign pontiff" is an elliptical expression. The vow is made to God to go wherever the pope orders (see [527]). From Montmartre in 1535 onward Ignatius and his companions desired to leave the disposition of themselves to the pope, since he knew best where the needs were greatest. Hence in their first profession in 1541, they vowed: "I promise a special obedience in regard to the missions as contained in the bull" (*Regimini* [4]); and this became the formula prescribed in *Cons* [527]. This well-known vow is treated further in [603–617]). Whether or not it adds to the obligations of all priests and

religious has been much discussed. At the very least it is an inspiring expression of Ignatius' spirit of intense desire to be closely and cooperatively associated with Christ and also with the pope as his vicar. See *AldamIntro*, pp. 246–249. The formula in which Ignatius expressed this spirit became, like other laws, the object of multiple interpretations and controversies.

12. "Ordinary" (*comun*), i.e., the manner of life is not that of lay persons, nor of older monastic orders which prescribed fasts and other austerities, but rather, therefore, like that of exemplary diocesan priests (*MonNad* V:156–157).

13. Here too is a difference from older orders. For the apostolic purposes he envisaged Ignatius established four classes or grades of members in the Society. The first class, the "professed," are the fully formed priests who have the three solemn vows of poverty, chastity, and obedience plus the fourth solemn vow of obedience to the pope ([12, 511]). The second class, the coadjutors, are of two kinds, spiritual and temporal: (1) the spiritual coadjutors are priests (in Ignatius' day of lesser learning than the "professed") and they are assigned to ministerial labors; and (2) the temporal coadjutors are "lay," the brothers who help in temporal or exterior matters such as cooking or farming ([13, 148, 149]). The third class, the "approved scholastics," are the Jesuit students who after their two years of novitiate have taken their simple but perpetual vows of poverty, chastity, and obedience, along with a promise to become full members as either professed or spiritual coadjutors after their studies and ordination ([14]). The fourth class, the "indifferent" or undetermined, are those who left it to their superiors to decide later whether they were to be priests or brothers ([15]). In modern times only rarely have applicants been admitted as thus indifferent. See also n. 54 on [510] below.

14. By taking his perpetual vows, at the end of the two years of training and testing in the novitiate. These vows included the promise to request definitive incorporation into the Society at the end of his studies and an additional year of spiritual training ([510, 516]). See also n. 55 on [510] below.

15. Ignatius concludes this chapter 4 of the *Examen* by his spiritual teaching on the love of the cross. His Christocentric viewpoint on this topic will be quickly recognized as virtually identical with that about the Third Way of Being Humble in *SpEx* [167] above. This is another of the aspects in his spirituality which to some seem negative and fright-

ening, at least at first sight. To be understood rightly, the affronts, abnegation of self, and injuries of which he speaks in either book must be fitted into his worldview of God's redemptive plan. Against that background they are seen as means to greater glory to God and eventually to greater happiness to the person who bears them for the love of God. One who is unwilling to bear them is not likely to show perseverance in the discouragements inevitably to be met in apostolic work. Ignatius does not ask the candidate to choose the injuries, false accusations, affronts, and the like for their own sake, as if they were good in themselves. They are accepted as means to higher ends. In the present case Ignatius states that genuine motive for the candidate just before the mention of injuries and false accusations: to become more like to Christ through love: "because of the love and reverence which he [Christ] deserves." See also note 81 on *SpEx* [167].

16. Aware that the ideal in [101] is too lofty to be expected of many a beginner, he presented it as a goal to be attained with passing time.

3. ON THE *CONSTITUTIONS*
The Preamble

17. "Writes upon hearts" (*corazones*): This sentence echoes Rom. 2:15 and 5:15, "the Law written in their hearts," where hearts means the persons. The Mosaic Law is a law exterior to human beings, and like it are the constitutions of religious institutes. External law gives information and commands but not always spiritual strength or inspiration. Such law is necessary for persevering and organized action or cooperation, but even so it cannot by itself make one holy unless one cooperates from within. His or her own interior decision to do the good works and the impulse of God's helping grace are both necessary (John 6:44, 15:4; Eph. 2:4–10).

18. On this practical procedure, see the Special Introduction above, pp. 276–277.

On Part III. Those in Probation in the Novitiate

19. More usually in modern times this two-year period is called the training of novices in a novitiate.

20. *Devoción*: a word which Ignatius used with great frequency in all his works. It expressed his attitude of profound respect before God and he used it with multitudinous connotations, often mystical.

Devoción is an affection for God that is prompt, compliant, and warmly loving. On its relation with other key phrases, see n. 4 on *SpDiar* [1], p. 437 above.

21. This spontaneous expression of Ignatius, simple as it is, contains the heart of his concept of what religious life is: total and irrevocable self-dedication to God through love. From this love of God flows love of the neighbor.

22. In [284] and [287] Ignatius gives a preliminary sketch of his concepts of obedience and poverty. He develops them at greater length later, especially in [547–552] and [553–581].

23. Constitution [288] contains another spontaneous expression of Ignatius' desire to live totally for God and to have his followers do the same (see [283] above and [813] below). A key idea of this God-centered attitude is his doctrine of a right intention. Synonymously called "pure" ([340] below), it is for Ignatius one "not . . . mixed with human motives" ([180]). This ideal recurs constantly throughout his writings. God should be the principal reason for whom we act or choose (*SpEx* [169]); and Ignatius' own dominant love of God often led him to express this in the language of love, e.g., the scholastics should pursue it "by seeking in their studies nothing except the glory of God and the good of souls" ([360]). God should be loved above anyone or anything else. However, in Ignatius' prudently balanced thought, this by no means excludes rightly ordered love for creatures, for they reveal God to us and he wants us to find him in them and by means of them, and to use them in proper manner by ordering them to God. For the love of God, we should esteem and use both the supernatural means and the natural, as Ignatius will bring out below in [360 and 361, 813 and 814]. See also above, *SpEx* [237] with n. 113; and Ignatius' disagreement with Juan Alvarez, who had expressed reluctance to use certain natural means: "One who thinks that it is not good to make use of such helps [natural resources] or to employ this talent [for diligent study] along with others which God has given him, under the impression that mingling such helps with the higher ones of grace produces a ferment or evil concoction, has not learned well to order all things to God's glory and to find a profit in and with all these things for the ultimate end, which is God's honor and glory" (*LettersIgn*, p. 192).

24. To "seek" or "find God in all things" is another key principle recurring throughout Ignatius' writings. It is intricately interwoven with his ideas on right intention. See *AldamIntro*, pp. 131–134. It was

largely through his habit of finding God in all things that he became a contemplative person "even while in action."

On Part IV. Instruction in Learning

25. With Part IV we begin to observe how Ignatius' worldview shaped his concept of Christian education, as was explained on pp. 278–279 above. Part IV, now containing 17 chapters, was composed in stages which reveal his expanding concept. Texts *a* of about 1546 and *A* of 1550 contain only the chapters presently numbered 1–6 and 8–10. *When first written* in or near 1546 they envisaged, as the very title of this part indicates, the formation of only the scholastics of the Society who were living in its colleges, i.e., domiciles in which classes were gradually added for the Jesuits. Then at Gandía in 1547 at the request of Duke Francis Borgia these classes were opened also to the youths of the region. At Messina in 1548 a college planned to become a university was opened for lay youths far more numerous than the Jesuits. The apostolic success from these colleges at Gandía, Messina, Rome (1551), and elsewhere opened up expanding horizons of possibilities to Ignatius' foresight. He saw that, in addition to educating his own scholastics, he could also train lay students who would be likely to participate capably and vigorously in the cultural and social life of the era and leaven society with the principles of Christ. Consequently the chapters of 1546 which envisaged only Jesuit scholastics were found to be applicable also to lay students, but also to need some supplements. With Polanco's help, Ignatius in 1553–1554 composed the present ch. 7 and chs. 11–17 on the universities. These chapters now explicitly envisaged the training of both Jesuit scholastics and "more especially" ([440]) extern students. (A few of these externs were preparing for the priesthood, e.g., in other dioceses or orders, but the vast majority envisaged lay life.) The new chapters were composed before Ignatius' death in 1556 and approved by General Congregation I in 1558. However, up to his death Ignatius did not yet go back and revise chs. 1–6 and 8–10 to make them express more clearly their applicability to extern students as well as Jesuits (see Lukács, in Clancy, *An Introduction to Jesuit Life* [St. Louis, 1976], pp. 286–307 and esp. 321–326; *ConsSJComm*, p. 171; *AldamIntro*, pp. 139–142). As a result his statements in chs. 1–6 and 8–10 often seem at first sight to envisage only Jesuit scholastics; but, with obvious and easy adaptations which the teachers or readers instinc-

tively made, they were being applied from 1547 to 1556 and thereafter also to extern students. More important still, all the 17 chapters reveal his ideals of Christian education, and these ideals are equally applicable to extern students whether clerical or lay, male or female, in the changed circumstances of later eras. In this work of adapting them to the education of lay students Ignatius himself led the way by example, as we can see in his letter of Dec. 1, 1551, to Araoz, among the Selected Letters, on pages 361–365 above.

26. In [307] Ignatius clearly directs the Society's educational efforts to the ultimate purpose of the students' lives, their salvation; and through it, to the greater glory of God. This is the ultimate aim of the Society's studies and schools. In the rest of Part IV he treats the proximate end, the means to form the young persons into "genuine students" ([361]). Here we once more see him fitting the training of the scholastics and the lay students alike into its place in his ascending hierarchy of intermediary ends leading to a capable, influential, and satisfying life on earth and to enriched eternity hereafter.

27. *Los scolares,* Latin *scholastici,* means students, some of whom were Jesuits and some externs. In most countries Jesuits not yet ordained are called "scholastics." The present translation turns *scolares* by "scholastics" when in a context it clearly means chiefly the Jesuit students, and by "students" when it refers chiefly to extern students whether clerical or lay, or to Jesuit and extern students together.

28. For the scholastics Ignatius legislated one hour of prayer daily, with methods variable according to personalities, but for the formed Jesuits he refused to assign a definite duration of prayer. Sections [340–345] contain his own legislation on prayer for those in formation, and [582–584] below that on prayer for the formed. On the modifications in later decades and centuries, see *DeGuiJes,* pp. 86–90, 169, 192–196, 205, 222, 227–229, 237, 552–554; *Documents of the 31st and 32nd General Congregations* (St. Louis, 1977), pp. 137–145; also, M. Fiorito, "St. Ignatius' Own Legislation on Prayer in the Society of Jesus," *Woodstock Letters* 97 (1968): 188–190.

29. Pure: i.e., not mixed. It is a synonym for "right" intention, on which see n. 23 on [288] above.

30. "Will be not less but rather more pleasing": This brief statement is a corollary flowing from Ignatius' far-reaching theological concept of apostolic spirituality. His concept can be compactly described as follows. A person serves or pleases God at some times by focusing attention on him in prayer and at other times by working for him and

one's neighbor through love. One should find God in all things and in all one's activities, and one ought to order all of these to God by means of a right intention. Ignatius' habit of "finding God in all things" is what led Nadal to call him a "contemplative even while in action" (*MonNad* IV:651–652). Here Ignatius' outlook is highly similar in many details to that of St. Thomas Aquinas, from whom he may have learned it. Thomas writes about Rom. 1:18 (*Commentary on Romans,* ch. I, lect. 5): "As long as a man is acting in his heart, speech, or work in such a manner that he is tending toward God, he is praying; and thus one who is directing his whole life toward God is praying always." Ignatius similarly writes (*EppIgn* VI:81): "In the midst of actions and studies, the mind can be lifted to God; and by means of this directing everything to the divine service, everything is prayer." According to St. Thomas, the works of the active life sometimes hinder the act of contemplation (*ST* 2, 182, 3); but one can remain a contemplative person, one in the unitive stage of spiritual growth whose dominant inclination is toward contemplation of God, even while one is engaged in apostolic activities. Such a person may "merit more by the works of the active life than another by the works of the contemplative life, e.g., if through divine love he or she consents to be withdrawn from the sweetness of divine contemplation for a time" to aid his neighbor (ibid., a. 2). In a similar vein Ignatius writes (*EppIgn* IV:127): "The distracting occupations undertaken for his greater service, in conformity with his divine will can be, not only the equivalent of the union and recollection of uninterrupted contemplation, but even more acceptable, proceeding as they do from a more active and vigorous charity." Similar texts are cited in Giuliani, *Finding God in All Things* (Chicago, 1958), pp. 3–24; J. Stierli, in *Ignatius of Loyola: His Personality and Spiritual Heritage,* ed. Wulf (St. Louis, 1977), pp. 135–163; Ganss, in *Woodstock Letters* 93 (1964): 161–164; also, " 'Active Life or Contemplative Life'?" *Review for Religious* 22 (1963): 53–66.

31. "Every eight days" was unusually frequent in the 1500s. Ignatius was an energetic promoter of more frequent Communion in the Church. See *DeGuiJes*, pp. 374–385.

32. I.e., the Little Office of the Blessed Virgin Mary.

33. This and many similar statements (e.g., in [307, 361, 400, 440, 448, 822,e] and the letter of 1551 to Araoz) enrich our understanding of Ignatius' concept of education. He took it up "to help souls," i.e., persons (*Autobiog*, 50). That is, his purpose was to form youths into cultivated persons who would be able and eager to take a capable part in

the social, cultural, and religious life of their era and leaven their environment with the principles of Christ.

34. *Facultades*: in the *Constitutions*, *facultad* means sometimes a branch of knowledge, learning, or teaching such as humanities or arts or theology (e.g., in [351, 446, 453]), and sometimes a group of professors who teach a given branch (e.g., in [498, 501, 502]). Either meaning implies or at least connotes the other. (See La Torre, *Constitutiones*, p. 150, fn. 3; Gioia, *Constitutioni*, p. 504.) In [446] a whole curriculum of theological branches is listed, and in ch. 12 ([446–452]) we find an entire curriculum of branches integrated toward a common objective: the humanities, arts (i.e., philosophy), and theology, with medicine or law also added insofar as they can contribute to the same objective, a scientifically reasoned Christian outlook on life. The humanities, philosophy, and theology would form the intelligent and good Christian person, and the medicine or law would make him or her also a capable and good medical or legal person. Our translation uses "branches" when *facultad* means chiefly an area of knowledge and "faculty" when it means especially the teachers of a branch. In some cases the choice must be arbitrary.

35. This chapter reveals Ignatius as an interested counselor trying to help the students devise efficient methods of study for their day. On the ages of youths admitted to the Society and its colleges in Ignatius' day, see *ConsSJComm*, p. 130; also the schematic arrangement below at [446–452].

36. On right intention, see nn. 23 at [288] and 29 at [340] above.

37. Notice in [360] and [361] the esteem of both the supernatural and the natural gifts. These ideas are developed also in Ignatius' well-known letter of 1547 to the scholastics at Coimbra (*LettersIgn*, pp. 128–129).

38. Constitution [366] springs from Ignatius' esteem for two features in "the method of Paris": a well-ordered curriculum and much self-activity (*mucho exercitio*) of the students. Elsewhere, especially in Italy, there was great lack of order. The students, not arranged in classes according to age or ability, often studied higher branches before acquiring a foundation in the lower ones. Often, too, there were no exercises, repetitions, or disputations to supplement the lectures (*MonPaed* [1985], pp. 70, 358).

39. On scholastic and positive theology see also *SpEx* [363] above with n. 159 on it. There he names Sts. Augustine and Gregory as positive doctors, and Peter Lombard, Thomas Aquinas, and Bonaven-

ture as scholastics. Scholastic theology was classified as speculative. By inductive and deductive methods and means it sought deeper understanding of God's revelation as found in Scripture and tradition. It was "faith seeking understanding" and in the twelfth and thirteenth centuries it was summed up in such works as the *Sentences* of Peter Lombard (1158) and the *Theological Summa* of Thomas Aquinas (d. 1274). These works fostered devotion as well as knowledge, and presented God's whole redemptive plan. They furnished a comprehensive outlook by which persons could guide their lives. In the 1300s and 1400s, however, many scholastic teachers fell too often into a decadent dialectical formalism. Their multiplied distinctions became irrelevant to the lives of ordinary people. Hence in the 1500's many humanists and reformers reacted against the scholastic teachers and their methods, often with scorn; and they put more stress on Scripture, sometimes taken alone or sometimes along with the Fathers. However, throughout the thirteenth, fourteenth, and fifteenth centuries Catholic scholars too were studying the Fathers (whom Ignatius terms "the holy and positive doctors" in *SpEx* [363]), and during his sixteenth century Catholic protagonists too, alongside the Protestants, were developing the study of Scripture, the Fathers, canon law, and other sources of Catholic belief. Their methods became known as "positive theology," and Ignatius was among the early writers to use this term. He saw the good in both scholastic and positive theology and presented the two as complementary. This thought of his is expressed briefly in *SpEx* [363] and is prescribed for his colleges and universities in *Cons* [351, 353, 366, 446, 464, 467]. Thus through his *Exercises* and his colleges or universities as guided by his *Constitutions* his attitude exerted for centuries a widespread influence on the teaching and study of theology. See M. Benitez, *La teología Española en el siglo XVI* (Madrid, 1976), pp. 181–187; *NCathEnc* 3:712, 714; 4:949; 14:42; *OXDCCh* , s.v. Scholasticism; *DalmMan*, p. 182.

40. This clarifying phrase is added by the Latin translators of 1558.

41. On this procedure, see "2. The Steps . . ." in the letter to Araoz, p. 362 below.

42. In applying his spiritual principles to this new area Ignatius, repeating again his aims in undertaking educational work, states explicitly that it is more especially for externs. He also expresses his hopes for the widespread social good such education may achieve.

43. Ch. 12 is a remarkable synthesis. In brief compass it shows the organizational structure which Ignatius had in mind for his schools.

Since approximately 1180, universities had been composed of four faculties. First was the lower faculty, which taught the branches of learning named the liberal arts (the trivium of grammar, rhetoric, and dialectic, and the quadrivium of arithmetic, geometry, musical theory, and astronomical theory). Next came the higher faculties teaching the professional branches of theology, law, and medicine. In the Renaissance, however, some of the liberal arts were being reclassified as a faculty of languages, and some as a higher faculty of arts or philosophy (*IdeaJesUn*, pp. 557–558; see also 33, 35). Ignatius used these structures and procedures by imitating the University of Paris. In a college he had his students study humane letters; for higher studies they should go "to the universities of the Society" ([394]). These universities are divided into three faculties: languages, arts, and theology ([498, 501]). Usually he founded his schools first as colleges with the lower faculty of languages, and often they became universities by adding the higher faculties of arts and theology. In the lower faculties the chief objective was to teach boys the art of speaking, reading, and writing Latin with facility and with elegance as far as possible, according to the Renaissance ideal of *eloquentia*. The higher faculties were those of (1) arts or philosophy, divided into the branches named in [451], and (2) theology, with instruction in scholastic and positive theology, canon law, and Scripture. (See the schematic outline facing p. 299). Ignatius' ideal was best realized in his cherished Roman College, which opened in 1551 and became a university in fact (though not yet in name) in 1553, when classes in philosophy and theology were begun with papal approval. Since 1584 it has been called the Gregorian University in honor of Pope Gregory XIII. Its history is interestingly told in P. Caraman, *University of the Nations* (Ramsey, 1982).

44. Since Ignatius' immediate purpose was the formation of future priests of his Society and also of other orders or dioceses, theology was considered the most important branch. In the early Jesuit universities not many lay students remained to study this branch. But since virtually all the teachers and administrators were Jesuits, the influence of theology and the worldview it imparts through syntheses like those of Peter Lombard or Thomas Aquinas filtered down to all the students clerical and lay in the faculties of humanities and philosophy. In the arrangement shown in ch. 12, theology so integrated the other branches that each of them contributed toward a scientifically reasoned Christian philosophy of life.

45. Ignatius' primary reason for the study of Latin was the necessity to read and write it and to speak it fluently if he was to learn or use theology. However, he also wanted the students to acquire the stylistic and rhetorical elegance so highly esteemed in Renaissance culture, as is seen in his letter of March 30, 1555, to a scholastic named Gerard (in *IdeaJesUn*, pp. 157; see also a letter of May 21, 1547, ibid., pp. 132–137).

46. As in the medieval universities, the arts or branches learned from natural reason are conceived here both as worthy of penetrating study in themselves ([381, 450]) and also as handmaids to theology ([447–451]). Thus Ignatius sees them as fitting into his hierarchy of ends leading persons to God.

47. Ignatius' principle for selecting ministries ([822–824]) is his manifest reason for ordinarily omitting elementary education, which was occasionally accepted because of special circumstances, especially in missionary countries (see, e.g., *MonPaed* [1901], p. 852). In a typical case, a boy might receive his elementary education from tutors at the ages of 5 through 8, then enter a Jesuit university and study languages from 10 through 13, arts from 14 through 18, and theology from 17 through 21, as is illustrated (with variations characteristic of the era) by the cases of Canisius, Bellarmine, Lessius, Corneille, and Calderón (*IdeaJesUn*, pp. 44–51, 68–73).

48. In Ignatius' universities any and all the faculties of the age could be present. In fact, however, faculties of law and medicine functioned only rarely in early Jesuit universities. The chief instance is the University of Pont-à-Mousson in Lorraine, opened in 1574. A course in law was given by a layman in 1577; and gradually a faculty of law formed under a lay dean. A similar faculty of medicine arose in 1582. See P. Delattre, *Les établissements des Jésuites en France* (Paris, 1810) 1:604–815; and Ganss, *The Jesuit Educational Tradition*, pp. 28–31. In the United States during the nineteenth and twentieth centuries six Jesuit universities established medical schools: Creighton, Fordham, Georgetown, Loyola of Chicago, Marquette, and St. Louis. Fordham and Marquette, however, later found it necessary to discontinue their sponsorship. Twelve Jesuit universities in the United States conduct schools of law. In the restored Society after 1814 many other faculties were added, such as business, dentistry, nursing, speech, etc.

49. This paragraph gave rise to successive drafts of a plan of studies (*Ratio studiorum*): Nadal's (1565?), Ledesma's (ca. 1575), and the more

concerted versions published by committees in 1586, 1591, and 1592 which culminated in the definitive *Ratio studiorum* promulgated by Aquaviva in 1599. It governed practice in Jesuit schools until the suppression of the Society in 1773. Through these successive drafts the Jesuits set up a school system more extensive than any previously existing in history. It was an organization of individual schools in close contact with one another, deliberately reviewing and evaluating classroom and administrative experience, and sharing and exchanging teachers on a large scale according to needs. Numerous *Rationes studiorum* were produced by Renaissance educators, but the Jesuit *Ratio* of 1599 was perhaps the most widely influential. It is, however, more a treatment of curricular organization and pedagogical procedure than of Christian educational theory. In the main it presupposed rather than expounded Ignatius' chief educational ideals, but these were in Part IV of his *Constitutions* and in the minds of the Jesuits who conducted the schools under the *Ratio*.

50. These words were added by General Congregation I in 1558.

51. Until well into the 1500s, Peter Lombard's *Sentences* was the most widely used textbook on theology, but in the first half of the sixteenth century the use of St. Thomas' *Theological Summa* was much furthered by the Dominicans (see *NCathEnc* 14:132–134). Ignatius was within this influence during his study of theology under the Dominicans at Paris in 1534. Ever afterward he and the early Jesuits, especially Nadal, had the esteem of St. Thomas manifested in the legislation contained in [484, 488]. On scholastic and positive theology see n. 39 on *Cons* [366] above.

52. The reason Ignatius forbade acceptance of tuition from extern students in Jesuit schools was the gratuity of ministries ([4, 398, 478, 816]). He clearly regarded educational work as a ministry or apostolate of the Society ([398]) and hence insisted that the teaching be given gratis to the students. However, he zealously sought endowments to support his colleges and universities. In most cases cities supplied these endowments; and many of the early Jesuit schools can be called "public schools" in the modern sense of this term. The Society long adhered to this policy of imparting instruction free, thereby occasionally incurring anger from other teachers who rightfully charged for their services, but in time it became impossible to conduct the Jesuit schools free. Hence papal dispensations permitting acceptance of tuition were granted in 1833 and 1853 (*InstSJ* 2:494, 519). On the history of gratuity of in-

struction, see A. Farrell, *The Jesuit Code of Liberal Education* (Milwaukee, 1938), pp. 436–440.

53. In ch. 17 notice how many officials Ignatius prescribed for his larger universities, such as Coimbra or Rome; also, how much consultation he desired ([501]). In his Society he established monarchical government but also abundant means of consultation, communication, and representation remarkable for his era.

On Part V. Incorporation into the Body of the Society

54. I.e., through the definitive incorporation which binds the scholastic to the Society and the Society to him. His first vows at the end of the novitiate were unilateral, i.e., they bound him to request this final admission at the proper time, but the Society could still dismiss him if sufficient reason should arise.

55. The four categories of membership, i.e., the classes or grades described in n. 13 on *Cons* [10] above. In [511] (not printed here) they are listed in a different order, that is, according to increasingly limited meanings of the term *Society*. They are: (1) the most comprehensive sense, all those living under the Society's obedience, including the novices; (2) the professed, the formed coadjutors whether spiritual or temporal, and the approved scholastics or brothers who have their first and unilateral vows, but are not yet "formed" by their bilateral final vows; (3) the professed and the formed coadjutors both spiritual and temporal who have final vows; these make up the "body" of the Society. It is what novices by their first vows promise to enter some years later by their final vows, which are bilateral, binding them to the Society and the Society to them; and (4) the professed of four vows, who form the central nucleus which is the Society in the most limited sense of the term. Part V treats of incorporation into the body of the Society by these final vows.

56. *Scuela del afecto*: Ignatius here prescribes a third period of training and probation (often called the tertianship; see n. 5 on *Cons* [2] above). It is a year to exercise prayer, virtues, and priestly ministries, and thereby to show suitability for the Society's ministries. His idea was novel and has been extensively imitated. Hugo Rahner (*DeGuiJes*, p. 37) and others perceptively think that it arose from his spiritual experiences at Vicenza, a "desert idyll" when he "had many spiritual visions and quite regular consolations; the contrary of what happened in Paris," his

465

period of studies (*Autobiog*, 95). The type of experiences Ignatius probably had in mind can be seen in Part IV, ch. 8, on instructing the scholastics in the means of helping the neighbor: e.g., preaching, hearing confessions, administering Communion, giving the Exercises, and teaching Christian doctrine [400–414]). Varying opinions exist about the meaning of *afecto*. A. de Aldama thinks that, contrasted as here with the intellect (*entendimiento*), it means merely the affective faculty, the will, which is perfected by moral virtues (*AldamIntro*, pp. 196–197, 286). That is basically true. However, acts of the affective faculty are generally accompanied by emotions, as Ignatius shows himself much aware, e.g., love, modesty, charity in [667,b], and "all virtues" in [725], kindness and gentleness in [727]; and to translate *afecto* merely by "will" seems not to do justice to the context or the historical situation. In 1558 Polanco translated *afecto* by *affectus*, "sentiments of affection, friendship, love" (Blaise, *Dictionnaire*, s.v.), especially in the phrase *affectus animi*, the soul as the seat of affections. Hence we translate by "heart," along with other modern versions which use *du coeur*, *del affetto*, *des Herzens*. Heart here has its biblcal meaning: the whole person, with intellect, will, and emotions. Almost all the activities listed in [400–414] bring with them emotions or consolations somewhat like what Ignatius had at Vicenza. Aquinas describes *affectus* as affection, related to benevolence, peace, and beneficence (*ST* 2-2, 80, 1 ad 2). Covarrubias in 1611 defined *afecto* as "passion of the soul" which overflows into the body; and modern Spanish dictionaries list passion, affection, etc., thus making *afecto* a synonym of *corazón*. On the later history of the tertianship see *DeGuiJes*, pp. 37, 235–237; *AldamIntro*, pp. 195–197; *ConsSJComm*, pp. 234–235; Mario Gioia, *Gli Scritti di Ignazio di Loyola* (Turin, 1977), p. 547.

On Part VI. The Personal Lives of the Incorporated Members

57. The value of celibacy embraced for the sake of Christ's Kingdom (Matt. 19:10–12) was presupposed by most Catholics of the 1500s as a necessary element of religious life, even though some humanists and the Protestants had attacked it. Moreover, the Society had no special way of its own for its practice. Hence Ignatius felt no need of lengthy treatment here. No one in his century seems to have expressed surprise at his brevity on chastity. The twentieth-century interest in psychological studies and problems pertaining to celibacy had not yet arisen.

58. The expression "angelic purity" was very ancient in the monastic tradition and it was natural for Ignatius to repeat it. Alluding to Matt. 22:29–30, Ignatius is urging a purity like that of the blessed in heaven. He is not implying that on earth the purity of men who have bodies can be identical with that of angels who do not have them.

59. In [547–552] Ignatius gives his final (1556) and most complete legislative expression of his concept of religious obedience. It contains also teaching which he distilled from earlier sketches, experiences, and thoughts, and treated at length in his classic letter of March 26, 1553, on obedience, in *LettersIgn*, pp. 287–295. See also *AldamIntro*, pp. 218–225; *ConsSJComm*, pp. 246–249. Espinosa Pólit, *Perfect Obedience* (Westminster, Md., 1947), has a thorough commentary on the classic letter of 1553. For a sketch of the historical development of religious obedience see David Knowles, *From Pachomius to Ignatius: A Study in the Constitutional History of the Religious Orders* (Oxford, 1963).

60. Ignatius' personalized concept of obedience grew naturally from his desire to cooperate with Christ in the spread of his Kingdom. The founder wanted to have a cohort of men ready for any task assigned anywhere in the world by the pope, whom he saw as the vicar of Christ; and he hoped to find many volunteers for service in this cause. Such an enterprise required obedience as a principle of unity and coordination. In his view, therefore, the foundation of obedience is authority derived from God through Christ to the pope, who in turn delegates it to subordinate officials such as bishops and religious superiors. What descends from God, at least in ordinary cases, is not new divine light on the problem under consideration, but the right to decide and command. This right is usually exercised after consultation, reflection, and prayer. These superiors, therefore, command "in the place of Christ" (*en lugar de Cristo*), but should do so according to "the pattern set by Peter and Paul" (1 Pet. 5:1–3; Phil. 3:17; 2 Thess. 3:7–9; 1 Tim. 4:12; Ti. 1:7); Formula of the Institute as in *Exposcit* [4]).

61. "Letter": i.e., a letter of the alphabet (*EppIgn* III:156). This example, found in *Apothegmata Patrum* of the fourth or fifth century (PG 65:296), is common in the monastic tradition (see, e.g., St. Benedict's *Rule*, ch. 5).

62. This statement that to be "perfect," obedience should comprise execution as reinforced by the will and even the judgment, expresses the essence or core of Ignatius' concept and is explained just below in Declaration C [550]. The similes of the corpse and staff were not in text

a of about 1547 but were added in text *A* of 1550 (*AldamIntro*, p. 219). Traditional in the literature of monasticism and perhaps found by Polanco, they were familiar and esteemed in the 1500s but are often less attractive today. All comparisons limp. Hence, what truly matters is to focus on the author's thought itself and distinguish it from the metaphors by which he illustrates it.

63. The idea of "blind obedience" is at least as old as the *Constitutiones monachorum* long attributed to St. Basil (see PG 13, col. 1409). Its meaning here in [547], its only occurrence in the *Constitutions*, has led to many debates (see Espinosa Pólit, *Perfect Obedience*, pp. 148–161; *AldamIntro*, p. 223). It surely entails a willingness to presume that the superior's order is right and prudent until some cogent reason to the contrary has become manifest. Other Ignatian texts reveal that for him the "blindness" was not total. The subject was expected to keep his eyes sufficiently open to see that there was no sin ([549]), and whether there were factors which should be represented to the superior (see [92, 131, 543, 627]); other references in *ConsSJComm*, p. 248.

What Ignatius truly desired to find in the subject was this complex: (1) the fundamental desire to learn and carry out God's will; (2) genuine religious indifference or impartiality in regard to what is commanded; (3) a willingness, as a guard against self-deception, to give the superior the benefit of possible doubts about the prudence of the command, at least until cogent reasons against it were examined, usually in dialogue; (4) recognition of the superior's right to make the final decision (see [810]); and finally (5) cheerful, wholehearted execution. Much the same procedure has been commended anew by Vatican Council II, Decree on the Renewal of Religious Life, no. 14.

64. The simile of the corpse appears in the Life of St. Francis of Assisi by St. Bonaventure (*Opera* 8:52). A staff is similar to an artisan's tool, which was used in the *Constitutiones monachorum* (ch. 22, no. 5, in PG 31, col. 1409).

65. In [550] is the very core of Ignatius' concept of *an act* of obedience with its three ascending degrees of perfection. In such an act execution of the command is the basic essential, the matter comprised by the vow. If a subject's act of obedience is to be raised to higher degrees of perfection, however, he must make it more effective through a lively concurrence of his own desire, by which he conforms his will to that of the superior. He will be aided toward this by inclining himself to see the prudence of the superior's command and to give him the benefit of possible doubts—at least until reflection or dialogue, in a genuine

and prayerful spirit of indifference, reveals something which he ought to represent to the superior ([543, 610, 627]). The subject ought also to recognize the superior's right to the final decision ([810]).

66. Ignatius wanted superiors to rule much as kindly fathers and as taking the place of Christ, so that as far as possible the relations between subjects and superiors would be firm but characterized by love ([551, 727, 810]), mutual esteem ([423, 551, 667]), and cordial and open communication ([91–93]). According to Ignatius' ideal, therefore, government by superiors should be paternal in the sense of their being kindly and inspiring filial confidence, but not in the sense that a superior should either exercise his authority in an authoritarian manner or bear himself toward his subjects as if they were still immature minors. See also the references to Scripture in n. 61 above.

67. Ignatius' esteem of evangelical poverty had an intensity and tenderness which remind one of St. Francis of Assisi's love of "Lady Poverty." This esteem arose, among other reasons, especially from (1) his enthusiastic embracing, already in his first conversion, of the mendicant spirit of St. Francis and St. Dominic which he found in Ludolph's *Life of Christ* and in Jacobus' lives of the saints, and (2) his antipathy to the prevalent avarice of so many of his contemporary ecclesiastics which was scandalizing and damaging the Church so much. On preserving poverty intact, see *AldamIntro*, pp. 225–228.

68. The words "or churches" here result from Ignatius' deliberation on poverty and his decision after the discernment recorded in his *Spiritual Diary* [50] for March 12, 1544. See pp. 218–219 in the Introduction. On the prohibition of fixed revenues and other technicalities in [555] see *AldamIntro*, pp. 228–230; on living on alms, ibid., 230–232.

69. "Any other rule": Just as [340–345] give Ignatius' legislation on prayer for those still in formation (see nn. 27 and 28 above), so [582–584] give it for the members already formed. He reached the formulation of these constitutions after much experience in directing others in prayer. This led him steadily to refuse to prescribe one universal rule obliging all the formed members to one specified duration of daily prayer ([582–583]). One reason was his disagreeable experiences with some members, such as Oviedo or Onfroy, who followed a tendency, then present especially in Spain and Portugal, to go to excess. There were other reasons too, which arose from his experience in guiding others whose temperaments or psychological needs greatly varied, and from his respect for individual differences. As Câmara says

of him: "The Father said that his opinion, from which no one would ever move him, was that one hour of prayer—[i.e., the hour which he had prescribed for the scholastics in [340]—was sufficient, it being presupposed that they are practicing mortification and self-abnegation; that such a one would easily accomplish more prayer in a quarter of an hour than another who is not mortified would achieve in two hours. . . . He thought there was no worse mistake in spiritual matters than to desire to lead others along the same path as one's own" (*FN* I:676–677; *DeGuiJes*, pp. 89, 167; see also nn. 28. 29, and 30 on [340] above and the references there).

70. The phrase "discreet charity" (*discreta caridad*), around which elaborate theories have grown, means simply the charity of a person who is discreet or prudent. Polanco coined the phrase, used it with Ignatius' approval, and turned it by *discreta caritas* in his Latin version of 1558. In [754] Polanco also used the term *prudente caridad* and translated it by "*prudentia cum caritate conjuncta*," i.e., charity controlled by prudence (*AldamIntro*, pp. 235–236).

71. In the 1500s many religious were singing the Office in choir and celebrating conventual Masses (chiefly inside their own monasteries and churches), as was proper according to their vocation which Ignatius always esteemed (see, e.g., *SpEx* [355]). He himself always loved the liturgy as practiced in his day and derived great devotion from it (see *FN* I:391, 636; II:337; also G. Ellard, "St. Ignatius Loyola and Public Worship," *Thought* 19 [1944]: 649–670). In many places, however, the Church's pastoral care of the people had almost collapsed, so that there were innumerable persons who could not understand the Latin of the liturgy and who consequently were receiving little or no instruction in the faith. Hence his aim was to organize a religious order whose proper work would be pastoral care of the people at large, and this apostolic end was his motive for excluding, with papal approval, the obligation of choral recitation of the Office, lest it interfere with the freedom and mobility of his men to work with the people outside the religious house when and wherever their needs arose ([586]). He did permit lengthier or more elaborate ceremonies when they furthered such pastoral care in the circumstances of his day ([587]). See *ConsSJ-Comm*, p. 262; *AldamIntro*, pp. 238–239.

On Part VII. The Distribution of the Members into Christ's Vineyard

72. In Ignatius' Spanish in the *Constitutions*, the word *mission* means an act of sending someone, the same as the Latin *missio* (*Aldam-Intro*, p. 249). Ignatius had in mind Christ's mission and dispersal of his apostles. Later the word acquired many other meanings, such as the errand which one was sent to accomplish, or an expedition to spread the faith, or the region where a missionary worked, or a charge or commission to do something.

73. This statement in [622,a] is one more slightly varied formulation of Ignatius' simple and fundamental criterion for election (*SpEx* [23. 152, 169, 184]), applied here to the choice of ministries: Which option is likely to bring greater glory to God? (We should recall that greater service to God also brings him greater glory.) All that follows in b, d, and f are applications of that chief criterion to cases which are often complicated.

On Part VIII. Their Union with the Head and among Themselves

74. *Cabeza*: In the *Constitutions* Ignatius' fundamental image of the Society is that of a body (*cuerpo*, e.g., in [135, 137, 322, 510, 512], with the general as its head (*cabeza*, e.g., in [137, 206, 512, 655, 666, 668, 671, 820, 821]), and with members (*miembros*). This image guides his terminology. *Miembros* is the term by which he habitually and most frequently designated all those who had enrolled under the general's authority, even novices, as can be seen in [135, 233, 322, 510, 511, 655, 666, 668, 671, 821]. On four occasions ([659, 660, 661, 701]), he calls members personally known to one another and associated in a common task "companions" (*compañeros*). Outside the *Constitutions* he often called Christ the head of the Society, e.g., in his *Spiritual Diary* [66] for Feb. 23, 1544: "Jesus, . . . since he is the head of the Society" (see also *FN* I: 204; II: 596). His concept pertaining to the Society closely paralleled that which he used about the Church as the Mystical Body of Christ. Ignatius conceives the Church as a body whose head is Christ, e.g., in his letter of Aug. 7, 1553, to the whole Society: "Since the order of charity, with which we ought to love the whole body of the Church in its head, Christ Jesus, requires that a remedy be applied especially to the member which is suffering from a more serious and dangerous

illness, we think that . . . the aid of the Society should be bestowed with special affection on Germany, England, and the northern nations" (*EppIgn* V:221). See also his letter of Feb. 23, 1553, to Emperor Claude of Abyssinia, which presents his ecclesiology in terms of the mystical body (*LettersIgn*, pp. 369–371).

75. Ignatius' usage of *de los ánimos* in [655], union "of hearts," should be carefully distinguished from his *de las ánimas* in [3], the salvation of the members' "souls" as meaning the persons or selves (see n. 16 on *SpEx* [23] and n. 6 on *Cons* [3] above). In 1558 Polanco discerningly translated *ánimos* of [655] by the Latin *animus*, the soul as the seat of feeling and affections, the heart, and *ánimas* of [3] by the Latin *anima*, the soul taken for the person or self—a meaning common in classical Latin and especially in Scripture (e.g., Acts 2:44). Ignatius' hope and ideal expressed here in [655] is a union of persons through their minds and hearts.

76. Sections [662 and 666] exemplify clearly Ignatius' concept of a hierarchically arranged series of superiors (see n. 60 on [547] above). This series also functions toward furthering unity.

77. This paragraph about the manner of commanding is written in Ignatius' own handwriting. Hence it was written by himself alone and shows us his own manner of commanding. See *AldamIntro*, p. 269.

78. The prescriptions in [673] have given rise to an immense amount of correspondence, of which the most important has been preserved in the archives of the Society in Rome. It has long been a mine of information for historians of the Society from Orlandini (1614) to the present. The project of publishing the most significant of these manuscripts and documents in the 133 volumes of the series Monumenta Historica Societatis Iesu, the Historical Sources of the Society of Jesus, was begun in Madrid in 1894 and transferred to Rome in 1929. See E. J. Burrus, "Monumenta Historica Societatis Iesu (1894–1954)," *Woodstock Letters* 83 (1954): 156–168.

79. Ignatius here uses the traditional term for a meeting of religious, "chapter." Usually, however, he employs the term "general congregation." This assembly is the highest legislative body in the Society beneath the pope.

On Part IX. The Superior General and His Government

80. Already in 1539 the early companions unanimously determined that the superior general whom they would elect was to hold office for

life (see *Cons*MHSJ I, 13, no. 14; 39, no. 14). The thirty-first General Congregation in 1965–1966 reaffirmed this prescription of [719]. However, it added clearer provisions for the general's honorable resignation in case he should become seriously and permanently incapacitated.

81. In this justly famous ch. 2 in which the founder sketches ([723–735]) his ideal of the superior general, he has also left an ideal which all the members of his order can well seek to approach (see [726]). Furthermore, he delineated here a "spirituality for superiors." The ideal has long been regarded as a self-portrait made subconsciously by Ignatius himself. Already in 1555 Câmara wrote about "the chapter of the Constitutions in which he [Ignatius] portrays the general, in whose case he seems to have portrayed his own self" (*Memoriale*, no. 226, in *FN* I:659). In ch. 64 of the *Regula monachorum* there is a sketch of the ideal of an abbot which is often taken to be St. Benedict's self-portrait.

82. *Afecto*: basically, the affective faculty, the will, which is perfected by moral virtues. However, acts of the affective faculty are often accompanied by emotions. See n. 57 on [516] above. Hence here, as there, we translate it by "heart." What perfects the general's heart is indicated in [725–728], e.g., "all virtues" in [725] and "kindness and gentleness" in [727].

83, *Providencia*: in Ignatius' usage this word means sometimes the vigilance of a court ([167]), sometimes the Church's guidance or provident care of her members ([22]), and sometimes, as here in [766], the similar care of the Society in regard to its general.

On Part X. The Preservation and Development of the Society

84. Well-being: i.e., keeping the Society what it ought to be. Part X sums up all the nine preceding parts. By bold strokes the founder recalls the important features of the Society's origin, organization, and spirit. For that reason Part X is perhaps the richest in spiritual doctrine (see *DeGuiJes*, pp. 139–151, esp. p. 146).

85. To be a closely united instrument in the hands of God from whom the true efficacy comes is a prominent and characteristic aspect of Ignatius' concept of an apostolic worker ([30, 638, 814]). This concept flows naturally from his desire to be cooperatively associated with Christ toward achieving God's redemptive plan.

86. In [813 and 814], notice the circular movement of Ignatius' thought: It starts from God, descends to creatures, then goes back to God, by ordering the creatures to God. This is another characteristic of his outlook, closely connected with his singleness of purpose or purity of intention in serving God (see, e.g., [283, 288, 360] and nn. 23 and 24 on [288]). In general, after his conversion at Loyola his thought can be observed to start with the Trinity and move downward toward service to human beings for the sake of glory to God, rather than to begin with creatures and then upward toward God by means of the "ladder of creatures" (*scala creaturarum*). See *Autobiog*, 27–30, 96; *SpEx* [101–109, 169, and 230–237] (where the gifts and blessings move downward from God because of his love and that is why they should excite one's gratitude and love toward God). Ignatius' dominant inclination was to see all things from God's point of view. Nevertheless, there is many another occasion when his thought does move from creatures upward to God to whom he is ordering them (e.g., the last half of *SpEx* [23] and *Cons* [340, 360, 361] above). But, as [814] clearly illustrates, this upward movement is a consequence of the first downward movement. He had great esteem for natural or temporal goods and hoped that human beings would consecrate the temporal order to God, i.e., perfect it so that it issues in greater glory to him than it otherwise would, much as Vatican Council II has urged (e.g., in The Church in the Modern World, nos. 4–6, 12, 34–39, 53–62; The Apostolate of the Laity, nos. 4–7, 13, 14). On this highly characteristic movement of Ignatius' thought see Hugo Rahner, *Ignatius the Theologian* (1968), pp. 1–31; J. Daniélou, "La spiritualité trinitaire de saint Ignace," *Christus* no. 3 (1956): 354–372; *BibThSpEx* pp. 327–331; Rom. 11:36.

87. When taken side by side, the typically Ignatian constitutions [813] and [814] make clear illustrations of his perspective and balance. He always saw the supernatural gifts, endowments, and means as by far the most important, but he also esteemed the natural gifts and means, the foundation on which the supernatural builds, and he desired his men to cultivate and use them for the sake of the supernatural. This perspective and balance are elements of great moment in his theory of apostolic spirituality.

88. For Ignatius' own exposition of the closely reasoned theological doctrine on which he based this statement, see the paragraph he wrote at the end of the first draft of the *Examen*, in text *a* (*Cons*MHSJ II:125), English in *DeGuiJes*, pp. 147–148.

89. *Seminario*, Latin *seminarium*: This word, which has the radical meaning of "a seedbed," took on the added meaning of "an institution to train youths." (In English this meaning appeared in 1581.) The success of the colleges founded by Ignatius to train his young men was an influential factor in the legislation of Trent on seminaries and in its implementation (see the references in *ConsSJComm*, p. 333). Furthermore, his hopes that vocations would come from his schools were richly fulfilled in his own and later eras. A large proportion of the Society's vocations have come from its schools and been a benefit also to its other ministries.

90. Prelate: one who by his office has ordinary jurisdiction in the external forum. Already in 1539 the future superior general was termed a "prelate" (*Cons*MHSJ I:13, no. 14; 39, no. 14; *Regimini*, [4]).

91. In 1546 King Ferdinand I desired to have Jay made bishop of Trieste. In his efforts to dissuade the king, Ignatius wrote that until then there were only nine professed, of whom four or five had already been proposed for bishoprics (*LettersIgn*, p. 112).

92. Ignatius' extensive measures to dissuade Pope Paul III from naming Jay a bishop are recounted in *LettersIgn*, pp. 111–113 and 115–120. For references to the cases of Borgia, Canisius, Laínez, and Bobadilla, see *ConsSJComm*, p. 335. To his opposition to acceptance of bishoprics Ignatius had one exception: bishoprics in mission lands where there was no danger of ambition or gain.

93. *Espíritu*: A word which Ignatius often uses to mean "spiritual life" or "spiritual progress" (*provecho spiritual*). See, e.g., [51, 60, 81, 93, 94, 101, 243, 417, 419, 819].

THE SELECTED LETTERS

Introduction

1. On this history see Iparraguirre in *Obrascompl*, pp. 641–643.
2. G. Dumeige, in *Saint Ignace: Lettres*, p. 10.

1. To Inés Pascual

3. Calixto de Sa, Lope de Cáceres, and Juan de Arteaga became disciples of St. Ignatius in Barcelona but did not remain with him beyond September, 1527. See *Autobiog*, 56, 80.

2. To Isabel Roser

4. Later on there was, however, one stormy period in this widely known case. After her husband's death, Isabel came to Rome in 1543 and with two companions asked Ignatius to be accepted under his obedience. He thought it inexpedient to begin a feminine branch of the Society and refused, but she successfully appealed to the pope and he commanded Ignatius to comply. Hence on Christmas, 1545, the three women pronounced solemn profession in the Society of Jesus in the chapel of Madonna della Strada. Ignatius received their vows and there was a feminine branch of the Society. Soon, however, Isabel made excessive demands on Ignatius and other Jesuits. Ignatius explained the frictions and disagreements to Pope Paul III. Thereupon he authorized Ignatius to dispense the three women from their vows, and later freed the Society from the regular care of religious women. The storm passed, she apologized to Ignatius, they parted, and neither harbored resentment against the other. Isabel entered a Franciscan convent in Barcelona, where she died holily in 1547.

A comprehensive account of Ignatius' relations with Isabel, including all the extant letters between them, is given with delicate and sympathetic insight by Hugo Rahner, *Ignatius: Letters to Women*, pp. 184–185; 262–295. See also *DalmIgn*, pp. 72, 88, 252–255.

5. No doubt one of the group of ladies who gathered about Ignatius in Barcelona and also gathered alms for him.

6. The legend of St. Marina, told, e.g., in PL 172, col. 1053 by Honorius Augustodunensis (fl. ca. 1120) and in the *Golden Legend* of Jacobus de Voragine for June 18, recurs frequently in medieval hagiography: A devout woman disguised as a man enters a monastery as a monk, is accused of misconduct, and is proved innocent after her death. In this story, called "a pious novelette" by the Bollandist H. Delehaye (*The Legends of the Saints* [New York, 1962], p. 51), variations are common; e.g., the heroine is called Pelagia, Eugenia, Euphrosia, Theodora, or Margaret. Ignatius may have read the account in the *Golden Legend*, or happened upon a version, probably in Paris, in which she is unnamed but made into a Franciscan; and since it aptly illustrated one aspect of his teaching on the third way of being humble, he inserted it for this purpose into his letter to Isabel Roser. See H. Rahner, *Ignatius: Letters to Women*, pp. 266–267; 523.

3. To Teresa Rejadell

7. The extant letters, hers and his, are beautifully presented in Hugo Rahner's *Ignatius: Letters to Women*, pp. 329–368.

8. On Lope de Cáceres, see n. 3 above.

9. On this section, which is similar to the treatment of consolation without preceding cause in the *Exercises*, see nn. 142 and 143 on *SpEx* [330–336] above.

10. Juan Castro (see n. 3 above) was a doctor of the Sorbonne to whom Ignatius gave the Exercises in Paris. He later became a Carthusian at Val de Cristo, near Segorbe, where Ignatius visited him in 1535.

4. To Magdalena de Loyola y Araoz

11. See H. Rahner, *Ignatius: Letters to Women*, pp. 114–116; García-Villoslada, *San Ignacio . . . nueva biographia* (Madrid, 1986), p. 51.

5. To Teresa Rejadell

12. See *DeGuiJes*, pp. 374–378; H. Rahner, *Ignatius: Letters to Women*, pp. 335–337; and n. 31 on *Cons* [342] above).

13. Ignatius is alluding to a jurisdictional dispute from 1513 to

1518 instituted by the Franciscans and settled by a bull of Leo X. It handed over the visitation of the convent of Santa Clara from the Franciscans to the Benedictines.

14. This opinion, which in the 1500s was wrongly attributed to St. Augustine, was in fact expressed by Gennadius of Marseilles (d. 494), who wrote: "To receive the Eucharistic Communion daily I neither praise nor blame. I am in favor of and even urge reception of Communion on all Sundays, on condition that the soul is free from the disposition of sinning" (PL 58, col. 994).

15. A book *De Sacramentis* attributed to St. Ambrose states: "Receive daily what can profit you daily. So live that you may be worthy to receive. One who is not worthy to receive daily is not worthy to receive yearly" (PL 16, col. 425).

6. To the Fathers and Brothers of Coimbra

16. That letter of 1544 is often called the "Letter on Perfection." The text is in *LettersIgn*, pp. 120–130. See esp. pp. 126–127.

17. The text is in *LettersIgn*, pp. 287–295.

18. Simão Rodrigues, one of Ignatius' first companions, who established the Society in Portugal.

19. This is possibly Ignatius' indirect attempt to stimulate Rodrigues to govern more responsibly in accordance with Ignatius' own principles.

20. *Sermo de virtute obedientiae ejusque gradibus* 41.4 (PL 183, col. 656).

21. *In Cantica* 19, 7 (PL 183, col. 866).

7. To Francis Borgia

22. On May 23, 1551, Francis was ordained in Spain at Oñate and celebrated his first Mass at nearby Loyola. He was elected third general of the Society on July 2, 1565. In that office he expanded the Society by organizing the missions existing in Asia and by starting new foundations in the Americas. He died on September 30, 1572, and was canonized on April 12, 1671.

23. These examples listed here are very similar to Ignatius' own personal experiences which he described throughout his Spiritual Diary in 1544. Thus they are also an indication that he was still experiencing them in 1548.

8. To Antonio Brandão

24. On that concept, see n. 30 on *Cons* [340] above.

25. Ignatius wrote this same prescription for scholastics in *Cons* [340], which in 1551 were not yet printed or promulgated.

26. Since the publication of Ignatius' letters (1903–1911) this paragraph has been quoted in almost all treatments on Ignatian prayer; e.g., by Stierli, in *Ignatius: His Personality*, pp. 145–146; Giuliani, *Finding God in All Things*, pp. 9–10. It shows very concretely what Ignatius meant by his oft-repeated idea of "finding God in all things."

27. The "tones" (*toni*) were a fixed model declamation or sermon which scholastics delivered as practice. It ran the gamut of feelings and modulations of voice.

9. To Jean Pelletier

28. See Lukacs' statistical list in Clancy, *Introduction to Jesuit Life*, pp. 302–303.

29. I.e., in their spiritual lives, or in spiritual progress.

30. On right intention, see n. 23 on *Cons* [288] above.

31. I.e., excessive dealings. Ignatius' own example is perhaps the best interpretation of this exaggerated word, possibly left unqualified through error.

32. See n. 25 above.

33. I.e., to religious or consecrated life. Right from the beginning, as this paragraph shows, Ignatius looked upon his schools as potential sources of recruits to the Society or other forms of consecrated life. He here points out a manner of dealing with this matter. The priests and the scholastics, whether teaching or merely studying, were unwittingly role models for the students. Some students would see the teachers as happy by doing worthwhile work and conceive a desire to be like them. From this would arise reflection, prayer, and instructive counseling which would clarify and foster the spiritual motivation, and eventual decision. Ignatius insisted that this final decision should be totally the youth's own—just as he did with the election in the Exercises. All through the Society's history many, probably most, of its vocations have come from its schools and thus provided manpower for its social, missionary, and other ministries.

34. They: i.e., the Jesuit staff members.

10. To Antonio de Araoz

35. I.e., the Jesuit scholastics. Since *Regimini* of 1540 and *Exposcit* of 1550 permitted endowed colleges to train the scholastics and were silent about colleges chiefly for externs, in 1551 the presence of some Jesuit scholastics as students was still deemed necessary. The topic was much controverted from 1556 to 1608, when the sixth General Congregation decreed that the presence of Jesuit scholastics was not required. See the digest of Lukács' extensive research on this topic, reprinted in Clancy, *Introduction to Jesuit Life*, p. 326.

36. Their age was ordinarily about 9 to 14 years. See the schematic outline opposite *Cons* [446] above.

37. "Al modo de Paris, con mucho exercitio": this phrase shows one of Ignatius' chief reasons for his fondness for this method. See n. 38 on *Cons* [366] above.

38. See n. 35 above.

REFERENCE MATTER

BIBLIOGRAPHY
INDEX

BIBLIOGRAPHY

All the works referred to in the present volume,
and a few others. It focuses especially on works in English.

I. BIBLIOGRAPHIES

Iparraguirre, Ignacio. *Orientaciones bibliográficas sobre San Ignacio de Loyola.* Subsidia ad historiam Societatis Iesu, no. 1. 2nd ed. rev. Rome, 1965.

Ruiz Jurado, Manuel. *Orientaciones bibliográficas sobre San Ignacio de Loyola. Vol. II.* (1965–1976). Subsidia ad historiam Societatis Iesu, no. 8. Rome, 1977. *Vol III.* (1977–1989). Subsidia . . . , no. 10, Rome, 1990.

Polgár, Lazlo. *Bibliographie sur l'histoire de la Compagnie de Jésus. 1901–1980. Vol. I. Toute la Compagnie.* Rome, 1980.

II. THE CHIEF PRIMARY SOURCES

MHSJ—MONUMENTA HISTORICA SOCIETATIS JESU, the Historical Records or Sources of the Society of Jesus in critically edited texts, most of them from the Society's archives in Rome. This scholarly series of 131 volumes was begun in Madrid in 1894 and transferred to Rome in 1929, where it is being continued by the Jesuit Historical Institute.

MI—Monumenta Ignatiana. The writings of St. Ignatius of Loyola.

Series I

EppIgn—S. Ignatii . . . Epistolae et Instructiones. 12 vols. Madrid, 1903–1911. The letters and instructions of St. Ignatius.

Series II

SpExMHSJ—Exercitia Spiritualia S. Ignatii . . . et eorum Directoria. Ed. A. Codina. Madrid, 1919. The *Spiritual Exercises* and *Directories.*

BIBLIOGRAPHY

*SpEx*MHSJ*Te*—Vol. I. *Exercitia spiritualia: Textus.* Ed. C. de Dalmases. 1969.
DirSpEx—Vol. II. *Directoria Exercitiorum Spiritualium (1540–1599).* Ed. I. Iparraguirre. 1955.

Series III

*Cons*MHSJ—*Constitutiones et Regulae Societatis Iesu.* 4 vols. The critically edited texts of the *Constitutions* and *Rules* of the Society of Jesus, along with copious introductions and notes.
*Cons*MHSJ I—Vol. I. *Monumenta Constitutionum praevia.* Ed. A. Codina. 1934. Sources and records previous to the texts of the *Constitutions.*
*Cons*MHSJ II—Vol. II. *Textus hispanus.* Ed. A. Codina. 1936.
*Cons*MHSJ III—Vol. III. *Textus latinus.* Ed. A. Codina. 1938.
*Cons*MHSJ IV—Vol. IV. *Regulae Societatis Jesu.* Ed. D. Fernández Zapico. 1948. Ancient drafts of various rules or directives.

Series IV

FN—*Fontes narrativi de S. Ignatio de Loyola et de Societatis Iesu initiis.* Ed. D. Fernández Zapico, C. de Dalmases, P. Leturia. 4 vols., 1943–1960. Vol. I, 1523–1556; II, 1557–1574; III, 1574–1599; IV: Ribadeneyra's *Vita Ignatii Loyolae* (1572). 1965.
Fontes documentales de S. Ignatio. Ed. C. de Dalmases. 1965.

In MHSJ, but not part of the Monumenta Ignatiana

MonNad—*Epistolae P. Hieronymi Nadal.* 6 vols. Vols. I–IV, ed. F. Cervós, 1898–1905. Vol. V, *Commentarii de Instituto S.I.,* 1962, and VI, *Orationis observationes,* 1964, ed. M. Nicolau. Letters and instructions of Ignatius' companion Jerónimo Nadal.

III. OTHER BOOKS

Aldama, Antonio de. *An Introductory Commentary on the Constitutions.* Trans. A. J. Owens. St. Louis, 1989.
———. *La Formula del Instituto de la Compañia de Jesús.* Rome, 1981.
Bangert, William V. *A History of the Society of Jesus.* 2d ed. rev. St. Louis, 1986.
Blaise, A. *Dictionnaire Latin-Français des auteurs chrétiens.* Strasbourg, 1954.

BIBLIOGRAPHY

Brou, Alexandre. *Ignatian Methods of Prayer*. Trans. W. J. Young. Milwaukee, 1949.

Burckhardt, Jacob. *The Civilization of the Renaissance in Italy*. New York, 1904.

Characteristics of Jesuit Education, The. Washington: Jesuit Secondary Education Association, 1987.

Cisneros, García de. *Ejercitatorio de la vida espiritual*. Edition Curiel. Barcelona, 1912.

————. *Book of Exercises for the Spiritual Life: Written in the Year 1500*. Trans. E. Allison Peers. Monastery of Montserrat, 1929.

Clancy, Thomas H. *An Introduction to Jesuit Life*. St. Louis, 1976.

Coathalem, Hervé. *Ignatian Insights: A Guide to the Complete Spiritual Exercises*. Taichung (Taiwan), 1971.

Covarrubias, Sebastián de. *Tesoro de la lengua Castellana o Expañola, segun la impresión de 1611*. Ed. Martín de Riquer. Barcelona, 1943.

Cusson, Gilles. *Biblical Theology and the Spiritual Exercises*. St. Louis, 1988.

————. *The Spiritual Exercises Made in Everyday Life: A Method and a Biblical Interpretation*. St. Louis, 1989.

Dalmases, Cándido de. *Ignacio de Loyola. Ejercicios Espirituales: Introducción, texto, notas y vocabulario por Cándido de Dalmases, S.J.* Santander: Sal Terrae, 1987.

————. *Ignatius of Loyola, Founder of the Jesuits: His Life and Work*. St. Louis, 1985.

Delattre, P. *Les établissements des Jésuites en France depuis quatre siecles*. 4 vols. Enghien-Weteren, 1956.

Directory of the Spiritual Exercises of Our Holy Father Ignatius: Authorized Translation. London, 1925.

Divarkar, Parmananda R., trans. *A Pilgrim's Testament: The Memoirs of Ignatius of Loyola*. Rome, 1983.

————. *The Path of Interior Knowledge*. Rome, 1983.

Documents of the 31st and 32nd General Congregations. St. Louis, 1977.

Dudon, Paul. *St. Ignatius of Loyola*. Trans. W. J. Young. Milwaukee, 1949.

Egan, Harvey D. *Christian Mysticism: The Future of a Tradition*. New York, 1984.

————. *Ignatius Loyola the Mystic*. Wilmington, 1987.

————. *The Spiritual Exercises and the Ignatian Mystical Horizon*. St. Louis, 1976.

BIBLIOGRAPHY

Farrell, Allan P. *The Jesuit Code of Liberal Education: Development and Scope of the Ratio Studiorum.* Milwaukee, 1938.

Fleming, David L. *The Spiritual Exercises: A Literal Translation and a Contemporary Reading.* St. Louis, 1972.

Frank, Francine W., and Paula A. Treichler, *Language, Gender, and Professional Writing.* New York: The Modern Language Association of America, 1989.

Futrell, John C. *Making an Apostolic Community of Love.* St. Louis, 1970.

Ganss, George E. *St. Ignatius' Idea of a Jesuit University: A Study in the History of Catholic Education.* 2nd ed. rev. Milwaukee, 1956.

————. *The Jesuit Educational Tradition and Saint Louis University.* St. Louis, 1969.

————. *The Constitutions of the Society of Jesus. Translated, with an Introduction and a Commentary.* St. Louis, 1970.

Gioia, Mario. *Gli Scritti di Ignazio di Loyola.* Turin, 1977.

Giuliani, Maurice. *Saint Ignace. Journal Spirituel: Traduit et commenté.* Collection Christus. Paris, 1959.

Gueydan, Edouard, en collaboration. *Ignace de Loyola. Exercices Spirituels. Traduction du texte Autographe.* Collection Christus, no. 61. Paris, 1985.

Guibert, Joseph de. *The Jesuits: Their Spiritual Doctrine and Practice.* Trans. W. J. Young. Chicago, 1964. 3rd ed. St. Louis, 1986.

————. *The Theology of the Spiritual Life.* Trans. Paul Barrett. New York, 1953.

Haas, Adolf, and Peter Knauer. *Ignatius von Loyola: Das geistliche Tagebuch.* Freiburg, 1961.

Harney, Martin P. *The Jesuits in History.* New York, 1940.

Hausherr, Irenée. *The Name of Jesus.* Kalamazoo, 1978.

Hernández Gordils, Emmanuele. *Que su santisima voluntad sintamos y enteramente la cumplamos.* Rome, 1966. Excerpts from a dissertation, Gregorian University.

Ignatius of Loyola, St. *Letters of St. Ignatius of Loyola.* Trans. W. J. Young. Chicago, 1959.

Ignatius, His Personality and Spiritual Heritage. Ed. F. Wulf. St. Louis, 1977.

Iparraguirre, Ignacio, and Cándido de Dalmases, eds. *Obras completas de San Ignacio.* ed. 4. Madrid: Biblioteca de Autores Cristianos, 1982.

————. *Vocabulario de Ejercicios Espirituales: Ensayo de hermenéutica Ignatiana.* Rome, 1972.

BIBLIOGRAPHY

Jaeger, Werner. *Paideia: The Ideals of Greek Culture*. Trans. Gilbert Highet. 3 vols. New York, 1941–1945.

Jesuit Higher Education. Essays on an American Tradition of Excellence. Ed. Rolando E. Bonachea. Pittsburgh, 1989.

Knauer, Peter. *Ignatius von Loyola: Geistliche Übungen und erläuternde Texte*. Übersetzt und erklärt von Peter Knauer. Leipzig, 1978.

———. See also Haas, Adolf, above.

Léon-Dufour, Xavier. *Dictionary of Biblical Theology*. New York, 1973.

Leturia, Pedro de. *Estudios Ignacianos*. Ed. I. Iparraguirre. 2 vols. Rome, 1957.

———. *Iñigo de Loyola*. Trans. A. J. Owen. 2nd ed. Chicago, 1965.

Longridge, W. H. *The Spiritual Exercises of Saint Ignatius of Loyola. Translated from the Spanish with a Commentary and a Translation of the Directorium in Exercitia*. London, 1919.

Ludolphus de Saxonia, *Vita Christi, ex Evangelio et approbatis ab Ecclesia Catholica doctoribus sedule collecta*. Ed. L. M. Rigollot. 4 vols. Paris, 1870.

McGinn, Bernard, and John Meyendorff, eds. *Christian Spirituality: Origins to the Twelfth Century*. New York, 1985.

McKenzie, John L. *Dictionary of the Bible*. Milwaukee, 1965.

Morris, John. *The Text of the Spiritual Exercises of St. Ignatius. Translated from the Original Spanish*. 4th ed. Westminster, Md., 1943.

Munitiz, Joseph A. *Inigo: Discernment Log-book. The Spiritual Diary of St. Ignatius Loyola*. London, 1987.

New Dictionary of Theology, The. Ed. Joseph A. Komonchak et al. Wilmington, 1987.

Nicolas, Antonio T. de. *Powers of Imagining: Ignatius de Loyola. A Philosophical Hermeneutic of Imagining through the Collected Works of Ignatius de Loyola with a Translation of These Works*. Albany, 1986.

O'Callaghan, Joseph F., trans. *The Autobiography of St. Ignatius Loyola*. Ed. John C. Olin. New York, 1974.

Ong, Walter J. *Ramus, Method, and the Decay of Dialogue*. Cambridge, 1958.

Oxford Dictionary of the Christian Church. Ed. F. L. Cross. 2nd ed. New York, 1974.

Palma, Luis de la. *Camino espiritual . . . de los Ejercicios*. Alcalá, 1626.

Pastor, Ludwig F. von. *History of the Popes*, vol. 13. St. Louis, 1924.

Petri Lombardi Sententiarum libri quattuor, Ed. Migne. Paris, 1853.

Puhl, Louis J. *The Spiritual Exercises of St. Ignatius. A New Translation*.

BIBLIOGRAPHY

Based on Studies in the Language of the Autograph. Westminster, Md., 1951, and Chicago, 1968.

Rahner, Hugo. *Ignatius the Theologian.* Trans. Michael Barry. New York, 1968.

———. *Ignatius: The Man and the Priest.* Trans. John Coyne. Rome, 1977.

———. *Saint Ignatius Loyola: Letters to Women.* Trans. K. Pond and S. A. H. Weetman. New York, 1980.

———. *The Spirituality of St. Ignatius Loyola. An Account of Its Historical Development.* Trans. F. J. Smith. Chicago, 1968.

Ravier, André. *Ignatius of Loyola and the Founding of the Society of Jesus.* San Francisco, 1988.

RB 1980: The Rule of St. Benedict in Latin and English with Notes. Ed. Timothy Fry. Collegeville, 1981.

Richards, Innocentia. See Vandenbroucke below.

Rusk, Robert R. *The Doctrines of the Great Educators.* 3rd ed. rev. London, 1965.

Schurhammer, Georg. *Francis Xavier: His Life, His Times.* Trans. M. Joseph Costelloe. 4 vols. Rome, 1973–1982.

Stanley, David. *A Modern Scriptural Approach to the Spiritual Exercises.* Chicago and St. Louis, 1967 and 1986.

———. *"I Encountered God!" The Spiritual Exercises with the Gospel of St. John.* St. Louis, 1986.

Tanquerey, Adolphe. *The Spiritual Life: A Treatise on Ascetical and Mystical Theology.* Trans. H. Branderis. Baltimore, 1930.

Tartaret, Pierre. *In Aristotelis philosophiam.* Venice, 1592.

Taylor, J. H. *The Literal Meaning of Genesis: An Unfinished Book. Translated and Annotated.* Ramsey, N.J., 1982.

Tetlow, Joseph A. *Choosing Christ in the World: Directing the Spiritual Exercises according to Annotations Eighteen and Nineteen. A Handbook.* St. Louis, 1989.

Toner, Jules. *A Commentary on St. Ignatius' Rules for the Discernment of Spirits.* St. Louis, 1982.

———. *Discerning God's Will: Ignatius Loyola's Teaching on Christian Decision Making.* St. Louis, 1990.

Torre, Juan de la. *Constitutiones Societatis Jesu Latinae et Hispanicae cum earum Declarationibus.* Madrid, 1892.

Tylenda, Joseph N. *A Pilgrim's Journey: The Autobiography of Ignatius of Loyola.* Introduction, Translation and Commentary. Wilmington, 1985.

Vandenbroucke, François, and Joseph Pegon. *Discernment of Spirits.* Trans. Innocentia Richards, from *Dictionnaire de Spiritualité* 3, cols. 1222–1291. Collegeville, 1970.

Westminster Dictionary of Christian Spirituality. Ed. Gordon S. Wakefield. Philadelphia, 1983.

IV. ARTICLES

Aschenbrenner, George A. "Consciousness Examen." *Review for Religious* 31 (1972): 13–21.

Buckley, Michael J. "Rules for the Discernment of Spirits." *The Way,* Supplement 20 (Autumn 1973): 19–37.

Burrus, Ernest J. "Monumenta Historica Societatis Iesu (1894–1954)." *Woodstock Letters* 83 (1954): 156–168.

Donnelly, Philip J. "St. Thomas and the Ultimate Purpose of Creation." *Theological Studies* 2 (1941): 53–83.

———. "The Doctrine of the Vatican Council on the End of Creation." *Theological Studies* 4 (1943): 3–33.

Fiorito, M. A. "Cristocentrismo del 'Principio y Fundamento' de San Ignacio." *Ciencia y Fe* 17 (1961): 3–42.

———. "St. Ignatius' Own Legislation on Prayer in the Society of Jesus." *Woodstock Letters* 97 (1968): 149–224.

Ganss, George E. "The Origin of Jesuit Colleges and the Controversies about Their Poverty (1539–1608)." In *Woodstock Letters* 91 (1962): 126–137, 142–143; reprinted in T. H. Clancy, *Introduction to Jesuit Life,* pp. 283–326.

———. "Thinking with the Church: The Spirit of St. Ignatius' Rules." *The Way,* Supplement 20 (1973): 72–82.

———. " 'Active Life or Contemplative Life'?" *Review for Religious* 22 (1963): 53–66.

———. "St. Ignatius and Jesuit Higher Education." Ch. 12 in *Jesuit Higher Education* (1989), pp. 154–159.

Kinerk, E. Edward. "Eliciting Great Desires: Their Place in the Spirituality of the Society of Jesus." *Studies in the Spirituality of Jesuits* 16 (November 1984).

Leturia, Pedro de. "Genesis de los Ejercicios de san Ignacio y su influjo en la fundación de la Compañía de Jesús." *Estudios Ignacianos* 2:3–55. Rome, 1957.

———. "Sentido verdadero en la Iglesia militante." *Estudios Ignacianos* 2:149–174.

BIBLIOGRAPHY

O'Malley, John W. "The Jesuit Educational Enterprise in Historical Perspective." In *Jesuit Higher Education. Essays on an American Tradition of Excellence*, ed. Rolando E. Bonachea, pp. 10–25. Pittsburgh, 1989.

———. "The Fourth Vow in Its Ignatian Context. A Historical Study." *Studies in the Spirituality of Jesuits* 15 (January 1983).

———. "The Jesuits, St. Ignatius, and the Counter-Reformation." *Studies in the Spirituality of Jesuits* 14 (January 1982).

Ong, Walter J. " 'A.M.D.G.': Dedication or Directive?" *Review for Religious* 11 (1952): 257–264.

———. "St. Ignatius' Prison Cage and the Existentialist Situation." *The Barbarian Within*, pp. 242–259. New York, 1962.

Quay, Paul. "Angels and Demons: The Teaching of IV Lateran." *Theological Studies* 42 (March 1981): 20–45.

Raitz von Frentz, Emmerich. "Ludolph le Chartreux et les Exercices de S. Ignace de Loyola." *Revue d'ascétique et de mystique* 25 (1949): 375–388.

Schneiders, Sandra M. "Spirituality in the Academy." *Theological Studies* 50 (1989): 676–697.

Solano, Jesús. "Cristología de las Constituciones." In *Ejercicios-Constituciones: unidad vital*, pp. 207–208. Bilbao, 1975.

Wickham, John. "The Worldly Ideal of Ignatius." *Thought* 29 (1954): 209–236.

INDEX

INDEX

Black Virgin shrine, 26
Bobadilla, 36
Bologna, 107
Bonachea, R.E., 450
*Book of Exercises for the Spiritual
    Life (Ejercitatorio de la
    vida espiritual),* by
    Cisneros, 26
Borgia, Francis, 346–349
Brandão, Antonio, 349–356
Brazil, 48
Buckley, Michael J., 423
Busa, Roberto, 118

Cáceres, 93, 102
Caiaphas, 170, 194
Calixto, 93, 94, 102
Calming of storm, 159, 189
Câmara, Luis Goncalves da, 10,
    41, 57, 58, 67, 68, 229
Capital sins, 126, 179, 389
Casting sellers out of temple, 188
Castro, 100–101, 102, 106
Catholic Church
    in 1500s, 10–11
    and evangelical poverty,
        217–218
    and Ignatius, 11, 13, 211–214,
        429–432
    and Jesus Christ, 43
    rules for thinking, judging, and
        feeling with, 211–214,
        429–432
Chanones, Juan, 26
Christ. *See* Jesus Christ
Christian doctrine, 40, 105–106
Christian education, Ignatius'
    theory of in the
    Constitutions, 48–49,

278–279. *See also*
    Education
    his ministry of, 361–365
    and Society of Jesus. *See*
        Education
Church. *See* Catholic Church
Circumcision, 185
Cisneros, García de, 26
City of God (Augustine), 18
Clare, St., 61
Classes of persons, three,
    156–158, 407–408
Coathalem, Hervé, 390, 399,
    404, 413, 415, 420, 423,
    424, 426, 427
Codure, Jean, 108, 109, 220
College of Montaigu, 36
College of Sainte-Barbe, 36
Communion, 135, 339–341
Confession, general, 135
Conscience
    daily particular examination of,
        130–131, 395–396
    general examination of,
        131–135, 395–396
Consolation and desolation,
    spiritual, 201–214,
    423–428. *See also*
        Discernment of spirits,
        rules for
    letter on, to Teresa Rejadell,
        339–341
    consolation without previous
        cause, 205–206, 427
Consolation, letters of
    to Isabel Roser, 327–332
    to Magdalena de Loyola y
        Araoz, 338–339
*Constitutions of the Society of
    Jesus,* background of

492

INDEX

Other Volumes in this Series